IntelliJ IDEA in Action

IntelliJ IDEA in Action

DUANE K. FIELDS
STEPHEN SAUNDERS
EUGENE BELYAEV
WITH ARRON BATES

MANNING
Greenwich
(74° w. long.)

For online information and ordering of this and other Manning books, please go to www.manning.com. The publisher offers discounts on this book when ordered in quantity. For more information, please contact:

> Special Sales Department
> Manning Publications Co.
> 209 Bruce Park Avenue   Fax: (203) 661-9018
> Greenwich, CT 06830   email: orders@manning.com

Ⅲ   Manning Publications Co.   Copyeditor: Tiffany Taylor
    209 Bruce Park Avenue   Typesetter: Denis Dalinnik
    Greenwich, CT 06830   Cover designer: Leslie Haimes

ISBN 1-932394-44-3

Printed in the United States of America
1 2 3 4 5 6 7 8 9 10 – VHG – 10 09 08 07 06

To my son Jake, who while too young to read this book,
will certainly enjoying coloring in it.

—D.F.

To my wife Michelle, whose support and understanding
never cease to astound me.

—S.S.

brief contents

contents

preface

It is often said that necessity is the mother of invention, and this was certainly the case on the cold winter day in February 2000 when JetBrains was founded. It had been nearly five years since the formal introduction of Java, and the tools market was already crowded with a myriad of development environments, all designed to provide a more convenient user interface for Java development. Although these early IDEs made it easier for developers to create applications, they delivered little functionality to alleviate the time-consuming tasks of coding or ensuring the consistency or excellence of design. As hard-core developers ourselves, we felt that the market lacked a satisfying development environment and we set out to create a tool that would assist professional developers to build complex applications.

Originally, we focused our efforts on restructuring code. As luck, or destiny, would have it, we were the first to make real progress in this area, and we became the first company to introduce commercial support for refactoring. The reigning IDE vendors took notice of us at this time, and soon afterward, all the major players were attempting to implement the technologies we had managed to bring to the industry forefront.

Later that same year, as the dot.com boom went bust and the overall quality of development tools for developers steadily declined, we saw a lot of ways we could improve on what others had failed to do. In January 2001, we introduced intelligence into the tools market with the release of IntelliJ IDEA, the first Java IDE that "thinks like a developer." With more capabilities and functionalities than anything the market had ever seen, IDEA took the concept of IDEs and developer tools to a new level.

And we were only getting started! Once we began to effectively compete in the tools space, the most important thing for us was to ensure that future releases of IDEA continued to have the robustness and capabilities that developers wanted and needed. The best way to accomplish this was to allow the developer community to meet and directly interact with IDEA's developers: we introduced our Early Access Program (EAP), which lets developers not only test our pre-beta builds for bugs but also argue for and request features that we implement. This approach works very well and many of IDEA's most powerful features have come into being as a result of the involvement and contributions of community members.

Ever since the initial release of IDEA, we have continued to add new features and capabilities to IDEA that remain true to its founding spirit. For us, nothing has been more central to our development philosophy than intelligence and usability. Creating a tool that helps developers code faster and increase productivity is our forte. Although we are proud to be recognized by industry mavens—IntelliJ IDEA has won virtually every major industry award over the past two years—what we value most is providing the industry with an intelligent IDE that developers have come to embrace. IntelliJ IDEA is now in its fifth generation, with the sixth currently in the works. I feel extremely proud of the work of our excellent development team, whose efforts I greatly appreciate. I express my personal thanks to all team members for their hard work.

It has been a pleasure working with the publisher and co-authors of this book to show how IDEA helps developers become better at building complex Java applications. Our objective was to bring to our readers a practical understanding of the many features of IDEA and how to unleash its full power. If you are familiar with IDEA, you will notice and appreciate that many of the new capabilities we added came directly from you. If this is your first time working with IDEA, or if you are simply curious to learn why so many of your colleagues swear by it, read this book and then try IDEA for yourself…you will wonder why it took you so long to quit doing things the hard way.

Develop with pleasure!

EUGENE BELYAEV

acknowledgments

We would like to recognize the support and collaboration of the many people who helped make this book possible. We acknowledge:

The development team at JetBrains, especially Serge Baranov and Ann Oreshnikova, for providing us with the latest in-depth information and for checking the book for technical accuracy. Working closely with the developers of IDEA gave us a deeper understanding of its magical powers, something that would not have been possible without them.

Our coworkers at Powered: Ron Green, Brandon Kearby, Mark Kolb, Katherine Beisner, and Trey Anderson, with whom we enjoyed learning the benefits of using IDEA for real world applications development.

Our publisher, Marjan Bace, for giving us this opportunity and suffering though the hazards of writing against a moving target; our editors, Susannah Pfalzer and Doug Bennett; our copyeditor, Tiffany Taylor; our proofreader, Barbara Mirecki; and our typesetter, Denis Dalinnik. Their insights, guidance, and expertise were invaluable to the completion of this book.

Arron Bates, for stepping in at the end of the project to provide much-needed assistance in finalizing the manuscript.

Our reviewers, whose comments, criticisms, and commendations advised, corrected, and encouraged us. Our deep appreciation is extended to: Jack Herrington, Mark Woon, Sean Garagan, Mark Monster, Bill Fly, Michael Yuan, and Jason McSwain.

Our friends and families for their unfailing support, assistance and tolerance throughout the long processes of writing and rewriting. Without them we could not have written this book.

about this book

Because you've decided to open this book, you probably already know that IntelliJ IDEA is a next-generation integrated development environment (IDE) for Java. As the term *IDE* implies, IDEA combines all the tools you need to develop Java software into a single application and interface. In other words, IDEA is a tool that helps you develop Java applications more quickly, easily, and intelligently. IDEA can help you with every phase of your project, from design and development to testing and deployment—provided you know how to make the most of it. This book will give you all the information you need to become an IDEA expert.

IntelliJ IDEA in Action is an independent and authorized book. This means the publisher, Manning, is independent of the vendor, JetBrains. It's authorized because from day one we have had the full cooperation, approval, and contributions of Eugene Belyaev and his team at JetBrains. We've had the best of both worlds in creating this book—complete editorial freedom to tell you everything you need to know about IDEA, and also the expert advice and assistance of the JetBrains team.

So, what's the big IDEA?

If you're already a user of IntelliJ IDEA, then by now you've discovered that it provides a powerful environment for managing your Java projects and source files as well as building and testing your applications. Its support for popular industry standards like J2EE, Ant, JUnit, XML, and various revision control systems ties together all the core aspects of Java development under a single tool.

Beyond the integrated tools, fancy editor, and snazzy project management features, IDEA provides a huge number of features aimed at increasing your productivity and improving your development experience. IDEA can help improve your efficiency by eliminating mundane and repetitive coding tasks, alerting you to errors before compilation, tracking code changes, and enabling powerful refactoring. By digging a little deeper into IDEA and embracing these features, you can become a more effective Java developer, because you're free to spend time on project design rather than code management.

Who should read this book

Without some educational investment on your part, however, IDEA can be just another editor. That, then, is the purpose of this book: not only to get you up and running quickly, but also to teach you how to use IDEA's multitude of powerful software development tools to their fullest advantage. We assure you that by digging into the many features, tips, and tricks covered in this book, you'll learn time-saving techniques or have at least one "Eureka!" moment that will make it worth your while many times over, even if you're an experienced IDEA user.

If you're new to Java development or a coder graduating from Notepad to your first real IDE, you'll find additional benefits in this text as we introduce you to the debugger, source code control, and code-generation tools you may not be familiar with. Mastery of these types of concepts is essential for taking your coding to the next level.

Our assumptions

That said, we assume you have at least some experience with Java and basic software development concepts. This is primarily a book about how to use IDEA, so we won't cover any particular Java technology too deeply. If there are areas you aren't familiar with (or don't care about), the structure of the book makes them easy to bypass.

This book is geared primarily to coders on the front line, but it can be useful to development managers who are evaluating IDEA or other development environments. Not only will it give you a good background on IDEA's capabilities, but it can also help you determine the best way to integrate IDEA into your team's development process.

What you'll find inside

The book is written in two main sections, divided into chapters in a manner that makes it easy for experienced users to jump straight to topics they want to dig deeper into while providing a logical, linear progression for users unfamiliar with IDEA and IDE development.

The first eight chapters cover the basics of working with IDEA. These chapters focus on getting started and hammering out your project from its basic components. This is the grunt work, the essentials, and where everyone new to IDEA should start.

The final chapters cover more advanced topics or areas of interest to particular types of developers, such as those working with Swing or J2EE. If you have a particular interest in these topics, you should feel free to skip ahead to chapters 9 and up, but we'll assume that you're comfortable working with other aspects of the IDE by this point.

Chapter 1: Getting started with IDEA

Many tools are required to help a developer create applications. Modern IDEs strive to bundle all these tools into a cohesive system, making access to the tools simpler and more productive. Chapter 1 introduces you to IDEA by demonstrating a simple programming task from implementation to execution. As complex as the software is, walking through this main development path allows new users to observe all the basic features they need to get their job done. Following up on the core knowledge, the rest of the book expands into the far corners of IDEA, showing you all the other features that will help increase your development efficiency.

Chapter 2: Introducing the IDEA editor

The most prominent feature of IDEA is the source code editor. If you've been using VI or Notepad to edit your Java source, we think you'll be pleasantly surprised at the number of conveniences IDEA offers over these tools. The IDEA editor can automatically format your source code, check it for syntax errors, and color-code Java keywords—all in real time as you type. The editor's awareness of code structure lets you navigate by method or block, collapse JavaDoc, hide inner classes, and take advantage of other conveniences. You can search and replace text, and even code usages, across your entire project. Compared to tools like a plain text editor, it's the difference between a nail file and a Swiss Army knife. This chapter introduces the editor's core features that will help you from day to day, line by line.

Chapter 3: Using the IDEA editor

After becoming familiar with the editor, you can knuckle down and get to work. The editor provides the means to write program code with a feature set like many others. However, the IDEA editor truly understands Java syntax and the Java API. This is where the editor can start to reduce your workload. If you forget the parameters for a method call, the editor can remind you. It can even bring up the JavaDoc for the method or class to give you additional insight. Convenient code-generation features eliminate the drudgery of creating accessor methods, implementing interfaces, and creating JavaDoc. Common coding tasks like iterating over the elements of an array are reduced to single keystrokes, thanks to the editor's innovative LiveTemplates feature. This chapter covers the power features within the IDEA editor.

Chapter 4: Managing projects

IDEA makes it easy to manage complex development projects. Through an innovative modular approach to project management, IDEA allows you to separate your application into discrete modules that can be developed, built, and tested independently. In addition, third-party resource packages are seamlessly combined with your own application through the use of handy code libraries. Dependency management ensures that nothing gets out of sync. Modules and libraries can even be shared across projects, promoting reuse and simplified project management. This chapter covers managing your projects.

Chapter 5: Building and running applications

The IDE is also used for compiling your project and making sure it runs. If you manage to create syntax errors, IDEA will help you locate them quickly and get them resolved. Integration with the Ant build framework lets you design powerful build scripts to automate not only the compiling but also the packaging and deployment of your projects. Building and running your project are covered in chapter 5.

Chapter 6: Debugging applications

Got bugs? Sure, you do. If you've been using `print` statements as your debugging tool of choice, you'll be surprised at how much more the debugger can do for you. IDEA's integrated symbolic debugger lets you examine running applications—even those running on an application server or a remote machine—to find out what's going on inside the program. Not only can you trace your program's execution, but you can also see the values of all program variables, evaluate expressions in the current context, and even change values to observe the effects on running code. The debugger is covered in detail in chapter 6.

Chapter 7: Testing applications with JUnit

You can help root out some of those nasty bugs that management is always complaining about, and keep them from coming back, by employing a suite of rigorous unit tests. IDEA supports JUnit, the de facto standard unit-testing framework for Java. With the IDEA test runner, you can run entire test suites, individual test cases, or individual tests with a single click. All of your unit test results are combined into a single report that tracks much more than a simple pass/fail. IDEA records the output generated by each individual test and tracks the amount of time and memory required to run each of them. JUnit and IDEA's unit testing support are discussed in this chapter.

Chapter 8: Using version control

IDEA also understands how to work with most popular version control systems, eliminating the need to manage your source tree from another tool. You can check out, edit, and commit files, as well as view their histories and examine the changes made between versions. Another innovation in IDEA is the *local history*, your own private source code control system that tracks your changes each time you successfully build the project or compile your unit tests. You can even tag your source with your own version label at any time, creating a fallback position when developing new features. You can view differences and roll back changes at any time, all without having to commit your code to the team's source code repository. The version control features of IDEA are discussed in chapter 8.

Chapter 9: Analyzing and refactoring applications

When you're ready to dig deeper, you'll want to check out IDEA's code analysis and refactoring features. For example, the code inspector tool can examine individual files or your entire source tree and locate redundant statements, missing JavaDoc comments, unused code, calls to deprecated methods, and other common design problems. It can even fix many of the problems it finds automatically!

IDEA's support for refactoring allows you to fine-tune your architecture without the headaches. For example, if you want to rename a class or move it between packages, IDEA will take care of moving the file and fixing all of the references to it. You can even reorder a method's parameters or change the signature without breaking all source code dependencies. With support for dozens of refactoring operations, IDEA enables you to keep your code clean and elegant in a way impossible to do by hand. This topic is covered in chapter 9.

Chapter 10: Developing Swing applications

Moving beyond basic text editing, IDEA adds a new graphical editor for building Swing interfaces. Using the Swing form designer, you can drag and drop components such as radio buttons and text fields directly where you want them on the interface. Then, you can easily configure the components' properties and tell IDEA how the graphical interface should be bound to your code. The development of Swing applications is covered in this chapter.

Chapter 11: Developing J2EE applications

If you do a lot of JSP, web, or EJB development, you'll be happy to know that IDEA hasn't forgotten about you. In fact, IDEA has some of the best J2EE development tools around. IDEA's code-aware features and refactoring support works inside JSP pages, and the editor has full support for tag libraries as well. You can take advantage of integrated support for Tomcat, WebLogic, and other web application servers to ease debugging and deployment. Web deployment tools make configuring and deploying web applications quick and painless. EJB tools make the creation of all the necessary interfaces and classes a snap. J2EE development is covered in chapter 11.

Chapter 12: Customizing IDEA

If you're like us, you're particular about your code layout, fonts, colors, indentation, beer, barbeque sauce, and other critical software development aspects. The folks at JetBrains must be, too, because IDEA is one of the most customizable tools we've ever seen. In chapter 12, we'll tell you how to adjust things to your liking.

Chapter 13: Extending IDEA

IDEA provides a number of convenient tools and accessories that span the functionality of the project. In chapter 13, we'll cover things like using bookmarks and macros, and extending IDEA using plugins and external tools.

Code conventions

The conventions described below are used throughout the book.

Terminology

We use the following styles throughout the text when describing the keystrokes and mouse combinations required:

- All of the shortcut key combinations that appear in the text represent those of the default keymap installed with IDEA on the Windows platform.

- When we want you to hold down one key along with another key or two, we list the two keys together with plus signs linking them, as in *Press **Ctrl+V** to paste the contents of the clipboard.* The keystrokes are always shown as uppercase, but that doesn't mean you should use the Shift key. If we want you to hold down the Shift key, we tell you to do so explicitly, as in *Press **Ctrl+Shift+N** to search the project files.*

- We tell you to *press* a key on the keyboard but to *click* or *double-click* your mouse.

- When we want you to hold down the Shift key and then click the mouse button, we ask you to *shift-click.* Likewise, we use the term *ctrl-click,* which means to hold down the Ctrl key while clicking your mouse button.

- On the Macintosh, the equivalent of the Alt key is Command.

- When we refer to a menu item, we use the vertical bar to indicate levels of menu hierarchy. For example, if we want you to select the menu item Class Name from the Code menu's Complete Code submenu, we would direct you to execute the **Code | Complete Code | Class Name** command. We always use the exact name and case of the actual menu entry and, where appropriate, specify the default keyboard shortcut in parentheses.

- Source code in listings or in text is in a `fixed width font` to separate it from ordinary text. Additionally, method names, class names, package names, and object properties are also presented using `fixed width font`.

Platform differences

Because it's an extremely common development platform, Microsoft Windows XP serves as the basis for all the screenshots in the book. If you're on another platform such as Mac or Linux, your interface may look slightly different. Additionally, we show IDEA in its default look and feel. If you've selected an alternate look and feel through the IDEA Preferences dialog, your interface will obviously look different.

With the exception of features new to 5, the screenshots in this text were created with version 4.5 under the Windows operating system. Version 5 of IDEA ships with a new look and feel, known as Alloy, and thus may appear slightly different. In addition, there maybe some slight differences between the versions 4.5 and 5 interfaces.

Callouts

Throughout the text are callouts that focus attention on various aspects of using the software. You'll encounter tips that point out clever or time-saving tricks, and warnings that alert you to particularly nasty situations you'd do well to avoid. You'll also see IDEA 5 callouts like this:

IDEA 5 At the time of the first writing, IDEA 5 was still in development. Although we have worked closely with JetBrains to ensure accuracy, some of the 5 features may have changed slightly before the final release. We added IDEA 5 callouts throughout the text to highlight the differences between versions 4.5 and 5.

Code downloads

Source code for all of the examples used in this book is available for download from the publisher's website www.manning.com/fields3.

Author Online

Purchase of *IntelliJ IDEA in Action* includes free access to a private web forum run by Manning Publications where you can make comments about the book, ask technical questions, and receive help from the authors and from other users. To access the forum and subscribe to it, point your web browser to www.manning.com/fields3. This page provides information on how to get on the forum once you are registered, what kind of help is available, and the rules of conduct on the forum.

Manning's commitment to our readers is to provide a venue where a meaningful dialog between individual readers and between readers and the authors can take place. It is not a commitment to any specific amount of participation on the part of the authors, whose contribution to the AO remains voluntary (and unpaid). We suggest you try asking the authors some challenging questions lest their interest stray!

The Author Online forum and the archives of previous discussions will be accessible from the publisher's website as long as the book is in print.

About the authors

DUANE K. FIELDS, web applications developer and Internet technologist, has an extensive background in the design and development of leading-edge Internet applications for companies such as IBM and Netscape Communications. With over 12 years' experience in software development, Duane currently works for upstart Internet company Pluck. He has published numerous articles on all aspects of Java applications development and is coauthor of the bestselling *Web Development with JavaServer Pages*. He is a Sun Certified Java programmer, is an IBM Master Inventor, and holds an engineering degree from Texas A&M University. Duane lives in Bastrop, just outside of Austin, Texas, with his wife and young son. He can be reached at his web site at http://www.duanefields.com.

STEPHEN SAUNDERS is a enterprise Java software engineer with a decade of experience spanning numerous industries, including knowledge management, financial services, and master data management. He's been using IDEA exclusively as his development environment of choice since version 1.0. He holds a BSc in Computing Sciences and a BA in English from Dalhousie University. Stephen lives in Halifax, Nova Scotia, on the rocky eastern shore of Canada, with his wife and their two young boys.

EUGENE BELYAEV is co-founder, president, and chief technology officer of Jet-Brains. With a PhD in Economics and a MS in Computer Science, Eugene has more than nine years of experience working with human-computer Interaction (HCI) as he has honed his skills at user interface design and software usability on a wide range of end-user application development projects. For the past five years, he has focused on creating and perfecting complex tools for developers in the real world. The popular Java IDE, IntelliJ IDEA, is one of his well-known creations. Eugene lives and works in St. Petersburg, Russia.

About the cover illustration

The figure on the cover of *IntelliJ IDEA in Action* is a "Subaltern Officer of the Janissaries." The Janissaries were elite troops that served as bodyguards of the sultan in the Ottoman Empire. The illustration is taken from a collection of costumes of the Ottoman Empire published on January 1, 1802, by William Miller of Old Bond Street, London. The title page is missing from the collection and we have been unable to track it down to date. The book's table of contents identifies the figures in both English and French, and each illustration bears the names of two artists who worked on it, both of whom would no doubt be surprised to find their art gracing the front cover of a computer programming book...two hundred years later.

The collection was purchased by a Manning editor at an antiquarian flea market in the "Garage" on West 26th Street in Manhattan. The seller was an American based in Ankara, Turkey, and the transaction took place just as he was packing up his stand for the day. The Manning editor did not have on his person the substantial amount of cash that was required for the purchase and a credit card and check were both politely turned down. With the seller flying back to Ankara that evening the situation was getting hopeless. What was the solution? It turned out to be nothing more than an old-fashioned verbal agreement sealed with a handshake. The seller simply proposed that the money be transferred to him by wire and the editor walked out with the bank information on a piece of paper and the portfolio of images under his arm. Needless to say, we transferred the funds the next day, and we remain grateful and impressed by this unknown person's trust in one of us. It recalls something that might have happened a long time ago.

The pictures from the Ottoman collection, like the other illustrations that appear on our covers, bring to life the richness and variety of dress customs of two centuries ago. They recall the sense of isolation and distance of that period—and of every other historic period except our own hyperkinetic present.

Dress codes have changed since then and the diversity by region, so rich at the time, has faded away. It is now often hard to tell the inhabitant of one continent from another. Perhaps, trying to view it optimistically, we have traded a cultural and visual diversity for a more varied personal life. Or a more varied and interesting intellectual and technical life.

We at Manning celebrate the inventiveness, the initiative, and, yes, the fun of the computer business with book covers based on the rich diversity of regional life of two centuries ago, brought back to life by the pictures from this collection.

Getting started with IDEA

1

Welcome to *IntelliJ* IDEA *in Action*. This book was written to introduce you to IDEA, one of the most innovative and intelligent Java integrated development environments (IDEs) available today.

IDEA is a fully featured IDE that has evolved beyond traditional IDEs by integrating modern best-practice features such as refactoring, intelligent code-editing assistance, and runtime analysis of code design. On the client side, IDEA sports a custom GUI Designer interface for rapid and uncomplicated interface design; on the server side, IDEA enjoys integration with J2EE technologies including industry-leading application servers. It's the only IDE in the industry that was originally built with the mission to enhance its users' productivity while providing a comfortable, customizable development environment to suit individual tastes and coding styles.

You may be new to Java programming, looking for a development environment that will help you learn the language. Or perhaps you're a seasoned developer who's used different IDEs in the past and likes to compare their features. Or perhaps you're an enterprise Java architect, looking for a development environment that's refactoring-friendly, provides tools for server development, and promises to improve your efficiency. Whatever your reason for choosing this book, we'll show you all the major functional components of the IDEA environment, and we'll help you begin developing in it as quickly as possible.

To lay the groundwork for future illustrations, and to provide a consistent example throughout the book, we'll introduce a sample application at the end of this chapter. As we progress through the book, we'll revisit that application, improve it, and extend it, with the goal of demonstrating the usefulness of some of IDEA's most compelling features.

1.1 *Installing and running IDEA*

Before we begin our exploration of IDEA's features and how they can be applied for effect, we're going to cover the basic installation and first-time execution of the software. Simply reading this book will help you learn about the IDE, but nothing beats first-hand experience with the tool itself. If you haven't yet downloaded, installed, and run IDEA, we encourage you to do so to make the experience that much more effective.

1.1.1 *Downloading the latest version*

If you don't yet have IDEA, you can download a copy of the latest version from the JetBrains web site (http://www.jetbrains.com/idea/download/), but you'll need a

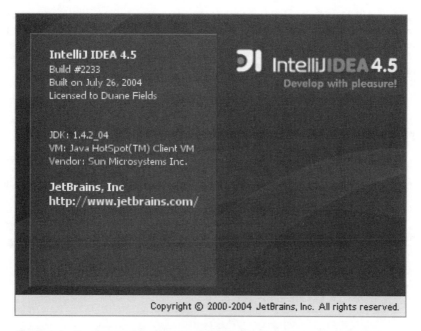

Figure 1.1   Here's an example of the IDEA About window from a version 4.5 installation. It shows the current version of the IDE, the specific build number, and the Java Development Kit and Java virtual machine under which the IDE is running.

license key to use it. IDEA requires a valid license key in order to function. If you haven't yet purchased IDEA, evaluation keys may be available from the JetBrains web site (http://www.jetbrains.com/forms/idea/download/evaluate); check there for details.

Once installed, IDEA periodically checks for updates and alerts you when one is available. Generally, updates take the form of a new distribution, so you'll end up running through the installer each time. If you ever have any question about the version you're running, use the **Help | About** command to open the window shown in figure 1.1. The **About** window shows you not only the version of IDEA you're running but also the Java version it's running under.

You'll need about 100MB for the application directory and another 100MB to 200MB for cache files. As far as RAM requirements go, the more the merrier! The bigger your project and the more files IDEA has to manage, the more memory you'll need. However, for all but the largest projects, IDEA runs comfortably on the recommended minimums per platform, as listed in table 1.1.

Table 1.1 **IntelliJ IDEA system requirements for all supported operating systems. Should any of this information change between versions, you can find the most up-to-date details on the Jet-Brains web site.**

Platform	System requirements
All platforms	256MB RAM minimum, 512MB RAM recommended 100MB hard disk space, plus at least 200MB for caches
Windows	Intel Pentium III/800MHz or higher (or compatible) Microsoft Windows 2003/XP/2000/NT 4.0 SP6a
Linux	Intel Pentium III/800MHz or higher (or compatible) Red Hat Linux Fedora/9.x/8.x/7.3 (Debian, Suse, Mandrake, Slackware, Gentoo, and other distributions with JDK 1.4.2 are also supported) GNOME or KDE desktop
Generic UNIX	Intel Pentium III/800MHz or higher (or compatible) Stable JDK 1.4.2 version available on platform
Mac OS X	1.42 GHz G4, G5 recommended Mac OS X 10.2 (Jaguar) or MAX OS X 10.3 (Panther) JDK 1.4.1 or JDK 1.4.2

IDEA supports the compiling, debugging, and running of your projects under any version of the Java Development Kit (JDK). To develop under a different version, you need to install that yourself, as described later in this chapter.

1.1.2 *Installing IDEA*

For Windows and UNIX users, the installer is a self-executing Java application. Run it by double-clicking its icon and following the installation instructions. You can go back to a previous step or cancel the installation at any time; nothing is installed until the final step of the process. Mac users have it easy: Just drag the IDEA icon from the distribution folder to your hard drive.

 In IDEA version 5.0, the UNIX distribution is now a packed archive instead of a self-executing file. To install the software, UNIX users need only download the archive and follow the instructions of the INSTALL.TXT file it contains.

Some of the steps described in this section don't appear during installation of IntelliJ IDEA 5.0, because some of the settings are stored in the user HOME by default. Other steps may have different sets of self-descriptive options.

Selecting an installation folder

The first important step of the installation process (after accepting the license agreement) is selecting an installation folder. The installer will suggest a reasonable default value, or you can use the file browser to pick your own. Be sure you choose a drive with plenty of room. If multiple users will need access to IDEA, make sure they have read access to this directory. Write access isn't required for this folder after installation.

If you're upgrading to a minor version of the same major release, you can safely install over the old one. If you're upgrading from a previous major release, install IDEA into a fresh folder. In either case, your settings will be automatically detected, because they're stored in the user HOME folder by default.

Choosing a cache folder

Next, select a folder that IDEA can use to store its cache files. To keep things speedy, IDEA analyzes and caches information about all your projects, your source code, your JDK, and any libraries you're using. This data can quickly add up, so we recommend selecting a drive with at least 100MB to 200MB of free space. Again, if you're installing the application for multiple users, make sure everyone can write to the selected directory.

Importing IDEA settings from a previous version

If you're upgrading IDEA from an older release, the installer can migrate your settings and license information to the new version. Select the option to import settings, and choose the installation folder of your previous version. Choose the directory that IDEA itself is installed in, not your personal settings directory. The installer will locate your personal directory automatically using the information stored in the installation directory. Your settings will be migrated during the installation process.

Creating product icons and shortcuts

In the next step, you have the option of choosing where to install the IDEA launch icon. Your choices will vary by platform, but all the usual locations (such as the Desktop or your platform's application folder) can be selected. If none of these locations is appropriate, you can choose a custom location or choose not to create any icons. If you wish to make the icon available to other users on the system, select the **Create icons for all users** option.

Associating project files with IDEA

As you'll learn in chapter 4, IDEA uses project files to keep track of your development projects. These files are given the file extension IPR (**I**dea **PR**oject file). If you choose to associate IPR files with IDEA in this step, you'll be able to open a project by clicking the project file—IDEA will launch automatically, loading the selected project.

You may assume that IDEA can associate itself with Java files so that they're automatically opened in IDEA. However, IDEA isn't just a Java file editor, so it needs to work within the context of a project.

Reviewing installation options

When you've finished making your selections, you have a final chance to review them. If you're happy with your choices, click the **Install** button to begin the installation. When it's complete, check out the ReadMe file or the JetBrains web site for the latest updates. You're now ready to run IDEA!

1.1.3 Running IDEA for the first time

To launch IDEA, double-click the shortcut created during installation, or run the IDEA executable for your platform from the bin folder of the installation directory. You can run only one instance of IDEA at a time: If you try to start a second one, you'll be reprimanded by the system. At first, you might see this as a limitation, but in chapter 4 you'll learn how to work on multiple projects simultaneously. If you have an existing project file on your file system, you can launch IDEA indirectly by double-clicking that project file.

The first time you launch IDEA, you'll be asked to enter the license key information given to you at the time of purchase, as shown in figure 1.2. If you have an evaluation key, IDEA will function the same way but will stop working once your evaluation period is over. If you later purchase a key or want to enter new registration information, you can do so by executing the **Help | Register** command.

> **WARNING!** IDEA won't allow you to use the same license key on two computers simultaneously. If IDEA detects another instance running on your local network, a warning dialog will appear and the IDE will shut itself down.

At this point, the software is licensed and running. If this is your first time starting the software, however, the **New Project Wizard** will appear after you've entered your license data. You'll create a new project as part of your first Java application in IDEA momentarily.

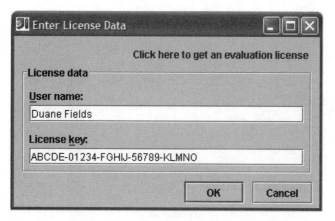

Figure 1.2 **You must have a valid license key to run IDEA. Make sure to type your license information exactly as you received it. Better still, use your platform's copy and paste functions to copy the key directly; that way, you'll avoid any spelling or typing errors.**

IDEA 5 The automatic segue into the **New Project Wizard** has been removed in IDEA 5.0. Instead, users starting the program see the new Welcome screen, described in more detail in section 1.3. The **Welcome** screen has a **Create New Project** button; when you click it, the **New Project Wizard** starts.

1.2 *Reviewing the IDEA interface*

The main IDEA window gives you access to all aspects of your project. Apart from the obvious source code editor component that dominates the window, IDEA provides a number of different panes and toolbars for accessing its various functions. Fortunately, these are all configurable, so you can design whatever interface layout you prefer.

1.2.1 *The main IDEA workspace*

An introductory look at a typical workspace is shown in figure 1.3. Remember, though, that this is but one particular layout—you'll be able to customize it to your liking. We'll introduce the main parts of the interface in this section.

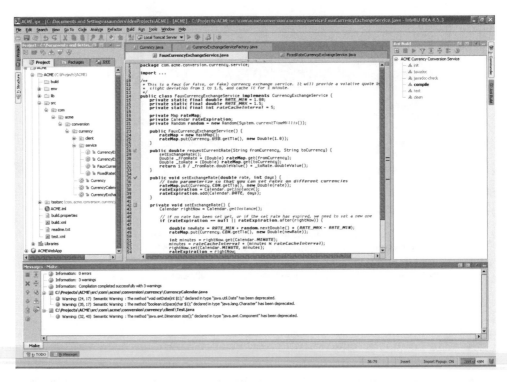

Figure 1.3   One of many configurations of the IDEA main interface. In this setup, the Project window is open on the left, the Messages window is open on the bottom, the Ant Build window is open on the right, and the main editor window consumes most of the screen.

1.2.2   The main menu bar

The main menu is used for executing most of the commands within IDEA, although a few commands are only accessible through the keyboard. One of IDEA's strengths is that you can control it entirely from the keyboard, so (if you're like us) you'll be using the menus less and less as you become accustomed to the environment. We'll be discussing IDEA's commands throughout the book.

1.2.3   The IDEA toolbar

Many of the most frequently used editing commands, like **Cut**, **Copy**, and **Paste**, are accessible through IDEA's main toolbar, shown in figure 1.4. There are also buttons for IDE-specific functions, such as **Make Project**, **Run**, and **Debug**. In addition, a unique control called the **Run/Debug Configuration Selector** lets you choose an application profile to run or debug. Selecting an item from the list and

Figure 1.4 The IDEA toolbar has icons representing basic file operations, Undo/Redo, Cut/Copy/ Paste, Search and Replace, backward and forward navigation, and project operations (such as Make/ Build, Run, Debug, and settings/configuration).

clicking the **Run** or **Debug** icon next to it runs the selected application. You'll learn how to define these profiles in chapter 5. If you prefer not to use the toolbar, you can turn it off by toggling its entry in the **View** menu.

1.2.4 *The source code editor*

Most of the IDEA main frame is reserved for the source code editor. More than just a simple text editor, IDEA's source code editor is fully aware of Java syntax, code formatting, and the classes and libraries available to your project. It assists you not only in writing code but also in finding and fixing errors.

Each file you open in the editor appears in its own tab at the top of the editor. Clicking a tab lets you switch between documents; alternatively, the keystrokes **Alt+Right Arrow** and **Alt+Left Arrow** cycle through the tabs. If you desire, you can create multiple groups of tabs, both horizontally and vertically. You can also split an editor into two panes in order to work on separate parts of a file simultaneously. You'll learn more about the editor and managing files in chapters 2 and 3.

> **TIP** You can use your platform's standard window controls to expand IDEA to occupy the full screen. If that's not enough for you, full screen editing mode can give you a little more room by removing the window's frame and controls. To toggle the full-screen mode on and off, use the **View | Full Screen** command or press **Ctrl+Alt+F11**.

1.2.5 *The tool windows*

Jutting out from the bottom and sides of the interface are IDEA's *tool windows*. These secondary windows come in a variety of flavors and provide access to very specific tasks in the IDE, such as project management, source code navigation, search results, and integration with revision control systems. Best of all, you can arrange them however you feel is most productive. We'll talk about managing tool windows in the next chapter and about the specific tool windows throughout the book.

1.3 Implementing "Hello, World"

IDEA is installed, and we've outlined the basics of the interface. Sounds like a great time to take the IDE out for a test drive. Let's walk through creating, building, and running the age-old "Hello, World" example to get a feel for how IDEA works.

1.3.1 Creating a project

All Java development done in IDEA occurs within the concept of a *project*. In IDEA, a project represents the context around a software development product. If you're working at home building open-source web photo album software, that album software is a project; if you work for a conglomerate and your department is responsible for maintaining an enterprise Java service layer API to other departments, that service layer API is a project. Project configuration and management is a key concept in IDEA, and we'll examine it very closely in later chapters.

IDEA 5

IDEA version 5.0 features a new **Welcome** screen when no active project is selected (see figure 1.5). This screen gives you quick access to the most logical starting points in the software. It's divided into three primary sections: **Quick Start**, **Documentation**, and **Plugins**.

The **Quick Start** section gives you one-click access to creating a new project from scratch or through your version control system, or to reopening a recently edited project. These options are also available through the **File** menu, but not quite as conveniently.

The **Plugins** section lists all the plugins installed in your copy of IDEA, including those bundled with the product. The plugins which feature the IntelliJ logo were created by JetBrains, the developer of IDEA. Others listed here were either installed by you or are third-party plugins bundled with your copy of IDEA. Click the **Open Plugin Manager** button to manage, update, or uninstall IDEA plugins.

To create a new project for the "Hello, World" application, do the following:

1 Select the **File | New Project** menu option from the menu bar (or alternatively, in version 5.0, click the **Create New Project** button on the **Welcome** screen).

2 The first dialog in the **New Project Wizard** appears and prompts you for a project name and the location on disk where the project file should be stored. In the dialog, enter HelloWorld as the name of your project, and

accept the default for the project file location. This default is typically under your home directory, which keeps your projects separate from those owned by other users of the system. If you'd like to relocate the project file somewhere else on the file system, click the ellipsis button (**...**) at the end of the text field. (The ellipsis button is often used in IDEA to select a file, directory, or class from the file system.) Click **Next** when you're finished.

3 The second dialog appears and prompts you for the target JDK of this project. Typically, you can select one of the JDKs on your machine that has been previously configured within IDEA, but a new installation of the software has none defined. The next step, therefore, is to configure IDEA to recognize and work with at least one target JDK on your system, as explained in the next section of the chapter. Click the **Configure** button to do so. Once you've configured the target JDK, you can return to setting up the "Hello, World" example.

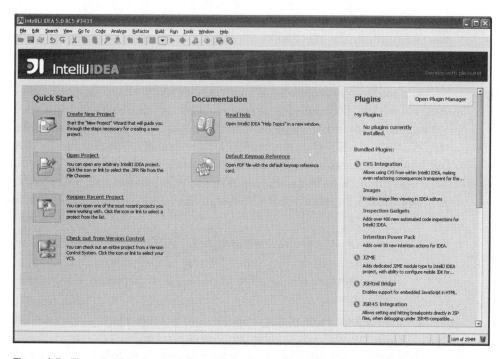

Figure 1.5   The new Welcome screen in version 5.0 provides immediate access to Quick Start, Documentation, and Plugins management features.

Installing and configuring a JDK

Before you can write your first line of Java code in IDEA, you must install and configure at least one JDK. IDEA ships with its own Java runtime environment (JRE), but it doesn't come with a Java compiler or an API library—and with good reason.

Unlike some development environments that integrate a particular version of the JDK, IDEA handles the inclusion of the project's underlying JDK in a modular fashion. It gives you the ability to develop with any JDK, including versions that haven't been released yet. This means you can use IDEA to develop applications for Java 1.2, Java 1.4, Java 1.5, and so on—at whatever patch level you require. Perhaps just as important, IDEA gives you the ability to use JDKs distributed by vendors other than Sun Microsystems. Obviously, any new features that are added to future versions of the Java language may require an update of IDEA in order to be fully supported.

If your system doesn't have a JDK installed, you need to download a copy from the Sun Microsystems web site (http://java.sun.com). Download the appropriate language and version for your system, but be sure to get the JDK, not the JRE (which only allows you to run Java applications, not develop them). When you're installing the JDK, be sure to install the source files (if they're included with your distribution). IDEA uses them to provide improved coding and quick-doc assistance.

We also strongly recommend that you download the documentation for your JDK. It's usually distributed as a separate package, due to its size, but you'll find it an invaluable resource. As you'll learn, IDEA can use the documentation to provide contextual help while you're developing. You can install these files anywhere, but it makes sense to install them into the JDK's root directory.

If you clicked **Configure** in step 3 in the previous section, you should see the **JDK & Global Libraries** window shown in figure 1.6. To configure your first JDK, follow these steps:

4   Click the plus button (**+**) at the top of the window to add a new JDK. This button works very much like the ellipsis button, but it's reserved for adding new entries to a list as opposed to populating a test field with a single answer.

5   The **Select Path** dialog appears and prompts you to choose a directory from the file system. Use the tree control to navigate to the home directory of your JDK installation (for example, C:\j2sdk1.4.2_08 for the latest release of the 1.4.2 JDK on Windows).

6 Click the **OK** button when the proper directory is selected. You'll return to the **JDK & Global Libraries** window, but a new Java version will be listed in the left panel, and a list of the class JARs will appear under the **Classpath** tab in the right panel.

The *Classpath* is the set of class directories and JAR files that make up the Java API and its extensions. By default, IDEA includes all the libraries and extension JARs included with the JDK. If you need to add additional libraries, click the **Add** button to do so, but you should never have to do this for any standard JDK. You should only include JDK-related libraries and extensions in this list. IDEA provides a different mechanism for configuring third-party shared classes (shared libraries), as we'll discuss in chapter 4.

The **Sourcepath** tab tells IDEA where it can find the source code associated with the class files specified in the first tab. You can specify not only directories but also JAR files. IDEA will automatically extract and parse the source files from the JAR file if specified. Including source files isn't required, but doing so improves IDEA's ability to provide inline help while coding.

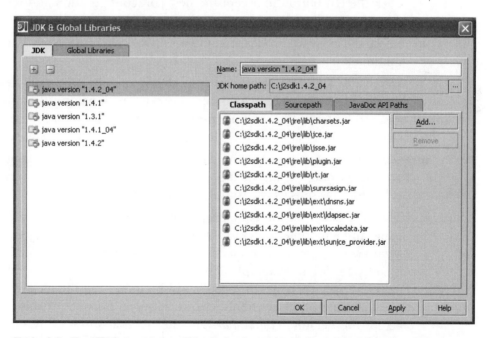

Figure 1.6   The JDK Setup window. This window is used to define each of the target JDKs on your local system. A target JDK is an installed JDK that can be used as the basis of an IDEA Java project.

The **JavaDoc API Paths** tab tells IDEA where it can find the HTML documentation that describes the target JDK's source code. Adding entries to the **JavaDoc API Paths** tab is also optional, but doing so gives you the ability to view documentation directly from the IDE. Specify the directories or JAR files where the JDK's documentation can be found. Alternatively, you can enter a URL that represents the root of the API documentation stored on a web server. IDEA uses this URL to locate the appropriate documentation if requested. For example, for JDK 1.4.2, you can use the documentation from Sun's web site by entering the URL http://java.sun.com/j2se/1.4.2/docs/api/index.html.

> **TIP**   If you install a new JDK at some point after IDEA has been installed and configured (or add the source or JavaDoc API documentation to an existing JDK), you can always come back to this configuration window through the **Settings** menu option.

Continue as follows:

7   Click the **OK** button to accept the new JDK configuration and return to the **New Project Wizard**.

8   Select the new JDK you just configured, and click the **Next** button to continue.

9   You're prompted to select either a single-module or a multi-module project. *Modules* represent a discrete piece of functionality within a project and can be reused in multiple projects. They're discussed in depth in a chapter 4; for now, select the single-module project and click **Next**.

10   You're prompted to select the type of module this project is concerned with developing. Again, we'll go into the differences in detail in chapter 4, but for now select **Java Module** and click **Next**.

11   The next dialog in the **New Project Wizard** prompts you for a module name and a module content root. This is a single-module project, so the wizard should reuse the project's name as the name of the module. This is sufficient for the example. The module content root is the directory where all the work on this project will be done; use the ellipsis button and following path-selection dialog to specify a new, empty directory, or accept the default. The *module file*—the file that stores all the module-specific settings—is typically stored in the module content root folder, but the **Change Directory** button at the bottom of the window allows you

to place it elsewhere (the default is fine for this illustration). When you're finished, click **Next**.

12 You're now prompted to specify the name of the directory where all the Java source files for your project are located. For a new project, you're specifying a new directory in which to put new files. The default is *src*, which is fine for this example. A src directory will be created beneath the module content root. Click **Next** to continue.

13 The last dialog prompts you to specify where the output from the compiler should be placed. When the source in src is compiled into classes, this directory is where those class files will be stored. The default is *classes* under the module content root, and this default is again fine for our example. Click **Finish** to complete the **New Project Wizard**.

IDEA will take a moment to scan through and parse all the Java classes known to your project (which, at the moment, are only the classes in the JDK). Let's push ahead with the project!

1.3.2 Making a Java class

We've laid the groundwork around the "Hello, World" project by defining where the files will live. Now it's time to create your first class. The following steps walk you through one of the many ways to create classes in IDEA.

For the purposes of this exercise, let's create a class called `HelloWorld` in the `com.acme.hello` directory:

1 The toolbar on the left side of the window contains two *tool window buttons,* **Project** and **Structure.** These represent *tool windows*: secondary windows within the interface that provide access and support for specific tasks. Generally, the **Project** tool window permits you to view and control your project, and the **Structure** tool window lets you view and maneuver around the structure of the current file in the editor; we'll examine each of the tool windows in greater depth in chapter 2. For now, click the **Project** tool window button to open that tool window.

2 The **Project** tool window opens, docked to the left side of the main window. Within that window, you can see a tree control representing the complex structure that is your project: its modules and its libraries. You need to navigate down to the source directory you specified in the **New Project Wizard**, because that's where your source code for new classes

will live. Open the HelloWorld subnode by clicking its attached plus sign
(**+**) or by double-clicking the node itself.

3   Within the HelloWorld module is a src directory marked by a folder icon
with small blue dot (and possibly a HelloWorld.iml file, if you didn't
change the default location of your module file; feel free to ignore that
file during this exercise). Right-click the folder to bring up a context
menu, and select **New | Package** from that menu. (Alternatively, you can
begin using IDEA's huge library of keyboard shortcuts: Press **Alt+Insert**
to open a New context menu.)

4   You're prompted for the name of this new package. Type in the name
com, and click **OK** (or press **Enter**). Doing so creates the first layer of the
package structure in your project.

5   Repeat the process in steps 3 and 4 to create the subpackage acme under
com, and then helloworld under acme.

6   With the com.acme.helloworld package created, right-click the hel-
loworld package icon and select **New | Class** from the context menu
(**Alt+Insert**).

7   Enter the name HelloWorld as the new class name, and click **OK**.

IDEA creates a simple Java source file with the appropriate package and class declarations. It also opens that file in the source code editor. Now that you have the
shell, you can edit the file to suit your needs. Add the main() method shown in
listing 1.1, but follow these steps to do so:

1   Inside the HelloWorld class, type the letters psvm and then press **Tab**. The
main() method should be roughed out for you by IDEA's Live Template
mechanism, a customizable code generation facility.

2   Inside the main() method, type the letters sout, and then press **Tab**.
Again, the call to println() is added for you, and your cursor is placed
within the double quotes, waiting for the String you wish to print.

Listing 1.1   A simple HelloWorld application, written in IDEA

```
package com.acme.helloworld;

/**
 * Created by IntelliJ IDEA.
 * User: ssaunders
 * Date: 1-Jun-2005
 * Time: 9:00:00 AM
```

```
 * To change this template use File | Settings | File Templates.
 */
public class HelloWorld {

    public static void main(String[] args) {
        System.out.println("Hello, World!");
    }

}
```

1.3.3 *Building the project*

Now that your class is finished, you can build the project. *Building*, in this case, involves compiling the Java source into a class file, but the task can be a much more complicated, multistage process for complex Java projects. Follow these steps to build your project:

1. Select the **Build | Make Project** menu option (or, if you prefer, click the **Make Project** button on the toolbar, or use the keyboard shortcut **Ctrl + F9**).

2. Because this is the first time you're building the project, IDEA recognizes that the directory where the compiler's output classes should go doesn't yet exist. Click **Yes** to let IDEA create the output directory for you.

That's it! If you navigate your file system and look in that output directory, you'll find a directory structure that matches the package structure in the **Project** tool window, and the `HelloWorld.class` in the `com.acme.helloworld` package.

1.3.4 *Running the project*

`HelloWorld` is a special Java class in that it has a `main()` method, an entry point that marks this class as a command-line executable. Consequently, you can directly run and test this class to ensure its behavior operates as expected. Follow these steps to run your class:

1. Select the **Run | Edit Configurations** menu option.

2. The **Run/Debug Configurations** window appears, allowing you to manage the different ways to execute and test code that you write. This sample is a simple Java application, so ensure that the **Application** tab is selected. If it isn't, click it.

3. Click the plus button (**+**) to create a new Java application run configuration. A new configuration is immediately added with the title Unnamed.

4   Change the name of the configuration from Unnamed to `Hello World` in the **Name** text field.

5   Click the ellipsis button (**...**) to the right of the **Main Class** text field. Doing so causes the **Choose Main Class** dialog to appear.

6   The **Choose Main Class** dialog allows you to select the class to execute either by name or by navigating the source tree. This project has only one class, so finding it is simple. Click once on the class name in the list, and then click **OK** to select it.

7   In the **Use classpath and JDK of module** drop-down list, select the **HelloWorld** module. Doing so tells IDEA that it should use the JDK associated with the `HelloWorld` module to execute the class.

8   Uncheck the **Display settings before running/debugging** option to prevent IDEA from showing this configuration screen every time you try to run or debug your project.

9   Click **OK** at the bottom of the **Run/Debug Configurations** window to execute the program. Doing so makes these options an acceptable configuration that you can subsequently run and returns you to the editor.

10   Be sure the `HelloWorld` run/debug configuration is chosen in the selector on the toolbar. To execute that configuration, select **Run | Run**. Alternatively, click the **Run** button next to the configuration selector or use the **Shift+F10** keyboard shortcut.

TIP   Now that you've seen the long way of defining a run/debug configuration, here's a quicker method: Right-click anywhere inside the class, and select the **Run HelloWorld.main()** menu item. Doing so creates a temporary run/debug configuration that can be used multiple times during the current IDEA session and can also be saved permanently if necessary.

Once you give the run command, IDEA executes the class, and the **Run** tool window automatically opens at the bottom of the screen. This tool window is responsible for displaying all the output from executed run configurations. The first line in the window shows the command line IDEA used to run the class, including all options and arguments. The last line shows that the process has exited normally and that you're not the victim of an infinite loop. And, if all has gone well, you should see a friendly "Hello, World!" between those two lines.

1.4 *The plot thickens*

Although this simple example is useful to get some hands-on experience with the IDE and to touch on a number of topics, it does nothing to help explore the deeper features of the software. To that end, we require a much more detailed project: not necessarily difficult, but complex enough to require the use of some of IDEA's more advanced features. Our discussions of those advanced features will be accompanied by an example of that functionality *in action* as applied to our running example.

1.4.1 *Welcome to ACME Incorporated*

Let's pretend that you're a staff engineer for the fictitious ACME Incorporated, and you've been tasked with building a Java application. The system required is responsible for providing currency exchange estimations based on exchange rates obtained from an undefined service provider. The client application and underlying implementation you provide must accept the user's request for exchange rates or actual exchange transactions, leverage the underlying service to determine the correct answer, and return those results to the end user. Some sample use-cases and requirements include the following:

- A user can request the exchange rate between two specified currency types (for example, rate of exchange from U.S. dollars to Canadian dollars).

- A user can request the conversion amount by specifying an amount in one currency and the currency to be converted to (for example, $5 U.S. converts to how many Canadian dollars?).

- A user can request a list of the currencies known by the system.

- The coupling to an exchange-rate service provider should be loose, so that ACME can switch between rate providers at will without requiring source code modification.

- The interface for the exchange rate service will be provided to you. It represents a common interface used by most of the rate providers.

1.4.2 *Starting the ACME project*

The first thing you need, to begin work on this product, is a new IDEA project. Select **File | New Project** to create a project representing the currency converter. Follow the process we outlined earlier for the `HelloWorld` example, because the two will be nearly identical for now. We'll return to the converter project definition to adjust it once you have more exposure to IDEA's feature set.

Name your project ACME, and make it a single-module project, containing only one Java module. Name that module `CurrencyConverter`, and accept the default names for source and classes directories.

Although many different implementations can fulfill the requirements, here are some possibilities that have their pros and cons. This isn't meant to be an ideal solution, remember, but rather one that helps expose you to the various features of IDEA:

- No requirement specifies that the list of currencies known to the system must be dynamic. Currencies can be hard-coded in the system, so you can have an enumerated-type class that represents both the definition of what a currency is as well as what currencies exist as far as the system is concerned.

- No user interface has been defined, so you can start with a simple command-line utility that takes arguments appropriate for the use-cases. You can always add more user interfaces later, and a command-line utility can help you test to see if your system works.

No matter what solution you eventually architect, the classes will be owned by ACME Incorporated and live in its source code repository. It's probably a safe assumption that ACME's Java products all live within the com.acme package structure. And, if this currency converter is a new project, there may not be an existing package that seems appropriate for its source code. In preparation for the new classes you're about to create, use the **Project** tool window to create a package tree that ultimately includes `com.acme.conversion.currency` and `com.acme.conversion.currency.client`.

1.5 Summary

IDEA boasts an impressive and extensive list of features for Java software development. The original name of the company producing IDEA was IntelliJ (now JetBrains), and it won't surprise you that we think IDEA is an extremely intelligent IDE. From automated code assistance to runtime code analysis, from continuous redesign support to an enabling extensibility framework, from sophisticated code navigation to modular project management, its features help simplify and speed up the process of software development. Trial versions of the software are available for download from the JetBrains corporate web site and aren't feature-restricted, allowing you to experience the full power of the software and gauge its effect on your own personal process before committing to it.

Ultimately, IDEA was designed to help Java software developers do their development work faster, better, and more effectively. As you explore the features of IDEA throughout the rest of this book, we'll show you how they help you do precisely that.

Introducing
the IDEA editor

2

In this chapter...

- A closer look at the IDEA main interface, including IDEA's tool windows
- Performing file operations
- Performing basic navigation, selection, and searching operations

The editor is the heart of the IDE. While developing in IDEA, you'll spend the bulk of your time working in the editor, so learning its features is the first step toward putting the environment to effective use. Many excellent editors are on the market, so it's only natural to wonder what makes IDEA's editor so special. This chapter will familiarize you with the editor's basic interface and editing capabilities, and the next will explore the features that truly set it apart.

2.1 *Exploring the IDEA interface*

Most of the IDEA window is dedicated to showing the contents of an open file and permitting you to edit it. In addition to that main panel, the editor window contains a number of screen artifacts that relate contextual information about the file you're editing. At the top of the window are the *editor tabs*; the *gutter* is the area to the left of the window, and the *marker bar* runs down the right side of the window. These can all be seen in figure 2.1.

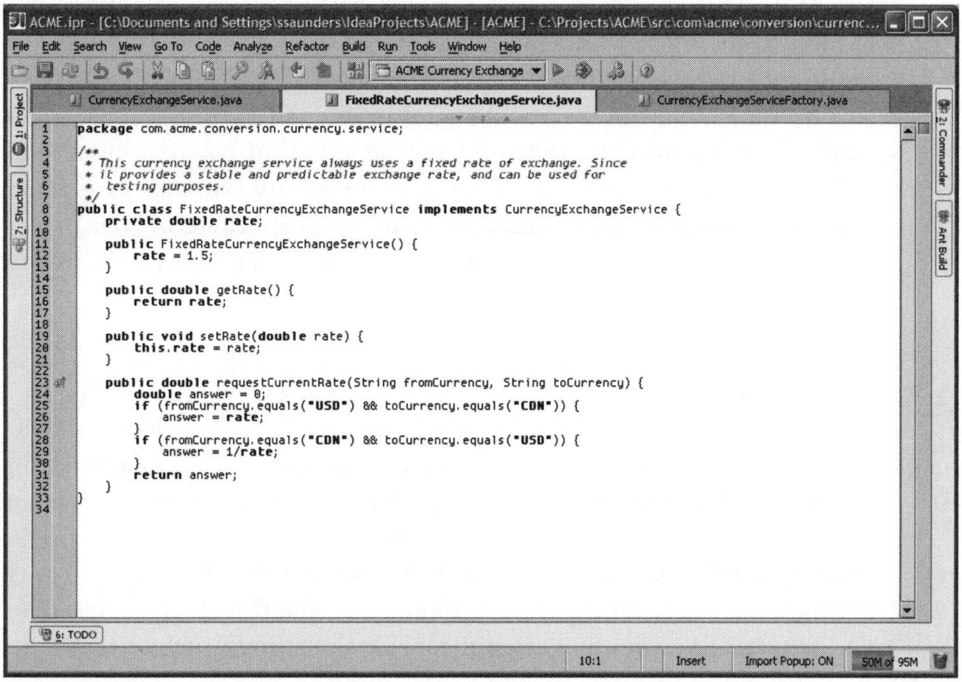

Figure 2.1 An example of the editor with multiple files open. Note the tabs for each file, the gutter on the left, and the marker bar on the right.

2.1.1 *Hanging out in the gutter*

The strip alongside the left margin of the editor is called the *gutter*. This isn't a derogatory term; the word comes from publishing circles and refers to the white space formed by the inner margins of a page. This area is used to provide additional information about your code. You may encounter various icons that identify information about the code structure, the meaning of which we'll cover later in the chapter. The gutter is also the location of code-folding outlines, scope indicators (both of which you'll learn about later in this chapter), and change bars (which are covered in chapter 8).

2.1.2 *Using the marker bar*

Opposite the gutter area, along the right-hand side of the interface, is the marker bar. It highlights errors and other items in your code with little multicolor tick marks, which indicate and let you navigate to those interesting points in your code. The position of the tick mark within the stripe indicates the relative position of the error or warning within the file—the bottom of the bar indicates the last line of the file, and the top of the bar the first line, regardless of the current window position or the size of the document.

The marker bar tracks more than just errors and warnings: It also tracks bookmarks, search results and highlighted usages, and (if you're using a version control system) changes made to the current document. Bookmarks appear as black tick marks, and the other features use the colors specified in your color scheme. Clicking any tick mark in the marker bar focuses the editor on the line indicated by the mark.

IDEA 5 You can now customize the colors used to display errors and warnings in the editor's error stripe. So, if red and yellow don't do it for you, or if you want to disable the indicators altogether, you now have the option to make changes. Bring up the **Colors and Fonts** settings panel, select the **Java** tab, and then choose either the **Error** or **Warning** formatting option from the list. Set the color you prefer for the **Error Stripe Mark** option, or disable the indicator for the selected type by deselecting the check box next to the option. Note that this change affects the display for the other file types that inherit from Java's settings, such as HTML and CSS.

2.1.3 *Using the editor tabs*

The IDEA editor is tab-based. Each file you open is displayed in its own tab of the editor window using the name of the file as the name of the tab. Hover your mouse pointer over the tab to display a tool-tip containing the full path to the source file. This information is also shown in the editor's title bar, but often it's too long to display in its entirety. Clicking a tab switches the main window to the contents of that file, allowing you to work on it. Your cursor position, history, undo, and other elements are tied to the file, allowing you switch back and forth between tabs without losing your place within a given file.

By default, the editor's tabs appear at the top of the editor, but you can change their location through the **Appearance** options of the IDE settings panel. The option **Editor tab placement** lets you move the tabs to the bottom, left side, or right side of the window. Placing the tabs on the left or right potentially wastes a lot of space on the screen, but you'll have to try it for yourself.

To select the current file for editing, click the tab to bring its contents to the front. In addition to clicking a tab to change the active document, you can use the keyboard shortcuts **Alt+Right arrow** and **Alt+Left arrow** to move through the editor tabs. Doing so lets you switch to another tab without having to use the mouse.

Moving between tabs

There are a number of ways to move between the currently open files in the editor, as summarized in table 2.1. It's important to understand the difference between the **Next/Previous Tab** and **Back/Forward** commands. The **Next/Previous Tab** commands move back and forth through the editor's tabs in the order they appear on the screen. These options provide a quick way to navigate back to a specific file without having to step through a navigation history. Alternatively, **View | Recent Files** (**Ctrl+E**) brings up a keyboard-navigable pop-up window displaying the most recently opened files. When you're moving between editor tabs, IDEA remembers your cursor's position within each opened file.

The **Back/Forward** commands don't pay attention to on-screen tab order, but rather move back and forth through your navigation history (much like a web browser). As you work on a Java project, you'll naturally jump from location to location, from file to file, in the course of editing. IDEA keeps track of these locations and lets you navigate through the list using the **Back** and **Forward** commands. The **Back/Forward** navigation commands are analogous to the **Undo/Redo** option for your navigation history, with the following distinction: **Back** and **Forward** control editor focus, whereas **Undo** and **Redo** alter your code by rolling back or reapplying changes.

Table 2.1 You can navigate between editor tabs in a number of ways: by retracing your steps in the editor's history, by using the manual Next Tab and Previous Tab operations, and by visiting recently opened files.

Operation	Shortcut	Description
Back	Ctrl+Alt+Left arrow	Steps backward through previous navigation operations
Forward	Ctrl+Alt+Right arrow	Steps forward through previous navigation operations
Next Tab	Alt+Right arrow	Changes the editor's focus to the editor tab to the right of the current tab
Previous Tab	Alt+Left arrow	Changes the editor's focus to the editor tab to the left of the current tab
Last Edit Location	Ctrl+Shift+Backspace	Steps backward through the locations of previous modifications (across any file)
Recent Files	Ctrl+E	Brings up a pop-up menu that lets you navigate to a recently opened file

TIP   You may want to consider Timur Zambalayev's excellent TabSwitch plugin for IDEA. This plugin emulates the Windows **Alt+Tab** feature (though it's mapped to **Alt+A** so it doesn't interfere), allowing you to cycle through the list of most recently used tabs. You can download it through the integrated Plugin Manager, accessed through the **IDE Settings** window.

How IDEA manages its editor tabs

When you open a file, a new tab appears in the editor window. If the file is already opened, its tab becomes selected as the active file. New tabs are added immediately after your currently selected tab. When the number of open tabs reaches the maximum allowed (as specified by the editor settings option **Tab limit**), the editor begins closing tabs to make room for the new files.

Tabs are closed in least recently used (LRU) order unless you've enabled the editor settings option **Close non-modified files first**. This option tells the editor to close any files you haven't changed first, presuming that you're probably through with them. When there are no more nonmodified tabs, tabs are closed least recently modified first.

If you want to ensure that a tab isn't removed from the editor window, regardless of its modification status or the order in which it was loaded, you can *pin* the tab to the editor by right-clicking it and selecting the **Pin Tab** option. An icon appears in the tab to show that it has been pinned. Select it again to unpin it. This feature is helpful in situations when you open a file for reference, not for editing, because it keeps IDEA from closing the file when you edit other files without touching it.

As you open more files, the editor creates additional rows of tabs as necessary to hold them all. An alternative option is available through the editor settings. The option **Editor tabs in a single row** forces the editor to display no more than a single row of tabs. If you have more open files than can fit in your window, the other tabs flow off the screen; you have to use the scrolling icons next to the tabs to reveal them. Enabling this option gives you more editing space if you have many open files.

> **TIP** If you don't like the editor's tabs, just change your tab limit to 1. This will effectively disable tabs. You can then use **View | Recent Files (Ctrl+E)** to switch between files. On the other hand, if you want IDEA to effectively never close your tabs, set the tab limit to an absurdly high number that you'll never encounter.

IDEA 5 A new option in the Appearance settings panel lets you completely disable the editor tabs. Select **None** as the value for the **Editor tab placement** option. This is similar in effect to the trick in Idea 4.5 of setting the tab limit to 1. You'll be working on a single file at a time.

Another new option called **Hide file extension in editor tabs** causes the editor tabs to show only the base name of the file you're editing. The file type icon is still present, so it should be easy to distinguish a Java file from a text file, and unknown file types still show their extensions. This option can save room in the interface and let you squeeze in a few more tabs up. You can also display the class or interface rather than the filename in the editor tab. This means that instead of the filename and icon, you see a class/interface name with the corresponding icon; depending on the class type (abstract, static, private, and so on), the icon modifiers are also shown to reflect the type.

Using tab groups to edit multiple files simultaneously

Tab groups let you create a variety of different editor layouts, allowing you to see and edit multiple files simultaneously. Creating a tab group splits the editor into two independent panes, which can be laid out either horizontally, as shown in figure 2.2, or vertically, as in figure 2.3.

To create a new tab group, right-click a tab and select either the **Split Tab Group Vertically** or **Split Tab Group Horizontally** option corresponding to the

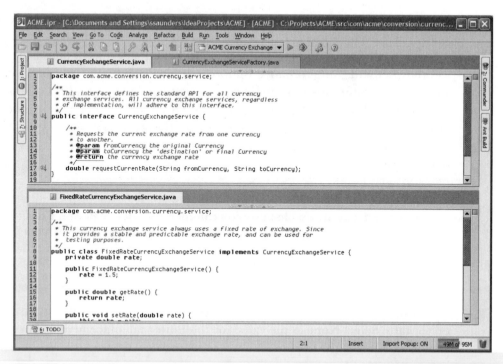

Figure 2.2 Tab group, split horizontally. In this view, you can see full lines from beginning to end, at the cost of the number of lines that appear on the screen at a time. It's a useful perspective for doing a line-by-line comparison between files.

orientation you want. (These options are also available through the **File** menu.) The new tab group appears with the selected tab as its first member. Note that you can have only two tab groups (meaning you can split the editor only once), so the **Split Tab Group Vertically** and **Split Tab Group Horizontally** options become disabled while active.

IDEA 5 In IDEA 5.0, you can now have an unlimited number of tab groups, which means you can see several files simultaneously or several places in the same file at once.

You can switch the orientation between the horizontal and vertical layouts by right-clicking any tab and selecting the **Change Tab Groups Orientation** option. You can move tabs between two tab groups by right-clicking the tab and selecting the **Move to Opposite Tab Group** option. When you close the last tab in a tab group, the editor returns to a single-pane layout.

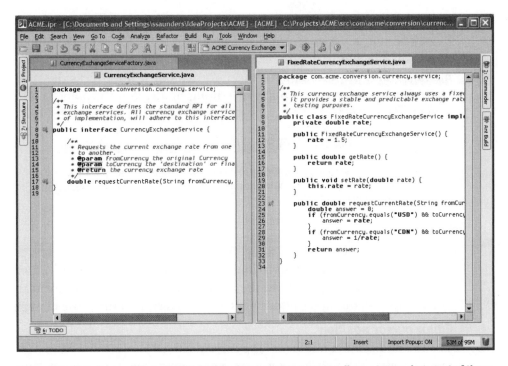

Figure 2.3 Tab group, split vertically. In this view, you can see more lines at once, but most of those lines scroll off the edge of the window. It's a useful perspective for comparing file structures or program flow.

IDEA 5 In IDEA 5.0, the ability to split an editor window has been merged with the tab grouping features. Among other benefits, this allows any file to be a member of several tab groups simultaneously. When you split the editor window into multiple panes in IDEA 5.0, you get two exact copies of the current editor window, complete with all the open editor tabs. Previously, these tabs would have been divided among the two tab groups.

To reflect this change, the term *tab group* has been replaced by the more generic *splitter* designation. Consequently, the menu option names for the splitting operations have been renamed slightly and moved under the **Window** menu, instead of **File**. For example, **Split Tab Group Horizontally** is now **Split Horizontally**, and **Change Tab Groups Orientation** has become **Change Splitter Orientation**.

2.1.4 Exploring the status bar

Below the editor, the status bar displays various feedback items (see figure 2.4). It shows the function of the currently selected menu item or action, displays error messages, and provides other status information. It also tracks the current row and column your cursor is on, your editing mode, and the amount of memory being used by IDEA.

Figure 2.4 The IDEA status bar, including message area, editor cursor position, read-only icon, insert/overwrite indicator, pop-up status indicator, memory usage, and garbage collection control.

Message area

The leftmost portion of the status bar is reserved for system messages, status information, and menu descriptions. It provides several types of information, depending on where you are in the application, including hints about the function of menu items, descriptions of error messages, and the cause of warnings.

Editor cursor position

The row and column number of the current cursor position are shown next to the message area. The first number is the row number, and the second is the column (the first column is column 1).

Read-only indicator

The lock icon in the status bar tells you that the current file is read-only. The file may be marked read-only by the local file system or by your version-control system, or the file may be located inside a JAR file. You can also lock any file temporarily by double-clicking the spot where the lock icon would normally appear. When a file is writable, no icon appears—the space is left blank. Unless a file is locked because it lives in a JAR file, you can unlock it at any time by double-clicking the lock icon to toggle its status.

When locked, a file of course isn't editable. You can't make changes directly through the editor or indirectly through refactoring or other operations. If you're using a version-control system (VCS; see chapter 8) that locks files you're not editing, you'll automatically be asked if you want to unlock them and notify the VCS that you're editing them.

Pop-up hints indicator

Pop-up hints are used in the editor to alert you to errors, provide API documentation, import necessary classes, and so forth. You'll learn about the various types of pop-up hints that IDEA provides as we progress through the book; for now, know that you can toggle them on or off by double-clicking the pop-up hints area of the status bar.

Toggling between insert and overwrite mode

The current text entry mode is indicated in the status bar by either the word **Insert** or the word **Overwrite**, and your cursor changes to a block cursor when you switch modes (unless you're using a block cursor by default, in which case it switches to the line cursor). You can toggle between the two modes by pressing the Insert key on your keyboard.

By default, the editor operates in insert mode. That is, as you type, characters are added into the document, pushing existing characters off to the right. IDEA also supports editing in overwrite mode, in which case your typing destroys any existing characters by typing over the top of them.

Monitoring memory usage

The memory indicator shows you how much memory IDEA has to work with. The indicator displays the amount of memory currently in use and the amount available. You can remove the memory indicator by disabling the **Show memory indicator** option located in the **Appearance** setting under **Window Options**.

This amount changes over time as you open more files, perform searches, and so forth. The amount may be misleading, however, because it indicates the *current* heap size and not the *maximum* possible heap size. Every Java program runs under a given memory configuration that specifies the minimum and maximum size of the Java heap. The VM keeps bumping up the heap size as needed until it reaches the maximum allotment. When the VM runs short of memory, it runs the garbage collector to free up space in the heap. If an application's maximum heap size is too small, it will spend lots of time in the garbage collector—this is bad news, because the program must stop everything while the garbage collector is running. If IDEA is running slowly and is frequently using all its memory, you may need to increase the size of the heap.

Once the VM claims some memory by growing the size of the heap, the memory is never returned to the system—even if it's subsequently freed by garbage collection. Therefore, it's important to pick a maximum heap size that is large enough to accommodate everything you need to do, without taking so much memory away from the operating system that it becomes unusable. Refer to chapter 12 for information about customizing your memory settings.

Forcing immediate garbage collection

You can request an immediate garbage collection by left-clicking the trashcan icon. Be warned that while the garbage collector is running, you won't be able to do anything else; your interface may appear to freeze while IDEA takes out the trash. Fortunately, this delay usually lasts only a few seconds.

Hiding the status bar

If you wish, you can remove the status bar altogether. To do so, toggle the state of the **View | Status Bar** option. Hiding it gives you more real estate but at the expense of the memory indicator and other information the status bar provides.

2.1.5 Exploring the tool windows

In addition to the editor, you'll find yourself spending a lot of time in IDEA's tool windows. *Tool windows* are the slide-out/dockable/detachable window panes used for everything from navigating your project tree to viewing the compiler's output. You'll learn about them throughout the book in due course; briefly, they have the responsibilities listed in table 2.2.

Table 2.2 Tool windows are secondary windows within the IDE that provide access to specific project functionality, such as searching, running/debugging, and build processes.

Tool window	Shortcut	Usage
Messages	Alt+0	Displays output from compilation and Ant builds
Project	Alt+1	Lets you navigate through your project files and source code
Commander	Alt+2	File-management tool that helps organize your files
Find	Alt+3	Displays results from search-and-replace operations and usage analysis
Run	Alt+4	Shows output from applications launched from within the IDE
Debug	Alt+5	Interactive, symbolic Java debugger
TODO	Alt+6	Tracks task reminders and other notes embedded in your source code
Structure	Alt+7	Presents a logical view of the code structure within the current file
Hierarchy	Alt+8	Displays hierarchy relationships between classes, superclasses, and interfaces
Ant Build		Lets you navigate and execute Ant build targets
Version Control		Version-control messaging and status window

continued on next page

Table 2.2 Tool windows are secondary windows within the IDE that provide access to specific project functionality, such as searching, running/debugging, and build processes. *(continued)*

Tool window	Shortcut	Usage
Dependency viewer		Presents a tree view of all dependencies of the selected code
Inspection		Displays the results of code analysis

Tool window fundamentals

Although they play different roles, IDEA's tool windows share common behaviors and features. Each tool window is represented by an entry in the Window menu and by a button in one of four tool window bars located around the main interface, as shown in figure 2.1. By default, inactive tool windows are hidden, and you won't even see their buttons in the interface. Windows like **Find** and **Run**, for example, aren't helpful when you aren't finding or running something. Other tool windows, like **Web** and **CVS**, may not be applicable to your project and will remain hidden. IDEA keeps down the clutter by hiding tool windows when they aren't in use.

Tool windows that aren't disabled can be accessed from the tool window bars that run down both sides and across the bottom of the IDE's main interface. Click the name of the tool window, and it extends out and appears. Right-click the name of the tool window, and you can set its options, including its mode and which tool window bar the control should appear on.

Tool window modes

Tool windows have several viewing modes, the principal ones being docked mode, floating mode, and undocked mode. This choice affects the windows' placement and behavior on the screen.

In docked mode, the tool window is displayed as part of the main window. It extends and retracts into the main window space, altering the size of the other windows around it (including the main editor window). You can resize it to take no more space than necessary, and that setting will persist as you close and reopen the tool window. The real benefit of this mode is that it ensures that all of IDEA's information and context is shown simultaneously: No information is lost from view because it's covered by a secondary window.

In floating mode, a tool window is detached from the main and displayed as a separate, free-floating window. It may be moved and resized to suit your personal preferences, but it always remains on top of the IDE's main window. This option gives you more control over your screen real estate, but at the cost of covering up parts of the interface with secondary windows.

Undocked mode isn't really a named mode; rather, it's the state of the window when you have both docked mode and floating mode turned off. Like docked mode, undocked mode features tool windows as part of the main window space, and they extend and retract from the tool window bars. Undocked tool windows don't alter the other windows in the IDE, however. Instead of pushing the other windows over, resizing them to make room, undocked windows overlay the remainder of the IDE, covering what's underneath.

In addition to these options, IDEA uses *pinning mode* to define the behavior of the window when focus is shifted away. If a window is pinned, it remains when focus is diverted elsewhere; if it isn't pinned, it disappears or retracts as soon as focus leaves. This lets you, for example, keep the **Project** window docked, pinned, and permanently visible while working in the editor, and yet have the **Search Results** window pop up separately and disappear as soon as you select a result from its list. When pinning mode is enabled, a pushpin icon appears. When the pin appears horizontal, pinning mode is disabled, and the window will disappear when you focus on another window. Alternatively, you can right-click the tool window bar icon or title bar of any active tool window to enable auto hide and other window modes. Pinning mode is applicable to both docked and floating modes, but not to undocked mode.

Accessing tool windows

The button's name and icon identify the tool window; for tool windows with shortcut keys, the number identifies their key mnemonic, as listed in table 2.2. Left-click the icon, select the window from the **Window** menu, or press **Alt** and the tool window's number to access the tool window. When open, a tool window's button is highlighted, alerting you that it's open even if it's obscured by other windows. Some windows reveal themselves automatically in order to alert you to new content. For example, when you're building an application, a message window—usually hidden from view—pops to life when a compilation error occurs.

To hide an active window, click its icon in the tool window bar or press its shortcut. Alternatively, you can click the minimize window icon in its title bar or use the **Window | Hide Active Window** command (**Shift+Escape**).

> **TIP** You can hide all the visible tool windows at once by pressing **Ctrl+Shift+F12** or selecting the **Window | Hide All Tool Windows** command from the main menu.

Docking and undocking tool windows

When you open a tool window, it slides out into the main interface, revealing its contents. By default, most of the tool windows are docked with the editor, as shown in figure 2.5. A docked tool window is displayed in an independent frame, allowing you to access the editor and tool window independently. Figure 2.5 shows an example of an interface with a single, tabbed editor and a docked tool window. You hold down the left mouse button and drag out the tool window to adjust its size. You can undock the tool window by clicking its undock window icon or by disabling the **Window | Docked mode** setting from the main menu. An undocked window slides over the editor rather than creating its own frame. Docked windows don't interfere with each other, allowing you to create a multi-pane interface customized to your liking. The same window shown in figure 2.5 can be seen undocked in figure 2.6.

Floating tool windows

If docking and sliding aren't enough for you, click the **Float** icon or toggle on **Window | Floating Mode** to break the tool window out of the interface completely. Now the window is independent of the main IDE window and can be

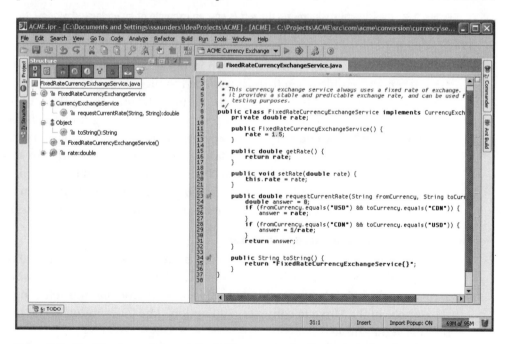

Figure 2.5 **The Structure window on the left is an example of a docked, pinned tool window.**

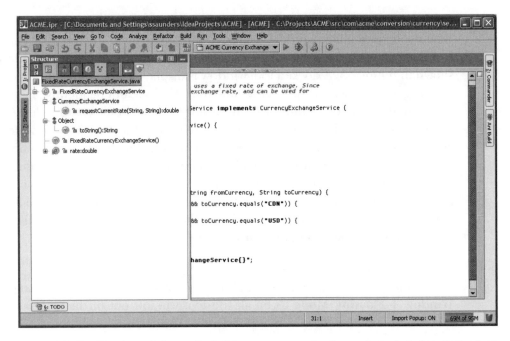

Figure 2.6 The Structure window on the left is now an example of an undocked window. Notice how it overlays (and obfuscates) the editor window underneath.

positioned wherever you'd like, as shown in figure 2.7. A floating window that is pinned remains visible when focus is returned to the editor. If pinning mode isn't selected, the window is hidden beneath the main frame. To un-float a tool window, click the **Fix** icon in its title bar, or toggle off the floating status with the **Window | Floating Mode** command; the window will return to the main interface.

Floating windows let you create a multiwindow interface (an MDI, in Windows parlance), if that's the type of thing you're into. Otherwise, you have the option of using floating windows only on those occasions when you need the contents of a window to remain on-screen while you continue to work in the main interface.

Moving tool windows to another bar

By default, none of the windows are rooted in the top tool window bar above the editor, so that toolbar doesn't normally appear. You can move any tool window to another tool window bar by right-clicking its icon or title bar and selecting one of the options in the **Move to** context menu option. The tool window's icon moves to the selected location.

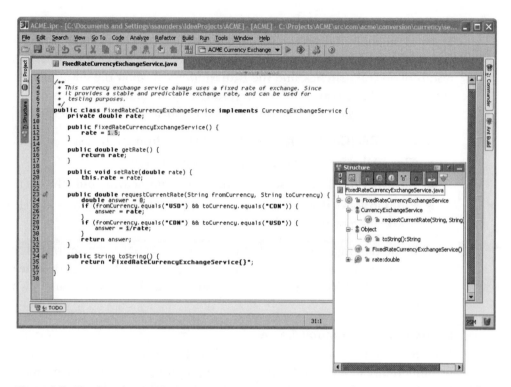

Figure 2.7 The Structure window at bottom right is an example of a floating tool window. It can be moved, placed, and resized independently.

Windows that live on the left and right tool window bars have a vertical orientation, whereas those at the top and bottom have a horizontal orientation. A horizontal orientation lets you see more columns without scrolling, and a vertical presentation is better for handling long lists. For this reason, windows like **Run** and **Messages** that contain wide output live along the bottom, but the **Project** and **Structure** windows are bound to the sides—although you're free to move them if you wish.

> **TIP**　Once you have arranged the tool windows in the locations (left, right, bottom, and so on) and with the settings you prefer (floating, pinned, and so forth), these settings are saved with your project. To use this configuration as the basis for all projects, select **Window | Store Current Layout as Default**. You can return to the default settings at any time through the **Window | Restore Default Layout** command.

Tool window tabs

Many of the tool windows can manage multiple sets of data simultaneously, if the **Open in new tab** option is selected. For instance, the **Find** window can display the results of several searches, and the **Run** window can show the output from several applications. In this case, each set of results appears in its own tab, as shown in figure 2.8. To manage your tabs, right-click any tab, and select one of these options:

- **Close Tab** (**Ctrl+Shift+F4**) closes this tab, losing any results it contained.
- **Close All** closes all the tabs, and the window too.
- **Close All But This** closes all of the other tabs, leaving only the current tab.
- **Pin Tab** locks the tab to the window, preventing it from being closed or overwritten by new results.

In addition to navigating tabs with the mouse, you can use the options in the tab's context menu to select the next or previous tab in the list. Or, you can use the shortcut keys **Alt+Right arrow** (next) and **Alt+Left arrow** (previous) while the window has focus.

Customizing tool window behavior

Each tool window's location, size, and display settings (such as docked, floating, or pinned mode) are saved with your project and are restored each time you use IDEA. This makes it possible to customize each tool window independently, based on its usage. For example, you might want to dock the **Debug** because you interact with the source code editor while using it, but undock the **Ant Build** window, which you use less frequently and only for brief actions. In the IDE settings, a number of additional tool window options are available through the **Appearance** settings panel:

Figure 2.8 Any tool window that produces output can store its output in multiple tabs, as shown in this figure. In this case, the results of multiple Find operations remain available in their own tabs.

- **Animate windows**—Deselect this option to disable the animation effect when revealing docked windows, giving them a little more snap.

- **Show window mnemonics**—Disable this option to remove the shortcut number from the tool window's icon.

- **Show tool window bars**—If disabled, the tool window bars and buttons disappear. Tool windows are still accessible through the Window menu and keyboard shortcuts.

- **Show buttons for disabled tool windows**—If enabled, this option shows placeholder buttons for inactive tool windows. The buttons are ghosted when inactive.

- **Use transparency mode for floating tool windows**—If enabled, floating windows become semitransparent (as determined by the transparency slider) when they lose focus. The timeout value specifies the number of milliseconds a window is inactive before it becomes transparent. This option is only available on Windows (see figure 2.9).

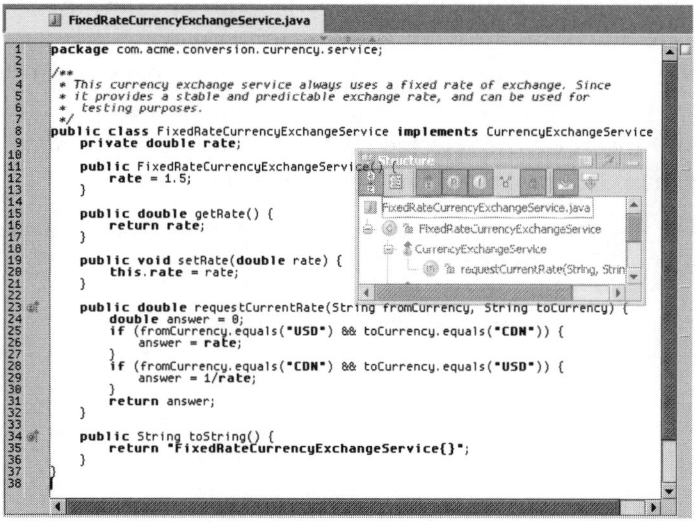

Figure 2.9 The Project tool window, configured to be both floating and transparent when not active. These settings let you work in the editor and yet see both the contents of the editor window and the tool window simultaneously.

2.2 *Using the IDEA editor*

Now that you have some familiarity with the screen artifacts and the functionality they represent, let's put that knowledge to practical use. You'll start by working on your currency converter project for ACME; then you'll apply some of IDEA's advanced, intelligent, Java-aware features and see how they might affect your development process.

2.2.1 *Writing the first ACME classes and interfaces*

Normally, the interface for the external service (such as the currency exchange rate service) would be defined for you already by some third-party library. Because this is a purely fictitious example, you'll have to define one yourself and then adhere to it. In light of that, let's assume that the interface is defined by a single method, requestCurrentRate(), which takes two String arguments that represent the three-letter acronym for the currency type (USD for the U.S. dollar, CDN for the Canadian dollar). The method returns a double that represents the rate of exchange between the two currencies. You can create a new simple interface in Java to represent this service, calling it CurrencyExchangeService and placing it in the com.acme.conversion.currency.service package using the **Project** tool window (right-click the service package and then choose **New | Interface**, or press **Alt+Insert** on the selected package). Once it has been created, you can edit the interface to have the code shown in listing 2.1.

> **Listing 2.1 The interface for requesting rates from a fictitious currency exchange rate service**

```
package com.acme.conversion.currency.service;

/**
 * This interface defines the standard API for all currency
 * exchange services. All currency exchange services, regardless
 * of implementation, will adhere to this interface.
 */
public interface CurrencyExchangeService {
    /**
     * Requests the current exchange rate from one currency
     * to another.
     * @param fromCurrency the original Currency
     * @param toCurrency the 'destination' or final Currency
     * @return the currency exchange rate
     */
```

```
    double requestCurrentRate(String fromCurrency,
                               String toCurrency);
}
```

There could be 100 different implementations of this interface, any of which you might be required to use. Rather than hard-code a specific implementation into the client code, let's request an implementation from an intermediary class. That way, you're not bound to a one specific service: the intermediary can pick and choose what implementation to provide each time a request is made. Create a CurrencyExchangeServiceFactory in the same package as the interface, and edit the file to look like listing 2.2.

Listing 2.2   The factory that will retrieve a CurrencyExchangeService for you

```
package com.acme.conversion.currency.service;

/**
 * This factory is responsible for providing a valid currency
 * exchange service upon request.
 */
public class CurrencyExchangeServiceFactory {

    public static CurrencyExchangeService getService() {
        // The body of this method should decide on and return
        //  a valid CurrencyExchangeService of some sort.

        // Until we either write one (or are provided one),
        // we can only return null here.
        return null;
    }

}
```

Finally, let's write a simple command-line program to use this factory and interface. Use the **Project** tool window to create a new package called com.acme.conversion.currency.client, and then create a new class in that package called CommandLineClient. Edit the file to look like listing 2.3.

Listing 2.3   The first implementation of your command line client

```
package com.acme.conversion.currency.client;

import com.acme.conversion.currency.service.CurrencyExchangeService;
import
  com.acme.conversion.currency.service.CurrencyExchangeServiceFactory;
```

```
public class CommandLineClient {
    public static void main(String[] args) {
        if (args.length != 2) {
            System.out.println("Requested parameters: " +
            "<source currency code> <target currency code>");
        }
        else {
            CurrencyExchangeService service =
               CurrencyExchangeServiceFactory.getService();
            double rate =
               service.requestCurrentRate(args[0], args[1]);
            System.out.println("Rate is " + rate);
        }
    }
}
```

Request currency
exchange service

Determine
exchange rate

Print calculated rate

Note that this command-line client won't work yet. You know the interface details, and you can easily create a client that uses that interface, but you still need an implementation of that interface to be provided by the factory. Save your work, and we'll discuss some of IDEA's features that can help you write that implementation.

2.2.2 Opening files into the editor

As discussed in chapter 1, the **Project** window gives you access to all the files in your project. You can double-click any recognized file (other than binary files, of course) to open it in the editor; alternatively, select the file and press **F4**. You can also load files into the editor through most of the other places where Java classes are referenced: for example, there are direct class references in result windows like compilation error messages, search usages windows, and so forth. When you see a class referenced somewhere, such as in a **Find** result tool window like that shown in figure 2.10, right-click and select the **Jump to Source** option from the context menu (or, again, press **F4**).

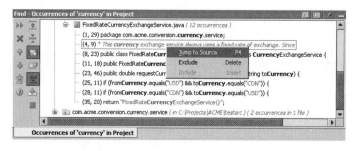

Figure 2.10
This Find tool window is the result of searching the project for usages of the word *Currency*. You can click the results to jump directly to the underlying source by loading it into the IDEA editor.

Figure 2.11
The Go To | Class command makes it easy to
load classes into the editor; all you have to know
is the names (or part of the names).

You can quickly load any Java class into the editor by using the **Go To | Class**
(**Ctrl+N**) command and entering the name of the class into the dialog box that
appears. As you type, matching entries will appear in the drop-down box, making
locating your file quick and convenient. Use the arrows keys or mouse to select an
entry, and then press **Enter** or double-click to load it. By default, only files that
are included in your project path are included. If you enable the **Include nonproject classes** option, however, your entire source path will be searched, including libraries and the JDK. The wildcard character (*) can be used anywhere in the
name to expand the search, as illustrated in figure 2.11.

> **TIP** The **Go To | Class** command is aware of the CamelHumps pattern (the
> typical use of upper- and lowercase letters in naming Java classes) and
> can use it to search for class names. For example, if you need to open the
> ArrayIndexOutOfBoundsException class, type AIOOB in the **Go To |
> Class** field, and IDEA will find all classes that follow the CamelHumps
> pattern. (Don't forget to select the **Include non-project classes** option,
> for this example to work!)

The **Go To | File** (**Ctrl+Shift+N**) command works the same way, but it loads files
by filename rather than by class name. You can see an example of this feature in
action in figure 2.12. This command can be used to load text, JSP, HTML, and
other text files. By default, Java files aren't included in the search results unless
you enable the **Include java files** option. Wildcard expansion is also supported
by this command.

Figure 2.12
The Go To | File command works exactly like the Go To |
Class command, but it operates on non-Java files.

TIP   The **Go To** commands support an extremely useful feature called *quick switching*. Let's say you use **Go To | Class** to find a specific class and enter the name, only to realize that it's not a Java class but an XML file you're searching for. If you press **Ctrl+Shift+N**, the pop-up quick-switches to the **Go To | File** pop-up and keeps your entered text in the field.

Reopening a recently opened file

You can reload a recently opened file by selecting the **View | Recent Files** command or by pressing **Ctrl+E** while in the editor. Selecting this option displays a dialog box containing a list of files you have opened recently. Files are sorted from most-recently opened to least-recently opened. You can use your mouse or the arrow keys to select a file to reopen from the list. The maximum number of files stored in the recent history list can be configured in the IDE settings by adjusting the **Recent files limit** option of the **Editor** settings panel.

How IDEA handles nonproject files

As discussed in chapter 1, IDEA was designed to work with your source files in the context of a module composed of well-defined source and class paths. This allows IDEA to understand the relationships between your source files, the module, and the rest of the project. Occasionally, you'll need to edit (or at least view) a file from outside your project. Perhaps you need to view a log file from an application server where your code is deployed or reference code in another project. Whatever the case, and wherever your file, you can use the **File | Open File** command to load the file into the editor. If the file is outside of your project, you'll have to live with some limitations:

- You can't use any of the code-analysis tools on the file.
- You can't refactor the file in any way.
- No error analysis is performed on the file.
- You can't compile the file if it's a Java source file.
- You can't reformat the code if it's a Java source file.

As you can see, you can edit the file, and that's about it. Allowing anything more would confuse the project situation, because IDEA wouldn't understand how the current code is supposed to relate to the rest of the project with regard to class paths and other dependencies.

2.2.3 *Saving your work*

One thing you may initially find disconcerting about the editor is the lack of ability to save a single file. IDEA works differently than you may be used to, because you don't have to explicitly save individual files.

When you exit IDEA, it saves your files automatically, so you never have to worry about manually saving your work. IDEA doesn't even alert you that a file has unsaved changes unless you've enabled the option to show asterisks in their tabs (found under the **Editor** group of **IDE Settings**). If you enable that option, files with unsaved changes are indicated by an asterisk symbol next to the name of the tab. When you're done editing your files, use the **File | Save All** command (**Ctrl+S**) to save the changes. IDEA executes a Save All operation when you close your project as well, so all active tabs are saved.

Closing files without saving them

If you don't want to save changes you've already made, you can close the tab by selecting one of the following options from the **File** menu or by right clicking any tab in the editor:

- **Close Active Editor** (**Ctrl+F4**) closes the file in the active tab only without saving any changes.
- **Close All Editors** closes all the editor tabs without saving any changes.
- **Close All Editors but Current** closes everything except the current tab.

Closing a file with unsaved changes doesn't discard your changes and return the file to its unmodified state, however. When you close a file with unsaved changes, your changes are preserved in the current editing session even though they aren't written to disk. If you reopen the file in the editor, your unsaved changes will be restored.

> **TIP** You can also close a tab by holding down the **Shift** key while left-clicking the tab, or by middle-clicking the tab if you have a three-button mouse.

 A new option in the **Window** menu lets you close all unmodified editor tabs with one selection. This is an easy and convenient way to clean up your workspace and close files that you opened for reference only. This operation is also available by right-clicking the tab bar in the editor or any individual editor tab and selecting **Close All Unmodified Editors**.

Auto-saving your changes

You have the option of letting IDEA save files for you on a regular basis. To enable this auto-save option, bring up the **General** options of the **IDE Settings**. Select the **AutoSave files** option, and specify the number of seconds of inactivity required to trigger a save. Once this option is enabled, the editor will automatically save any changes to your file after you stop using the mouse or keyboard for the specified amount of time.

Saving files when you leave the editor window

A related option in the **General** settings, **Save files on frame deactivation**, is particularly useful. This option automatically saves all of your editor's open files for you each time you deactivate the IDEA window by switching to a command prompt or other application window. It's a good idea to enable this option if you're compiling or building outside of IDEA and frequently forget to save your changes before building. Of course, the downside is that sometimes you'll end up saving changes you might not have been ready to save, but hey—that's what version control is for, right?

Reverting your changes

If, after working with a file, you change your mind and want to back out all of your unsaved changes, select the **File | Reload from Disk** command. It reloads the current file, throwing out any changes you made during the current session. This option is unavailable if there are no unsaved changes in the current file.

> **TIP**   For a more powerful way to back out your changes, see section 8.3, "Using IDEA's local history" in chapter 8.

Exporting your files to HTML format

The **File | Export to HTML** option lets you create a color-coded, hyperlinked HTML representation of your source files. This command acts on the currently active file, or the currently selected file or directory in the **Project** view. This option re-creates the view you see in the editor window as an HTML document, complete with full syntax colorization. This isn't JavaDoc; it's the source code itself, with pretty formatting and all the necessary escaping applied. Keep in mind that the resulting HTML code won't be useful as source code—it's full of HTML markup, so it won't compile—but it makes a great reference. For example, you might consider posting a Web-accessible copy of your source tree on your

Figure 2.13 You can view an HTML marked-up copy of source code using Internet Explorer.

intranet or distributing it with your application as reference material. You can see some sample output in figure 2.13.

The **Generate hyperlinks to classes** options in the **Export to HTML** dialog can be enabled to create hyperlinks to all the local class references. This option is applicable only when you're exporting an entire directory or package of source code, which can be accomplished by enabling the **All files** option. This makes it possible to navigate through the entire source tree from the comfort of your web browser. Specify the output directory where you want your HTML files generated. The files will follow the package structure, and the files' extensions will be changed appropriately.

2.2.4 *Printing your file*

The command **File | Print** creates a hard copy of a file. You can either select a file or directory in the **Project** view or print the active file in the editor. You can customize the following options shown in figure 2.14:

Figure 2.14
Need to bring a print out of your latest bug fix to tomorrow's status meeting? Use the File | Print command.

- **Font** specifies the font type and size to use for printing the document text.
- **Show line numbers**, if enabled, includes line numbers in the output.
- **Draw border**, if enabled, draws a box around the entire page.
- **Color printing**, if enabled, uses your color scheme when printing.
- **Syntax printing**, if enabled, includes your color scheme font options and text effects.
- **Word wrap (Advanced)** enables word wrapping.
- **Margins (Advanced)** lets you tweak the margins of the printout.

When you click the **Print** button, you're shuffled off to your platform's native Print dialog, giving you a chance to further customize your printer's settings. Unfortunately, IDEA has no Print Preview function, but many printer drivers provide their own.

2.2.5 *Navigating in the editor*

Table 2.3 summarizes the basic navigation keys. In addition, you can use the mouse to position your cursor manually anywhere in the source file. IDEA also keeps a history of your recent navigation steps, much like a web browser. You can move back and forth through your previous steps by choosing **Go To | Back** (**Ctrl+Alt+Left arrow**) and **Go To | Forward** (**Ctrl+Alt+Right arrow**) from the main menu.

TIP Sometimes you aren't interested in your previous navigation steps but rather wish to return to the last place you made a change in your code. You can return the cursor to the location of your last edit by pressing **Ctrl+Shift+Backspace** or by selecting **Go To | Last Edit Location**. This command even works from within another file. Using it multiple times continues to move back through your editing history, edit by edit.

Table 2.3 Like most mature editors, IDEA provides a number of keyboard shortcuts for navigation within a file, including a few specific to code navigation (such as method-by-method and brace-by-brace navigation).

Shortcut	Moves the cursor...
Alt+Down, Alt+Up	To the next/previous method in a Java file or the next tag in an XML or HTML file
Home, End	To the start/end of the line
Ctrl+Home, Ctrl+End	To the start/end of the file
Page Up, Page Down	Up/down one page
Arrow keys	In the appropriate direction
Ctrl+Page Up, Ctrl+Page Down	To the top/bottom of the screen
Ctrl+M	To the middle of the screen
Ctrl+Alt+Left arrow, Ctrl+Alt+Right arrow	Back/forward one navigation step
Ctrl+Shift+BackSpace	To the previous edit position
Ctrl+[, Ctrl+]	To the code block's start/end
Gtrl+G	To a line
F2, Shift+F2	To the next/previous highlighted error

Enabling the Home and End smart keys

Normally, the **Home** key moves your cursor to the start of a line: the first column. However, if the **Home smart key** option is enabled through the editor settings, the **Home** key jumps to the logical start of the line, instead, which is defined as the first nonspace character. Think of this option as redefining the **Home** key to go to the start of the code rather than the start of the line. Pressing the **Home** key again places you at the first column, so both behaviors of the key are still accessible.

The **End** key normally moves you to the end of the current line. As with the **Home** key, enabling the **End smart key** option changes the **End** key's behavior so it moves to the logical end of the line rather than the physical end. However, the logical and physical end of a line are usually the same, except when you're on a blank line. On a blank line, the logical end should follow the indentation appropriate for the current line. So, the **End smart key** option adds this indentation (as defined in your code style) and moves into it, positioning the cursor at the new end (and logical beginning) of the line.

Scrolling the editor view

Scrollbars appear on the right and bottom borders of the editor window as needed. If you have a mouse with a wheel, you can use it to scroll up and down (as well as the usual on-screen controls).

You can also scroll the editor window using just the keyboard. Use **Ctrl+M** to center the view on the current line, and use **Ctrl+Up** and **Ctrl+Down** to scroll the view up and down one line at a time. The system will also scroll the editor view automatically as you reach the edge of the visible area either through typing or through navigation.

You can scroll the view an entire screen at a time by clicking inside the scrollbar track anywhere other than on the scrollbar itself. Clicking above the scrollbar scrolls up one screen, and clicking below moves down a screen. This is equivalent to using the navigation keys **Page Up** and **Page Down**.

Jumping to a specific line number

You can jump to any line number directly by using the **Go To | Line** command or by pressing **Ctrl+G**. You'll be prompted with a dialog box, into which you type the line number you wish to jump to. This is an absolute line number, not a relative one, so you can't jump back or forth a specific number of lines. If the line number you enter is greater than the number of lines in the file, you'll go to the last line of the file. As discussed earlier, you can add line numbers to the editor window display through the editor settings.

IDEA 5 You can now disable many of the editor's advanced mouse options through the **Advanced mouse usages** group in the editor settings panel. You can selectively enable drag-and-drop support, dynamic font sizing, and camel-hump selection by checking the appropriate options.

2.2.6 *Making text selections*

The basic way to select text is through the standard practice of dragging out a selection with the mouse. With the keyboard, you can hold down the **Shift** key in combination with any of the navigation and movement keys described in the previous section to drag out a selection along with the cursor. For example, **Ctrl+Shift+Page Down** selects everything from the cursor position to the bottom of the screen. From the main menu, you can also select **Edit | Select All** (**Ctrl+A**) to select the entire contents of the file.

> **TIP** To select an entire line, click in the gutter area next to the line, or triple-click the line itself. You can also drag your mouse over the gutter to select a block of lines.

By far the most useful selection tool is listed only in the Keymap settings, not in any of the menus. It's the modestly named **Select word at caret** command (**Ctrl+W**). Although pressing **Ctrl+W** does select the current word, this command is much more powerful than its name suggests.

With each successive press, the selection grows to include the selection's next level of containing code. For example, if you place your cursor inside the expression of a conditional block, successive **Ctrl+W** presses expand the selection from a single word, to the contents of the expression of which it's a part, to its entire conditional block, to its containing method body, to the method itself, to its containing class, and so on.

If you already have a selection, pressing **Ctrl+W** expands the selection to include the entire logical block of code. For this reason, we prefer to think of this feature as "expand selection to include containing block" rather than selecting the current word. The command **Unselect word at caret** (**Ctrl+Shift+W**) works the same way, only in reverse: Each successive press shrinks the selection a level. If you've enabled the CamelHumps option in the editor settings, the selection grows and shrinks on logical word boundaries.

> **WARNING** This feature is so useful, and can become so imprinted on the part of your brain responsible for typing, that it can cause problems outside of IDEA. On Microsoft Windows, many other applications map **Ctrl+W** to mean "close the current window" (on the Mac, the command is **Cmd+W**). We can't tell you how many times while writing this book we tried to use **Ctrl+W** to expand a selection inside Word or Internet Explorer—only to close the application! Worse yet, it took two months to figure out the real cause of the "applications-keep-trying-to-close-themselves" virus we were convinced we'd contracted. You might want to remap this key combination in the Keymap settings panel if you have the same problem.

IDEA 5 Another handy new feature in IDEA 5.0 is the ability to easily reorganize your code by relocating a selected line, a block of code, or an entire method declaration by moving it up and down in relationship to the existing code structure. For example, moving a method up within the code relocates it between the two previous methods. To use this feature, select the code you wish to relocate using any of the traditional means (such as repeated **Ctrl+W** actions) and then execute the **Code | Move statement up** or **Code | Move statement down** action. Alternatively, you can use the much more convenient **Ctrl+Shift+Up** and **Ctrl+Shift+ Down** shortcuts.

2.2.7 *Using IDEA's undo and redo mechanism*

You'll find the seemingly standard **Undo** operation, along with its twin **Redo**, at the top of the **Edit** menu and in the main IDEA toolbar. Behind its mild-mannered facade hides a powerful editing feature. There are the standard keyboard shortcuts, **Ctrl+Z** (Undo) and **Ctrl+Shift+Z** (Redo), as well as a special bonus set, **Alt+Backspace** and **Alt+Shift+Backspace**—options you may find more convenient to press, if somewhat less familiar.

You're probably familiar with the basic operation of the **Undo** and **Redo** commands. **Undo** backs out the last change you made to the document. **Redo** does just the opposite: It undoes the last **Undo** command. Note, however, that it doesn't repeat the last operation—it only restores the document back to the state before the previous undo. Each time you press **Undo**, you back out the previous change, moving back in time as it were. Pressing **Redo** of course moves you forward until there are no more changes to reapply. You're free to undo or redo as long as you want, but when you exit the application, you lose your undo history.

IDEA's **Undo** feature has one important difference from those you may be used to: It's smart about deciding what sort of activity constitutes an undoable step. It doesn't just back out the last typed character, it uses your editing activity to determine the most logical places to break actions into steps. A number of events are used to signal the end of a logical step, including these:

- Pressing **Enter**
- Using the mouse to reposition the cursor
- Using any of the navigation shortcuts
- Cutting, pasting, or tabbing

This functionality makes the undo/redo mechanism extremely convenient, because its concept of an operation will more closely match your own (for example, "undo the last line I wrote" as opposed to "undo the last letter I typed"). However, it doesn't stop there. The undo mechanism also understands how to undo complex operations such as creating and deleting files, refactoring code, and reformatting your source. Some of these operations involve multiple subsystems, all of which are undone in a single operation. For example, when you rename a class, not only does the class declaration block have to change, but the name of its source file and its version control system entry must change as well. When you undo or redo complex operations like these, IDEA always asks you to confirm your decision.

2.2.8 Cutting, copying, and pasting

The toolbar includes entries for the **Cut**, **Copy**, and **Paste** actions; they're also on the **Edit** menu and the editor's context menu. Each of them has two identical sets of keyboard shortcuts; the choice is yours, because they do the same thing:

- **Cut—Ctrl+X** or **Shift+Delete**
- **Copy—Ctrl+C** or **Ctrl+Insert**
- **Paste—Ctrl+V** or **Shift+Insert**

Because IDEA uses the system clipboard, you're free to cut and paste text between applications. This also means that anything you put into the clipboard remains there even after you exit the application and that any other cutting and pasting on the system affects your clipboard entries in IDEA. IDEA only supports plaintext clipboard entries, so any rich text (such as text from a web page) is stripped of formatting before insertion.

> **TIP** Being aware of the requirements applied to the `String` literals in Java code, IDEA eases your job when you copy or paste `String` values. Quotes and other special symbols are automatically escaped when you paste strings. In addition, the redundant escape symbols are removed when you cut or copy `String` values into the clipboard. So, you can use the clean value anywhere, and outside IDEA.

IDEA has an extended clipboard mode that remembers recent clipboard selections and lets you paste from any one of them. To access the extended clipboard, select the **Paste** option from the **Edit** menu or context menu or by pressing **Ctrl+Shift+V** or **Ctrl+Shift+Insert**. As long as your clipboard isn't empty, you'll see the dialog shown in figure 2.15.

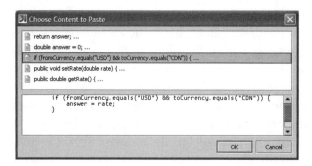

Figure 2.15
The extended clipboard stores your previous clipboard selections, allowing you to choose from several selections when pasting.

The list at the top of the dialog contains one-line summaries of your past clipboard entries, with the most recent entry at the top. You can select any clipping and view its contents in the preview window below the list. To paste an entry, select it and press **Enter** or click the **OK** button, or double-click the entry as a shortcut. The extended clipboard format is also supported by some native applications, which can share their data with IDEA and vice versa.

> **TIP**   You can compare the most recent contents of the clipboard with the current selection by selecting **Compare with Clipboard** from the editor's context menu. This command launches the diff tool viewer, which is described in more detail in chapter 8.

You can control the maximum number of stored clipboard entries through the editor settings under the **Limits** group. When you reach your limit, the oldest entry is removed from the list. You can manually edit the list of items by selecting any entry and pressing the **Delete** key to remove it from the clipboard.

> **TIP**   You can use **Cut**, **Copy**, and **Paste** with the files and packages in your **Project** view. A cut and paste is analogous to moving a file, whereas a copy and paste creates a new file using the copied one as a template. These operations are shortcuts for the **Move** and **Copy** refactorings, which are discussed in more detail in chapter 9.

IDEA 5   Even the **Copy** command has a few new tricks in 5.0. For starters, X-Windows users will appreciate that IDEA now supports standard X-Windows style copy and paste actions under that environment. You highlight the text to be copied, switch to the location where you want to copy, and press the middle mouse button to paste.

Copy also now works inside lookup lists, such as those that appear on **Ctrl+N** or during code completion. Any selected item in the list can be copied to the clipboard via **Ctrl+C** shortcut and then pasted, say, in the editor, even as a fully qualified name (if appropriate).

A new command, **Copy Reference (Ctrl+Alt+Shift+C)** from the **Edit** or popup menu, lets you place a logical copy of a symbol (such as a method, variable, or class) into the clipboard. When you later paste the reference, perhaps into another source file, IDEA correctly references the original symbol, adding the necessary class or package qualifiers as required.

2.2.9 *Searching for and replacing text*

Like any good editor, IDEA provides extensive search and replace capabilities. However, many of the situations in which you're used to using search and replace have been made obsolete by IDEA's refactoring features. For example, refactoring lets you rename methods, variables, and even entire classes, while automatically correcting all references to them. We'll talk about refactoring in chapter 9.

Performing an incremental search

The most basic (and, some say, handiest) of IDEA's search commands is the incremental or *type-ahead* search. It's really more of a navigation feature than a search feature. This type of search lets you jump to a matching term in the current document. To begin a search, choose the **Search | Incremental Search** command (**Alt+F3**).

You won't see a proper dialog box, only a little **Search for** floating prompt. Begin typing the word or phrase you want to find: With each keystroke, the search is updated, instantly taking you to the next match within the current file. If no more matches are available, the search term changes from black to red. If the search term is black, there are additional matches; you can use the **Up** and **Down** arrow keys to move between the search results. You can press **Escape** or any navigation key to stop the search.

By the way, a form of incremental search also works in many other areas of IDEA, such as the **Project** window: just start typing to activate it.

> **TIP** To repeat the last incremental search, press **Alt+F3** twice in succession. The first press brings up the search prompt, and the second recalls the last search term.

Searching within the active editor

If you need a search with a little more control than is offered by the incremental search, you can use the standard search tool, accessed through the **Search | Find** option, the **Find** toolbar icon, or the shortcut **Ctrl+ F**. This action displays a **Find Text** window, as shown in figure 2.16.

Figure 2.16 The Find operation searches only the currently opened file in the editor, using the options and scope you specify in this window.

> **TIP** If you have a current selection when you bring up the search window, it will be prepopulated as the text to find.

Enter the text you want to search for in the **Text to find** field. This field accepts text directly, but it also has a history drop-down that remembers your recent search terms. The dialog's options let you control the various search options:

- **Case sensitive**, if selected, finds only results matching your search text exactly, in terms of upper- and lowercase letters. Otherwise, case isn't considered when searching for matching text.

- **Whole words only**, if enabled, requires the entire search term to appear alone, surrounded by the start of a line, a space, a tab, or some other punctuation (for example, if you type fox and enable this option, then *foxtrot* won't be found as a match). This option is disabled when using regular expressions.

- **Regular expressions** interprets the search text as a regular expression rather than a simple text match. IDEA uses the JDK 1.4 regular expression library for parsing the regular expression, which is very similar to Perl 5 regular expression syntax; refer to the Java SDK documentation (specifically, the java.util.regexp.Pattern class) for information on writing regular expressions.

- **Scope** specifies the search's scope. If you select the **Selected text** option, the search only occurs within the current selection (if any) rather than the entire document (as specified by the **Global** option).

- **Direction** specifies the search direction for finding successive matches (forward or backward).

- **Origin** specifies the starting location for the search: either from the current cursor location to the end of the file or from the beginning of the file (**Entire scope**).

Click the **Find** button to begin your search. If there aren't any matches, you're informed of this sad fact. Otherwise, the first match relative to your starting point is selected in the editor window, and your cursor is repositioned to that point. To navigate to the next match, select **Search | Find Next (F3)** or **Search | Find Previous (Shift+F3)** to go back to the previous match. When you reach the end of your matches, you have the option of looping through them again.

Searching for a specific word in the editor

The **Find word at caret** search is a shortcut for performing a search for the current word. Select (or place your caret on) a word, select **Search | Find Word at Caret** or press **Ctrl+F3**, and you're off. This action behaves exactly like the standard search but requires an exact match on the word you're searching for; and you aren't given the chance to change any of the search options. **F3** and **Shift+F3** navigate to the next and previous occurrence of the term.

TIP   When searching Java code, you can also use the **Search** menu's **Find Usages (Alt+F7)** and **Find Usages in File (Ctrl+F7)** commands to find actual usages of a symbol rather than just a string match.

Performing a search and replace

As you can see in figure 2.17, the only difference between the search dialog and the replace dialog is the added ability to specify a replacement term and an option to preserve the original case of the replaced text (for example all caps or initial caps). To begin a search and replace, select **Search | Replace,** press **Ctrl+R**, or click the **Replace** icon on the main toolbar.

If the operation finds matching text, the editor navigates to the first match and prompts you with a dialog box to specify how to proceed. Your choices are as follows:

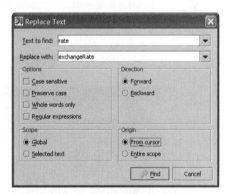

Figure 2.17   The Replace operation uses options that are almost identical to those of the Find operation. And, similarly, it operates on the currently opened file in the editor.

- **Replace** substitutes the current match with your replacement text and moves to the next match.

- **Skip** ignores this match and continues to the next one.

- **All** replaces all the rest of the matches without asking, ending the search-and-replace operation.

- **Cancel** aborts the search-and-replace operation. Any replacements already made are kept.

TIP   The **Replace Text** window is regular-expression capable, just like the **Find Text** window. You can, for example, use a regular expression in the **Text to find** text field that contains grouped sequences and then use back references in the **Replace with** text field.

Search across a project

IDEA gives you the ability to search for matching text in all the files in your project or, if you prefer, a particular directory hierarchy. You do so through the **Search | Find in Path** command (**Ctrl+Shift+F**), whose dialog box is shown in figure 2.18.

As you can see, you have some of these same options as in a single-file search, but your scoping control has changed. Now you can choose between the entire project, a specific module, and a specified directory. You can use the drop-down to choose a module or the file browser control to select the folder to search (and then, optionally, enable the **Recursively** option to search any child directories of your selected directory). Additionally, the **File mask** option restricts the search to files matching a certain naming pattern. Click **Find** to begin the search.

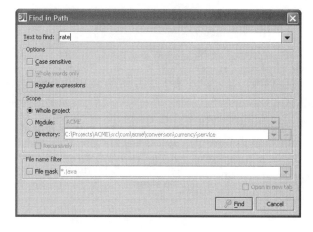

Figure 2.18
The Find in Path operation expands the scope of the Find operation and lets you specify a single directory, a recursive directory, a complete module, or the whole project as the scope of the search.

If matches are found, a **Find** tool window opens, as shown in figure 2.19. If you're searching a large number of files and get tired of waiting, click the **Background** button in the search progress window; it lets you work on other items while IDEA keeps searching. You can follow the search's progress in the status bar; when it's complete, the results appear in the **Find** window.

> **TIP**   When the Find process is running in the foreground, you can cancel it with the **Stop** button in the resulting dialog. Once the process has been put into the background, you can cancel it by clicking the **Stop back-ground search** button in the **Find** tool window's toolbar.

Working with the search results window

The results of your search are displayed in the **Find** tool window once the search is complete. If a set of search results already appears in the **Find** window, it's over-written unless you've enabled the **Open in new tab** option when creating your search. The results window shown in figure 2.19, for example, has one set of search results, denoted by the lower tab labeled *Occurrences of 'rate' in Project*. Additional search result sets would create additional tabs next to this one.

The results view includes an entry for each matching line of text found in your search path along with a reference to its location in your project. The numbers next to each entry are the row and column of the start of the match within the file. The matching terms are shown in bold. You can control the display of the results using the various options on the **Find** window's toolbar, as summarized in table 2.4.

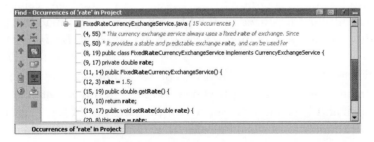

Figure 2.19   Results from a Find in Path operation are shown in the Find tool window on a tree control. The results are logically organized into directories (for non-Java files) or packages (for Java files).

Table 2.4 The Find tool window has a number of operations that affect its behavior and your view of the search results.

Icon	Action	Shortcut
▶▶	Rerun search	Ctrl+F5
✖	Close tool window	Ctrl+Shift+F4
⬆	Navigate to previous occurrence	Ctrl+Alt+Up
⬇	Navigate to next occurrence	Ctrl+Alt+Down
🖐	Export to text file	Alt+O
?	Help	F1
⬍	Expand all	Ctrl+Numpad+
⬍	Collapse all	Ctrl+Numpad+
📦	Group by packages	Ctrl+P
📦	Group by modules	Ctrl+D
⬇	Merge duplicated lines	Ctrl+F
⬇	Scroll to source	

A particularly useful option is **Group by package**. If this option isn't selected, all of your search results are organized by the file they come from. Enabling **Group by package** adds another level of hierarchy, organizing each file by the package it lives in.

You can navigate through the search results one at a time in the editor by double-clicking a match (single-clicking if you've enabled **Scroll to source**), right-clicking the match and selecting **Edit Source**, or pressing the **F4** key. You can also use the right-click menu to perform version control operations, as discussed in chapter 8.

Clicking the **Rerun** icon (**Ctrl+F5**) executes the search again, updating the results if need be. If your edits have removed any of the matches or created new ones, the changes appear in the **Find** window.

Replacing text across a project

The command **Search | Replace in Path** (**Ctrl+Shift+R**) works similarly to the **Replace** command discussed earlier in terms of replacing matches and like the **Find in Path** operation in terms of the results window it returns. As before, you see all the matches in the **Find** window, but you're taken to the first match and immediately prompted with a dialog that offers the following options:

- **Replace** replaces the current match with the replacement text you've specified and moves to the next match.
- **Skip** moves on to the next match, leaving the current one unchanged.
- **All in This File** replaces all matches in the file containing the current match and open in the editor with your replacement text, and moves on to the next file with matches.
- **All Files** replaces all matches across all files.
- **Cancel** closes this replacement dialog and returns to the **Find** window.

From this dialog, it would appear that you have three choices: step through each match one by one, replace everything, or replace nothing. If you have many results, you'll be glad to hear that there is a more selective (and faster) way of processing your replacement selections. When you close the replacement dialog and return to the **Find** window, three buttons appear at the bottom of the window:

- **Do Replace All** replaces all nonexcluded matches. You may exclude any subset of the found files that you wish, including entire packages, classes, or methods. Items can be excluded from the context menu or by selecting them and pressing **Delete**.
- **Replace Selected** performs a replacement on the currently selected matches.
- **Cancel** aborts the entire process. Any replacements youve already accepted remain replaced, but you can use the Undo operation to revert them.

2.3 *Summary*

IDEA's editor is a full-featured editor with most of the functionality you expect to find in any world-class editing package. It supports such features as tabbed-file editing, tab grouping, a recent file list, and the like. In addition, IDEA uses the gutter and the marker bar to provide real-time information about the state of the edited file, providing useful features that are uncommon in other editing applications. All of IDEA's operations can be reassigned to preferred keystrokes and mouse clicks in the IDE's settings, so it's not necessary to relearn commands when you begin using this editor.

IDEA uses tool windows to provide access to functionality not directly embedded in the editor itself. Many of the tool windows deal with operations whose scope exceeds that of a single file, such as project navigation. Because you can also customize the location, docking style, and behavior of these windows, they can be adjusted to best suit an individual user's needs.

Ultimately, migrating from another editor to IDEA's editor should be a relatively painless procedure, and the IDEA editor is easy to learn and use.

Using the IDEA editor

You can use any editor to write Java code. The factor that distinguishes IDEA's editor is its *intelligence:* the editor's awareness of the nuances of the Java language and the set of powerful features that are enabled through that awareness. These features allow you to perform difficult tasks easily and thus improve your speed and efficiency in developing Java software. This chapter will go beyond IDEA's basic editing capabilities and explore the most useful of these intelligent features.

3.1 What makes IDEA the intelligent editor?

IDEA understands Java.

The IDE has a fundamental understanding of the Java programming language. It understands the basic concepts of classes and packages. It knows the primitive data types, and it knows that they aren't treated the same as fully fledged objects in the system. It knows about Java language syntax, about inheritance and overriding, about interfaces, about reflection and delegation, about arrays and collections and iterators. It knows about visibility modifiers, and nested loops, and exception handling. And it knows about all the silly little mistakes that humans make when they program in a software language.

And, knowing all this, it's able to provide incredibly useful features that no simple editor can hope to emulate. It can navigate around the package and class hierarchy with ease (where most other editors are only familiar with the file and directory hierarchy). It can provide inline documentation while you write, to demonstrate proper method call parameters and API usage. It can generate common code for you, saving you the time of writing mindless, formulaic code again and again. And it can analyze your code as you write it, looking for common mistakes that we all fall into. In some cases, it can even suggest how to fix the code… or *it can fix it itself, if you want it to.*

Be warned. It may even know Java better than you do.

3.2 Using code folding

Code folding is an editor feature that lets you hide portions of your source code that are irrelevant to the current task or otherwise distracting. You can collapse an arbitrary selection, an expression, a single line, a method, or even an entire class. Folding code you aren't interested in makes reading the source code simpler, because you only see the relevant lines. For example, in figure 3.1, the contents of one of the `if` clauses and a previous method have been folded.

Folded code is displayed as a shaded ellipsis, whereas folded blocks also retain their opening and closing delimiters. You can control the color and style of the

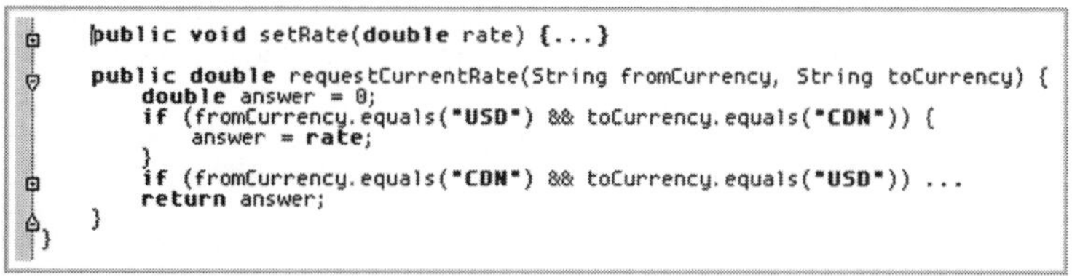

```
public void setRate(double rate) {...}

public double requestCurrentRate(String fromCurrency, String toCurrency) {
    double answer = 0;
    if (fromCurrency.equals("USD") && toCurrency.equals("CDN")) {
        answer = rate;
    }
    if (fromCurrency.equals("CDN") && toCurrency.equals("USD")) ...
    return answer;
}
}
```

Figure 3.1   IDEA's code folding feature lets you collapse arbitrary sections of code to a single line.

folded code through your color scheme. Previewing the contents of a folded area is also very easy: Move your mouse pointer over the folded region, and its contents appear in a pop-up tool-tip. You can left-click your mouse while viewing the preview to unfold the code. When you move your mouse away, the preview closes. Table 3.1 lists all the operations related to code folding.

The icons next to the gutter (see figure 3.1) form an outline used to control code folding. All JavaDoc blocks, methods, inner classes, and import blocks (those with more than one line, anyway) are bounded by code folding outlines, making it easy to collapse and expand them. A plus-sign icon indicates previously folded code that you can expand by clicking the icon. A minus icon delimits a block of foldable code. Notice that the minus icons are in little arrow shapes; when you click one of these icons, the area between the arrows collapses into a single line.

Personally, we find the little icons a distraction, but you can turn them off through the **Editor** settings by disabling the **Show code folding outline** option. You can still use the code-folding feature through the **Folding** submenu in the **View** or editor context menu. These actions are available even if you have the code-folding outlines enabled, allowing you to use the menu options if you wish. Plus, the menu options give you more control than the outlines, letting you fold arbitrary selections.

Table 3.1   Summary of all the operations related to folding and expanding code, including their keystrokes. These operations are usable regardless of whether the code-folding outline is displayed in the editor's gutter.

Operation	Keystroke	Description
Expand	Ctrl+NumPad+	Expands the method, class, or other foldable region of code at the caret.
Collapse	Ctrl+NumPad-	Folds the method, class, or other foldable region of code at the caret.

continued on next page

Table 3.1 Summary of all the operations related to folding and expanding code, including their keystrokes. These operations are usable regardless of whether the code-folding outline is displayed in the editor's gutter. *(continued)*

Operation	Keystroke	Description
Expand All	Ctrl+Shift+NumPad+	Expands all folded regions throughout the entire current source file.
Collapse All	Ctrl+Shift+NumPad-	Folds all foldable regions throughout the entire current source file.
Expand JavaDocs	unmapped	Expands all folded JavaDoc regions in the current source file.
Collapse JavaDocs	unmapped	Folds all foldable JavaDoc regions in the current source file.
Fold Selection	Ctrl+.	Folds the current selection. This option lets you fold arbitrary selections of code, even in the middle of a line.
Fold Code Block	Ctrl+Shift+.	Folds a current block of code, even if that block doesn't typically have code folding handles (for example, fold an `if` or `while` code block).

You can also expand any folded region by clicking it with the mouse. Code folding is purely a function of the IDE. It doesn't affect your source code in any way.

In the **Editor** settings, you can select categories of code that should be folded by default on file opening. These settings affect any newly opened files but not currently opened or recently opened files. Under the **Code Folding** options group, you can choose to collapse the following areas of code automatically:

- **File header**—Folds comments at the top of the file
- **Imports**—Folds blocks of two or more import statements
- **JavaDoc comments**—Folds all your JavaDoc comments
- **Method bodies**—Folds all your methods, leaving just the method signatures
- **Simple property accessors**—Folds getter and setter methods
- **Inner classes and Anonymous classes**—Folds these types of classes
- **XML tags**—Folds the body contents of XML tags (applies to XML files, not Java files)

3.3 *Navigating through your Java code*

When working with Java code, it's often useful to navigate around your document tree by using the code's structure rather than by moving to the next page, the end of the line, and so forth. IDEA doesn't just let you type Java code; it can interpret your code's structure dynamically, so it understands a variable reference when it sees it. This lets you navigate using the code structure, following method calls and other code elements to take you where you want to go.

3.3.1 Navigating between methods

Because Java classes are largely composed of a number of methods, it's convenient to jump around the file method by method. You can quickly jump to the start of the next method in the editor by selecting **Go To | Next Method** or pressing **Alt+Down**. Conversely, **Go To | Previous Method** (**Alt+Up**) can be used to go the other direction, toward the beginning of the file.

> **TIP** In the **Editor** settings, enable the **Show method separators** option to add a line graphic between each method in the editor. Doing so provides a visual indication of where each method begins and ends.

3.3.2 Navigating to a symbol's declaration

In Java, a *code symbol* is any named code reference—for example, a method or instance variable. When you're working in the editor, it's often handy to navigate back to where the symbol was first declared, making it easy to understand its place in the world and its relevance to the rest of the code. In the editor, you can jump back to the initial declaration of a symbol with the **Go To | Declaration** command (**Ctrl+B**). You can use this command anywhere a symbol is referenced, even from inside another class or within JavaDoc comments. You can use this feature with any of the Java code symbols:

- Methods
- Classes
- Instance variables
- Class variables
- Local variables
- Method parameters

A related command, **Go To | Type declaration** (**Ctrl+Shift+B**), takes you to the declaration of the symbol's type rather than the symbol itself. (This command has no effect on symbols that reference any of the primitive types.) For example, let's presume that the class `FixedRateCurrencyExchangeService` has an instance variable named `defaultCurrency`, which holds an object of type `Currency`. If you move the cursor to any usage of the `defaultCurrency` variable and execute the **Go To |**

Declaration command, your cursor moves to the initial declaration of the variable, inside the `FixedRateCurrencyExchangeService` class:

```
public class FixedRateCurrencyExchangeService
implements CurrencyExchangeService {
    private Currency defaultCurrency;
    double rate;
    ...
}
```

If you execute the **Go To | Type declaration** command on a reference to `default-Currency`, you're instead taken to the declaration of the symbol's type—that is, the `Currency` class.

```
public final class Currency {
    public static final Currency USD = new Currency("USD");
    public static final Currency CDN = new Currency("CDN");
    ...
}
```

TIP To view a symbol's declaration without moving the caret, hold down the **Ctrl** key and hover your mouse over the symbol. The statement that declared the symbol will appear in a tooltip window. Likewise, to view the declaration of a symbol's type, hold down **Ctrl+Shift** and hover with the mouse pointer. **Control**-clicking the symbol navigates you to that declaration! This is one of the easiest and most often used ways of navigating around the Java class tree.

 A new Quick View feature in IDEA 5.0 lets you see the code behind the symbol at the caret. To activate it, place the caret at the symbol you're interested in and select the **Code | Quick Definition Lookup** action (**Ctrl+Shift+I**). This option displays the implementation in a pop-up window, and you can use its toolbar buttons to navigate to the source file if you wish. If multiple implementations are available, you can switch between them using the drop-down at the top of the preview window. This feature is a good alternative to **Go To | Declaration** (**Ctrl+B**) when you want to quickly review the implementation and not necessarily load it into the editor.

3.3.3 *Navigating to a symbol by name*

The feature that lets you navigate to a symbol by name is similar to the **Go To | Class** and **Go To | File** commands you've already learned about. The **Go To | Symbol** command (**Ctrl+Alt+Shift+N**) lets you navigate to the declaration point of any symbol in the project, including classes, methods, instance variables, and so forth with just the symbol's short name. It also supports wildcard expansion, as illustrated in figure 3.2; in the figure, we've brought up the list of all the symbols in our project that contain the substring *serv* (the match is case insensitive.) You can expand the search to include your libraries as well, by enabling the **Include non-project symbols** option in the search dialog.

As you type, the suggestion list brings up the first 30 matching symbols. Using the mouse or arrow keys, select the symbol you're interested in, and you'll be whisked away to its declaration point. Like most of IDEA's suggestion boxes, this one is limited to a few dozen selections; if the symbol you're hunting for isn't listed, try specifying a more unique search term.

IDEA 5

In version 5.0, IDEA has added a couple of nice enhancements to the ability to navigate to a class, file, or symbol by name through the **Go To** menu. First, if the term you enter doesn't find any matches within the Project, IDEA implicitly activates the option to extend the search to the Java classes and other libraries in use for your project. Very handy!

Second, you can see additional matches when your search returns more than one page of results. If the last row of your search results is an ellipsis (…), this indicates that the results were truncated. Pressing **Enter** or double-clicking the ellipsis loads an additional page of results. You can repeat as necessary to load additional matches.

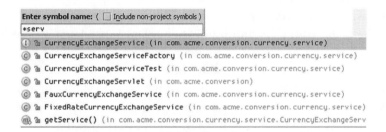

Figure 3.2   The Go To | Symbol feature lets you navigate to the declaration point of any symbol in your project with just its name.

As you start typing characters in the text field, the lookup dialog appears, suggesting names that match that pattern. Because the most common use of these functions is to type the *beginning* of a symbol name, IDEA inserts a virtual asterisk at the end of your pattern, meaning that the pattern matches all symbols beginning with that pattern. Alternatively, you can match the ending of symbol name by providing an extra space at the end of the pattern string. Finally, the lookup dialog is also aware of camel-case and can search for symbols based on capital letters. For examples, see table 3.2.

Table 3.2   Semantic of pattern matching in the Go To Class/File/Symbol pop-up dialog

Pattern	Matches
serv	Symbols beginning with *serv*, such as `Servlet`, `Service`, and so on
*serv	Symbols with the substring *serv* anywhere within their name, such as `Http-Servlet`
serv (with trailing space)	Symbols ending with serv, such as `ProtoServ`
AIOOB	Symbols starting with *AIOOB* camel-case (A*I*I*O*B*), such as `ArrayIndex-OutOfBoundsException`

3.3.4 *Navigating with the structure view pop-up*

If you know the name of the method in the current source file you want to edit, you can use the structure view pop-up to get there quickly. The pop-up menu, shown in figure 3.3, is accessed by choosing **View | File Structure Popup (Ctrl+ F12)**. This window lists all of the current file's classes, methods, and fields in alphabetical order, grouped by classification. You can double-click or use the arrows keys to choose the method to edit. You'll be taken to the beginning of the method's declaration.

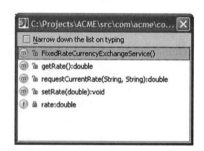

Figure 3.3   The structure view pop-up makes it easy to navigate the code structure of the current class.

An easier method, however, is to enable the **Narrow down the list on typing** option by clicking the checkbox or using the mnemonic. When it's enabled, you can begin typing the name of the entry you want to edit. As you type, all of the methods that don't start with the name you've entered so far are removed from the list. This makes it easy to navigate the structure of a large source file without having to take your hands off the keyboard.

The structure view tool window offers a similar but more thorough and configurable view of your code's structure. It's a powerful tool not only for navigating your source code but also for understanding your code's architecture. For quick navigation, the structure view pop-up is generally easier to use than the full-blown tool window.

3.3.5 *Navigating to an overridden/implemented or overriding/implementing method*

When a method is overridden by a subclass or overrides some method itself, it's marked by an appropriate icon in the editor's gutter bar (see table 3.3). You can hover over those icons to learn their origin. The same goes for abstract methods and interfaces: You can click any icon to navigate to the supermethod or implementation. In addition, you can use the **Go To | Super Method** command (**Ctrl+U**) to visit the supermethod, if any, of the method your cursor is currently inside.

Figure 3.4 The editor makes it convenient to track down method implementations.

Methods in interfaces, abstract methods, or concrete methods with multiple overriding implementations let you access all of their implementations. Clicking the icon presents you with a menu, allowing you to choose which implementation to visit; for example, figure 3.4 shows a host of implementations of the `ObjectInputStream` class. Alternatively, you can use the commands **Go To | Implementations** (**Ctrl+Alt+B**) and **Go To | Called Implementations** (**Ctrl+Alt+Shift+B**). The latter lets you limit your selections to implementations used in the current project.

Table 3.3 The method hierarchy icons appear in the gutter to indicate how this method interacts with the hierarchy tree.

Gutter icon	Description	Action
⊙↑	This method is overriding a method defined by its superclass.	Click to navigate to the overridden method.

continued on next page

Table 3.3   The method hierarchy icons appear in the gutter to indicate how this method interacts with the hierarchy tree. *(continued)*

Gutter icon	Description	Action
	This abstract or interface method is implemented by one or more descendents.	Click to navigate to an implementation of this method, selecting from a list of all implementations.
	This method is implementing a method required by an implemented interface or parent abstract class.	Click to visit the interface or abstract class that defined the method.
	This method is being overridden by one or more of its subclasses.	Click to navigate to one of the overriding methods, selecting from a list of classes if there are multiple overriding classes.

TIP   You can include mouse button clicks and double-clicks, including the center button, in your shortcut combination. By default, the following mouse button shortcuts are defined:

- **Ctrl+Button1 click** (or Button2 click)—Go to declaration
- **Ctrl+Shift+Button1 click**—Go to type declaration
- **Ctrl+Alt+Button1 click**—Go to implementation
- **Ctrl+Button2 click**—Go to definition

You can change these shortcuts or define other combinations through the **Keymap** control panel in **IDE Settings**. Setting up your own keyboard shortcuts is covered in chapter 12.

3.4 *Analyzing your Java code in real-time*

IDEA supports on-the-fly error analysis, alerting you instantly to any problems with your source code (see figure 3.5). This feature can greatly improve the efficiency of your coding sessions by eliminating the endless cycle of edit, compile, fix syntax errors, compile, fix more errors, compile, ad infinitum.

IDEA's error analysis doesn't just alert you to errors, however. IDEA also warns you about suspect code such as unused variables or other conditions that may indicate a logic error on your part. In IDEA's customizable **IDE Settings**, in the **Errors** panel, you can adjust IDEA's definition of what is a warning and what is an error. For example, invalid JavaDoc tags are considered an error condition by default, whereas you may prefer to flag them as warnings (or not flag them at all).

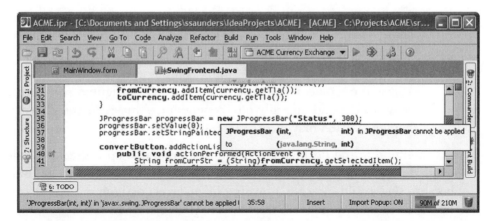

Figure 3.5 IDEA's ability to analyze your code syntax in real time means fewer compile-time errors, more time programming, and less time building and debugging. Syntax errors are spotted within a few moments of your typing them and are immediately flagged for inspection. Note the stripe (or *marker*) in the marker bar on the right, the wavy line under the erroneous code, and the tooltip that explains the problem.

3.4.1 *How IDEA alerts you to problems in your code*

Any problems discovered in your code by IDEA are highlighted in the editor window with your selected color scheme. By default, errors appear in red, or with wavy underlines, depending on the type of error encountered. You can see the reason for the problem by hovering over the error, as shown in figure 3.5, where we've made an invalid constructor call to the JProgressBar.

Errors and warnings are also indicated by little red or yellow tick marks in the right margin of the code editor in the area known as the *marker bar*, also shown in figure 3.5. Hovering over a tick mark gives you a brief description of the problem, and clicking it moves your cursor to the problem's location in the source code.

3.4.2 *Monitoring the status of the current document*

Notice the document status indicator in the upper-right corner of the editor content window, at the top of the error stripe. This square indicates the current state of your document. It can be in any one of the following states:

- **Clear**—Document has not yet been analyzed. Particularly long classes may take a few moments to be analyzed when you first open them.
- **Green**—Everything's fine (as far as IDEA can determine). No syntax errors or warnings are present.

- **Yellow**—Warnings found. One or more warnings, such as an unused import or variable, have been detected. The source will probably compile but may warrant further investigation.

- **Red**—Errors found. The code won't compile due to errors in Java syntax or invalid references. Note that if you haven't configured your project correctly, such as adding all your dependent libraries to the classpath (see chapter 4), IDEA may incorrectly report some valid calls as errors.

Pay attention to the document status indicator, and keep it green! It's always a good idea to reexamine your source code if it has been flagged with any warnings, because they could indicate a missing or incorrect assignment elsewhere. IDEA has saved us many times with this feature.

3.4.3 *Navigating between problems in the current file*

The **Go To | Next Highlighted Error** (**F2**) and **Go To | Previous Highlighted Error** (**Shift+F2**) commands allow you to navigate through all the errors (and warnings) in the current file. When you reach the end of the file, you loop back around to the first problem from the top. This is a convenient mechanism for finding, reviewing, and editing all your code problems at once.

3.4.4 *Controlling the reparse delay*

To configure IDEA's error-handling options, bring up the **Errors** section of the **IDE Settings**, as shown in figure 3.6. The first configurable option in the **Errors** settings is the **Autoreparse delay** option. This value indicates the number of milliseconds IDEA waits to check for errors after you stop typing. The default value should be adequate, but you can adjust it as you see fit. Remember, though, that if you set this value too low, IDEA will begin flagging errors aggressively, possibly even before you even finish typing a keyword. Your circumstances may vary, but we recommend setting this to around 1000ms (which means it only starts marking things as errors once you take a real pause).

3.4.5 *Configuring IDEA's warning levels*

Under the **Errors** settings, you can see a list of the different types of problems that IDEA looks for in your code. All the problems listed in these settings are technically just warnings, because they pertain to code that is syntactically correct and will compile. The purpose of the **Errors** settings is to give you the opportunity to treat certain warnings as more serious or less serious. You can do this by adjusting each condition's warning level designation in its drop-down list:

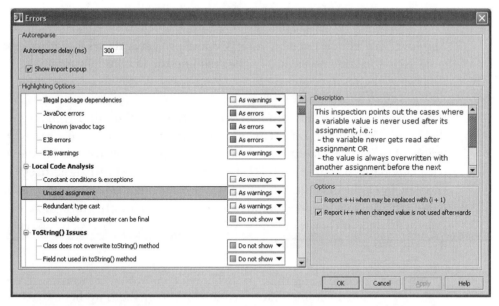

Figure 3.6 The Errors configuration screen lets you control how each questionable condition is visually denoted within IDEA. Don't care about redundant typecasts? Don't show them. Despise unused variables? Categorize them as an error so they'll stand out.

- **As warnings**—Treat this problem as a warning in the error stripe.
- **As errors**—Treat this problem as an error in the error stripe.
- **Do not show**—Ignore this problem.

You should tweak these settings based on how critical you consider conditions to be to your project. For example, if you're creating a public API, you may place a lot of importance on the JavaDoc and increase its warning level to be treated as an error. This calls more attention to the problem in the editor than just a warning.

IDEA 5 The **Errors** settings panel in version 5.0 has been extended to include all code analysis conditions tested during code inspection. Likewise, the warning and error conditions are tied in with your code inspection profiles, allowing you to name and manage multiple error profiles. Because of the huge number of code analysis conditions built into IDEA, a filter has been added to help narrow down the list. For example, if you only want to find conditions related to threading, type `thread` into the filter to narrow the list to those items whose name, description, or category name matches this term.

3.5 *Getting help from the JavaDoc and API references*

The JavaDoc API reference for your JVM and project is always just a few keystrokes away. Now you have no excuse for not reading the documentation!

3.5.1 *Viewing method parameters*

If you need to know what parameters the method you're calling requires, execute the **View | Parameter Info** (**Ctrl+P**) command when your cursor is within the braces of the appropriate method call. A pop-up window will display the method parameters (or the entire method signature, if the **Show full signatures** option is enabled in **Code Completion** settings). If more than one method matches the name (and any parameters already passed to the method), all possible combinations are listed, as shown in figure 3.7. You can navigate between the parameters with the **Tab** and **Shift+Tab** keys.

TIP   If you're using third-party libraries, and you want to have access to extended parameter information for the methods in them, make sure you include these libraries' sources in the project source path. Otherwise, you'll be able to only view the parameter types and not their names.

You can specify a couple of parameter-related options under the **Code Completion** settings control panel. The first option, **Autopopup**, automatically displays a

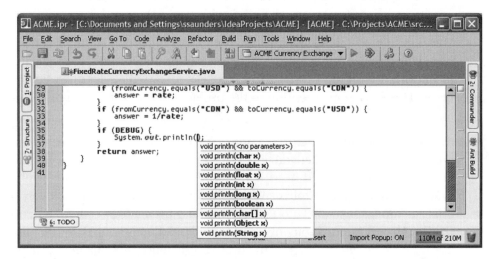

Figure 3.7   Viewing parameter information shows you what parameters are required for the method you have selected.

list of the parameter types required by the method you're calling after the specified number of milliseconds has passed. The **Show full signatures** option, if enabled, also includes the method name and return type (if the source code is available).

3.5.2 *Viewing the JavaDoc*

If you need help on the usage of any symbol (class, method, field, and so forth), place your cursor on the symbol and execute the **View | Quick JavaDoc** (**Ctrl+Q**) command. You'll be presented with the JavaDoc reference for the symbol. In the example shown in figure 3.8, you can see the JavaDoc reference for the Double class. Notice that you don't need to go the symbol's original definition, because IDEA determines the class for you. The JavaDoc comes directly

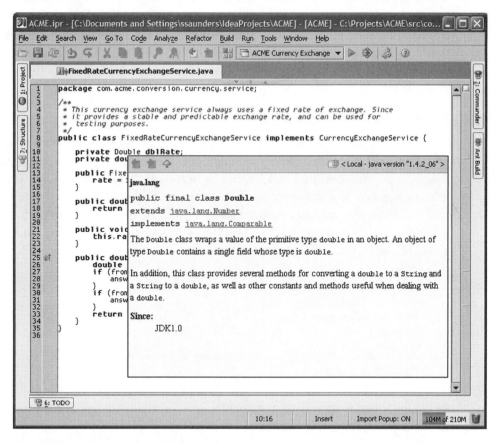

Figure 3.8   Using Quick JavaDoc is a handy way to read a class's JavaDoc without switching to an external browser.

from source code specified in your project settings. If no JavaDoc is found in the source (or you don't have the source), then only the method's signature information is displayed.

The Quick JavaDoc window is fully navigable. In our example, you can click the link to the `java.lang.Number` class to view its JavaDoc. Once you navigate to another element, a small toolbar appears in the Quick JavaDoc window, allowing you to navigate back and forth and to view the JavaDoc in a browser window.

Viewing the full JavaDoc in an external browser

For a little more information, you can use the **View | External JavaDoc** (**Shift+F1**) feature to view the JavaDoc of any symbol with your browser in its native HTML format. The editor locates the JavaDoc by searching your JavaDoc entries for the symbol's containing class. Of course, this only works if you have added and made IDEA aware of the appropriate API documentation. This command handles local JavaDoc files as well as those hosted on a web site, provided you have set up your JDK with a reference to the JavaDoc files as described in chapter 1.

3.5.3 *Creating JavaDoc comments*

IDEA provides a number of features to help you generate and maintain your Java-Doc. IDEA will get you started by stubbing out the JavaDoc of any method for you. Simply type the opening block comment brace `/**`, and press Return. IDEA will add the applicable parameter attributes and the `throws` clauses where necessary, and will close the comment automatically. You can disable this behavior in the **Editor** settings by disabling the **JavaDoc stubs** option under the **Smart Keys** group. Here's what IDEA generated for the `requestCurrentRate` method:

```
/**
 *
 * @param fromCurrency
 * @param toCurrency
 * @return
 */
public double requestCurrentRate(String fromCurrency,
  String toCurrency) { ... }
```

Now all you have to do is add any explanatory text and descriptions of the parameters and return type. IDEA will alert you to any errors in syntax or usage for your JavaDoc.

You can customize IDEA's handling of JavaDoc syntax-checking in the **Errors** section of your **IDE Settings**. Here you can specify whether problems with JavaDoc should be considered errors or warnings (or ignored) as well as tell IDEA about any custom JavaDoc tags you're using. IDEA's refactoring tools (see chapter 9) will even keep your JavaDoc in sync if you rename method parameters or otherwise alter the method signature.

> **TIP** Code completion (described in the next section) also works on both standard and custom JavaDoc attributes. You can use the code inspection tool described in chapter 9 to search for missing JavaDoc across your project.

As soon as you have your new JavaDoc block, it becomes immediately available via the **Quick JavaDoc** command, described earlier. Just position the caret at the method name, and press **Ctrl+Q**: The newly created JavaDoc will be opened for review.

3.5.4 *Generating your project's JavaDoc reference*

IDEA provides a graphical front-end to the standard JavaDoc tool, allowing you to generate your project's JavaDoc. Execute the **Tools | Generate JavaDoc** command to bring up the Generate JavaDoc window, as shown in figure 3.9. You can elect to generate JavaDoc for the entire project (all source trees) or for a particular package. The Scope slider determines what level of documentation

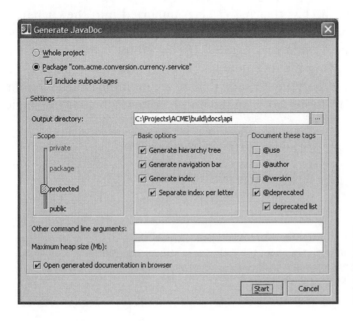

Figure 3.9
IDEA's Generate JavaDoc window provides an easy interface for configuring how your JavaDoc API documentation should be created.

to generate. You can find a full explanation of JavaDoc and the JavaDoc generation options with your JDK documentation.

3.6 Code completion

With a few quick keystrokes, IDEA's code-completion and code-generation features can stub out a method, create a new variable, or find the right method to use. The objective of IDEA's code-completion and code-generation features isn't to attempt to write your code for you, as some rapid prototyping tools attempt to do. Those types of code wizards and program generators rarely produce designs that are as useful or maintainable as you'd hope. IDEA instead uses code generation as more of an assistance mechanism, eliminating the drudgery of common coding tasks with predictable outcomes.

3.6.1 Using IDEA's code-completion features to do your work for you

IDEA has a built in code-completion feature that can save you a lot of typing by suggesting appropriate code for you. As you'll see, IDEA can fill in method and field names, find appropriate parameters, and so forth. Not only does it save you some typing, but this feature also serves as a way of reminding you what API calls are available.

Auto-importing required packages

When you reference a class that hasn't been imported into the current source file, IDEA helps you by trying to locate the class in your Classpath and add it to your list of imports. As shown in figure 3.10, the editor prompts you to accept the import by displaying the fully qualified name of the class it plans to import. Press **Alt+Enter** to import the class; or, if there are multiple matches on the class name, select the class to import from the list presented. Whether the single class

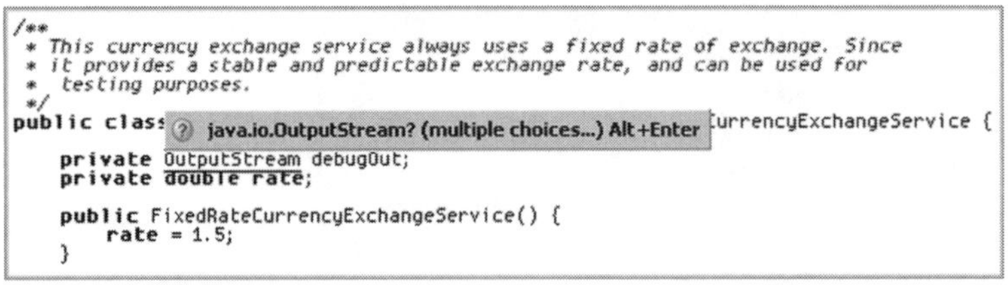

```
/**
 * This currency exchange service always uses a fixed rate of exchange. Since
 * it provides a stable and predictable exchange rate, and can be used for
 * testing purposes.
 */
public class [?] java.io.OutputStream? (multiple choices...) Alt+Enter urrencyExchangeService {

    private OutputStream debugOut;
    private double rate;

    public FixedRateCurrencyExchangeService() {
        rate = 1.5;
    }
}
```

Figure 3.10   Because IDEA knows about the entire class structure of your project, it can suggest appropriate import statements when it notices classes without them, like this OutputStream class.

or the entire package is imported depends on your code style settings for importing classes.

IDEA finds these required imports in the existing files and prompts for you to import them *without moving your cursor,* thereby not interrupting your current editing session.

> **TIP** You can disable the pop-up hints and auto-import requests temporarily by double-clicking the **Import Popup** entry in the status bar, next to the memory indicator. Double-click again to turn them back on.

IDEA 5 A new option in the **Editor** settings panel, **Add unambiguous imports on the fly**, improves IDEA's import management. If you select this option, IDEA won't bother to ask you whether you want to import a referenced class; if there is only a single possible match, IDEA will add it.

Using basic code completion

Basic code completion completes the names of classes, methods, fields, and the Java keywords anywhere in the current visibility scope when you invoke **Code | Complete Code | Basic** (**Ctrl+Space**). In the example shown in figure 3.11,

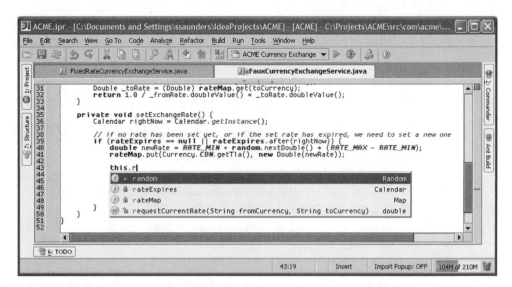

Figure 3.11 Code completion lists all the possible alternatives based on context. In this case, it lists all variables that are in scope and begin with the letter *r*.

we've typed the letter *r* and invoked basic code completion. All of the parameters, fields, and methods in the current scope that begin with the letter *r* are shown in the completion suggestion list. Scroll down the list with the arrow keys and press **Enter**, or make the appropriate selection by double-clicking it.

TIP   To help you enter code even faster, IDEA has an option called **Autocomplete common prefix** that's enabled by default. This option scans all methods and fields during auto-completion and looks for common prefixes. In the previous example, if you type *rat*, IDEA will recognize that only two fields match that pattern (rateExpires and rateMap) and that both of these share the common prefix *rate*. IDEA will then automatically complete the prefix in the editor, saving you typing it manually. This feature is very visible—and very useful—in classes with many similarly named members.

IDEA 5   Code completion in version 5 has been enhanced to work with custom file types. If you have specified a list of keywords in your custom file types, then IDEA offers these up as code-completion possibilities when working with files of that type. Keep in mind that, unlike Java code completion, IDEA isn't aware of the structure and semantics of custom file types, and it offers any of the keywords as a completion option, legal or not.

You don't have to begin your code completion on a blank line. You can invoke it anywhere. For example, in figure 3.12 (see code line 43) we have invoked code completion immediately after the get in the call to rightNow, an instance of Calendar, resulting in a list of all the reachable Calendar methods that begin with the

Figure 3.12   When in the context of a method name, code completion lists the methods of the class that fit the pattern. In this case, because the cursor falls after the letters *get*, it lists all the accessor methods of the Calendar.

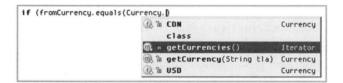

Figure 3.13 Because a field or a method reference can follow a dot, invoking code completion in that context lists all accessible method invocations and all accessible fields.

prefix `get`. This is an excellent way to narrow down the list of options or browse the list of available properties of a class.

> **TIP** When you press **Enter** or double-click the mouse to accept a completion from the suggestion list, the completion is inserted to the left of the caret, preserving the source text; think of this as insert mode. If you press the **Tab** key, however, the selected completion is used to replace the symbol at the caret with the selected suggestion; think of this as replacement mode.

Similarly, if you invoke basic code completion directly after an object dot separator, all of that object's accessible methods and fields appear in the suggestion list. An example of this behavior can be seen in figure 3.13.

> **TIP** You can use the **Quick JavaDoc** command (**Ctrl+Q**) to view the JavaDoc for the currently selected completion.

Using basic code completion to create variable names

When you invoke basic code completion as part of a field, parameter, or variable declaration, IDEA suggests a name for your new reference, using the item's type to generate a list of suggested names. An example is shown in figure 3.14; here, we're creating a new local variable of type `FixedRateCurrencyExchangeService`.

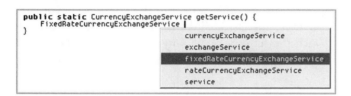

Figure 3.14 Code completion can also be used to suggest a variable name when you're creating a new variable.

The types and style of suggested names can be controlled through your **Code Style** settings, as discussed in chapter 12.

TIP   If you have defined local variable prefixes/suffixes in your **Code Style** settings, the suggested variable names appear with the specified prefix and/or suffix.

Using SmartType code completion

The SmartType code-completion command works similarly to basic code completion, but it can filter its list of suggestions to include only those whose type is applicable to the current context. You invoke SmartType through the **Code | Complete Code | SmartType** command (**Ctrl+Shift+Space**). SmartType completion can only be used in situations where an appropriate type can be determined; for example:

- On the right hand of assignment statements
- In variable initializers
- In return statements
- In a method call's parameter list
- After the new keyword in an object declaration

Figure 3.15 shows SmartType completion being used inside the method call to after(), which requires an argument of type Date. As you can see from the suggestion list, only two appropriate Date objects are reachable in the current scope: expiryDate and warningDate.

```
Calendar today = Calendar.getInstance();
if (today.getTime().after()) {
                        expiryDate    Date
                        warningDate   Date
```

Figure 3.15   SmartType completion works similarly to basic completion, but the list is pruned to eliminate any entries that don't contextually match the appropriate class.

TIP   SmartType completion automatically highlights the selection it thinks is the most appropriate. You can further limit the code completion suggestions by typing in the first few letters of the completion you want to accept. As you type, the list shrinks to include only those completions beginning with the letters you've entered. Press the **Backspace** key to erase any characters you've typed, and the list will expand appropriately.

Class name completion

Class name completion works similarly to basic completion, but it only completes on class and interface names. Unlike basic completion, which only completes the names of class reachable by the current source, class name completion searches all the classes in your project. If the class isn't currently imported, the auto-import mechanism discussed earlier handles it. To complete a class name, choose the **Code | Complete Code | Class Name** command (**Ctrl+Alt+Space**).

3.6.2 Completing brackets, braces, parentheses, and quotation marks with smart completion

A number of options in the **Smart Keys** option group of the **Editor** settings help you when inserting paired symbols such as braces, brackets, and quotes. For either of the **Insert pair }** and **Insert pair %> in** JSP options you enable, the editor automatically indents the pair's closing symbol when the opening symbol is entered and the **Enter** key is pressed. The appropriate level of indentation is determined by your **Code Style** settings.

The **Insert pair bracket** (including parentheses) and **Insert pair quote** options work a bit differently. When they're enabled, the editor automatically adds the appropriate closing symbol for you as soon as you type the opening bracket or quote. One handy feature is that if you delete the opening brace of an empty set, the closing bracket or quote is also deleted.

> **TIP** You can automatically complete the current line with the shortcut **Ctrl+Shift+Enter**, which moves the cursor to the end of the line and adds any required closing punctuation (quotes, parenthesis, and so on) and the trailing semicolon.

3.6.3 Commenting out code

You can comment out the current line of source code with the command **Code | Comment with Line Comment (Ctrl+/)**. If the current line is already commented, the command uncomments it. In Java, line comments start with double slashes (//).

You can comment out multiple lines of code in one of two ways: You can either select a series of lines and use the **Code | Comment with Line Comment** command (**Ctrl+/**) to comment out each line with line comments, or you can use **Code | Comment with Block Comment (Ctrl+Shift+/)** to apply a block comment to your selection. In Java, block comments are delimited by the symbols /* and */.

This feature isn't limited to Java files. IDEA can also insert comments into the predefined supported file types like JSP, HTML, XML, and so on. Auto-commenting is even available when you're editing an arbitrary file type for which you have specified the line- and block-level comment delimiters, described in more detail in chapter 12.

 The **Code | Comment Line** and **Code | Comment block** actions work with custom file types as well as IDEA's built in file types in version 5.0.

3.6.4 *Reformatting code*

You can reformat your code to use your current code style selection at any time by selecting the **Tools | Reformat Code** (**Ctrl+Alt+L**) command from the main menu. A dialog box will appear, as shown in figure 3.16, in which you can change the scope of the reformatting to include the file, your selected text, or all the files in the directory. When you're ready to go, click the **Run** button. IDEA will use all of your code style options to layout the spacing, indentation, and other properties. This makes it possible to switch code styles in the middle of a project and to reformat the entire source tree. Refer to chapter 12 for information about configuring your code style settings.

 The **Reformat Code** action was moved from the **Tools** menu to the **Code** menu in version 5.0.

If you select the **Optimize imports** option, IDEA also rewrites and rearranges your import statements. It uses your code style settings to determine exactly how you prefer them, but in general it removes unused imports, decides whether to

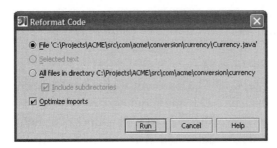

Figure 3.16
The reformatting feature can keep your whole project strictly adhered to a specific code style.

include individual classes or entire packages, and arranges them in the order specified under the Imports options of the **Code Style** settings.

It's also possible to apply the **Reformat Code** command to an entire module. To do so, open the **Project** tool window (**Alt+1**), select a module to be reformatted, right-click, and select **Reformat Code** from the context menu.

> **WARNING** If you try to reformat a large source tree at once, make sure you bump up the amount of memory you allocate to IDEA, at least temporarily—this operation can be memory intensive.

3.6.5 *Customizing IDEA's code completion settings*

You can customize the behavior of IDEA's code completion features through the **Code Completion** control panel of the **IDE Settings**. A screenshot of the settings panel is shown in figure 3.17.

Adjusting case sensitivity

Under the **Code Completion** option group, the first option is **Case sensitive completion**, which lets you adjust the degree to which IDEA considers case when

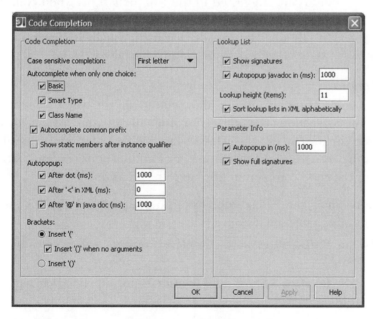

Figure 3.17 You can customize the behavior of IDEA's code-completion features in the Code Completion settings window.

generating code completions. For example, if you enter the prefix *get*, should it match methods starting with just the prefix get, or those starting with Get, GET, and GeT, as well? The available choices are as follows:

- **All**—The case of all letters is considered when determining a match (the most restrictive option).
- **None**—Case is never considered (the least restrictive option).
- **First letter**—Only the case of the first letter in your match prefix is considered.

Autocomplete options

The **Autocomplete when only one choice** option tells IDEA that when there is only one possible completion, it shouldn't bother showing a suggestion list—it should accept the sole completion. You can enable this option for each type of completion individually by enabling the box next to each type.

The **Autocomplete common prefix** option takes effect when all the code-completion suggestions begin with a common prefix. If it's enabled, the common prefix is automatically completed for you in the editor.

The **Show static members after instance qualifier** option determines whether static fields and methods are suggested in the completion list when completing on an instance variable. If this option is disabled, only instance methods and fields are suggested (it's disabled by default, because it usually isn't recommended that you refer to the static members from instance variables).

Autopopup options

The options in the **Autopopup** group allow you to specify where, when, and if code completion suggestions are offered to you without your asking for them. There are three circumstances in which you can enable Autopopup completion. After each option, you can specify the number of milliseconds you must stop typing in order for the code completion pop-up to be offered:

- **After dot**—Show the auto-complete pop-up against an object's methods and fields after a dot separator.
- **After '<' in XML**—Show auto-complete pop-up tags (according to the DTD) in XML.
- **After '@' in JavaDoc**—Show auto-complete pop-up JavaDoc tags inside JavaDoc comments.

Brackets options

These options dictate how the code-completion features handle brackets when inserting a method call. You can elect to insert the full set of brackets or only a single opening bracket. In either case, your cursor is positioned just after the opening bracket at the end of the completion operation. If you select the opening bracket option only, you have the additional option of going ahead and inserting both brackets in the single case where the called method takes no arguments.

Lookup list options

These four options dictate the behavior of the items in the suggestion list:

- **Show signatures**—If enabled, methods are shown with full signatures, including their parameters. If disabled, methods appear in the suggest list by name only.

- **Autopopup JavaDoc**—If enabled, the quick JavaDoc for the currently highlighted selection appears after the specified number of milliseconds.

- **Lookup height**—This option indicates the maximum number of entries that the completion list can contain.

- **Sort lookup lists in XML alphabetically**—If enabled, XML tag completion lists the tags alphabetically rather than the order specified in the DTD.

3.7 Using IDEA's code-generation tools

We've looked at IDEA's code-completion features, which help you fill out method calls, name variables, and other operations. Now we'll discuss IDEA's code-generation features, which go a step further by creating entire methods for you.

3.7.1 Generating constructors

To access the constructor code-generation feature, execute the **Code | Generate** command (**Alt+Insert**) and select the **Constructor** option from the pop-up menu. The constructor generator lets you create class constructors that accept arguments that are then assigned to field variables. You need to create your fields first. Pick the fields you wish to include in your constructor (see figure 3.18): You can hold down the **Ctrl** key to select more than one, or press **Shift** to select a range of parameters. Click **OK** to create your constructor. It will appear in your source code at the location specified in your **Code Style** settings, usually at the top of the class under your field declarations. If you don't want any arguments to your constructor, click the **Select None** button instead of **OK**.

Figure 3.18
Constructors are trivial to write, so IDEA can do it for you. The constructor generator needs to know which fields are instantiated by the constructor, and it uses this window to let you pick them.

TIP   The generated constructor's parameters will appear in the same order that they appear in the constructor dialog. If you want to reorder them later, you can use the **Change Method Signature** refactoring discussed in chapter 9.

In the example shown in figure 3.18, we've selected one field to serve as our argument. The code generated by this selection is as follows:

```
public CurrencyExchangeBean(Currency startingCurrency) {
    this.startingCurrency = startingCurrency;
}
```

TIP   If you have defined parameter prefix/suffixes in your **Code Style** settings, the generated parameter names appear with the specified prefix and/or suffix.

3.7.2 *Generating accessor and mutator methods*

Like the constructor generator, the accessor and mutator generators work against your existing fields. Accessor and mutator methods are used to provide users of the class with the ability to get and set the values of internal fields without having direct access to the fields. Using accessors and mutators instead of direct field access is desirable because it makes it possible to change the class's implementation without affecting its public API. Some tools, such as reflection, JSP, and the JavaBeans API, are based around the getter/setter model and expect a standard method signature. For example, to get and set a property of type `double` named `rate`, IDEA generates the following methods:

```
public double getRate() {
    return rate;
}
```

```
public void setRate(double rate) {
    this.rate = rate;
}
```

Notice that the setter method accepts only a single argument, as required by the JavaBeans API. The accessor and mutator method generator creates these types of methods from your field variables automatically, making the process quick and painless. From the code-generation pop-up (**Code | Generate** or **Alt+Insert**) you can select one of the getter/setter options:

- **Getter**—Creates accessor methods for getting the current value of selected fields
- **Setter**—Creates mutator methods for setting the specified value to selected fields
- **Getter and Setter**—Creates both the get and set methods for selected fields

You can see an example of this feature in action in figure 3.19. For each field selected, an appropriate set of getters and/or setters will be created and inserted at the cursor.

> **NOTE** If accessor and/or mutator methods already exist for any of the class's fields, these fields don't appear in this dialog.

3.7.3 *Generating hashCode and equals methods*

This feature helps you avoid one of the most common Java pitfalls: failing to override the `equals` and `hashCode` methods together. According to the Java specifications, if two objects are equal according to the `equals` method, then calling the `hashCode` method on each of the two objects must produce the same integer result. Otherwise, bad things can happen, especially with regard to collections.

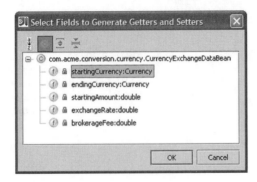

Figure 3.19
Another trivial yet common coding task is the creation of accessors and mutators for your class's fields. IDEA's code generator lets you generate them all automatically with one command.

The generator also generates much safer and efficient versions of these methods than most people have the patience to write, especially if you have many fields to consider.

> **NOTE**   If these methods are already defined in the class, IDEA informs you with the corresponding dialog.

From the generator pop-up, select the option to create hashCode and equals methods. Doing so launches a wizard with three steps (see figure 3.20).

In the first step, select the fields that should be used to determine equality. Each of the selected field's values will be compared, and objects will be considered equal only if all the field values specified here are equivalent. Click **Next** to continue.

In the second step, select the fields that should be used to generate the hash code for the object. In keeping with the specification requirements, you can't include fields in the hash code that aren't in the equals method, so the list contains only the fields you selected previously. By default, they are all selected, but you can disable some of them if necessary without violating the equality rule. Click **Next** to continue.

In the third step, select the fields that you can guarantee contain non-null values. This step is optional, but if you know a value will never be null (for example, a constant, or a value defined in the constructor), then the generated code will skip the check for null for a small improvement in efficiency. Click **Finish** to complete the wizard and generate your methods. The code generated by our example can be seen in listing 3.1.

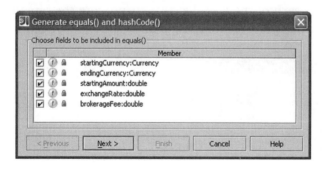

Figure 3.20
The code generator needs to know which fields are used to determine equality within the equals and hashCode methods of the class.

Listing 3.1 Once chosen, the fields are used in proven algorithms to implement the `equals` and `hashCode` methods.

```java
public boolean equals(Object o) {
    if (this == o) {
        return true;
    }
    if (o == null || getClass() != o.getClass()) {
        return false;
    }

    final CurrencyExchangeDataBean currencyExchangeDataBean =
        (CurrencyExchangeDataBean) o;

    if (exchangeRate != currencyExchangeDataBean.exchangeRate) {
        return false;
    }
    if (startingAmount != currencyExchangeDataBean.startingAmount) {
        return false;
    }
    if (endingCurrency != null
            ? !endingCurrency.equals(
                currencyExchangeDataBean.endingCurrency)
            : currencyExchangeDataBean.endingCurrency != null)
            return false;
    if (startingCurrency != null
            ? !startingCurrency.equals(
                currencyExchangeDataBean.startingCurrency)
            : currencyExchangeDataBean.startingCurrency != null)
            return false;

    return true;
}

public int hashCode() {
    int result;
    long temp;
    result = (startingCurrency != null
                ? startingCurrency.hashCode() : 0);
    result = 29 * result + (endingCurrency != null
                ? endingCurrency.hashCode() : 0);
    temp = startingAmount != +0.0d
                ? Double.doubleToLongBits(startingAmount) : 0L;
    result = 29 * result + (int) (temp ^ (temp >>> 32));
    temp = exchangeRate != +0.0d
                ? Double.doubleToLongBits(exchangeRate) : 0L;
    result = 29 * result + (int) (temp ^ (temp >>> 32));
    return result;
}
```

3.7.4 *Overriding methods in your superclass*

You can override any of your parent class methods by using the **Code | Override Methods** command (**Ctrl+ O**). This command presents you with a list of methods you can override, grouped by the classes that first defined the method. Only methods that have not already been overridden, and that are accessible from your subclass, are shown. An example with several ancestors is shown in figure 3.21.

Select the method (or methods) you wish to override, and IDEA will create the methods for you. By default, the body of the method calls the superclass's method, resulting in no change in behavior. You'll have to add a useful body to the method yourself, of course.

If you enable the **Copy JavaDoc** option, then the JavaDoc from the overridden methods (if any) is copied into your source file. Otherwise, no JavaDoc will be generated.

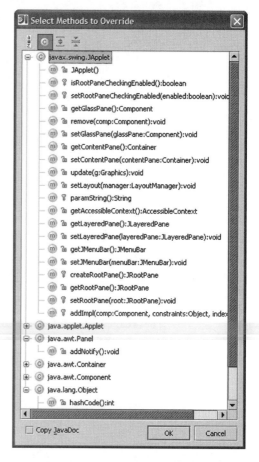

Figure 3.21 There's no need to fear specifying the wrong method signature when you're trying to override a method. Using the Override Methods command shows you a list of every inherited method and will insert any subset of them directly into your current class.

3.7.5 *Implementing methods of an interface*

The **Code | Implement Methods** command (**Ctrl+I**) is very similar to the **Override Methods** command. When it's executed, you're presented with a list of methods that your class needs to implement, because either it has declared itself as implementing a particular interface or it's extending a class with abstract methods.

In the example shown in figure 3.22, we've called the command from a class that is declared as implementing the MouseListener and MouseMotionListener interfaces, and we're required to implement seven methods. Select one or more

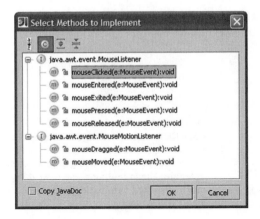

Figure 3.22
The Implement Methods operation creates a master list of all methods not yet implemented that are defined by interfaces related to your class, and allows you to choose any subset of them to implement.

methods to implement, and click **OK**. IDEA will stub out the methods, using default return values for primitives and nulls for objects. As with the **Override Methods** command, select the **Copy JavaDoc** option if you want to duplicate the JavaDoc from the interface or abstract method you're implementing.

3.7.6 *Creating delegation methods*

The **Code | Delegate Methods** command lets you create methods that delegate behavior to one of your class's fields or methods. You generally create delegation methods to access information or implement behavior that is a part of one of your fields, without having to expose that field directly. To create a delegation method, you select the field you want to delegate to and then the methods of that object that you wish to delegate. Take for example figures 3.23 and 3.24, which show both steps.

Figure 3.23
To delegate a series of methods through your class to a contained object, IDEA first prompts you to select the object to be delegated to.

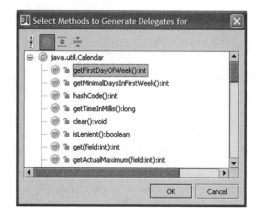

Figure 3.24
Once IDEA knows what object is being delegated to, it prompts you for the set of methods (that is, the subset of the underlying object's API) to delegate. These methods and their delegation mechanism are automatically implemented in your current class.

In our example, a `CurrencyCalendar` class has a field of type `Calendar` called `calendar`. This is the underlying calendar implementation, and we want to give users of the `CurrencyCalendar` class access to some of the `Calendar`'s functionality without exposing the `calendar` field directly. To do this, we create a new method that wraps the `calendar`'s `get()` method, delegating the request to `calendar`. The resulting new method looks like this:

```
public int getName(int field) {
    return calendar.get(field);
}
```

3.7.7 Enclosing a block of code

You can use the **Code | Surround With** (**Ctrl+Alt+T**) command to wrap a selected block of code with one of the Java constructs such as an `if`, `while`, or `try`/`catch` block. Select the block of code you want to surround, and then activate the command. A menu like that in figure 3.25 will appear. Use your mouse or the shortcut key (listed next to each entry in the menu) to wrap your code block.

3.7.8 Customizing code generated by IDEA

You can use the Code Templates tab in the **File Templates** editor in **IDE Settings** to customize the code generated for you by the editor's code-generation features. A number of preexisting entries are defined. You can only edit the existing entries; you can't remove them or create new ones. Each template type defines its own variables, which may be

Figure 3.25
Many of the basic control and flow structures in Java can be generated by selecting a bunch of code and invoking the Surround With operation.

used when designing your template. These are listed in the description area of each code template:

- **Catch Statement Body**—Template for filling in the body of a catch statement generated by the **Code | Surround with** command (**Ctrl+Alt+T**). By default, this template prints a stack trace.

- **New Method Body**—Template used when new methods are created. By default, this template returns a default value based on the return type of the method.

- **Implemented Method Body**—Template used when creating a new method through the **Code | Implement Methods** command (**Ctrl+I**).

- **Overridden Method Body**—Template used when creating a new method through the **Code | Override Methods** command (**Ctrl+O**).

3.8 Programming by intention

IDEA has many code-completion features designed to ease the development process while at the same time improving the quality of the code you write. Code-completion features like SmartType completion only appear when you specifically request them. Another feature, intention actions, is always working silently in the background.

3.8.1 What are intention actions?

Sometimes we can get ahead of ourselves while programming. We reference classes we haven't yet imported, assign values to variables we haven't defined, make calls to method we haven't written, and so forth. Technically, these could be considered mistakes, but they're mistakes made with the best of intentions.

This is where intention actions come in. When IDEA suspects a possible problem with your code, it does much more than bring the problem to your attention. If possible, it also suggests a solution for you. As an added bonus, IDEA can carry out its recommendations on your behalf: It can change the way variables are assigned, create missing references, and much more. Each of these operations is known as an *intention action*. An intention action is an action that IDEA performs for you because it knows what you intended to do.

A special class of intention action is called a *Quickfix* intention, denoted by the little exclamation point in the intention light bulb. Quickfixes correct errors in syntax or other problems that would prevent IDEA from building the class. For example, if your class name doesn't match the name of its containing file, a Quick-fix intention appears and offers to rename one or the other into compliance.

3.8.2 Why and when IDEA suggests intention actions

When IDEA encounters a syntax error or other portion of code that it believes it can assist you with, it alerts you with the intention action alert symbol, which looks like a little light bulb, flush left on the page. An example is shown in figure 3.26, where we're trying to return a long value from a method with a return type of int.

Figure 3.26   The light bulb icon suggests that IDEA has an idea: an intention, a way to solve the bad code.

Because any given line of source code may trigger several different intention action alerts, the alert icon appears only when your cursor is on the affected region. In our example, the alert is displayed only when the cursor is on the line with the return keyword. Note that although this alert is centered on a syntax error, in some situations IDEA offers intention actions for code that is syntactically correct as well; it does so if it has a suggestion about how to optimize the code or improve its structure or can logically deduce a common operation you might wish to perform.

3.8.3 Using intention actions to fix errors

The primary purpose of intention actions is to fix problems and oversights in your code. For example, in figure 3.27, when we try to return a long value from a method with a declared return type of int, IDEA not only flags the syntax error before the compiler catches it, but also offers two possible suggestions based on what we may have intended to do. In our example, IDEA suggests that we either cast the returned value to an int, thereby satisfying the method signature, or change the method signature to return a long value, as shown. Whichever action we take, IDEA implements the change. You'll learn how to invoke these actions a little later.

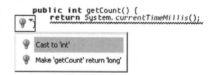

Figure 3.27   When a problem highlighted by an intention has multiple solutions, IDEA presents them in a short drop-down list for your review.

3.8.4 Using intention actions for code completion

Intention actions do more than fix mistakes. Once you're familiar with the types of intention actions IDEA provides, you can use them to perform code completion or act as programming shortcuts. For instance, if you make a call to a method that doesn't yet exist, IDEA's intention actions will offer to create the method for you.

With this in mind, you can make a call to the method you wish you had, and let the intention actions stub it out for you. It's amazing how much repetitive work like defining variables, casting objects from collections, and importing packages can be eliminated by relying on the intention features of IDEA to do the grunt work.

Counting on intention actions quickly becomes a natural and efficient way to program. Instead of trying to understand all the methods, instance variables, and other elements up front, you can let intention actions define them as you need them.

3.8.5 *Choosing an intention action to execute*

When you see the intention action alert, your next step is to select which, if any, intention action you want to perform. IDEA never tries to fix the code for you without your approval. To review IDEA's suggestions and accept an intention action, click the light bulb icon or press **Alt+ Enter** to view the suggestion list. IDEA will present a list of possible intention actions via a drop-down menu sourced from the light bulb icon. Only intention actions that will result in valid code are shown in the list. In figure 3.28, we're trying to assign a value to an undeclared field.

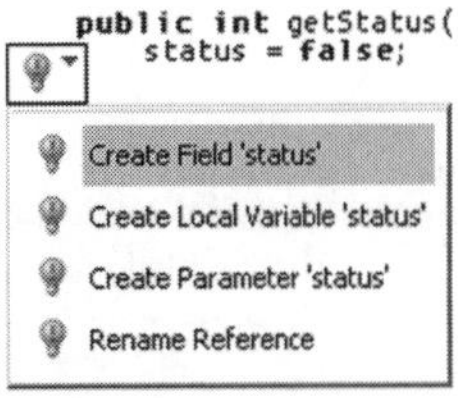

In this example, there are four possible intention actions from which to select. Use the mouse or keyboard

```
public int getStatus() {
    status = false;
```

- Create Field 'status'
- Create Local Variable 'status'
- Create Parameter 'status'
- Rename Reference

Figure 3.28 When you select an option from the intention action drop-down, IDEA will modify your code to implement the suggested fix.

to select one of them, and IDEA will automatically implement the changes. Although most conditions are applicable to only one or two intention actions, this situation has four possible solutions. Briefly, the four options in our example will perform the following actions:

- **Create Field**—Creates a new boolean field called status
- **Create Local Variable**—Creates a new boolean local variable called status
- **Create Parameter**—Adds a new boolean parameter called status to the method
- **Rename Reference**—Changes the assignment to another, existing boolean reference in scope

Select the option that matches your intended purpose for the code. If none is appropriate, you can press **Escape** to close the intention action list and leave the code unchanged, or you can make your own changes.

3.8.6 *Disabling intention alerts*

If desired, you can disable the alert for any type of intention action. You may want to do this if you find that one of IDEA's intention actions isn't suited to your style of programming, and you don't wish to be continually alerted to its availability. To disable any action you encounter, bring up the suggestion list by clicking the alert icon or by pressing the **Alt+Enter** shortcut. Click the light bulb icon next to each action listed in the suggestion list to toggle its status from on to off. Clicking the icon again will enable the action once again.

Once disabled, that intention action's availability will no longer cause the intention action alert icon to appear in the editor. However, you can still perform the intention action by using the **Alt+Enter** key combination while in the area that you suspect to bring up the suggested action list. Because using this key combination makes the intention action list appear, it also lets you turn a suppressed alert back on.

IDEA 5   New to the **IDE Settings** options is the **Intention Settings** panel (see fig. 3.29). This panel lets you browse through IDEA's lists of intention actions and selectively enable or disable them. Each intention action's behavior is described, and a before-and-after example illustrates its effect on your code. The blinking box in the before example indicates the code whose presence will trigger the intention action.

If a particular intention action annoys you constantly, you can disable it by deselecting its entry in the action list. You can disable entire groups of intentions by deselecting the box next to the group name.

3.8.7 *Exploring some common intention actions*

IDEA supports literally dozens of different intention actions that span all areas of development. There are intention actions for correcting errors, optimizing class structure, working with exceptions, building EJBs, and much more. We won't cover them all here, but we'll highlight some of the ones you're most likely to encounter in your day-to-day programming. Knowledge of IDEA's support for these actions will let you anticipate their usage, allowing you to use them as shortcuts to performing common operations.

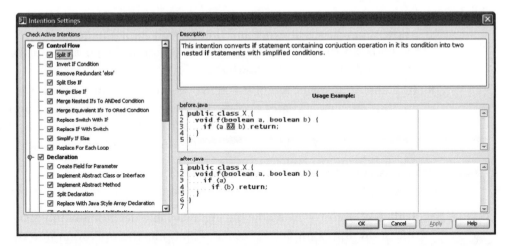

Figure 3.29   IDEA 5 lets you explore and control your intention actions in its new Intention Settings configuration window.

The following are common exception-related intentions:

- **Move catch up**—Reorganizes a `catch` statement among multiple catches so that the most specific exception is caught first. For example, an `IOException` should be caught before its ancestor `Exception`.

- **Surround with try/catch**—Available when an uncaught exception is detected. Generates a `try/catch` block around the offending call, catching the appropriate exceptions.

- **Add exception to catch**—Available inside a method with an existing `try/catch` block. Adds a `catch` block for a currently uncaught exception to the existing `try/catch` block.

- **Add exception to throws**—Available when code inside a method can generate an uncaught exception. Adds the exception in question to the `throws` clause of the method signature.

These are some of the common method-related intentions:

- **Fix method return**—Changes the method's signature to declare a return type matching that of the returned value.

- **Create method from usage**—Available when your code attempts to call a nonexistent method. Creates a new method whose parameters and return type are inferred from the context of the method call attempt.

- **Implement methods**—Available in classes that implement an interface or whose superclass is abstract and that haven't implemented all the required methods. Creates stub method implementations. Equivalent to the command **Code | Implement Methods**.

- **Implement abstract method**—Active when inside an abstract method of an abstract class. Locates classes that extend the abstract class and stubs out the method in them, if they haven't implemented it already. This is useful when you're adding a new method to an abstract class with a number of existing concrete classes.

The following are common variable- and assignment-related intentions:

- **Split declaration**—Available during a variable declaration and assignment operation, for example `int count = 0`. Splits the operation into two lines of code: declaration of the variable alone, followed by an assignment of the value to the variable on the next line.

- **Variable type fix**—Changes a variable's declared type to be compatible with an assignment operation. For example, if you try to assign a `boolean` to an `int` variable, this action changes the declared variable type to `boolean`.

- **Create field from parameter**—Appears inside an object's constructor that has unused parameters. Creates a new field (an instance variable) based on the unused parameter, and uses the constructor to initialize its value.

- **Create field/variable/parameter from usage**—Introduces a new variable based on an assignment or usage in context. Depending on the context, you can create fields, local variables, and method parameters.

Finally, here are a few other intention actions you'll probably encounter:

- **Fetch external resource**—Appears in the XML editor when the document references an external resource, such as a DTD. Downloads the resource to the local server so that IDEA may use it for validation purposes. You can review or edit the selection in the Resources area of the IDEA settings.

- **Ignore external resource**—Like the previous action, but tells IDEA to not attempt to validate against the resource nor warn you about it in the future. To un-ignore a resource, remove it from the ignore list in the **Resources** area of the IDEA Settings.

- **Invert if condition**—Available on conditional statements (position your caret at the `if` keyword to activate). Inverts the condition, and swaps the body of the conditional with the `else` block (or the code following the conditional). The resulting operation is logically equivalent.

- **Remove redundant cast**—Removes a cast that is unnecessary because the cast value is already of the correct type.

- **Add type cast**—Casts a reference to the expected type as allowed to satisfy the conditions. For example, if you're pulling a `String` from a collection and assigning it to a local variable, IDEA casts the value from an object to a `String`.

3.9 *Continuing the ACME project*

If you want to use this command-line interface, to test the system if for no other reason, you'll need a `CurrencyService` against which to test. That's where the bulk of the functionality lies; all the program will do, ultimately, is provide a facility to call that service and provide the results through an effective user-interface. Let's mock up a false service called `FixedRateCurrencyExchangeService` in the `com.acme.conversion.currency.service` package. Follow these steps:

1   Using the **Project** tool window, right-click the service package and use **New | Class** (**Alt+Insert**), naming the class `FixedRateCurrencyExchange-Service`.

2   Make this class implement the `CurrencyExchangeService` interface by modifying the class declaration to include the `implements Currency-ExchangeService` clause (don't forget, you can use Class Name Completion [**Ctrl+Alt+Space**] to fill this name in for you). As soon as you do, IDEA marks the class declaration with a red wavy underline, indicating an error (there's also a red marker in the marker bar). Hovering your mouse over the offending code tells you that your class doesn't implement the interface it claims to. Of course it doesn't—you haven't implemented the methods yet.

3   Rather than looking for the `CurrencyExchangeService` interface, activate the **Code | Implement Methods** option (**Ctrl+I**). The ensuing dialog shows a very small tree: Your class is implementing one interface, and that interface has but a single method defined. Select the method, and click **OK**. You'll be returned to the editor. (Alternatively, you can press **Alt+Enter** on the wavy error, and IDEA will suggest solutions to the error using intention actions, including **Implement methods**.) In any case, the method is implemented for you automatically, and the error

demarcation is removed. The focus of your cursor is left within the body of the new method. Delete the default body, and you'll give the service some functionality.

4   Let's make the service return a fixed rate of 1 US dollar to 1.50 Canadian dollars for now. This means that if someone requests a USD to CDN conversion, the rate returned will be 1.5; if someone requests a CDN to USD conversion, the rate will be the inverse: 2/3, or 0.66. A fixed value will make the converter easy to test. You'll store that value in a private variable called `rate` and initialize that value in the class constructor. Move your cursor inside the class definition and add the line `private double rate;` to add the field.

5   Select the **Code | Generate** menu option to bring up the pop-up (**Alt+Insert**). Why write when you can generate?

6   Choose the **Constructor** option, and then click the **Select None** button, because the constructor won't take arguments.

7   Inside the constructor, set the rate to be 1.5 with the line `rate = 1.5;`. Choose the **Code | Generate** option again to generate getters and setters for the `rate` variable.

8   We haven't discussed what to do if you're passed currency acronyms in the implemented `getCurrentRate()` method. There's a lot more error-checking you could implement here. For now, you'll just return a zero, but we'll revisit that implementation in a short while. For now, edit your service class to look like listing 3.2.

9   One more alteration you can make is to have the currency exchange service factory from Chapter 2 return an instance of this fixed rate factory. Open the `CurrencyExchangeServiceFactory` class—possibly with the **Go To | Class** command (**Ctrl+N**)—and change the line inside the `get-Service()` method to read as follows:

```
return new FixedRateCurrencyExchangeService();
```

NOTE   If you notice errors or intention actions as you work, feel free to stop and investigate them. Don't forget to try out some of the features outlined in this chapter, such as the following:

■ *Code completion*—Type `fromCurrency.` and then press **Ctrl+ Space** for basic completion, and select `equals()` from the list of options.

- *Intentions*—Omit the declaration of the answer variable, and let IDEA note that answer = rate isn't a valid line. Select **Create Local Variable 'answer'** from the intention pop-up, and initialize it to zero.

Listing 3.2 A basic implementation of a `CurrencyService` for the ACME project

```
package com.acme.conversion.currency.service;

public class FixedRateCurrencyExchangeService
    implements CurrencyExchangeService {

    private double rate;

    public FixedRateCurrencyExchangeService() {
        rate = 1.5;
    }

    public double getRate() {
        return rate;
    }

    public void setRate(double rate) {
        this.rate = rate;
    }

    public double requestCurrentRate(String fromCurrency,
                                     String toCurrency) {
        double answer = 0;
        if (fromCurrency.equals("USD") &&
    toCurrency.equals("CDN")) {
            answer = rate;
        }
        if (fromCurrency.equals("CDN") &&
    toCurrency.equals("USD")) {
            answer = 1/rate;
        }
        return answer;
    }
}
```

3.10 *Summary*

IDEA is a mature and sophisticated IDE for the Java language whose feature set can be compared favorably against any modern editor on the market. It boasts a clean and intuitive editor, a highly configurable workspace, and a series of stable features that we'd wager are relatively common among the lion's share of IDEs.

Beyond all this, however, is IDEA's intelligent understanding of Java code. Its caching mechanism permits it to read an entire project and all its dependent libraries and intelligently maintain the complex interconnected expanse of it all that we have no hope of maintaining in our own minds. Because of this fundamental characteristic, IDEA is able to provide many more valuable features like real-time code analysis as you type, multiple suggested intention actions when it notices problems in your code, and smart/contextual code complete. And these features only touch a small portion of IDEA's utility.

Managing projects 4

In this chapter...

- Creating and managing projects in IDEA
- Using modules to create efficient projects
- Using libraries to manage third-party components

Work in IDEA begins with the concept of a project. A project encapsulates all your source code, library files, and build instructions into a single organizational unit. Since version 4.0, IDEA's modules and libraries let you segregate larger, complex projects in more manageable structures that can share common code. Modularized projects are also a great benefit when you're building enterprise applications composed of several different components with complex interdependencies. Even if you've used an older version of IDEA extensively, we recommend that you not skip this chapter due to the fundamental changes in project management.

4.1 Understanding IDEA's project strategy

When you work on source code in IDEA, you do so in the context of a *project*. Because everything in IDEA revolves around the project, it's important to have a firm understanding of how and why IDEA handles projects the way it does.

4.1.1 Examining the IDEA project hierarchy

If you've never used an integrated development environment (IDE) like IDEA before, you may not immediately understand why you have to define a project before diving into your work. Remember, however, that IDEA isn't a simple text editor; it's a Java development environment. As such, you can't just start typing in your source code willy-nilly. First you have to create a project.

What is a project?

A project in IDEA is an organizational unit that represents a complete software solution. Your finished product may be decomposed into a series of discrete, isolated modules, but it's a project definition that brings them together, relates them with dependencies, and ties them into a greater whole.

Projects don't themselves contain development artifacts such as source code, build scripts, or documentation. They're the highest level of organization in the IDE, and they define project-wide settings as well as collections of what IDEA refers to as *modules* and *libraries*.

What is a module?

A *module* in IDEA is a discrete unit of functionality that can be run, tested, and debugged independently. Modules contain the development artifacts for their specific task; this includes such things as source code, build scripts, unit tests, documentation, and deployment descriptors. IDEA supports different types of modules, from plain Java applications to web apps, EJB modules, and so on. For many projects, a single module will suffice.

What is a library?

A *library* is an archive of compiled code that your modules depend on. Such an archive is typically represented as a JAR file or an expanded JAR in a directory. Libraries may optionally contain references to source files and API documentation: Including these references doesn't alter the usage of the library in any way, but it does add valuable information to the editor during class navigation and inspection. Examples of libraries include a DBMS vendor's private JDBC driver, or an open-source XML parser.

4.1.2 *Selecting different types of modules*

IDEA provides four distinct types of modules, which fall into two categories: basic Java modules and enterprise Java (or J2EE) modules. This chapter covers the first category; we'll reserve discussion of J2EE modules until chapter 11. As a head start, here's the purpose of each of the available module types shipped with IDEA:

IDEA 5 With version 5.0, this list has been expanded. Now there are six types of modules, roughly categorized into basic/standard Java (J2SE) modules, J2EE modules, and J2ME modules.

- *Java modules* are the simplest module type and represent a basic Java application project, whether it's a command-line tool, a Swing application, or a JAR library. When configuring this type of module, you can specify a set of Java source paths that will be compiled to a single class folder. We'll discuss using and configuring this type of module in detail in this chapter. The basic capabilities of this module are carried over into the web module.

- The *web module* is an extension of the Java module that adds support for web applications. In addition to providing the ability to create and build Java sources, it lets you edit your web application's deployment descriptor, build and deploy it to your application server, and configure other web application capabilities. You create a web module for each web application in your project. Web modules will be discussed in detail in chapter 11.

- An EJB *module* lets you design and package a collection of Enterprise Java-Beans. EJB modules will be discussed more fully in chapter 11.

- A J2EE *application module* is different than the other module types discussed so far. The J2EE module type is primarily concerned with packaging J2EE applications for deployment as enterprise archive (EAR) files. As such, it references Web and EJB modules that it packages for deployment.

IDEA 5 IDEA version 5.0 comes with two new module types: J2ME modules and IntelliJ Plugin modules. A J2ME module is a module suited for working on micro applications (such as for mobile technologies), and an IntelliJ Plugin module provides you with a correctly configured module for developing your own IDEA extensions.

4.1.3 *Selecting a project structure*

Because it's the module that defines a set of source files, a typical project must be composed of at least one module (you can create a project with no modules, but it's useless until the first module is added). For many projects, a single module is all you need. For more complex projects, especially J2EE projects or software suites composed of several discrete applications, a multi-module structure is more convenient. Separate modules let you build and test each piece separately while maintaining a common configuration. You obtain three primary benefits from breaking your project into modules:

- Reusability and sharing of modules between projects
- Improved project structure
- Module specific features

One benefit of the IDEA's modular projects is that a module can be shared among several projects if the need arises. Take, for example, a collection of utility classes that you'd like to share among several different types of projects. By putting them into their own module, you can easily add it to your other projects while maintaining the ability to develop it independently.

Modules can be built, tested, and versioned independently, so they're a great way to reduce the complexity of large projects. You can choose to compile and test a single module for example, without waiting on the rest of the application to be built. In addition, you can take a single module from many in a complex project and place it into a second project by itself, allowing you to remove the overhead and distraction of the larger project.

Modules in IDEA come in several different flavors, each designed with a particular type of application in mind. These application-specific modules extend the capabilities of IDEA to support new types of applications and to assist in their development and deployment. Web modules offer one-click deployment, whereas the J2EE module packages your application into an EAR file. No doubt future releases and third-party extensions to IDEA will add new types of modules.

Imagine you're building a Microsoft Office–style suite of office applications consisting of spreadsheet, word processor, and presentation designer applications. One natural way to model this project is to create a separate module for each application in the suite along with a module representing a set of utility functions common to all three applications.

4.2 Working with projects

Project creation is simplified with the assistance of the **New Project Wizard**, a process you've already run through with the creation of your "Hello World" and ACME projects. Things have a habit of changing over time, however, and it's a rare project that doesn't need some sort of reconfiguration during its lifetime. Ongoing project maintenance is handled through IDEA's **IDE Settings** window, which lets you change almost every aspect of the project you're working in.

4.2.1 Creating a new project

You create a new project by selecting the **File | New Project** command to launch the project wizard. The project wizard takes you through the steps required to set up a basic project and, if you desire, set up the project's initial module. When you first launch IDEA, it automatically directs you to the **New Project Wizard**.

IDEA 5   In version 5.0, the number of steps (as well as the order of the steps) of the New Project creation wizard may not match those described here for version 4.5.

Specifying the name and location of the project

In the first panel of the **New Project Wizard** (see figure 4.1), you're asked to specify the name of the project and the folder where the project file will be created. The name of the project file will be the name of the project plus the .ipr extension, so if you have specific requirements concerning spaces (or lack there of) in your filenames, take appropriate action. There is no requirement that your project file be located anywhere in particular, but you must consider several factors when choosing a location:

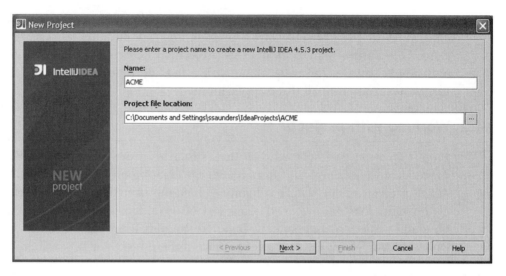

Figure 4.1   Step 1 of the New Project Wizard involves choosing a project name and a location to store the IPR file.

- You'll have fewer problems sharing or relocating your project if you keep all of your project's file and components at the same level or below the project file itself.
- If you'll be maintaining your project file in a source control system, it's convenient to place the project file in the root of your source control project.
- Keeping all of your project files in the same folder makes it easier to find and access them; likewise for your module files. However, doing so may be less convenient with regard to your source code control system.

If the folder you specify for the project doesn't exist, the wizard asks you if you wish to create it. Remember that you're specifying the folder where the project file will be created, not the name of the project file itself (this is created automatically and is always the same as your project name). When you're ready, click **Next** to continue.

Selecting a project JDK

In the second step of the **New Project Wizard** (see figure 4.2), you're asked to specify which JDK to use for the project. (Refer to chapter 1 for instructions on configuring JDKs for use within projects.) Make your selection, and click **Next**.

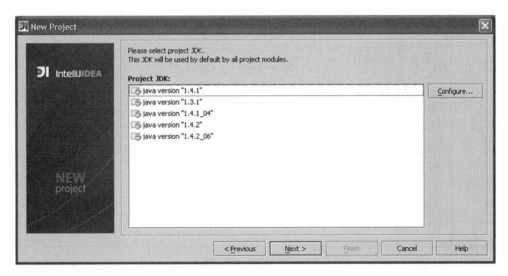

Figure 4.2   Step 2 of the New Project Wizard involves selecting a target JDK for the project.

Your choice of JDK determines which compiler and API library are used to build your project, unless a module specifically overrides this setting.

Selecting a single or multi-module project

At this point, the **New Project Wizard** has everything it needs to create a new project. However, without any modules, a project is just an empty shell and not very useful. This step lets you create your initial module (through the wizard) by selecting the first option **Create single-module project** and clicking **Next** (see figure 4.3).

If you want to create a multi-module project, or if you want an empty project to which you'll add modules later, select the second option **Create/configure multi-module project**; doing so changes the **Next** button to a **Finish** button. Click **Finish** to exit the wizard. The project is created, and you're taken to the **Add Module Wizard** to create or import modules. Creating and importing modules into your project is covered in the next section of this chapter.

4.2.2 Managing project settings

Along with its global settings and preferences, IDEA maintains a collection of settings specific to each project you define. These settings define not only the project's contents and behavior but also related information such as your source code control settings and compiler behavior. You can access these settings by

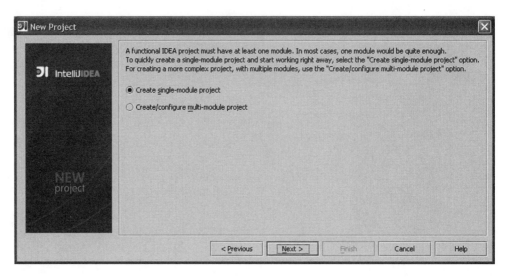

Figure 4.3 Step 3 of the New Project Wizard lets you choose between a single-module and a multi-module project.

selecting **File | Settings**, by using the shortcut **Ctrl+Alt+S**, or by clicking the **Settings** icon in the main toolbar (the wrench and machine nut). Doing so brings up the **Settings** control panel, shown in figure 4.4. The project-specific categories for the currently active project are shown at the top of the panel; global IDE settings are listed in the lower half. We'll cover the details of customizing IDEA through the settings panels in chapter 12.

The project-specific options that you can specify include defining the list of modules involved in the project, the compiler to use for building the project (and some of its options), the version control system configuration for the project, the code style to which the project adheres, and a few options controlling the behavior of the IDEA GUI Designer.

Configuring paths

The **Paths** settings panel is the main control panel for configuring your project. However, as you can see in figure 4.5, this control panel is sparse when no modules are present (you'll see another screenshot of this window shortly with modules in it, for comparison). This is because the modules, not the project, manage the development artifacts like source folders, dependent libraries, and so forth. The module list lets you add and remove modules from the project; it's discussed in the next section.

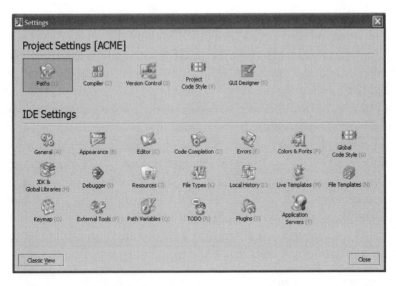

Figure 4.4 **The Settings window lets you control project-specific settings as well as general IDE settings. The two categories are separated for convenience, as shown here.**

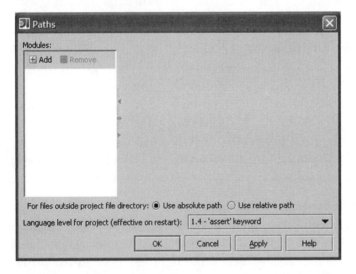

Figure 4.5 **The Paths window lets you control a few project-specific settings, as shown here, but it's principally used to configure the paths of the project's included modules (for a project with modules defined, see figure 4.13).**

The first option allows you to select between absolute and relative paths. If a module, library, or other referenced file is located outside the project file's directory, IDEA uses either the absolute path or the relative path (relative to the project file) to reference them, depending on which option you've selected in the project's path options. For files within the project directory, relative paths are always used to make project files as portable as possible between machines. This setting is also available on a module-by-module basis, should that become necessary.

The other setting lets you to configure the language level for the project. The default language level is 1.3, but you can use 1.4 or 1.5. Language level 1.4 enables the `assert` keyword, introduced in JDK 1.4. By default, Java compilers disable this keyword, because it wasn't a reserved keyword prior to JDK 1.4 and may cause conflicts with older source code. Similarly, language level 1.5 enables some of the new JDK 1.5 features, such as the `enum` keyword and autoboxing. If you alter the language level, you must restart IDEA in order for the option to take affect.

Configuring compiler settings

The **Compiler** settings panel lets you control build-related options such as whether to generate warnings, passing additional parameters to the compiler, and so forth. The details of the settings configured through this panel will be covered in chapter 5.

Configuring version control settings

The **Version Control** settings panel lets you integrate your version control system with your project. Because this is a project-level setting, you're free to use different source code control systems for different project or tweak the behavior of each from project to project. Note that IDEA also maintains a set of global settings for version control shared from project to project, such as the location of your source code repository. These settings are also accessed via this panel. Using and configuring your version control system with IDEA is covered in chapter 8.

Configuring project code style settings

The **Project Code Style** settings panel lets you override the code layout and formatting styles used for this project. IDEA maintains a detailed set of code formatting options that are shared between projects unless overridden through this panel. The **Code Style** settings let you specify everything from the size of your indents to the spacing around method calls and operator symbols. Code style settings are covered in chapter 12.

Configuring GUI Designer settings

The options in the **GUI Designer** settings panel pertain to IDEA's GUI Designer tool, which makes building user interfaces in Swing relatively painless. Using the GUI Designer and configuring its options is covered in chapter 10.

Configuring project template defaults

When you create a new project, the initial settings are based on project template settings maintained by IDEA. To edit these settings, select the **File | Template Project Settings** command to reveal a subset of the **Settings** panel (figure 4.6). IDEA lets you specify default settings for the compiler, version control, code style, and GUI designer options. Once set, all new projects begin with these default settings. Because the options in these panels are identical to those used when configuring an existing project, we'll defer discussing them in detail until we come to their usage throughout the book.

Saving your project settings

IDEA automatically saves project settings, so there is no need (or opportunity) to explicitly save your project. The newly defined settings are applied immediately, so you don't need to restart IDEA or close and reopen project to make them effective.

Reopening a project

When you start IDEA, it automatically reopens the last project you worked on, unless you've disabled the **Reopen last project on startup** option under IDEA's **General** settings. You can open an existing project by selecting the **File | Open Project** command and selecting the IPR file corresponding to your project. Or, if

Figure 4.6 The Template Project Settings window lets you specify defaults for most project-specific settings. These defaults are applied to all new projects you create.

you've used the project recently, it's listed in the **File | Reopen** submenu, which maintains a list of the most recently used projects.

Working with multiple projects

When you attempt to work on a project while one is already open, IDEA asks if you wish to open the project in a new frame. If you want to work on multiple projects simultaneously, click **Yes**. Otherwise, click **No** to close your existing project and open the new one.

When you open multiple projects, each is loaded in its own IDEA frame. The two projects are completely independent; other than letting you cut and paste between the application windows, they can't share data. To close a project, select the **File | Close Project** menu option.

> **WARNING** Regardless of how many projects you have open at once, only a single instance of IDEA is running, so all open projects must share the same memory space. You may need to bump up the amount of memory allocated to IDEA if you plan to frequently have multiple projects open at once.

4.2.3 Working with project files

IDEA stores the configuration data for projects and their components in plaintext XML files, making it easy to manage, edit, and share project configuration data with others. IDEA creates three different types of files: the project file, the workspace file, and the module file.

Project files have an .IPR extension and contain information core to the project itself, such as the names and location of its component modules, compiler settings, Ant configurations, and so forth. You can click an .IPR file to launch the project in IDEA. By default, this file is created at the root of the project.

Along with each project file, IDEA creates an .IWS file to store your personal workspace settings. This file remembers the placement and positions of your windows, your VCS and History settings, your Run/Debug configuration targets, and other data pertaining to the development environment. This file is always created alongside your project file. If this file is deleted, it's regenerated automatically, unlike the project .IPR file.

Module files are created for each module you defined and have the .IML extension. The module file stores all the path and dependency information associated with the module. Its exact contents depend on what type of module it is. By default, module files are located in the module's content root folder.

4.3 Working with modules

Although the project may be the center of attention, the module does all the work. Without a module, your project has no source code, no output, nothing other than a collection of configuration preferences. Like projects, modules often require alterations after their initial creation. Their participation in a project, as well as their individual internal settings, is controlled through IDEA's Settings interface.

4.3.1 Managing project modules

Modules are managed from within the project's **Paths** settings panel. The list of modules associated with the project is shown along the left side of the panel. IDEA gives you options for adding, removing, and editing the list of modules.

Adding a new module to your project

When you create a new project, the project wizard gives you the opportunity to define your first module as part of the project setup. Alternatively, to add new modules after the initial project creation, select **File | New Module**. Either way, the process is the same, beginning with the **Add Module Wizard**, shown later in figure 4.9.

Importing a module into your project

In the first step of the **Add Module Wizard** you have two options: You can create a new module from scratch or import an existing one into your project by selecting the **Import existing module** radio button. Select the path to the module's .IML file by either typing it in or clicking the ellipsis button to select it via the file requestor.

When you import an existing module, you're really just adding a reference to it. The module isn't copied into the project's root folder or altered in any way. The module is always stored in a single location. This allows a single module to be shared by multiple projects.

IDEA 5 Since version 5.0, IntelliJ IDEA provides the ability to automatically convert Eclipse and JBuilder projects into its own format.

Removing modules from the project

You can remove a module from a project by selecting it from the module list and then clicking the minus button in the toolbar. This only removes the module reference from the project and doesn't delete or affect the module file or its contents. You can add the module again by using the **Add Module Wizard** and selecting the **Import** option.

Managing dependencies between projects

When you're building a multi-module project, you may end up with modules that rely on the output of one or more of the other modules in the project. For example, a module representing the installation artifacts and scripts for a packaged product may depend on the module representing that product. In order for IDEA to build your project successfully, you must specify all such dependencies. Click the **Dependencies** tab at the top of the **Paths** settings window for the dependent module, as shown in figure 4.7.

All the other modules in the project are listed, along with a checkbox for each. Select the modules the currently selected module relies on to build or function properly. Any attempt to build the selected module automatically triggers builds of its dependencies. Likewise, a change to one of the module's dependencies triggers a rebuild of the dependent module.

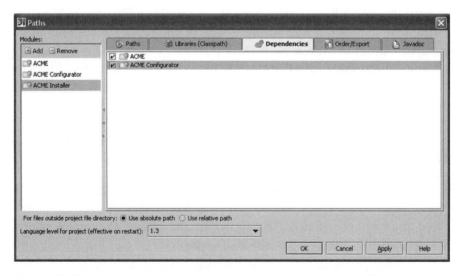

Figure 4.7   Dependencies between modules need to be specified so that IDEA can determine which modules require rebuilding when the build command is invoked.

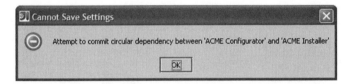

Figure 4.8   Circular dependencies make projects impossible to build, so IDEA prevents you from defining them.

Circular dependencies aren't allowed: Module A, for example, can't depend on Module B if Module B depends on A. Larger circular dependencies are likewise not permitted. If you create a circular dependency, IDEA warns you and keeps you from applying your changes, as shown in figure 4.8.

IDEA 5   Version 5.0 allows circular dependencies, but it warns the user that they aren't recommended. Version 5.0 is capable of analyzing such dependencies and can assist in correct organization of the build process for such projects.

4.3.2 Creating a Java module with the module wizard

The primary module used by IDEA for everything other than J2EE applications is the *Java module*. The Java module covers everything from a simple command-line utility, to Swing applications, to libraries with a public API but no direct user interface. Being a generalist, it doesn't provide much in the way of special application support the way the J2EE modules do. We expect that in the future, specialized extensions of this module type will be available to ease the creation of common application themes. Even so, the features of the Java module form the core of the other module types and are important to learn.

Specifying the type of module to create

If you choose to create a new module from scratch, select the module type from the list in the **Add Module Wizard** (figure 4.9), and click **Next** to continue. This chapter focuses on the Java module; the other module types are covered in chapter 11.

IDEA 5   The **Add Module Wizard** looks different in version 5.0; it supports two new types of modules.

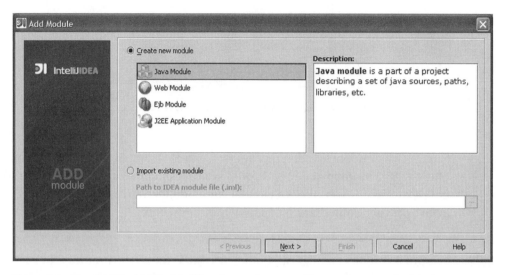

Figure 4.9   Step 1 of the Add Module Wizard prompts you to either create a new module from scratch or select an existing module on disk (represented by an IDEA module file, extension .iml).

Specifying the module file's name and location

The next step in the **Add Module Wizard** is much the same as the similar step in the **New Project Wizard**. As shown in figure 4.10, it lets you specify the name and

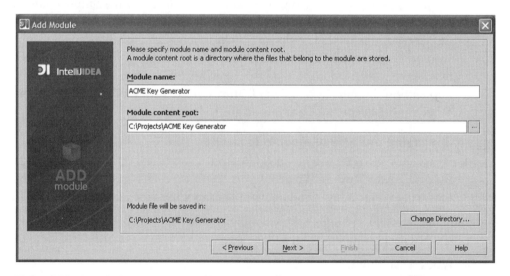

Figure 4.10   Step 2 of the Add Module Wizard involves naming and specifying a location for your new module.

location of the module file you're creating. In addition, however, it wants the location of the module's content root folder.

The module's content root folder is the folder that contains all the files that make up the module, including Java source files, Ant files, scripts, resources, and other related files. In the next step, you'll have the chance to specify a subfolder of your module's content root folder for source code.

By default, IDEA creates your new module's content root folder as a subdirectory of your project's root folder, based on the module's name. You can change the location manually or by clicking the ellipsis button to select an alternate location. Likewise, IDEA assumes that you want your module's IML file to be located in the content root folder, but you can change this by clicking the **Change Directory** button.

> **TIP** Although it isn't required, the default project/module layout is recommended. Keeping your modules contained within their projects not only helps you stay better organized but also makes sharing them with others easier, because it eliminates absolute path problems. This approach also makes it easier to check your entire project into your source control system. One exception is situations where you're sharing modules between several projects, in which case it may make sense to locate modules above the project level.

Specifying the Java source folder

IDEA needs to identify the root of the folder (or folders) that contain your Java source files. In the **Add Module Wizard** dialog shown in figure 4.11, you're required to specify the subfolder that contains them. This folder path is relative to your module's content root folder, and IDEA will create it if it doesn't already exist.

This folder forms the root of your Java package hierarchy. You can direct IDEA to use an existing source directory by clicking the ellipsis button and navigating the directory browser to the right location. If you want to specify additional source folders, you can do so through the project's **Paths** settings, discussed a little later.

You don't have to store your sources in a subfolder: You can enter a period (.) as your source path to mark the entire content root folder as a source folder. Of course, this means any auxiliary files are mixed in with your Java source files, which can make things confusing.

If you don't want to specify a source directory, or you aren't ready to create it now (you can always add it later), select the **Do not create source directory** option.

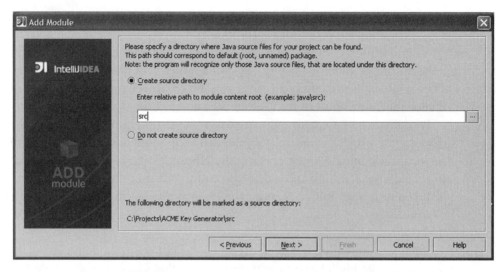

Figure 4.11   Step 3 of the Add Module Wizard prompts you to specify the main source folder where Java source files can be found.

TIP   If there are already Java source files in the directory structure of the module's content root folder, IDEA automatically searches the directory tree for Java source code. All of the root directories of the Java package structures it finds are automatically provided as options for source folders. This is handy when you download a full project from CVS or another source and want IDEA to use the structure already provided.

Specifying the compiler output path

In the next step of the **Add Module Wizard**, you need to specify the folder you want to compile to. Regardless of how many source folders you define in your module, they will all build their class files into the folder you specify here. If your project includes multiple modules, you may want to compile all of them into the same output folder; but by default IDEA picks a subfolder of your content root folder, as shown in figure 4.12. (More on how all this works in a bit.)

When you click the **Finish** button, your new module is created.

4.3.3 *Managing Java module settings*

The **Add Module Wizard** does a fine job of creating a basic module, but you'll probably need to fine-tune your module settings. The definition of a Java module includes a content root folder, source and output paths, libraries, a dependency mapping between it and other modules, and documentation.

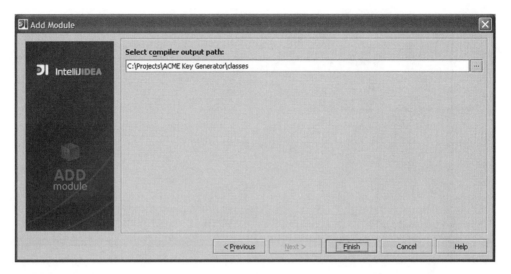

Figure 4.12 Step 4 of the Add Module Wizard prompts you to specify the directory where the compiler output (the class files generated from your Java sources) will be placed.

You can also access these settings by selecting **File | Settings**, by using the shortcut **Ctrl+Alt+S**, or by clicking the **IDE Settings** icon in the main toolbar (the wrench and machine nut), as shown earlier in figure 4.4. All module-specific configurations are found under the **Paths** icon on the **Paths** configuration screen shown in figure 4.13. This screen lets you configure a project by adding and removing modules from that project, and it also allows you to configure the included modules. Each module has configuration options for its **Paths**, **Libraries (Classpath)**, **Dependencies**, **Order/Export** (of the classpath) and **Javadoc**.

Configuring the content root folder

Modules have at least one content root folder, selected at creation time through the **Add Module Wizard** as you've just seen. All the files and paths that make up your module must fall under a content root folder. You can create additional content root folders if your module's files and folders are spread out in several directories. For most projects, this won't be necessary; one content root folder with subfolders for source code, class files, and so forth, will suffice.

The left panel in the **Paths** tab in figure 4.13 shows all the path folders defined for the currently selected module. These paths are organized by the content root folder they belong to, because some modules have more than one content root folder. You can add more content root folders by clicking the **Add Content Root**

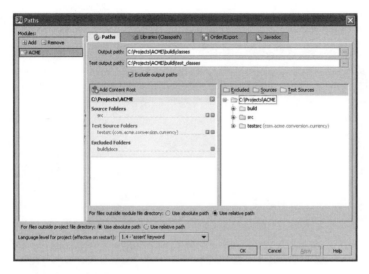

Figure 4.13   The Paths window is used to specify which directories in your modules contain Java source for production, Java source for testing purposes, and artifacts that should be excluded.

button. Content root folders can be removed easily by clicking the cross icon to the right of the content root item in the panel and confirming its removal.

Each content root folder contains folder paths under three important designations:

- *Source folders* contain Java source files.
- *Test source folders* contain Java source files related to testing only.
- *Excluded folders* are folders that IDEA should ignore when searching, compiling, and performing other similar actions.

Understanding source folders

When you designate a folder as a source path, you're telling IDEA that this folder and its subfolders contain Java source code that should be compiled as part of the build process. The top of this folder is considered the root of a package hierarchy; .java files in it are considered part of the default package, whereas subfolders designate a standard Java package structure.

Test source folders are singled out for special treatment so you can keep code used for testing (such as unit tests) separate from the production code. This makes it easy to package your application for distribution free from any testing-related code. We'll look further into IDEA's support for unit testing in chapter 7.

Understanding excluded folders

Excluded paths let you hide certain folders from IDEA. Files in folders designated as excluded aren't parsed, watched, searched, or compiled by IDEA. Typical candidates are temporary build folders, generated output, logs, and other project output.

> **TIP** You can use the **Compiler** settings control panel to hide individual files or folders from the compiler without excluding them from the rest of IDEA. Doing so makes it possible to have source folders that are parsed and accessible for editing without having to compile them.

Configuring folders within the content root folder

The right panel of the dialog in figure 4.13 is used to locate and manage folder allocations within the content root folders. Selecting a content root item in the list shows the corresponding folder structure on the right side. To add a folder to the content root, click to select the folder in the panel, and then click the folder type button: **Excluded**, **Sources**, or **Test Sources**. The folder is added to the current content root folder selected, and its color is updated to reflect its status. You can remove folder items from the content root folder by clicking the cross button to the right of the folder items.

> **TIP** You can do most of the actions of adding and removing folders from the content root item in the right panel. Right-clicking a folder displays a list of options that define what type of folder the selection can become. Selecting the same option again returns it to normal folder status. As an extra bonus, you can add new folders to the project by right-clicking and selecting the **New Folder** option.

Configuring source folders

Adding and removing source folders may be all that most projects require. However, because source folders are known to hold Java source files, the smart people at JetBrains have taken things a step further. Typically, source files exist in a subdirectory that matches their package structure, and thus source and test source directories are assumed to map to the default package. Some people think that's overkill for a module that specifies a single package that's deeply nested. Rather than create an arbitrarily deep directory structure to satisfy this convention, IDEA lets you specify a package root prefix, which means the package tree in that directory starts in the package you define and not the default package. In figure 4.13, the testing source directory is using a package root prefix.

Setting the package root prefix for a source folder (either a testing source folder or otherwise) is easy. Click the **P** button, and you'll see a dialog where you can type the package prefix. IDEA takes this prefix into account when compiling, viewing source, and other such tasks.

Understanding and configuring output paths

For each of the two types of source folders, IDEA maintains a separate output path for use during compilation. When you build the module, test sources are compiled to the test output path, and standard source files are compiled to the regular output path. Both output paths are automatically added to your project's classpath. You configure the output paths by editing the text in the paths at the top of the **Paths** editing dialog. For convenience, you can also use a visual file browser by clicking the ellipsis buttons to the right of each path.

Excluding output paths

You can add both output paths to your list of excluded paths by selecting the **Exclude output paths** option. (This option is enabled by default.) The output paths are still considered part of your classpath for running and debugging your project; but because they're generated by IDEA, there's typically no need for them to be monitored, searched, and so on.

4.4 *Working with libraries*

Using IDEA's library features makes it easy to manage the often-burdensome task of building applications utilizing third-party toolkits. IDEA manages not only the classes and JAR libraries for you, but the source and reference documentation as well. IDEA supports three different library configurations, which determine the scope and reusability of the library within your environment:

- *Project libraries* are defined within a project for its exclusive use.
- *Module libraries* are defined within a module for its exclusive use.
- *Global libraries* can be used by any project.

4.4.1 *Understanding library basics*

The three types of libraries supported by IDEA are configured and behave a bit differently, but they perform the same mission and share many of the same traits. Figure 4.14 shows the interface for configuring global libraries; it's essentially the same for all types of libraries. In many ways, configuring a library is similar to the

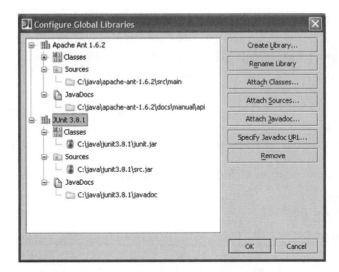

Figure 4.14
The Configure Global Libraries window demonstrates how a library is defined by a collection of class files, optional source files, and optional JavaDoc files. These files may be part of an exploded directory or packaged in an archive such as a JAR or ZIP file.

process of configuring your JDK from chapter 1; you specify a set of class files and then optional source and JavaDoc reference files.

Understanding class folders and JAR files

Every library must have at least one class folder or JAR archive added to it. When you add a library to a module or project, you're adding the library's classes to its classpath. Without class files, a library wouldn't do anything. Click the **Attach Classes** button, and select a directory of class files or a JAR archive of class files to add class path entries to the library. You may add multiple class entries if necessary.

Now, any module or project that uses this library will automatically recognize the classes and include them in the classpath when running or testing your application. Classes are all that is required to create a library, but if you attach source code or JavaDoc entries as described next, you'll gain further advantages.

Adding library source code

If the source code for the classes in the library is available, you should use the **Attach Source** button to add it to the library, even if you only have a portion of it. IDEA won't attempt to use the source code to rebuild the library; it only uses the source code to provide the same level of integration with libraries as it does with your own classes. When source is available, IDEA can provide inline documentation through the use of JavaDoc it extracts from the source code; it can also use the original parameter names in method signature help. In addition, IDEA lets you drill down into the source code (marked as read-only) while editing.

Adding JavaDoc reference

Like the source code reference, JavaDoc entries are optional. If they're present, you can use IDEA's **View | External JavaDoc (Shift+F1)** command to quickly load the JavaDoc for the method or class referenced at the cursor into your browser.

> **TIP** Instead of folders, you can specify JAR or Zip archives that contain your class files, source folders, and JavaDocs. Just remember that the root of the archive should correspond to the root of the Java package structure. IDEA's file requestor lets you expand archives and select individual folders if you don't want to include the entire archive.

4.4.2 Adding libraries to the project

The **Libraries** tab of the project **Path** settings provides access to the selection and configuration of libraries (see figure 4.15). In addition, you can create global libraries outside the project through the **JDK & Global Libraries** control panel under the IDE Settings.

Adding global libraries

Global libraries exist outside the project and are available for use by any module, in any project on your machine. Global libraries were designed as a way to encapsulate third-party packages that, while not compiled as part of your application, are required to run it. Examples of this might be your web application server's JSDK implementation, a set of JDBC drivers, a third-party plugin API, and so on.

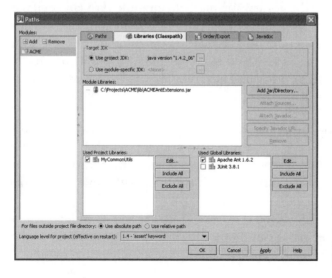

Figure 4.15
The Libraries tab of the Paths configuration window lets you specify module, project, and global libraries.

You add global libraries to a project by enabling them for each module that requires them. Once configured, you'll see each global library listed in the **Used Global Libraries** section of your module settings. To include a global library in the currently selected module, select the check box next to the name. The **Edit** button next to the list lets you edit exiting global libraries as well as include new ones.

Adding project libraries

Project libraries have the same look and feel as global libraries but are created at the project level. Therefore, they're only available to modules in the current project. If the module exists in more than one project, it doesn't share the project library in the other project. Available project libraries are shown in the **Project Libraries** list; like global libraries, they can be selected and deselected on a per-module basis.

Adding module libraries

Module libraries are defined within a particular module and are available to that module only. However, they can be carried with the module from project to project. Module libraries are anonymous; they aren't given individual names like global and project libraries, because the list of module libraries is the classpath for this module, with optional source file and JavaDoc attachments. Module library entries are often used to include items like resources, property files, and other non-class file entries into your project. They're also useful when the JAR files that make up your library are included as part of the module itself rather than in an external directory.

> **TIP** Use IDEA's path variables feature (described later in this chapter) to make it easy to relocate, share, and upgrade libraries. Create a path variable pointing to the root of the library's installation folder; then each user can create a path variable corresponding to the libraries location on their machine.

Specifying search order (modules, classes, libraries)

In some situations, the order of items for the module's classpath may be important: for example, when one of your libraries is pulling in an older version of a class you require, or properties files in a library JAR conflict with one another. Whatever the situation is, you can use the **Order/Export** tab, shown in figure 4.16, to help correct the problem. Use the **Move Up** and **Move Down** buttons to reorder the module's classpath entries appropriately. Notice that in addition to your

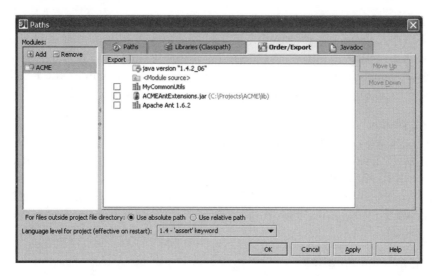

Figure 4.16   The Order/Export tab of the Paths configuration window can help you deal with issues such as classloading conflicts by explicitly setting which directories and class archives are loaded/searched first.

libraries and module class files, the module's sources and the JDK are also included in the list.

This window also includes an **Export** checkbox for each included library. By selecting this checkbox, you signify that the library should be exported to all other modules that have dependencies on this one.

4.4.3   *Migrating projects from IDEA 3.x*

Between version 3.x and version 4.x of IDEA, significant changes were made in the files that store the definition and configuration of projects: Version 3.x and previous lack the concept of a module. When you attempt to open an older-format IDEA project file, IDEA does its best to convert the project to the new format. Note, however, that there is no going back from this step; the older version of IDEA will no longer be able to read the project. As a convenience, IDEA creates a backup copy of the old project file by appending *_old* to the original filename.

When converting to the new format, IDEA creates a new project with a single Java module including all the source paths and libraries present in the original project. Any classpath entries are converted into module libraries, in accordance with the current way of thinking.

Because of conceptual differences between the two versions, some projects may suffer from conversion problems or missing elements. In particular, any paths in 3.x projects that don't follow under the project root will be missing from the updated project file. Fortunately, this is an uncommon configuration and is easy to correct.

4.4.4 Sharing projects with others

All project files can be shared among a team of developers. Although you can certainly distribute copies of them, your best bet is to place these items under source code control along with the rest of your project's files to ensure that they're always up to date. You probably don't want to share workspace (IWS) files, because they contain information specific to each developer's IDE.

By default, all path-related settings in the project file are stored relative to the project file itself; the same is true for module files. This allows for easy relocation of projects and modules and lets each developer use their project from any location they choose. Any items outside the project or module directories (such as third-party libraries and your JDK settings) are stored by IDEA as absolute paths. This obviously can cause problems between machines. There are several possible solutions:

- Whenever possible, keep the content of your modules under the same path as the module file itself.

- In your project settings, set the option **For files outside project directory** to **Use relative paths**. This will avoid the use of absolute path names, making your project files easier to share between individuals. Modules have a similar option. You still need to make sure that each developer's source tree is arranged similarly in order for the paths to resolve correctly.

- Use path variables, as described next.

4.4.5 Using path variables

Path variables are project-independent macros defined in your IDE Settings. Any time IDEA encounters a path that includes a path variable reference (path references, like other variables in IDEA, are delineated by a pair of dollar sign characters), it uses your path variable settings to resolve the actual path.

Path variables allow you to hide the locations of files outside of your project or modules behind a named variable whose value can be changed on each installation of IDEA. This enables developers to share projects containing absolute path references.

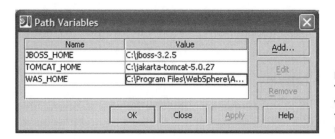

Figure 4.17
The Path Variables configuration window lets you define variables that make your project and module files more portable.

Using path variables to facilitate shared projects

Path variables are particularly useful when you're working with third-party libraries. For example, if your project uses the JDOM XML libraries, stored on your machine as C:\libs\jdom-1.0.0, all references to files below the root folder (its classes, sources, and JavaDocs) can instead be derived from the logical folder $JDOM_HOME$. Then, users of the project can define the actual location of the JDOM home directory on their own workstation, allowing IDEA to resolve the path correctly.

Creating and editing path variables

You manage your collection of path variables, and create new ones, through the **Path Variables** section of the **IDE Settings**. A typical example is shown in figure 4.17. In this example, we've configured copies of home folders for third-party libraries as well as our application server and Java Servlet SDK. Using this settings panel, you can add, edit, and remove path variables at any time. When you add a path variable's value, you're asked to select the directory value using the directory requestor—you can't edit the values by hand. This ensures that variables resolve to actual directories.

Using path variables in your project

IDEA automatically uses any path variables you've defined in your setup, replacing corresponding path references in your projects and modules with the path variable reference. Note that if you're sharing your project with other developers, you've now required them to define the path variables as well. Otherwise, IDEA won't know how to resolve the path correctly, in which case the path (with the path variable visible) will be

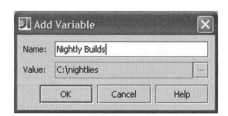

Figure 4.18   Adding a new path variable is as simple as specifying a name and choosing a path.

shown in red to alert the user to the missing path variable. Note that after you define the missing path variable, IDEA may require you to close and reopen the project before recognizing it.

4.5 Using the Project tool window

The first tool window we'll discuss in detail is probably the one you'll use most often. The **Project** window lets you navigate, edit, and explore the contents of your project's module and source files. All the files that are part of your project (and their libraries) are accessible from this view, organized by their parent modules. Figure 4.19 shows a typical example.

4.5.1 Understanding the Project and Packages views

The two tabs at the top of the **Project** window let you switch between a module/file oriented view of your project and one representing all the available packages and classes that make up your source trees. (A third tab, which we'll talk about in chapter 11, gives you a J2EE-oriented view of web and enterprise applications. This tab only appears when your project contains these types of modules.) The **Packages** tab is unique in that it pays no attention to module boundaries or file-system structure. Instead, it provides a combined view of your entire source path, organized into the logical

Figure 4.19   The Project tool window, navigating in Project mode. This view provides an overview of the directory structure that forms your project, including all modules and libraries.

Java package structure. An example **Packages** view is shown in figure 4.20.

4.5.2 *Configuring the Project window*

The options toolbar (see figure 4.21) along the top of the **Project** window lets you filter the **Project** views to your liking. These settings are saved along with your project and restored each time you open it. Note that some of the options aren't relative for all views.

Flattening packages

The **Flatten Packages** option removes the hierarchy from your package structure and collapses package families into their flattened form, as you might see them referenced with the code itself. As you can see in figure 4.22, this view is much more compact then the hierarchical view, allowing you to fit more packages within the view than normal. In the **Project** view, this only affects library entries; source directories remain in their file-system structure.

Showing and hiding middle packages

The **Hide Empty Middle Packages** option, available only when the **Flatten Packages** option is engaged, eliminates an empty package hierarchy. For example, if all your classes reside in the com. acme.conversion.currency package,

Figure 4.20   The Project tool window, navigating in package mode. In this view, the boundaries and divisions of disparate modules, directories, and libraries are hidden. It shows the project strictly as a set of packages and classes.

Figure 4.21   The Project tool window's options toolbar includes these buttons: Flatten Packages, Hide Empty Middle Packages, Show Members, Autoscroll to Source, Autoscroll from Source, Show Structure, Show Modules, and Show Libraries Contents. Most tool windows use a toolbar control like this for setting and unsetting options.

Figure 4.22
When the Flatten Packages option is enabled, the package view of the Project tool window shows top-level directories with package names instead of a deep directory structure. In this example, the Show Members option is also enabled, which adds nodes for methods and fields of each class to the overview.

enabling this option hides the three empty levels of packages above the `currency` directory. If your package structure is deep or complex, this option can give you back lots of real estate. It's also smart enough to not hide empty packages at the lowest or highest levels of hierarchy, because you probably intend to use these eventually (hence, the term *middle* packages.)

When you're using the **Flatten Packages** option, a new option has been added to the **Project** view: **Abbreviate Qualified Package Names**. Enabling abbreviations shortens the package name considerably by replacing the leading package names with single letters. For example, the package `sun.net.www.protocol.http` becomes `s.n.w.p.http`. This saves you real estate, at the expense of readability.

The **Compact Empty Middle Packages** option lets you ignore empty packages for more convenient display. Its view is very similar to the **Flatten Packages** view, except that packages containing no classes are omitted from the tree. For example, if a project includes source code in the `com.texism` and in the `com.`

texism.examples.book packages, but no code at any other package level, this option shows only two packages on the tree: com.texism and com.texism.examples.book. The com and com.texism.examples packages are not shown. For all practical purposes, this option enables package flattening for empty package structures. This option is only available when you haven't enabled the **Flatten Packages** option.

Showing and hiding members

Want even more fine-grained access to the items in your project? Enabling the **Show Members** option exposes the methods and fields that belong to each class listed in the **Project** view, as shown in figure 4.22. Double-clicking a field or method item in the list loads its class's source file and positions the cursor at the point the member is declared. This is an excellent way to quickly explore the structure of your code and navigate right to the method of interest. However, it takes up a lot of room, so there is the alternative structure view, which we'll get to in a second.

Configuring autoscrolling to source

Enabling the **Autoscroll to Source** option turns all those double-click navigation operations we've mentioned into single clicks. Selecting any item in the **Project** window takes you to that item in the editor. It even works with keyboard navigation: Arrow around the tree, and watch the editor follow you.

The inverse option—**Autoscroll from Source**—provides the opposite functionality: While you navigate your code in the editor, the current semantic item (class, method, or field) is automatically selected in the **Project** window.

> **TIP** With the **Project** window active, begin typing the name of the class, method, or field you want to navigate to. The selection automatically selects the next matching item. Then, use the up and down arrows to navigate between matching items.

Showing class structure

An alternative way to examine class members is handled by the **Show Structure** option. Enabling the **Structure** view adds a panel to the bottom of the **Project** view (as shown in figure 4.23) that exposes the structure of the selected class. This gives you the ability to navigate directly to a particular method without eating up the whole window. You can even resize the pane as necessary. For even more

Figure 4.23
Enabling the Show Structure option in the
Project tool window dedicates a portion of
the tool window to a more detailed view
into the class currently open in the main
editor window.

structure fun, IDEA provides a dedicated tool window (the aptly named **Structure** window). We'll discuss the particulars in chapter 9 when we talk about analysis and refactoring.

Showing modules

The **Show Modules** option is available only in the **Packages** view. Enabling it adds the module structure pack to the **Packages** view, grouping packages under their parent module. Even if two modules share common packages, the class files appear only under the module whose source path they're defined in.

IDEA 5 The **Project** view now lets you group your project's modules into a tree structure of your choosing. This is purely for organizational purposes; but it can be convenient if your project includes many different modules, because you can selectively collapse and expand the groups you're working with at any given time.

To group a module, right-click the module in the project browser and select the **Move Module to Group** option, either selecting an existing group, creating a new group, or moving the module outside of all the existing groups. Creating a module grouping adds nodes to the project tree, allowing you to customize your view. Your code structure and the locations of your modules and source files are unaffected by the grouping operations.

Showing library contents

The **Show Libraries Contents** option, applicable only to the **Package** view, toggles the inclusion of library classes into the view. When enabled, classes that live in libraries appear in the package structure, although they're read-only. By default, IDEA assumes you're more interested in editing and navigating among your own classes, but this option can be handy in some circumstances.

IDEA 5 A new **Favorites** tool window has been introduced in the new release. It's basically a shelf where you can store an ad hoc selection of modules, packages, classes, files, or libraries for quick access. It's like a mini version of the **Project** browser. You can even create multiple groups of favorites (represented by tabs in the **Favorites** view) to further organize things.

To add an item to your list of favorites, right-click the item either in the **Project** view or through its symbol in the editor and select the **Add to Favorites** option from the context menu. Here you have the option of placing it into one of your existing groups of favorites or creating a new one.

4.6 *Summary*

Project configuration and management is an important aspect of software design, and any worthy IDE provides functionality to address this need. Without it, an engineer may as well be writing software in a plain text editor. The creators of IDEA have invested much thought and effort into making the project-management feature set within their IDE support the needs of their audience.

IDEA uses the concepts of projects, modules, and libraries to decompose the traditional concept of a software project. Projects are the highest level; they equate roughly to the products you're trying to produce. Modules are wholly contained subcomponents—individually buildable, runnable, and testable—that can be assembled into a larger solution. Libraries are static modules that aren't dynamically built or altered but that can be leveraged within the context of a module. By defining these layers and making them self-contained and modular (as Java components are touted to be), software designers can begin to reuse code in multiple projects and also manage that task with a minimum of effort.

Building and
running applications

5

In this chapter...

- Building your project and compiling source code
- Extending IDEA's building and packaging capabilities with Ant
- Running applications within IDEA

With all the project management and code authoring to one side, no project comes to life unless you build it. Bringing together the perfectly written (and bug free?) project source code, external libraries, and configuration information is part of this process. IDEA provides all the facilities required to compile, assemble, and run your application within the IDE. To compile and execute your application, you can use IDEA's built-in project management tools, which automatically track files in the project that need to be compiled. For final packaging or more involved build processes, you can enlist the help of Ant, the popular open source build tool. With its high degree of integration with the Ant build tool, IDEA can help create and manage Ant build scripts. This chapter will illustrate using its abilities directly from within IDE.

5.1 Building a project

At some point, it's time to stop coding, build your project, and see if it runs. You don't need to leave IDEA, however. Along with helping you write your application, IDEA gives you the ability to easily compile, assemble, and run your application directly from the IDE. Using IDEA's internal compilation tools can give you a productivity boost; having IDEA track and compile your source code means that compiling one file or an entire package is quick and simple.

5.1.1 How IDEA builds your project

When IDEA builds your project. it performs a number of operations:

- It compiles Java code in your module's source paths to your project output folder.
- It compiles Java code in your module's test sources paths to your test output folder.
- It copies any resource files it finds in your source paths into your output path.
- It reports any problems that it encounters to you through the Messages window.

You'll learn more about each of these steps in this section.

Understanding the steps in the IDEA build process

IDEA is intelligent about how it performs its builds. It has two goals: compile only the files that have changed, and make sure all dependencies on other source files and modules are resolved. This makes for builds that are as fast and as safe as possible. Before compiling, IDEA must determine which files are *dirty* and require recompilation. The basic steps it follows in determining which files are dirty are as follows:

1 Calculate which files have been modified since the last build, and mark them dirty.
2 Track down dependencies of any of the modified files, and mark them dirty.
3 Determine which modules are affected, and mark them as dirty.
4 If any dirty modules have dependencies, mark them dirty as well.
5 Locate modified files in dirty modules.

Specifying a project's output path

When you set up your project, you specify an output directory to hold your compiled Java classes. The output path is required to build your project. If you're using a version control system, you should generally specify an output path that doesn't fall under its control. You won't be checking compiled class files into the repository, so it will confuse things to have them show up as unregistered files in your tree. Most version control systems let you ignore entire directory hierarchies, so you may wish to ignore your output folder. Your output directory is automatically added to your project's Classpath.

Keeping test classes separate using your test output path

When setting up your project properties, IDEA gives you the option of isolating your test classes into their own output path. Keeping them separate ensures that your test classes don't end up as part of your final release when you JAR up your output class folder. When you run your application from within IDEA, your test output path isn't included (unless you're running unit tests, of course). This ensures that no dependencies between your production code and test classes sneak in. You'll learn more about creating test classes in chapter 7.

Handling resource files

Resources are files used by your application that aren't Java classes or libraries. Common examples of resources include property files, icons, bitmaps, DTDs, and XML files. These files are typically loaded from your application's Classpath through the `ResourceBundle.getBundle()` method (for property files and resource bundles) or the `loadResourceAsStream()` method of `ClassLoader` for icons and other files. These and other resource fetching schemes rely on the resource files being in your program's Classpath, even though they obviously aren't Java classes. As part of the build process, IDEA copies all your resource files from your source directories into the output directory, preserving whatever directory structure they exist under (relative to the source path). IDEA relies on the name of the file to determine which files are resource files. By default, it recognizes the following file extensions:

- `.properties`
- `.xml`
- `.html`
- `.dtd`
- `.tld`
- `.gif`
- `.png`
- `.jpeg`
- `.jpg`

You can customize this behavior through the **Compiler** control panel (discussed in the next section), located in the **IDE** Settings. The **Resource patterns** field specifies a regular expression used to identify which files are resources. You can easily add your own extensions to the list or modify the default selections.

5.1.2 *Setting up a compiler*

A number of compilation options are available through the **Compiler** control panel of the **IDE Settings**. Select the **Compiler** option to bring up the configuration panel, shown in figure 5.1. The compiler properties are saved with your project, allowing you to use different compilation setups for different applications.

 The **Compiler** configuration panel in version 5.0 may look slightly different and include some additional options. Figure 5.1 shows the **Compiler** configuration panel from version 4.5.

> **TIP** If you're using Java 1.4 or later and want to enable the use of the `assert` keyword, you must do so in the project's **Paths** settings panel. This is disabled by default to maximize compatibility with older source code.

Excluding paths from compilation

If your project path includes files that you wish to specifically exclude from the compilation process, add them to the list of excluded entries in the central part of the **Compiler** dialog. You can add individual files as well as directories. Be sure to

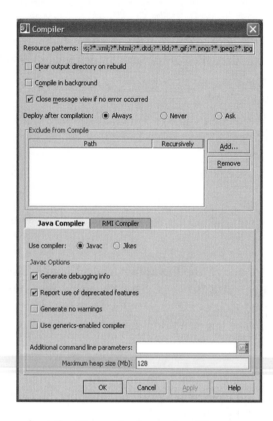

Figure 5.1
Project-specific compiler settings are controlled through this window.

select the **Recursively** option if you want all subdirectories under a folder to be excluded as well. Be advised, however, that if some of the sources you've excluded are also dependencies of source code being compiled, they will be pulled in and built by the compiler as needed—regardless of their exclusion status. If files fail to compile for but aren't critical to the project, you may add them to the exclusion list until they're fixed, allowing the build to complete the compilation of the rest of the project. The same is true if your project includes source files that you don't want compiled into your output folder.

Selecting a Java compiler

The area below the excluded paths list in the **Compiler** dialog lets you configure the settings for the compilers supported by IDEA. Currently, IDEA supports the Javac compiler (the compiler included with the JDK as configured for your project) as well as Jikes, the popular open source Java compiler. You must select a compiler for use in your project. Regardless of your choice of compiler, the class files will be nearly identical and compatible with the Java VM.

Using the Jikes compiler

The Jikes compiler isn't included with IDEA. To download a copy (it's free), visit http://jikes.sourceforge.net. Jikes is available for all the platforms supported by IDEA, and more. Jikes offers several advantages over Javac. First and foremost, it's an extremely fast implementation of the Java compiler. This is mainly due to the fact that it's written in C and is thus a native application for the platform it's running on. When we say *fast*, we mean it can run an order of magnitude faster than Javac: Running Jikes for the first time and registering its speed is a little disorientating.

Jikes' compilation rules are strictly by the book—they follow the Java language specification to the letter. If you encounter an error, it will likely quote the pertinent section and paragraph number from the language spec. Jikes also lets you do dependency checking and perform incremental compilations (a feature that is unnecessary when running from IDEA, because IDEA performs its own dependency checks). To enable Jikes, select the **Jikes** radio button in the **Compiler** dialog (see figure 5.2), and enter the path to the Jikes executable on your system.

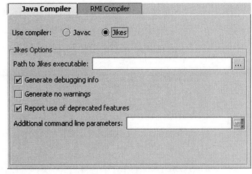

Figure 5.2 The options in the Compiler configuration window change to reflect your compiler of choice. This figure shows the Jikes options.

Setting compilation options

IDEA lets you tweak the compilation as you desire. The following compilation options are common to both Javac and Jikes:

- **Generate debugging info,** if enabled, makes the compiler include the information necessary to run this class in the debugger. See chapter 6 for more information about the debugger and generating debugging info.

- **Report use of deprecated features** enables warnings about deprecated methods, classes, or fields encountered by the compiler. Your build will succeed, but a warning message will be displayed in the compiler's output window.

- **Generate no warnings** disables the compiler's built-in warnings about suspicious language usage.

- **Additional command line parameters** lets you enter arguments to be passed to the compiler via the command line (refer to your compiler's documentation for valid options).

The Javac compiler has these additional options:

- **Use generics-enabled compiler** enables the use of *generics*, if supported by your compiler. J2SE 5.0 supports the use of generics (also known as *parameterized types*).
- **Maximum heap size** controls the size of the heap available to the Java process that launches the compiler. If you're compiling a particularly large or complex project, you may get out-of-memory errors and be required to increase the amount of memory allocated to the compiler.

Compiling your application in the background so you can keep working

Both the Javac and Jikes compilers offer you the option of building in the background. This goes for building the entire project as well as a single file. Unless this option is enabled, the compiler displays a modal dialog when active, tracking the progress of the compilation as shown in figure 5.3. This dialog gives you a constantly updating status report, but you can't do anything else while compiling. Click the **Background** button to push the build into the background and regain control. This has the same effect as enabling the **Compile in background** option from the **Compiler** settings panel. (Of course, compilation is a fairly intensive operation, so on many machines you won't be able to do anything else anyway.)

Deleting all the files from the output directory

If you enable the **Clear output directory on rebuild** option in the **Compiler** dialog, IDEA automatically deletes all the files in your output folder when you rebuild. Using this option isn't necessary to ensure a clean rebuild—IDEA's dependency tracking should handle that—but it ensures that unused or renamed classes that may cause problems aren't left behind.

Figure 5.3
The Compile Progress dialog keeps you apprised of status of the active compilation process.

5.1.3 Building an application under IDEA

IDEA makes building your application easy and straightforward, once you've configured your project and modules successfully. You have the option of building individual modules, the entire project, or an individual file. IDEA uses the term *make* to describe the process of compiling your class files to the appropriate output directories, in homage to the classic build tool, make.

Building an individual module

To build a single module of your project, right-click the module in the Project window and select **Make Module**; or, select the **Build | Make Module** command if you're currently editing a file that belongs to the module you want to build. If the module has dependencies on other modules, these too will be built if necessary.

Building the entire project at once

You can build all the modules in your project at once by selecting the **Build | Make Project** command (**Ctrl+F9**). IDEA automatically compiles all the modified source files and their dependencies throughout the project. Your source files are compiled to your output folder and your test sources to the test folder. Any resource files are copied to your output folder as well.

Compiling individual files or packages

You can compile any individual file or package by right-clicking its entry in the **Project** window or in the editor for the current file and selecting the **Compile** option. Alternatively, you can select **Build | Compile** (**Ctrl+Shift+F9**). The selected file (and any dependencies) are compiled to the appropriate output directory. This is a good option when you want to run or test an individual file without building the entire project (or when you can't build the project because it's completely broken at the moment).

Rebuilding the entire project from scratch

A *rebuild* of a project is distinguished from a normal build in that IDEA recompiles all your source files, regardless of whether they appear to need rebuilding. To rebuild your project, select the **Build | Rebuild Project** menu option. This action is sometimes known as a *clean compile*, because it ensures that all your class files are up to date. Of course, it takes longer than the incremental build, so you don't want to do it every time. You should rebuild your project any time you introduce major changes to your project structure. IDEA's good about recognizing dependencies, but in unusual circumstances it can miss something. This command lets you avoid the issue.

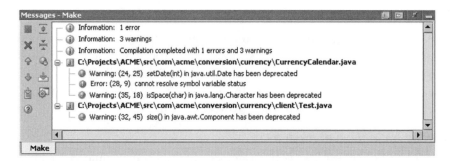

Figure 5.4 Status and results of your build are delineated in the Messages tool window. This figure shows the Javac summary of a failed build that produced one error and three warnings during compilation.

> **TIP** You should always perform a clean build if you have changed your JDK, your project's Classpath, or libraries.

5.1.4 Reviewing the results of the build

When you begin a new build, whether compiling a single file or building your entire project, IDEA opens a **Messages** window to display the results of the build, as shown in figure 5.4 for Javac or figure 5.5 for Jikes. All the information gathered during the build process, including errors, warnings, and other messages, is neatly organized into a message tree in this window. Successive compiling actions on your project or source files show the **Messages** window only if there are errors or warnings from the compiler. Successful compiling actions in the future will only show a success message in IDEA's status bar. Finding out quickly that your files compile properly means you can continue the important task of writing source code with little interruption.

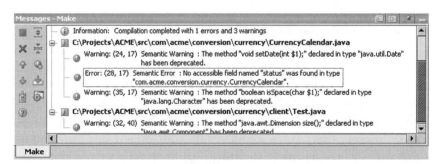

Figure 5.5 The Jikes compiler produces different status, warning, and error messages than the JDK's Javac compiler, but IDEA is able to show them in much the same fashion.

At the top of the message tree in the **Messages** window, IDEA displays summary information about the status of the build, including the number of errors and warnings encountered. Following that are all the compilation errors, grouped by the source file responsible for generating them. The toolbar buttons on the left side of the window are helpful for sifting through the various messages.

Interpreting compilation messages

The **Messages** window displays two types of messages: errors and warnings. The difference between the two is that an error prevents the file from being compiled, but a warning doesn't (although it may indicate a real problem in your code). Each type of problem has its own icon, along with an error message generated by the compiler. The two numbers that precede each message are the row and column number where the problem was encountered.

Resolving compilation errors

IDEA makes it easy to track down and resolve any compilation problems you encounter. Double-click any error message in the **Messages** window to jump straight to the source of the problem. If you enable the **Autoscroll to Source** option, a single click will suffice. Alternatively, use the **Messages** window buttons to move through the error messages. The shortcuts **Ctrl+Alt+Up** and **Ctrl+Alt+Down** are even better—keep pressing them until you've visited (and, we hope, corrected) all the errors, and then try again.

Saving a record of compilation problems

The **Export to Text File** button in the **Messages** window toolbar (**Alt+O**) lets you create a plaintext version of the compilation report and save it to a file, as shown in figure 5.6. You can print this file and bring it to the next dev meeting or leave it on the desk of that guy who always breaks the build.

> **TIP** You can use the **Export to Text File** feature as an easy way to capture the compiler output through the clipboard, so you can paste it into an e-mail or other application. Select the errors you're interested in, and then click the **Copy** button to add them to the clipboard.

5.2 Extending IDEA's build system with Ant

In recent years, the open source tool Ant has become the de facto standard for building Java projects. Like its venerable ancestor make, Ant is a tool for building and packaging your development project. Built on Java and XML, Ant is easy to

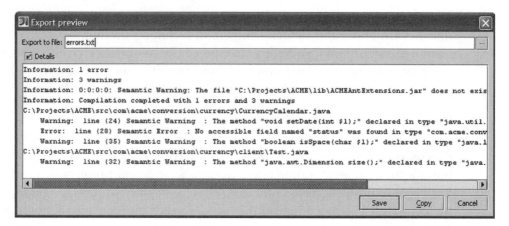

Figure 5.6   **In the event that you need the contents of the Messages window brought outside the IDE—to print, to email, to log for future reference, to post details in a bug-tracking suite, and so on— the Export to Text File feature will assist.**

use, flexible, and platform independent. As such, IDEA relies on Ant to extend the application building process beyond basic compilation. IDEA does much more than just allow you to run Ant scripts: It provides close integration with Ant, blending it seamlessly into the development process.

5.2.1   *Introducing Ant*

Although it isn't particularly difficult to learn, the language and syntax of Ant are beyond the scope of this book. For those not familiar with this technology, we'll present a brief introduction here so you can understand its relationship with IDEA; perhaps we'll also persuade you to investigate its details further. Manning has published a book on the subject, *Java Development with Ant*, which provides all the details on this popular development tool. You can also find additional information on Ant at the official Ant web site, http://ant.apache.org.

The power of Ant

Ant is a Java command-line tool that uses an XML file to script the process of compiling and packaging your code into a finished application, library, or other end product. Ant is an ongoing project of the Apache Software Foundation. As such, it has become the tool of choice for many open source projects including Tomcat, the reference implementation of Sun's Java Servlet API.

If you're familiar with `make`, a tool originally developed for the UNIX environment, you already have a good background about what Ant is trying to accomplish.

Ant attempts to solve the same problems as make, while avoiding its two biggest shortcomings: a confusingly ancient syntax and platform dependencies.

Like make, Ant relies on a *build file* to direct the actions you wish to perform; but instead of a shell script, Ant uses a platform independent XML file. Unlike make, the steps defined in Ant's build file enumerate the logical activities, not explicate system commands, which must be carried out to build the application. The platform-independent Ant software takes care of performing the actions, which it calls *tasks*, regardless of the platform it's running on.

Using Ant with IDEA

As you've learned in this chapter, IDEA provides an efficient and easy way to use system for compiling your projects and modules. IDEA tracks dependencies automatically and provides excellent tools for tracking down and resolving compile-time problems. IDEA is more than capable of compiling your project.

However, successfully compiling your project is only the first hurdle. At a minimum, most production applications must be packaged with documentation, source code, and other components into something distributable to the end user. Some applications require other more involved steps such as initializing a database, running a local script file, or archiving the previous release. This is where Ant comes in.

Ant comes bundled with dozens of different tasks you can use to complete or extend the build process, including the ability to interact with your source code control system, FTP server, and much more. Best of all, Ant is *extensible*; you can download or create additional tasks if necessary through the Ant API. Here are just a few of the scenarios that Ant can handle:

- Copy, delete, and move files
- Change file permissions on your build output
- Launch coverage tools like JProbe and JDepend
- Run the Javac, Jikes, and Rmic compilers
- Generate JavaDoc and XML/XSLT-derived documentation
- Push files to remote FTP or web servers
- Send email build notifications and log build errors
- Perform linefeed conversions and text search/replace operations
- Commit files to revision control systems
- Execute SQL operations to populate databases
- Control preprocessors like JavaCC, ANTLR, and iContract

Working with build files and targets

As we've mentioned, Ant takes its cues from an XML build file, typically named build.xml. An Ant build file is a collection of *build targets*. Each target defines a series of sequential tasks, which are executed to perform some specific task. For example, a target might create a JAR file from a collection of class files or generate documentation via an XSLT transform.

A target can also specify dependencies on other targets in the file. If a target has dependencies, the dependent targets are executed first. If a target's job is building a JAR file, for example, a likely dependency is the target in charge of compiling the project's source. If any dependent targets fail, execution of the build stops immediately, and errors are reported back to the user. Listing 5.1 shows an example of a very simple build file that compiles Java source code and archives it into a JAR file.

> **Listing 5.1   A simple Ant build file that can compile classes into a JAR file**

```xml
<project name="Example" default="dist" basedir=".">
  <property name="src" value="src"/>
  <property name="build" value="build" />
  <property name="dist" value="dist"/>

  <target name="compile" >
    <mkdir dir="${build}"/>
    <javac srcdir="${src}" destdir="${build}"/>
  </target>

  <target name="dist" depends="compile">
    <mkdir dir="${dist}"/>
    <jar jarfile="${dist}/example.jar" basedir="${build}"/>
  </target>
</project>
```

Each task in the Ant toolkit performs a different operation and requires different arguments. As you saw in an earlier example, the task for compiling looks different than the task that makes directories. Ant is good at operating on large groups of files, such as source code and output folders. It has a sophisticated pattern-matching scheme that lets you group different types of files together by status, type, or location.

Each target in an Ant build file is given a unique name. This name is used not only to relate dependencies between targets but also to direct execution. When you invoke Ant, you specify the target you wish to run. This lets you create a series of targets designed for different purposes. For example, one target may build your JAR files, and another uses XSLT to create documentation. Each Ant build file defines a default target, as well, which is used if a target isn't specified when Ant is invoked.

Using system properties for more flexible build scripts

The behavior of Ant tasks can also be parameterized through the use of system properties. The build file syntax provides a mechanism for using property values at runtime and also reacting to their presence (or absence). This makes it possible to build sophisticated build processes. Properties can be passed in explicitly, gleaned from the environment, or set in the Ant build file in response to certain conditions such as the absence or presence of a particular library.

5.2.2 *Improving your build process with Ant*

As we mentioned earlier, IDEA provides integration with the Ant framework for extending its build and packaging capabilities beyond compilation. Ant is included with IDEA, so no special setup is required to use it. Refer to the IDEA web site for the latest word on bundled versions, because IDEA releases updated versions from time to time.

By using Ant rather than its own proprietary build system, IDEA ensures that your project's build steps remain flexible and platform independent. Ant provides a smorgasbord of functions, and many developers are already familiar with Ant, making the development of the build files easier. When you're designing an IDEA build project, you can implement a number of possible Ant integration strategies.

Using IDEA for compiling and Ant for packaging

You can stick with IDEA's standard project and module builders for compiling your classes, and create Ant targets for your packaging and deployment tasks, which IDEA alone has no way of doing. With this approach, you achieve the tightest possible integration with the IDE, making editing and compiling your classes straightforward and efficient. You can choose to compile source files individually when necessary, and you get fast build times because IDEA is constantly tracking your file's dependencies and modification times. Ant then sticks to its core strengths, providing excellent packaging capabilities. In this strategy, Ant is used for all the steps IDEA can't handle on its own, either before or after compilation occurs.

One potential downside of this approach is that it requires a running instance of IDEA in order to compile and build the project. If some developers on the project aren't running IDEA, or if you wish to create automated nightly builds, then this may not be the best strategy.

Using Ant for both compiling and packaging

Alternatively, you can rely exclusively on Ant for all your build requirements, including compilation duties. With this approach, you abandon the built-in compiler and use Ant as your exclusive build mechanism. This has the benefit of completely decoupling your build process from the IDE and ensuring that you can continue to produce automated builds and support various development environments.

The primary downside to this approach is a decrease in speed, especially with large projects. Not only must Ant scan your entire project before compiling to determine which files have changed, but after the build, IDEA must resynchronize its file cache to learn what files Ant has introduced or updated. In addition, overhead is associated with starting and executing the Ant process. And, there is no easy way to force Ant to compile an individual file if necessary. The effects of this behavior on the speed of your build vary from system to system and project to project.

Supporting compilation in either Ant or IDEA as necessary

A combination of the two ant-integration approaches, this option means a little more work but provides the most flexibility. The basic idea is to use both Ant's and IDEA's compilation features along with Ant's packaging and deployment capabilities, to achieve the best of both worlds. When it's necessary or convenient to build outside of IDEA with Ant (such as when you're executing a nightly build), do so. When you're running IDEA, however, feel free to enjoy the speed and convenience of its internal project builder. In either case, Ant remains in charge of other build tasks.

The complication is making sure that IDEA and Ant don't step on each other's toes. One way to do this is to have Ant and IDEA use different output paths for compiling their files, ensuring that the two build mechanisms remain separate. If necessary for your packaging process, create additional Ant targets designed to be called from IDEA in order to prepare files for packaging. You can simplify the matter if you rely on Ant to do everything for your final package builds, compilation and all, using IDEA's compiler only during daily development.

5.2.3 Working with Ant build files

To do anything with Ant through IDEA, you must have an Ant build file that defines the steps required to build your project. IDEA can be used to create new Ant build files as well as work with ones from existing projects.

Editing build files with IDEA

As you can see in figure 5.7, IDEA provides more than just syntax highlighting for Ant build scripts. It can also complete tag and attribute names, generate closing braces, and detect error conditions such as undefined properties or missing attributes. Errors show up as error marks in the marker bar, just as Java errors do. Here are some of the other helpful features provided by the editor when you're working on Ant files:

- **Go to | Declaration (Ctrl+B)** on a target reference jumps to the target's definition.
- You can navigate the target hierarchy through the structure view.
- **Refactor | Rename** can be used to change the names of targets and automatically correct all references (more about refactoring in general in chapter 9).
- Code folding can be used to hide target bodies and aid navigation.
- **Tools | Reformat** reformats and indents your file appropriately.
- **Tools | Validate** double-checks your syntax.
- **View | Parameter Info (Ctrl+P)** shows you acceptable tag attributes.
- **View | Context Info (Alt+Q)** displays the current block's definition if it's off screen and not visible.

Creating a new build file

Creating an Ant build file is no different than creating any other type of file in IDEA. You must remember that Ant build files are written in XML, and you'll need to specify the appropriate extension. The file can be located in any directory,

```
<target name="javadoc-check">
    <uptodate property="javadoc-uptodate"  targetfile="${basedir}/build/docs/api/index.html">
        <srcfiles dir="${basedir}/src"/>
    </uptodate>
</target>

<target name="test" depends="compile">
    <mkdir dir="${basedir}/build/test"/>
    <m           description      dir}/build/testresults"/>
                 dir
    <j                            y="true" haltonerror="false" haltonfailure="false"
                 id               /build/test">
                 taskname         ="xml" usefile="true"/>
                                  d="project.classpath"/>
                                  . acme.test.CurrencyConversionTestSuite"/>
    </junit>

    <junitreport>
        <fileset dir=".">
            <include name="TEST-*.xml"/>
        </fileset>
        <report todir="${basedir}/build/testresults"/>
    </junitreport>
</target>
```

Figure 5.7   IDEA provides automatic completion for tasks within Ant build files.

but it's best to keep it close to the project. To create a new build file, follow these steps:

1. In the **Project** window, select the directory in which you wish to create the build file.

2. Right-click the directory, and select **New | File** (**Alt+Insert**).

3. Specify the name of the build file with an XML extension.

The editor's XML and Ant awareness make it a great platform for developing build files, but the design of the targets and steps is up to you. For IDEA to treat XML files as Ant build scripts (and provide the Ant-specific extensions that come with the designation), the XML build file must be added to the **Ant Build** tool window, described in the next section. If you don't include the file in the **Ant Build** tool window, IDEA treats it as a regular XML file with only basic support.

> **WARNING** The Ant build file editor flags any references to property values not explicitly defined in the file, even though they may be valid at runtime. You can appease the editor by setting up default values for every external property referenced in the build file. Any values present in the system will override these default values anyway.

Generating the Ant builds

Since version 4.5, IDEA provides the ability to automatically generate Ant build files, based on your project structure. Using **Build | Generate Ant Build** is a good start, especially if you're new to using Ant. This command can generate a single Ant file that builds your entire project or a series of Ant files that build each individual module. Once generated, the files can be edited, customized, and maintained as per normal.

The **Generate Ant Build** dialog also gives you the option to either back up or overwrite previously generated files and to enable the compilation of IDEA's UI forms. IDEA custom UI form designer and the implications of using it on your build scripts are dealt with in chapter 10.

The Ant Build window

The **Ant Build** window is where you interact with your project's build files. The window is accessed by clicking the **Ant Build** icon on the right margin of IDEA or by selecting **Window | Ant Build**. Initially, this window appears empty, because you haven't added any build files to the project yet. Briefly, here's what each of the buttons in the Ant toolbar does:

- **Add** adds an Ant build file to the project.
- **Remove** removes the currently selected Ant build file from the project.
- **Run** executes the selected build file or Ant target.
- **Filter targets**, if enabled, enables the target filter to hide unwanted targets.
- **Expand all** expands the tree to show all the targets under each build file.
- **Collapse all** collapses the tree to show only the build files themselves.
- **Properties** opens the **Build File Properties** dialog, where you can modify the execution properties for the currently selected build file.
- **Help** opens help related to the **Ant Build** window.

Adding a build file to your project

To add a build file to a project, click the **Add** icon on the Ant toolbar and select your build file with the file requestor. You must select an existing build file; one won't be created for you automatically. After you add a build file, the window looks something like figure 5.8.

You can add more than one build file to an IDEA project, should you decide to break up your build into several components. Each file you add is listed in the **Ant Build** window under the project name specified in the build file. Don't confuse this with the name of your IDEA project; this name comes from the value of the name attribute of the Ant build file's `<project>` tag (the root tag for an Ant build). The actual name you select is arbitrary. Under each build file is a list of the build targets defined in it. Right-clicking a build file's name displays a context menu, which gives you several options:

Figure 5.8 The Ant Build tool window provides access to all your build file's targets. The tool window buttons let you add and remove build files from IDEA's list of known build files, execute a selected Ant target, filter available targets, expand and collapse the tree, edit properties, and view help.

- **Run Build** executes the default target (we'll discuss this shortly).
- **Jump to Source** (**F4**) loads the build file into the editor window.
- **Remove** disassociates the build file from the project but leaves the file untouched (it isn't deleted).
- **Properties** (**Alt+Enter**) opens the build properties dialog, analogous to clicking the Properties button on the Ant toolbar.

Viewing the Ant build targets

The default build target is shown in a bold font. It's specified in the Ant build file through the `default` attribute of the project task. This target is executed if you click the **Run** icon with no target selected or double-click the name of the build file. The targets listed in a normal font are the primary targets. Any target in your build file that has a `description` attribute specified is considered a primary target. The targets in the lighter color text are the secondary targets. Typical Ant scripts contain many targets that aren't meant to be called directly and are used like subroutines by the primary build targets. It's a good practice to specify a description for all targets that can be called directly.

> **TIP**   If your build targets have a value specified for the `<description>` attribute, passing your mouse pointer over any such targets in the **Ant Build** tool window displays the value of the description in the handy form of a tool tip.

5.2.4 Executing Ant targets

From within IDEA, you can easily execute build targets, review the results of compilation, and navigate directly to any errors encountered. You can even automatically trigger the execution of Ant build targets upon IDEA events such as compiling, launching, or debugging an application from within IDEA.

Running a build target

The most straightforward way to execute an Ant target is to double-click on it in the **Ant Build** window or select it with the mouse and click the **Run** icon. Doing so executes the target and displays the results in the **Messages** window, as we'll discuss later. Right-clicking an Ant target and selecting the **Run Target** option has the same effect.

An alternative way to execute Ant build targets is to select them from the main **Build** menu. Each Ant build file you've added to your project is added as a submenu to the bottom of the **Build** menu's choices, with all the primary targets listed as child selections. Selecting one of these target menu items is the same as double-clicking the target from the **Ant Build** window.

Executing a target from a keyboard shortcut

It can also be handy to create a keyboard shortcut for an Ant target. Doing so makes it easy to execute common build targets with a single key. The primary Ant targets for each Ant file in your project are listed as actions in the **Keymap** control panel, accessible from IDE **Settings** (see chapter 12). Each Ant target in the project is listed under the **Keymap** editor's **Ant Targets** hierarchy. To assign a keyboard shortcut to an Ant target, follow these steps:

1 Right-click the target in the Ant Build window to access its context menu.

2 Select the option **Assign Shortcut** to bring up the **Keymap** dialog.

3 Click **Add Keyboard Shortcut**

4 Press the key combination you wish to assign to the build target.

5 If desired, enable a second keystroke and enter it as well.

6 If there are no conflicts, click **OK** to commit the assignment.

Automating the build process with Ant target triggers

As alluded to earlier in the chapter, it's possible to integrate Ant with other aspects of IDEA such as its built-in compiler, debugger, and execution features. Each target can be individually configured to automatically run in response to several different types of triggers, all linked back to the IDE.

Using compilation triggers to add Ant to the build

If you're relying on Ant targets to complete critical steps of your build, you'll want to configure a compilation trigger. You can configure Ant targets to execute before or after IDEA's internal compiler has completed executing. You can also execute the target both before and after, if the need arises. If a compilation fails, Ant targets linked to the end of the compilation aren't executed. Note that this compilation trigger only applies to the built-in project builder, not to any compilation your Ant build performs. Any target dependency based on Ant directed compilations should be specified as part of your Ant file.

To establish a compilation trigger, right-click the target you wish to run and select either **Execute on | Before Compilation** or **Execute on | After Compilation** from the menu. Your choice will be reflected with a checkmark beside the enabled option. Selecting an option again removes the trigger. When active, the trigger is listed in the **Ant Build** window in parentheses next to the target name, as a reminder.

Using execution triggers to execute Ant targets before running or testing

When you're using IDEA's execution feature to launch, debug, or test applications (discussed later in this chapter and in the next chapter), you may need to execute an Ant target before or after doing so to prepare your project if you're relying on Ant's functionality. This can be accomplished with the use of an *execution trigger*. You assign an execution trigger by right-clicking the target in the **Ant Build** window and selecting **Execute On | Before Run/Debug** from the menu, which brings up the dialog shown in figure 5.9.

From the dialog, select the types of executions you want to trigger the selected Ant target. The execution types supported by IDEA are presented as a tree structure. A checkmark by the execution type (Application, Applet, JUnit, and so forth) indicates that all execution configurations of that

Figure 5.9   The Execute On feature for Ant build files lets you add complex scripting elements to almost any stage of the code-build-test process in IDEA.

type will by default trigger your Ant target. For example, if you select JUnit, the Ant target you select will execute before (or after) any JUnit configuration is run. If you've defined configurations for a particular type, they're listed under it, allowing you to narrow the scope to particular configurations only (more about **Run/Debug** configurations later in this chapter).

5.2.5   Following Ant's progress in the Messages window

When you execute an Ant target, it displays its output progress to a tab in the **Messages** window. Each build file gets its own tab, but all executions against that build file reuse the tab, destroying any messages already there. You can maintain the messages tab for a file by right-clicking the tab name and selecting the **Pin Tab** command. Briefly, the toolbar buttons perform the following tasks:

- **Rerun (Ctrl+F5)** executes the build target again. This is a quick way to build again after fixing any errors you encountered.

- **Pause Output,** when enabled, suspends output from the Ant build process, even though the Ant process itself continues to execute. Click this option again to resume the display of output.

- **Stop** aborts a currently running build.

- **Previous Error/Warning (Ctrl+Alt+Up)** navigates to the source of the previous error shown in the **Messages** window.

- **Next Error/Warning (Ctrl+Alt+Down)** navigates to the source of the next error shown in the **Messages** window.

- **Help** accesses Ant-related help.

- **Toggle tree/text mode** changes the **Messages** view between a structured tree view and plaintext.

- **Show All Messages** displays all available messages. This can create a very large list of messages, because it shows every step the Ant process has taken. Enabling this option can be useful when you're debugging Ant scripts.

- **Expand all (Ctrl+NumPad +)** expands the message hierarchy to view all entries.

- **Collapse all (Ctrl+NumPad -)** collapses the message hierarchy to only show the root targets.

- **Auto scroll to source**, if enabled, loads the source file into the editor at the source of an error, warning, or message you select in the **Messages** window. This goes for both compilation messages, which loads source files, and Ant messages, which loads the build file.

Selecting the view mode

Most Ant builds generate a number of results and messages. Even if you don't encounter any problems, you can still use the Ant **Messages** window to follow the progress of the build. You have your choice of two different views: a tree view and a text view. Both show the same data, but in different ways.

In tree mode, the results of the Ant build are displayed as a hierarchy of messages rooted at the Ant targets that generated them. Each step in the Ant build process is shown, regardless of whether it produces output or error messages. By default, targets are expanded only if they have produced meaningful output (such as a compilation error). You have the option of collapsing or expanding individual nodes or the whole tree en mass via the toolbar. A typical example of an Ant build in tree mode is shown in figure 5.10.

In the example shown in figure 5.10, a problem was encountered with the Ant target `compile`. As you can see, there was an invalid variable name. The source file reference and compiler error message are shown, along with the location within the Ant script where the error originated, just as with the built-in compiler. Double-clicking either of these messages will take you to the offending

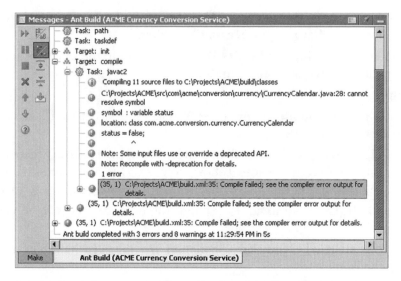

Figure 5.10 A Messages window reports on the progress of the build and lets you navigate directly to any errors or warnings reported by the compiler. This is the tree view of the Ant results.

spot. If you've enabled the **Autoscroll to Source** option on the toolbar, only a single click is required.

In text mode, output is shown more or less as Ant's raw output, with little formatting. However, you can still link straight to the source of any compilation problems encountered, as shown in figure 5.11, which is the text-mode version of the build operation you saw earlier.

Messages in verbose mode

The **Show All Messages** button controls the amount of data Ant displays in the **Messages** window. If you have ever played Zork or the other classic text games from Infocom, you're probably familiar with the term *maximum verbosity*. This button enables Ant's version of maximum verbosity, which lists the status and result of just about every step of the build process. It's great for debugging Ant scripts, but you'll generally want to leave this off, because it slows things down and creates clutter.

By default, IDEA runs all Ant builds with Ant's default level of verbosity. To modify this level for a build file, specify additional Ant command-line parameters in the **Build File Properties** dialog discussed later in this chapter (for the particular values, refer to the Ant documentation).

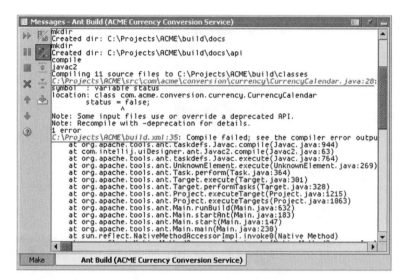

Figure 5.11 This is the text view of an Ant Messages window, which more closely resembles traditional Ant output.

Navigating through errors and warnings

The **Previous** and **Next Error/Warning** buttons in the **Messages** window work just like those in the native IDEA compiler window. They load the appropriate source file and jump directly to the origin of each error in turn. This is equivalent to clicking the hot links in the **Messages** window, but much handier. Even handier are the keyboard shortcuts **Ctrl+Alt+Up** and **Ctrl+Alt+Down**, which are active from the main editor window. They let you step through (and, we hope, fix) any compilation errors without having to jump back to the **Messages** window between edits. When you've completed your edits, click the **Rerun** icon to try again.

5.2.6 Controlling Ant's behavior

To control how IDEA runs your Ant script, access the **Build File Properties** dialog (figure 5.12) by clicking the Ant toolbar's **Properties** button or right-clicking the name of the build file and selecting **Properties** from the context menu.

At the top of the dialog, the full path to your build file is displayed, along with several global options:

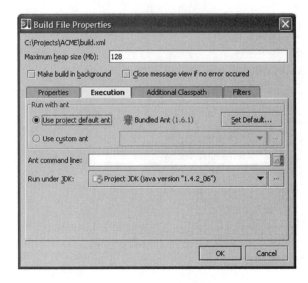

Figure 5.12
The Build File Properties dialog lets you control Ant's execution options and environment.

- **Maximum Heap Size** controls the amount of memory allocated to the Ant build process. If your Ant process fails after running out of memory, you should increase this value. The default value of 128MB is usually sufficient, but it may be too low if you're using Ant to generate JavaDoc or compile extremely large projects. Ant's memory allocation is independent of the amount of memory used by IDEA and is released once the Ant process has completed.

- **Make build in background** runs Ant in the background, enabling you to work on other things during the build. If this option is unselected (the default), Ant displays a modal progress dialog during the build. Be warned that compiling is often processor intensive, so IDEA may appear unresponsive during compiles if you enable this option. You'll need to experiment with this option in your environment to see if it's useful for you. You can also build in the background by clicking the **Background** button of the modal dialog, although this only applies to the build currently in progress.

- **Close message view if no error occurred** tells IDEA that you don't want to see Ant's **Messages** window if the build completes without any errors. If you get tired of closing that window after each successful build, enable this option. If it's selected however, you won't be given the opportunity to review Ant's output for successful builds.

TIP   To use Jikes as your Java compiler under Ant, set either the `compiler` attribute of `javac` tasks in your build file or the global option `build.` `compiler` to `jikes`. Otherwise the compiler bundled with your JVM will be used. In either case, the Jikes executable should be in Ant's execution path.

Specifying runtime properties

The **Properties** tab of the **Build File Properties** dialog (figure 5.13) lets you pass information to your Ant builds. Any values specified here are exposed via Java system properties. This is the equivalent of using the –D option when launching Ant from the command line. These properties are exposed to both the Ant process itself and any code launched from within the build file. System properties are often used to provide configurable behavior to build files or applications, such as a destination directory, database password, and so forth.

Using macro values as system properties

In addition to hard-coded values, IDEA lets you specify dynamic values for system properties via its extensive macro capabilities. *Macros* are logical values evaluated by IDEA at runtime. They let you avoid hard-coding project specific paths and other information into your Ant scripts. For example, if one of your Ant targets needs to copy files to a certain folder of your development tree, you can use a macro to pass in the path information dynamically, allowing the script to run in any environment, not just yours.

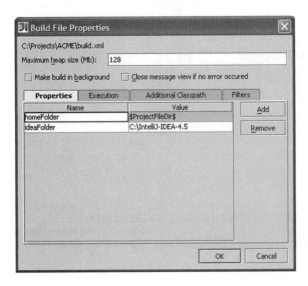

Figure 5.13
You can specify system properties for Ant's environment through the Properties tab.

Macros are delimited on either side by dollar signs. For example, in figure 5.13, the `homeFolder` property is being set to the same directory where the IDEA project file is stored, via the macro `$ProjectFileDir$`. A full list of macros is available through the **Build File Properties** dialog.

To use a macro as a property value, follow these steps:

1 On the **Properties** tab, click the **Add** button to create a new system property or select an existing one from the list.

2 Select the **Value** column.

3 If you know the name of the macro, you can type it here; or, click the plus icon to browse the available macros, as shown in figure 5.14. Use the preview window to see how the macro will be evaluated at runtime. Note that some macros are for use in other parts of IDEA and are unavailable for use as system properties. These off-limits properties show up empty in the preview window.

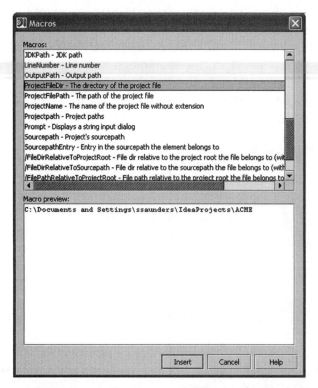

Figure 5.14
Macros make it easy to create portable Ant build files.

Setting execution options

The **Execution** tab of the **Build File Properties** dialog (figure 5.15) is used to control how IDEA launches the Ant build process when invoked. Ant is a Java program, and it's executed outside of the main IDE. Special integration hooks allow IDEA to transparently monitor and control the entire Ant process. This loose coupling lets IDEA easily support new versions of Ant as they become available.

Here's how to use these options.

- **Run with Ant** controls the Ant version that will be used to execute your build file. If you select **Use project default ant**, the default Ant version is used; if you select **Use custom ant**, you can use the drop-down control to select any version of Ant that has been configured/registered in IDEA. Ant configurations can be controlled by the nearby ellipsis button.

- **Ant command line** lets you include command-line parameters that affect the invocation of Ant. You can include any special Ant parameters here with the exception of -logger. Format of the parameters is identical to using them on the command line: Precede them with a hyphen (-), and separate parameters with a space.

- **Run under** JDK lets you choose the JDK you wish to use for running Ant targets for this build file. The selected JDK not only determines the VM Ant is run under but also determines which version of the Java API is used during compilation. You can use the ellipsis button next to the combo box to configure your system's JDK installations.

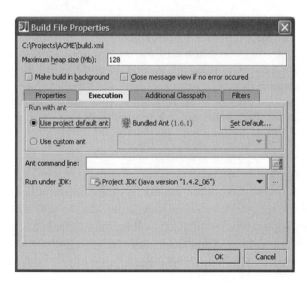

Figure 5.15
The Execution tab is used to control Ant's runtime behavior.

Setting Ant's Classpath

The **Additional Classpath** tab of the **Build File Properties** dialog lets you add libraries and Classpath entries to Ant's runtime environment. Ant loads its Classpath to your project separately, so you may need to modify these settings to get your Ant script to run properly under IDEA. The reason is that Ant build scripts should be made as if they were to be run from the command-line Ant tool outside of IDEA. This means the scripts themselves should be written in such a way that they configure themselves to load the libraries they require.

To add a JAR or directory to the additional Classpath, click the **Add** button and browse to the desired JAR or directory. Select the item, and click **OK**. As a convenience, you can hold down the **Ctrl** key and select multiple resources at a time. Sometimes you may have many JAR files in a single directory that you need to add to the Classpath. If this is the case, click the **Add All in Directory** button, and select the directory in the directory browser. Clicking **OK** with this option adds the directory into the Classpath list. It appears as a typical directory; but when Ant runs, it loads all the JAR files contained in that directory into the additional Classpath.

The other features in this dialog reorder and remove items in the additional Classpath. The order of the Classpath can be important; by selecting one or more items in the list and clicking the **Move Up** or **Move Down** button, you can change the order in which Ant loads the resources. Finally, removing an item from the Classpath is a simple matter of selecting the item and clicking **Remove**.

> **NOTE** Many of Ant's optional tasks require additional libraries that must be added to the Classpath in order to function. If your targets will be using XSLT, for example, you must add the `xalan` library or other XSL package to Ant's Classpath. Although you could add the library into the **Additional Classpath** dialog as just described, it's handier to set up Ant externally in case you ever need to run Ant scripts outside of IDEA. See Ant's documentation for details on task requirements.

Controlling the target list view

Most Ant scripts are composed of many targets, some of which are used internally by other targets and weren't designed to be called directly. By default, the Ant **Build** window displays all the targets defined in your build file. To limit the list of targets, click the **Filter targets** button on the Ant toolbar. The default filter shows only the primary targets. To modify the filter and select specific targets to appear, select the **Filters** tab of the **Build File Properties** dialog, as shown in figure 5.16.

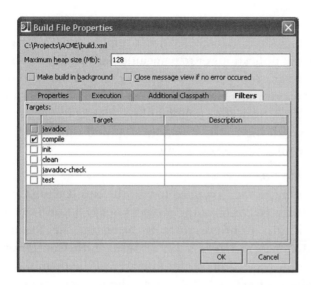

Figure 5.16
IDEA gives you the ability to specify
which Ant targets are important to you
and filter the rest so that they don't
clutter your tool window.

All the targets defined in the build file are listed in the **Filters** tab, along with their description if one is present in the build file. If the checkbox to the left of the name is selected, the corresponding target is listed in the **Ant Build** window when the filter is applied.

NOTE   IDEA lists your Ant targets in the order in which they're defined in your build file. To change the order of the list of targets in the **Ant Build** window, you must edit the build files and change the order of the targets in the files.

5.3   *Running your project*

IDEA makes it very convenient to run your application directly from within the IDE. Often it's easier than running it outside of the IDE, because IDEA automatically specifies the appropriate Classpath entries. You can run many different types of applications from within IDEA, including command-line applications, Swing applications, and even web applications.

Although we'll be talking about running applications in IDEA, technically IDEA only launches them: The applications run in their own VM. For each class that you wish to be able to run from within IDEA, you need to set up a separate configuration profile. This profile is called a *Run/Debug configuration*, and it's stored in your project's workspace file. The configuration profile specifies the class to run, additional VM arguments or options, as well as any other specific attributes required for running your application.

5.3.1 *Managing Run/Debug configuration profiles*

Any project in IDEA may include different executable applications. Your project may be composed of several applications or may include performance tests, code generators, database loaders, or other utility programs that you may run during development. IDEA lets you run any program with a valid Java main method defined, just as you would run from the command line. The configuration profiles give you a way to store all the runtime options required with your project, making it easier to run the program the next time.

Accessing the configuration panel

To define a new configuration profile, you need to visit the **Run/Debug Configurations** dialog. There are two ways to access the project's defined Run/Debug configurations: Select **Run | Edit Configurations** to bring up the **Run/Debug Configurations** panel, as shown in figure 5.17; or select **Edit Configurations** from the end of the drop-down selections in the Run area of the main toolbar.

The **Run/Debug Configurations** dialog shows all the configuration profiles defined in the current project. The tabs across the top of the panel are used to select the different types of configuration profiles supported by IDEA, although in this chapter we'll focus on the **Application** tab:

- **Application** runs command-line or Swing applications launched via a main() method. More information on running Swing applications can be found in chapter 10.
- **Applet** runs Java applets through either an applet viewer or a web page and your local browser.
- **JUnit** executes unit tests written against the JUnit testing framework. Running unit tests is covered in chapter 7.
- **Remote** specifies configurations for debugging Java applications running outside of IDEA, such as on an application server. Remote debugging is covered in chapter 6.
- **JSR45 Compatible Server is** used for running or debugging applications running inside a JSR45-compatible application server directly supported by IDEA's web server integration features, covered in chapter 11.
- **Tomcat Server** is used for running or debugging applications running inside a Tomcat application server directly supported by IDEA's web server integration features, covered in chapter 11.
- **Weblogic Instance** is used for running or debugging applications running inside a Weblogic application server directly supported by IDEA's web server integration features, covered in chapter 11.

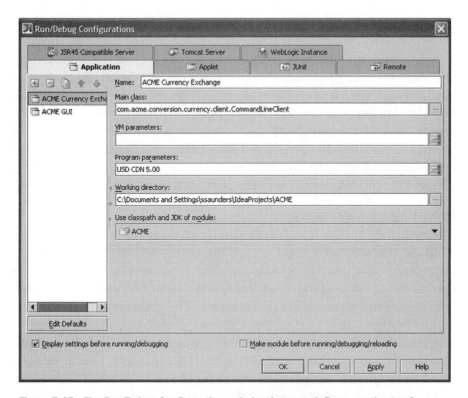

Figure 5.17   The Run/Debug Configurations window lets you define named sets of contextual information about how to run and debug your applications, making the actual act of running or debugging as simple as a single mouse click.

 In version 5.0, two additional tabs have been added: configurations for J2ME applications and for IntelliJ IDEA Plugin sandboxes.

Creating a new configuration profile

To create a new configuration profile, make sure the **Application** tab is selected in the **Run/Debug Configurations** window, and click the **Add** (plus sign) icon to create a new entry in the configuration list. If you've already created some configuration profiles, you can use the **Copy** icon to duplicate an existing profile to use as a starting point. The new profile is created without a useful name, so assign one by editing the **Name** field. This name is used to identify the profile in the **Run/Debug** drop-down list on the main toolbar and can be anything you'd like. Next, you need to specify the class containing the main method you'll be executing.

You can either enter the fully qualified name of the class into the **Main class** field yourself or click the browse icon next to the field to have IDEA help you. The browser brings up a list of all the classes in your project that have an appropriately defined main() method, as shown in figure 5.18. Select the class you wish to run, and click **OK** (or press **Enter**) to have IDEA fill in the field with the name of the selected class. You can also begin typing the name of the class, and IDEA will reduce the list by showing only the classes that have names starting with the letters typed. Note that all IDEA wants in this field is the class name—it doesn't need the main() method tacked onto the end. Alternatively, select the **Project** tab and navigate the project tree to find the appropriate class, as shown in figure 5.19.

Specifying VM parameters

The next field in the **Run/Debug Configurations** window, VM **parameters**, is optional. You only need to put something in this field if you require parameters to be passed in to the VM in order for your application to run correctly. Typical options define system properties, increase the heap size, and specify garbage-collection options for tuning VM performance. The contents of this field are passed to the VM when IDEA launches the application. In the example in figure 5.17, we aren't passing any VM properties in this configuration; however, we could easily pass one to increase the size of the heap. IDEA may also pass in other options based on your IDE settings. For example, if you've specified a particular file encoding, IDEA passes this to the VM through the appropriate system property.

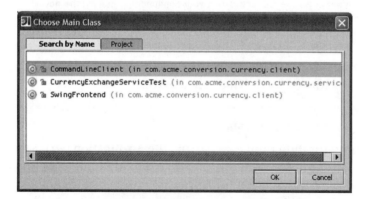

Figure 5.18 You can choose a class with a main() method by searching the entire project tree by name. The applicable classes are listed here alphabetically, with their package shown for reference. Expressions in the top text field filter the list to include only classes whose names match the expression.

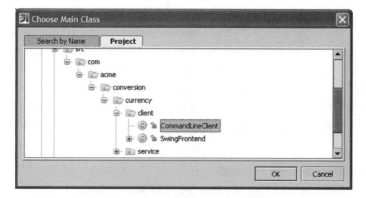

Figure 5.19 Alternatively, you can choose the class with a `main()` method by navigating your project tree. Folders represent packages, just like in the Project tool window.

Enter your options into the field if required, or leave it blank if you don't need any. If you need more room to type, click the icon next to the field to access a larger text entry dialog.

Specifying program arguments

You can configure the list of arguments passed to your program. Enter in the arguments into the **Program parameters** field in the **Run/Debug Configurations** window just as you would when running the application from the command line. These values are passed to the `main()` method through the arguments array required by the `main()` method signature.

If arguments contain spaces, surround them with quotes. If your program doesn't require any arguments, leave this field blank.

Setting the working directory

The *working directory* serves as the current directory for the application while it's running. Essentially, it specifies which directory you want to change to before running this application. If your application will be accessing local files, this directory determines the starting point for all relative file paths for both input and output. You don't need to worry about how your working directory relates to the location of your class files or your project; IDEA will figure out how to set up the Classpath appropriately. If your application isn't working with files, then it doesn't matter what you set your working directory to in the **Run/Debug Configurations** window. By default, IDEA sets it to the same directory as your project file.

Setting the Classpath and JDK

In order to select the JDK and the Classpath for running an application, IDEA provides the list of modules as configured for this project. Selecting the module from the drop-down list in the **Run/Debug Configurations** window provides the Classpath and JDK as configured for that module. Changing the list of selectable modules requires reconfiguring the modules for the current project. See chapter 4 for information regarding adding modules to and removing them from your project.

Modifying application default settings

If you have a complicated set of arguments and parameters, you can save time by changing IDEA's default application settings. Click the **Edit Defaults** button underneath the list of configurations on the left in the **Run/Debug Configurations** window to bring up the default settings dialog. You can specify a default class, program parameters, VM parameters, working directory, and which module's JDK and Classpath should be used for all newly created application profiles.

> **TIP**   If you're editing a class with a valid `main()` method, you can create a Run/Debug configuration for it by right-clicking and selecting the **Create <*classname*>.main()** option. Doing so brings up a configuration profile dialog prepopulated with information for running the current class. You can also create a Run/Debug configuration by right-clicking a class in the **Project** window.

Managing the list of configuration profiles

Using the icons above the list of configuration profiles in the **Run/Debug Configurations** window, you can remove items, copy them, and reorder the list. Click the remove icon to delete configuration profiles that you no longer need. Use the arrow icons to reorder the list. The order of the configuration profiles determines how they appear in the **Run/Debug** drop-down list on the main toolbar. As we mentioned earlier, the copy icon creates a copy of the currently selected profile, allowing you to use it as a template for a new configuration profile.

Run/Debug options

The **Run/Debug Configurations** screen includes a couple of checkbox options at the bottom. The first, **Display settings before running/debugging**, instructs IDEA to pop up the settings panel you've been working with each time you run an application in IDEA. This gives you a chance to tweak the settings, perhaps adding new arguments or changing the working directory, for example, before executing the profile. The second option, **Make project before running/debugging/reloading**, triggers an automatic build of the project before executing. Enabling this option makes sure any source files that have changed are recompiled appropriately. If there have been no changes, your program will run. If you've enabled any Ant targets to run as part of your build, they will be executed as well.

> **WARNING** Both the **Display settings before running/debugging** and **Make project before running/debugging/reloading** options are global settings for the project. There is no way to enable these options differently for each configuration.

Creating multiple configurations for the same class

You aren't limited to creating one configuration profile for each Java class that you want to execute. You're free to create as many different configuration profiles as you need, specifying different working directories, program parameters, or VM settings. Doing so lets you create several combinations of settings to run your application with different arguments. For example, if you use an executable to initialize your database that takes the database URL from a command-line argument, you can set up separate targets for initializing your development and testing databases. The only restriction is that the names for the configurations must be different, because the name is the only identifier for a given profile.

5.3.2 *Executing a Run configuration*

Once configured, you can run your application by first selecting the appropriate configuration profile. Because the configuration contains all the details of the running state—including the class to run, its arguments, its working directory, and the like—the configuration needs no additional data to execute. It has essentially become accessible via a single mouse-click or keystroke.

Selecting a configuration profile

On the IDEA toolbar, select the configuration profile you want to run from the drop-down list next to the **Run** icon, as shown in figure 5.20. Then, click the **Run** icon to start or select the **Run** option from the **Run** menu, or press **Shift+F10**. If you've enabled the option to show the settings panel before running, your program will run after you click **OK** to close the settings window. If you've enabled the option to build the program before running, it will begin the build and, if successful, launch the application. Otherwise, IDEA will directly launch your program. The output generated by the program appears in the **Run** tool window, which we'll discuss in the next section.

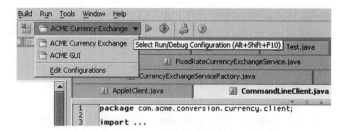

Figure 5.20 **The Run/Debug Configuration drop-down selector on the main toolbar lets you choose a configuration and then run or debug it. The selector also contains an entry that lets you edit those configurations.**

> **TIP** If you've created a Run/Debug configuration for the file you're currently editing, you can also right-click in the editor and select **Run** from the context menu to execute it.

Using temporary configuration profiles

Occasionally, you'll want to run or debug a class without having to bother with defining a new configuration profile for it in your project. You may do this for infrequently run applications or while testing new code that you don't intend to run again. You do so by right-clicking inside the editor or on a file in the **Project** window and selecting the **Run** (or **Debug**) option. This action adds a temporary configuration profile to the project, using the default application settings, and immediately executes it.

Temporary configuration profiles appear with a ghosted icon and lighter color font in the **Run/Debug** drop-down list on the main toolbar and in the **Run/Debug Configurations** dialog. They work the same as any other configuration profiles. If you need to change arguments or settings, you can do so through the **Run/Debug Configurations** dialog.

To convert a temporary configuration profile to a permanent one, you can use any of these three methods:

- Select the **Save <<*Class Name*>>** option at the bottom of the **Run/Debug** drop-down list on the tool bar.
- Click the **Save Configuration** button in the **Run/Debug Configurations** dialog.
- Select the **Save <<*Class Name*>>.main()** option in the context menu when the class is opened in the main editor window.

NOTE There can only be one temporary configuration for the current project. If you create a new temporary configuration without saving the existing one, the existing configuration will be overwritten. Make a habit of saving useful configurations, because they can be easily overwritten if left in a temporary state.

5.3.3 *Using the Run window console*

The **Run** tool window appears whenever you launch an application from within IDEA. It displays any output generated from the program as well as provides a mechanism for entering any input required. You can see an example of the **Run** window in action in figure 5.21.

Understanding output in the Run window

Any output generated from the running program appears in the **Run** window console. The color of the text indicates the source of the output:

- **Black** indicates output sent to the System.out stream.
- **Red** indicates output sent to the System.err stream.
- **Green** indicates input received from the console, presumably from you.

As you can see from the example, if you're so unfortunate to encounter a stack trace, IDEA links stack trace entries back to the original source file and line number. Click to load the source file into the editor, and position the cursor at the appropriate line number. If you need to copy the output of the application, right-click in the console and select **Copy Content** to place a copy of the entire output into the clipboard. If you've selected some text, this option is replaced with the command **Copy Selection**, which limits the copy operation to the

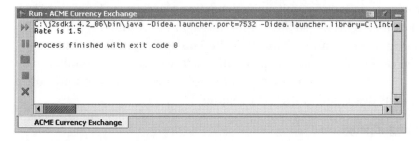

Figure 5.21   The Run tool window displays the output of the running process, color-coded by output stream and hyperlinked back into your source code, making the investigation of uncaught exceptions faster and easier.

selected text. To clear the output, right-click inside the **Run** window and select the **Clear All** command.

Running multiple programs at once

The output from your application appears in a tab inside the **Run** window that's named after the configuration profile you used to run the program. If you rerun the application, the output uses the same tab inside the **Run** window. Running different applications causes their output to use separate tabs. You can keep the output of an application, even if you rerun it, by pinning the tab. To do so, right-click the tab and select the **Pin Tab** option. An icon appears on the tab to indicate that the tab will neither be closed nor overwritten. You can right-click the tab and toggle off the pin if you wish.

When multiple tabs are present, you can right-click any of them to perform the same type of tab-management command available to the editor tabs. You can close one tab, all tabs, or all but the current tab. You can also navigate between them via the context menu or by pressing **Alt+Right** and **Alt+Left**.

> TIP   You can close any tab by holding down the **Shift** key while clicking it. Alternatively, if you use a three-button mouse, click the tab with your middle mouse button.

Stopping a program or suspending its output

To stop a program that is out of control or otherwise has no way to stop itself, click the **Stop** icon in the **Run** window. The process is interrupted and should exit immediately. If you try to close the tab of an active process, IDEA stops the process first (after having you confirm the decision). You'll also find a **Pause Output** button in the **Run** window toolbar. This button temporarily suspends the output of the program to give you a chance to examine the output. It acts as a toggle button: Click it once to pause the output and again to resume.

It's important to understand that the **Pause Output** button suspends output from the program but not the program itself, which keeps running in the background. To pause a running program, you must load it application into the debugger as described in the next chapter.

Rerunning a program

You can rerun any application whose tab is still available in the **Run** window. To do so, select the tab, and then click the **Rerun** icon in the **Run** window's toolbar, or press **Ctrl+F5**. The program will be run again using the same settings used initially. This is a time saver when you're fixing bugs. Make sure you've enabled the option to build the project with each run, and then pin the tab. Now you can fix bugs and continually rerun the application as needed.

5.4 Expanding the ACME project

Now, the practical question: How does this material apply to the ACME project? If you had a full development team with numerous interdependent projects on the go, you might want to leverage existing modules written by other people in the CurrencyConverter. Unfortunately, the simplicity of the example precludes such complexities. You can, however, integrate a third-party library relatively easily.

5.4.1 Adding a library to the ACME project

The Log4J project can be found at http://logging.apache.org. It's an open source software framework for logging application debugging messages. It defines an API that permits sophisticated logging to be enabled at runtime with requiring modification to the application binary. It was also designed to have a minimal impact on performance, so that source code with Log4J API calls can be included in production code without incurring a heavy performance cost. You'll use IDEA's modular library mechanism to include Log4J into the project and then put some logging code into the service.

The first step is to retrieve Log4J from its official web site. In your web browser of choice, visit http://logging.apache.org and navigate to the **Download** section. Download the software release (for example, at the time of this writing, the archive containing the binaries and source files was called jakarta-log4j-1.2.9.zip). Save and expand it to some directory on your local file system.

Follow these steps to add the library to IDEA and then include that library in your ACME module:

1   Select the **File | Settings** option (**Ctrl+Alt+S**) to open the **Settings** window.

2   Click the **Paths** icon to open the **Paths** configuration window.

3   CurrencyConverter should be the only available module in the ACMECC project, but if it isn't, ensure that the CurrencyConverter module is selected in the **Modules** list on the left side of the window.

4   Click the **Libraries (Classpath)** tab to bring the libraries configuration panel to the front.

5   In the **Used Global Libraries** area of the panel (bottom right), click the **Edit** button to configure the library definitions.

6   In the **Configure Global Libraries** window, click the **Create Library** button to create a new global library.

7   Give the library an appropriate name (such as `Log4J 1.2.9`) in the **Library name** text field.

8   Navigate to the Log4J JAR file containing all the Log4J class files (typically, in the dist/lib directory under the log4j home; for example, C:\jakarta-log4j-1.2.9\dist\lib\log4j-1.2.9.jar). Click **OK**.

9   Click the **Attach Sources** button, and select the src/java directory under the Log4J base install directory as the source location. Click **OK** to complete the operation.

10 Click the **Attach Javadoc** button, and select the docs/api directory under the Log4J base install directory as the JavaDoc location. Click **OK** to complete the operation.

11 Click **OK** to accept the new library definition.

12 Ensure the Log4J library has an enabled checkbox next to its entry in the **Used Global Libraries** section of the panel. Enable it if it isn't already so.

The library is now configured and available within the scope of your module. To prove it, return focus to the editor pane, and select the **Go To | Class** menu option (**Ctrl+N**). Type in the word `Logger`, and it will highlight in red, indicating that there's no such class in your module—but select the **Include non-project classes** checkbox, and IDEA will find a series of classes starting with `Logger` in your libraries, the first of which is `org.apache.log4j.Logger`. Accept the choice by pressing **Enter**, and IDEA will open that file—a non-editable source file found within a referenced library—in the editor window.

IDEA 5 In version 5.0, if the requested class isn't found in the project, IDEA searches in nonproject classes automatically, without your needing to explicitly select the corresponding checkbox.

5.4.2 *Improving and running the ACME project*

Let's make `CommandLineClient` a little more intelligent. You already know that it expects two arguments: the two currencies for which the exchange rate is being queried. The client requests a rate from the service only if both arguments are specified. Let's modify the application so that if a third argument is provided, it specifies a value or amount of the first currency. In this case, the client should return not just the rate but also the actual value of the conversion (so, for example, the inputs USD CDN *5.00* represent a request of the exchange rate from US dollars to Canadian dollars, plus the actual Canadian dollar amount if 5.00 US dollars were exchanged at that rate).

Using any and all of the features you've seen so far, update your `CommandLineClient` code to look like listing 5.2.

Listing 5.2 A revamped version of the command-line currency exchange client

```
package com.acme.conversion.currency.client;

import com.acme.conversion.currency.service.CurrencyExchangeService;
import com.acme.conversion.currency.service.CurrencyExchangeServiceFactory;

public class CommandLineClient {
    public static void main(String[] args) {
        if (args.length != 2 && args.length != 3) {
            System.out.println("Requested parameters: " +
            "<source currency code> <target currency code> " +
            "[amount to exchange]");
        }
        else {
            CurrencyExchangeService service =
                CurrencyExchangeServiceFactory.getService();
            double rate = service.requestCurrentRate(args[0], args[1]);
            System.out.println("Rate is " + rate);
                if (args.length >= 3) {
                    double oldAmount = Double.parseDouble(args[2]);
                    double newAmount = oldAmount * (1/rate);
                    System.out.println(oldAmount + " " + args[0]
                    + " is " + newAmount + " " + args[1]);
                }
        }
    }
}
```

Annotations:
- **Number of arguments must be 2 or 3** — `if (args.length != 2 && args.length != 3) {`
- **If 3 arguments, execute additional code** — `if (args.length >= 3) {`
- **Convert number into a double** — `double oldAmount = Double.parseDouble(args[2]);`
- **Conversion calculation** — `double newAmount = oldAmount * (1/rate);`

For those of you paying attention, *this code contains an intentional bug!* Chapter 7 covers debugging and testing, so we'll catch it there. The code is, however, in perfect shape to run.

To run the executable within IDEA, you need to create a Run/Debug configuration that represents this context. Follow these steps to set up the configuration:

1 Select the **Run | Edit Configurations** menu option.

2 Select the **Applications** tab.

3 Click the **Plus** icon (+) to create a new, unnamed configuration.

4 Enter `Simple Exchange Request` in the **Name** text field.

5 Either type the fully qualified class name of `CommandLineClient` into the **Main class** text field, or click the ellipsis button (**...**) to select the class from a list or tree.

6 Enter the string `USD CDN 5.00` into the **Program parameters** text field.

7 In the **Use classpath and JDK of module** drop-down, select the `Currency-Converter` module.

8 Ensure the **Make module before running/debugging/reloading** checkbox is enabled.

9 Click **OK** to save your configuration.

You can now run your command-line program from the main toolbar in IDEA. To do so, select **Simple Exchange Request** from the drop-down list in the toolbar, and then click the **Run** button to its right to execute the command.

5.5 *Summary*

The most important stages of development are arguably those stages you can't avoid. Compiling and running your application is certainly one of these stages. IDEA provides the facilities to use IDE-specific means to build and run your application, and it also provides the integration with the most popular open source build solution, Ant.

If the end goal is to go from A to B, from writing your application to have it run, then using IDEA's built-in tools is obviously the quickest way to go. Alternatively, if your goal is to use a popular build tool so that the means of building the application is no longer coupled to the IDE, then the Ant integration in IDEA is made for you. Ant build scripts written with the help of IDEA can let you build from an external command line or even automate processes running on a remote server.

Probably the most remarkable aspect, and the most important, is the ease of use of these features. IDEA strives to make the most-used features the easiest to use. In little time at all, you'll find compiling and running your application (including using Ant) almost invisible; you'll use these features without thinking.

Debugging applications

6

We'd all like to think that we never make mistakes. No matter how good a developer you are, if you write programs then you also write bugs—it's an unavoidable fact of life. The question isn't whether you'll need to debug your program, but how you plan on going about doing it. Many beginning programmers rely on `System.out.println()` to show them what's happening inside their program, but more sophisticated developers understand the benefits of using a debugging tool. The debugger included with IDEA is a powerful, easy-to-use tool for examining a running program to determine what's happening (or not happening) behind the scenes. After reading this chapter, you'll never need to rely on print statements again.

6.1 Introducing the debugging process

In this section, we'll introduce the basic concepts of using a symbolic debugger to analyze Java programs. If you're familiar with using such tools, and you just want to understand how the IDEA debugger works, feel free to skim ahead to the next section.

6.1.1 Finding and fixing bugs with a debugger

We must start with some bad news: A debugger can neither find nor fix bugs. If it could, we'd all have a lot more free time. No, you'll need to find the bugs on your own, either through testing or pure luck (if you call getting big nasty stack traces lucky). Although the debugger won't fix bugs for you, it's immensely helpful in tracking them down and understanding what you must do to fix them.

A *debugger* is essentially a tool that can tell you what's going on inside the Java VM as your program is executing. It lets you start your program and then walk through it, method by method or line by line, using a process known as *stepping through the code*. Executing your code this way lets you slow things down and monitor your application's progress. Each step of the way, you can examine the state and contents of your application's variables and object references. The process can answer burning questions like, "What is the value of the variable x at the start of this method?", "Where did that null pointer exception come from?", and "How did I get here?"

Once you suspect a bug is lurking in your code, it's time to bring out the debugger. Before you begin hunting down bugs, it's important to know exactly what you're looking for and to have an idea where you may find it. In the wild, you'll encounter several different species of bugs, and the debugger can help you track down all of them.

Syntax errors

Syntax errors are the bugs you're probably most familiar with. We bet the first program you ever wrote consisted primarily of syntax errors. (Heck, we still work with some guys like that.) *Syntax errors* are invalid statements or code structure that the Java compiler can't make sense of. In other words, they're just plain wrong.

Examples of syntax errors include referencing a variable that doesn't exist or passing the wrong number of parameters to a method. Thanks to the real-time syntax analysis feature of IDEA's editor, you'll probably catch most of these errors before they get to the compiler, but occasionally one will slip through.

Bugs of this type surface during compilation and therefore can't affect running code. The debugger is designed for analyzing programs that run, and it can't help fix compilation problems like syntax errors—you're on your own for that. It will, however, help determine the cause of any *runtime errors* you encounter.

Runtime errors

Runtime errors stick out like a sore thumb; you can't miss them. They can rear their ugly heads at any time, often with dramatic explosions of stack traces and cryptic error messages. The JVM throws a runtime error when something unexpected happens, like trying to read off the end of an array or encountering a null where an object was expected. In Java, these issues are called *exceptions*, and they come in many varieties. Some exceptions you'll handle yourself; others will bubble up and be handled by the VM or your application server. (Of course, its idea of handling an exception may be to shut down the application.)

Once you've encountered a runtime error, you can use IDEA's debugger to investigate its cause. If you have access to a stack trace or log message for the exception, it may help narrow down the source of the problem, possibly even giving the exact line number. But as we said, exceptions are inherently unexpected— so the question is, what happened that wasn't expected? By executing the program in the debugger, you can follow its progress, test your assumptions, and observe the program data in a state of suspended animation. All of these features should help you determine what went wrong.

Logic errors

Logic bugs are trickier beasts because they may not be readily apparent. With a logic error, your application seems to work fine, but the outcome isn't as expected. For example, if your new sorting method generates lists of data that aren't properly sorted, you probably have a logic error.

Like runtime errors, the key to resolving logic errors is being able to peek under the covers of the running program. By examining the contents of your supposedly sorted list at each step of execution, you can try to determine the issue at hand.

Race conditions

A *race condition* is a bug caused by an unexpected dependency on the relative timing of events. For example, if an instance variable is accessible by two threads simultaneously, one thread may interfere with another's use of the class. While this situation may not cause a problem every time you run your application, the potential is always there. Bugs tied to race conditions only cause a problem when the timing is just right (or just wrong, depending how you look at it). Race conditions are often the result of threading problems; to help you find them, IDEA gives you the ability to examine all of your application's threads when searching for the problem.

The dreaded Heisenbug

As with particle physics, the attempt to examine a system tends to alter its behavior in some way. *Heisenbugs*, a take-off on the Heisenberg uncertainty principle, are bugs that seemingly disappear or change their appearance when you try to track them down in the debugger. Although using a debugger is for the most part a non-invasive process, be aware that it can affect your running code in terms of timing and concurrency. In particular, applications will run slower under the debugger, which may cause bugs to run for cover when you try to seek them out. Race conditions and threading-related bugs are particularly susceptible to this effect.

6.1.2 *Preparing your code for debugging*

One nice thing about working with a debugger to root out problems is that you aren't required to modify your source code, recompile, use a special VM, implement a magic interface, or write your code in any particular style. The debugger takes advantage of monitoring technology built into the Java platform. You do, however, have to follow a few rules to make sure that the debugger can operate correctly with your classes.

Generating symbolic debugging information

When you build your application, the compiler converts all your pretty Java code into a tight bundle of Java byte code. A debugger works by tracking the byte code's execution and reporting on the original source code references that generated it. This relationship between byte code, your code symbols, and their original source files and line numbers is called *symbolic debugging information*, and it isn't strictly required by the JVM to run your program. After all, the JVM doesn't care that line number 3,310 from the file LogonEventListener.java added 1 to the value of the variable `logins`; it just executes the byte code to make it happen.

But you do care—unless you speak byte code. That is why when you compile your application, you must tell the compiler to preserve this information and save it as part of the generated class file. Fortunately, this is the default mode in most compilers, but you must be aware of this fact when specifying your compilation options. Why would you ask the compiler to omit this information? Because doing so reduces the size of your class files and may help protect the class files from reverse engineering. For this reason, some developers choose to compile their application twice, creating a debug version (which they keep) and a production version (which they deploy). For the production version, they omit the symbolic debugging information for the reasons stated earlier.

Compiling the latest version of your code

Given that the debugger works by mapping the running byte code to the original source code, it stands to reason that the two must be in sync. If your source code has been modified since you compiled and executed your application, then the debugger is unable to accurately report on its progress. When lines of executing source don't match up to your local source, things can get very confused, very quickly. We've all been caught watching the debugger step through yesterday's class with today's source. For that reason, it's best to always perform a clean build of your application before firing up the debugger, to make sure everything is properly updated.

Gathering third-party source code

If you're using any third-party libraries and have their source code, it's a good idea to add it to your project. Sometimes during your debugging you'll want to follow the program flow into these libraries to understand where a problem is occurring. (Maybe it's a bug in a vendor library and not your fault!) If you have access to all the source code, you'll more easily be able to tell what's going on.

Disabling the JIT

The just in time compiler (JIT) is a component in the VM that helps improve the performance of running applications. It works by caching generated machine code in memory and reusing it to speed up execution of the program. When doing so, however, you lose your ability to generate meaningful stack traces, even though the debugger may still work. If a problem arises in executing the cached machine code, the stack trace will only display the unhelpful reference *in compiled code*.

Therefore, you may want to turn off the JIT while debugging in order to more clearly follow what's happening in the case of a problem. Options vary by VM, but generally you can disable the JIT by launching the VM with the parameter compiler=none. JDK 1.4 is smart about this type of thing, and it makes sure methods with breakpoints in them aren't optimized by the JIT; this is supposed to eliminate this problem in the debugger.

Setting breakpoints

When you launch your program in the debugger, it runs uninterrupted until it hits a breakpoint marker. A *breakpoint* is a logical code reference that causes the debugger to suspend the program (or take some other action) when it reaches that point. Once suspended, you can use the debugger's tools to examine the state of your program. You can then advance the program to the next breakpoint or the next line of code at your leisure.

Generally, you'll set up breakpoints in your code to suspend the VM just as your program enters a section of code that you suspect is the source of a bug. Then you can follow the program step by step and make sure things are going as expected.

Breakpoints are markers known only to IDEA and the VM. They aren't saved in your Java source or built into your generated class files. Therefore, breakpoints can be set or cleared as needed, at any time—even while the program is running. You may need to set them before launching your program, for example, should you wish to stop its execution early. Conversely, you may wish to toggle breakpoints on and off throughout the debugging session as you try to narrow down the problem.

6.1.3 Debugging your source code

Once your code is compiled and ready to go, you launch the application in the debugger to begin your bug hunting at the first breakpoint. From there, you can peek at what's happening inside your application. We'll discuss the details of using the debugger in the next section of this chapter.

Launching your application in the debugger

When you use IDEA's debugger to launch your program, you're actually running your program with the VM's debug mode enabled. In debug mode, the VM continually reports information about the state of your program to the debugger, which in turn displays the data to you in a meaningful way.

> **WARNING**   IDEA uses the Java Platform Debugger Architecture (JPDA), a technology built into the Java2 platform, as a source of debugging information. If you're developing an application using Java 1.1 or earlier, you won't be able to use the debugger.

Stepping through your program

The debugger allows you to step through each line of source code at whatever pace you desire. This lets you follow each step logically, evaluating the results and observing program flow. You can choose to examine every line as it's executed or skip ahead to meaningful parts of the code you wish to observe more closely.

Examining the values of variables and program state

As you step through the program, you have the opportunity to examine the internal values of your classes to see if they contain what you expect them to. You can peek inside collections and arrays, evaluate the output of methods, and examine instance variables. The debugger also presents information about the current state of execution, the call stack, and your program's threads in order to help you understand exactly what your program is doing.

Changing data values on the fly to observe the results of potential changes

Beyond strict observational capabilities, the debugger also lets you tweak values on the fly in order to observe the results. For example, you can force a method to return false instead of true, and observe the outcome; or skip to the end of a loop by incrementing its counter.

6.2 Working with breakpoints

Breakpoints are source code markers used to trigger actions during a debugging session. Typically, the purpose behind setting a breakpoint is to suspend program execution to allow you to examine program data. However, IDEA can use breakpoints as triggers for a variety of different actions, as you'll learn in this section. Breakpoints can be set at any time during the debugging process, including prior to launching your program in the debugger. Your breakpoints won't affect your Java source code files directly, but breakpoints and their settings are saved with your IDEA project so you can reuse them across debugging sessions.

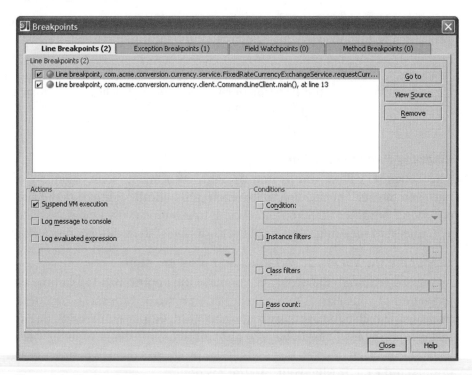

Figure 6.1   The Breakpoints configuration panel lets you manage all your breakpoints in one place.

6.2.1 *Managing breakpoints*

You can manage breakpoints through the **Breakpoints** panel, shown in figure 6.1, which is accessible through the menu option **Run | View Breakpoints** (**Ctrl+Shift+F8**) as well as through the corresponding icon on the Debug window toolbar.

Working with different types of breakpoints

IDEA lets you create four types of breakpoints. Each is managed through its own tab in the **Breakpoints** panel. The number beside each type of breakpoint indicates the number of breakpoints defined for that type. IDEA supports the following types of breakpoints:

- **Line breakpoints** are assigned to a particular line of Java source.
- **Method breakpoints** act in response to the program entering or exiting a particular method.

- **Exception breakpoints** are triggered when a specified exception is thrown.
- **Field watchpoints** allow you to react to any access or modification of specific instance variables.

Each of these breakpoints addresses different debugging needs and has its own individual settings. In this section, we'll address some of the concepts common to all types of breakpoints. We'll discuss each type of breakpoint in detail in the following sections.

> **TIP** The easiest way to create line breakpoints in your application code is to click the gutter area next to the line of interest. If you **Alt+Click** the gutter area, the appropriate breakpoint type will appear. Its type depends on the context of the current line. You can remove a breakpoint by clicking its icon in the gutter area. The keyboard shortcut for toggling breakpoints is **Ctrl+F8**.

IDEA 5 Here's another gem for 5.0 that makes it easy to set up logging breakpoints. Select an expression or symbol you want to log during debugging, and then **Shift-Click** in the gutter next to the line where you wish to set the breakpoint. Doing so automatically creates a breakpoint that doesn't suspend the VM but only logs the value of the expression to the debugging console.

Navigating back to the breakpoint's source

For method and line number breakpoints, you can use the **View Source** and **Go to** buttons to visit the source code the breakpoint references. The **View Source** button loads the source into the editor, and the **Go to** button also closes the **Breakpoints** panel and switches focus to the editor.

Breakpoint icons

When a breakpoint is set, the editor displays a breakpoint icon in the gutter area to the left of the affected source code. Each type of breakpoint is represented by its own icon in the editor, as shown in table 6.1. The icons indicate both the type and status of the breakpoint. You can place your mouse pointer over a breakpoint icon in the gutter area of the editor to review the breakpoint's settings, including information about its type, location, and action. In some cases, it's possible for multiple breakpoints to apply to the same line, in which case the icons line up next to one another, expanding the gutter area as required.

The icons also serve as convenient shortcuts for managing your breakpoints. Clicking the icon removes the breakpoint. Successive use of **Alt+Click** the icon toggles its state between enabled and disabled. Right-clicking the breakpoint icon provides a context menu with three options:

- **Disable** (like **Alt+Click**) temporarily disables the breakpoint.
- **Remove** permanently removes the breakpoint.
- **Properties** lets you configure the breakpoint in the **Breakpoints** panel.

Table 6.1   The editor displays the status of your breakpoints in the left gutter. The icons allow you to immediately tell the type and status of the breakpoint without requiring a visit to the Breakpoints configuration window.

Icon	Description
	A breakpoint
	A disabled breakpoint
	A verified line breakpoint (visible only during an active debug session)
	An invalid line breakpoint (visible only during an active debug session)
	A field watchpoint
	A disabled field watchpoint
	A verified field watchpoint (visible only during an active debug session)
	An invalid field watchpoint (visible only during an active debug session)
	A method breakpoint
	A disabled method breakpoint
	A verified method breakpoint (visible only during an active debug session)
	An invalid method breakpoint (visible only during an active debug session)

Runtime breakpoints

When you run the debugger, it prepares and evaluates the configured breakpoints. When this happens, the breakpoint becomes either *verified* or *invalid*, and the icon in the gutter area updates to reflect this state. If the breakpoint is refused and becomes invalid, in most cases it means there was an absence of debugging information or the information doesn't correspond to the source code. In some cases, recompiling your sources may solve the sync problem.

Removing and disabling breakpoints

You can permanently remove any breakpoint from your project by selecting its entry in the **Breakpoints** panel and clicking its tab's **Remove** button. To temporarily disable a breakpoint without removing it, deselect the checkbox next to its definition. You can also remove and disable individual breakpoints through their icon by clicking and **Alt+Clicking**, as described earlier.

IDEA 5 You can now use drag and drop to reposition breakpoints in your code. Grab the breakpoint with your mouse, and drag it to its new home.

6.2.2 Working with line number breakpoints

If you've worked with other debuggers, you're already familiar with *line number breakpoints*. These are the most common type of breakpoints and are a staple of the debugging process. Quite simply, they're used to target a particular section of code for debugging.

Breaking at a line number

Line number breakpoints are triggered when the program reaches the specified line of source, before the line is executed. It's possible to define a line breakpoint that is never reached during program execution, in which case it's ignored.

Setting or unsetting a line number breakpoint is easy. Bring up the source file in question in the editor, position the cursor anywhere on the line you wish to target, and do one of the following to toggle the breakpoint on or off:

- Choose **Run | Toggle Line Breakpoint** (**Ctrl+F8**).
- Click in the gutter area next to the line.

Once set, a line number breakpoint remains in the project until it's removed. Note, however, that the breakpoint is assigned to the line number, not to the code. Moving or altering the line of code moves its corresponding breakpoint, but the breakpoint obtains an invalid status until you reload the class.

Line breakpoints can only be set on lines of code that can be executed by the VM. Comments, declarations of fields or methods, and empty lines aren't valid locations for line breakpoints. If one of your breakpoints is invalid, it appears with the invalid breakpoint icon during your debugging session and is ignored.

> **TIP** If the debugger shows some of your breakpoints as invalid even though they're assigned to lines of code you know to be executable, your source code may be out of sync with the running application. Try recompiling your application and rerunning the debugger. You can even avoid recompiling and restarting your application by using IDEA's HotSwap feature, which lets you reload classes within a running debug session (via the **Run | Reload Changed Classes** command).

6.2.3 Working with method breakpoints

Method breakpoints allow you to target your debugging sessions by the method, rather than by line number, that you wish to investigate. They let you follow program flow at the method level as well as check entry and exit conditions. Unfortunately, relying on method breakpoints can slow down the application you're debugging, so use them sparingly.

Setting a method breakpoint

You create a method breakpoint by placing your cursor inside the method in question and selecting **Run | Toggle Method Breakpoint** from the menu bar. The method breakpoint icon appears in the gutter area next to the method declaration.

It doesn't matter where inside the method your cursor is when you place the breakpoint. The breakpoint applies to the method as a whole, and the icon always appears next to the declaration statement. Left-clicking the icon removes it, whereas right-clicking brings up a context menu allowing you to modify the breakpoint's properties.

You can also **Alt+Click** the gutter area next to the line where the method is declared, to set a method breakpoint basing on the context of the line.

Breaking on method entry or exit

In the **Watch** group of the **Method Breakpoints** options panel are two checkbox options: **Method entry** and **Method exit**. These selections control the points in the method access at which the breakpoint's action is triggered. You must enable at least one of these method trigger conditions, both of which are on by default. Select or deselect the boxes as required.

6.2.4 Working with exception breakpoints

Exception breakpoints allow you to tell the debugger to respond to thrown exceptions. Unlike the line number and method breakpoints, which require specific source references, exception breakpoints apply globally to the exception condition, not to a particular code reference. Exception breakpoints are a great shortcut to finding the source of problems stemming from a `Throwable` condition deep in the bowels of your code, without the fuss of having to track down the exact source of the problem yourself. (What can we say? We're as lazy as the next guys.)

Breaking when a certain exception is thrown

Because of their global nature, you must use the **Breakpoints** dialog to create exception breakpoints. Select the **Exception Breakpoints** tab, and click the **Add** button to create a new breakpoint. You're presented with a dialog for selecting the exception you wish to break on. You can select any `Throwable` class from your Classpath. Once a breakpoint is set for a particular type of exception, its action is triggered when the exception is thrown anywhere in the code. If this is too aggressive for you, you can narrow the scope through the use of class filters.

> **TIP**   A very handy feature is the **Any Exception** option of the **Breakpoints** dialog. It's a global option that can't be removed, only disabled. Activating this option breaks the execution of the application at any point where it causes an exception, even if no breakpoint is explicitly set for that exception. Using **Any Exception** quickly illustrates any exception paths in the application's execution.

Differentiating between caught and uncaught exceptions

The **Notifications** option group for exception breakpoints provides options for responding to caught and uncaught exceptions. By selecting some combination of these two options, you can control the type of exceptional condition that should trigger this breakpoint. If a box is deselected, exceptions in that situation won't trigger the debugger action.

6.2.5 Working with field watchpoints

Field watchpoints allow you to target your debugging search to specific instance variables. For example, if at the end of a complicated process you're ending up with an obviously wrong value on one of your fields, then setting up a field watchpoint may be the quickest way to determine the origin of the fault.

Adding a field watchpoint through the Breakpoints configuration window

Typically, you set up a field watchpoint from the editor when the caret is on the line of the field declaration. Select **Run | Toggle Field Watchpoint** from the main menu, or **Alt+Click** the gutter area next to that line. You can also set a field watchpoint through the **Breakpoints** dialog. Select the **Run | View Breakpoints**

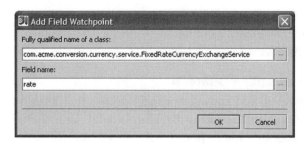

Figure 6.2
Adding a field watchpoint is an easy way to track changes to an instance variable over time.

menu item to bring up the **Breakpoints** dialog (or press **Ctrl+Shift+F8**), and select the **Field Watchpoints** tab. Like the other types of breakpoints, any currently defined field watchpoints are listed here. Click the **Add** button to bring up the **Add Field Watchpoint** dialog, and specify the class and field name you want to break on. The class name you provide here must be fully qualified. Using the selection buttons next to each field makes this process easier, because you can navigate to the desired class and field by name or through a tree view of your project.

Once added, your field watchpoint displays a corresponding icon in the editor's gutter area. It behaves like other breakpoint icons: It can be disabled, enabled, or removed directly from the gutter area.

> **TIP** You can set field watchpoints directly through the editor. To do so, right-click the line with declaration of the field you want to watch, and then select the **Toggle Field Watchpoint** option from the context menu. This sets the breakpoint and opens the **Breakpoints** dialog.

Adding a field watchpoint while debugging

There is another way to add a field watchpoint. Although it's more convenient, it can only be used once a debugging session is underway. After you've suspended your application, you can add a field watchpoint for an instance variable by right-clicking its icon in the frame view and selecting the **Add Field Watchpoint** menu item. This command creates the appropriate field watchpoint and opens the **Breakpoints** dialog. In addition, it prepopulates the instance filter (described in the next section) with the instance ID of the field's source object.

Breaking on field access or modification

Regardless of how you set up your field watchpoints, you must specify under which circumstance you want the debugger to trigger the breakpoint. These options are located in the **Watch** group of the **Breakpoints** dialog panel.

The first option, **Field access**, tells the debugger that you wish to trigger the breakpoint any time the field is accessed. This could involve initialization, read access, or write access. The second option, **Field modification**, says that you only care about changes to the field. Simple read attempts won't cause the breakpoint to trigger. You must select at least one of these options.

6.2.6 *Setting conditional breakpoints*

Breakpoints needn't be absolute. You can also create breakpoints that take effect only under certain conditions and situations. This gives you a much finer degree of control, allowing you to spend more time debugging and less time stepping through program code.

Breaking only when a certain condition is true

This option lets you specify a logical condition for activating the breakpoint's action. The condition is any valid Java expression that evaluates to a `boolean` (`true`/`false`) value at runtime. This expression is evaluated in the context of the current line, so it can use any available fields, methods, or variables available at that point. For example, any of the following represent valid `boolean` expressions, assuming the referenced variables are accessible at the breakpoint:

```
time >= 100
user.getRoleId() == STUDENTROLE
response != 0 && response > 12
```

Notice that these are expressions, not lines of code or statements—don't end the expression with a semicolon. To set the break condition, enter the expression in the **Condition** field of the **Conditions** option group, and enable it by selecting the appropriate checkbox. Your expression isn't validated until the debugger reaches it, so type carefully! If you make a mistake and enter an invalid expression, you'll be notified when it's reached and given the option of breaking.

> **TIP** You can use IDEA's code-completion features to help construct your expression.

Breaking only for certain instances

The **Instance filters** option lets you activate a breakpoint for particular instances of the class within the VM. Each object in the VM is assigned an instance ID at creation time. You can see this instance ID in the debugger's view of the stack frame as the number following the @ sign next to an object reference. Unfortunately, you can't predict the instance ID value—it's not necessarily sequential. Instance IDs change from run to run, so this conditional breakpoint setting must be reset with each run.

When enabled, the breakpoint applies only to an object's instance whose ID is included in the instance filter list. This option is useful for following the progress of a single object instance as it travels through code paths shared with many other instances, such as when you're working with objects in collections.

Breaking only for certain classes

You can use class filters to narrow the scope of breakpoints so they apply only to particular classes. Simple wildcard expansion can be used to match the fully qualified class name. The filter format is limited to either an exact match or a pattern match beginning or ending with an asterisk. For example:

- `com.acme.conversion.currency.Currency` matches a single class, `Currency`.
- `com.acme.conversion.currency.*` matches all classes in the `currency` package and its subpackages.
- `java.*` matches all classes in the core `java` packages.
- `*Listener` matches any class whose name ends with `Listener`.

To create a set of class filters for a breakpoint, enable the **Class filters** option and type in the pattern or list of patterns delimited by spaces. By using a minus sign before a pattern, you can exclude matching class(es) from the scope.

As an alternative to typing, you can click the ellipsis button next to the text box to show the **Class Filters** dialog; there you can specify the set of patterns using the IDEA's *find class by name* feature.

Breaking after a certain number of passes

This option lets you create breakpoints that become active only after they have been reached a certain number of times. To enable this condition, enter a numeric value in the **Pass count** field of the **Conditions** option group, and select the checkbox. The **Pass count** value is the threshold for enabling this breakpoint, meaning that the breakpoint is active for all subsequent passes once this threshold has been crossed. It doesn't specify which execution pass to debug, but rather the number of passes to skip before debugging.

This option is useful for debugging loops or other lines of code that are called repeatedly. For example, if you want to examine the last iteration of a loop that runs 10,000 times, but you don't feel like stepping through it for an hour, set the **Pass count** option to 9,999 to trigger your debugging action on the last iteration.

WARNING   The **Pass count** condition is mutually exclusive with any other conditional operation.

6.2.7 *Configuring breakpoint actions*

By default, new breakpoints are configured to suspend the program to let you examine it in the debugger's frame viewer. In addition, IDEA lets you create breakpoints that generate console messages when triggered.

Suspending the program

The **Suspend** VM **execution** action tells the debugger to pause the program's execution when the breakpoint is reached, assuming any conditions that have been assigned to it have been met. Once suspended, the top stack frame is shown in the debugger's frame view. From that point, you can examine the program's state or use the debugger's stepping functions to resume execution (you'll learn about these functions in detail later in this chapter).

Logging a message to the console

Enabling the **Log message to console** option lets you display the reaching of the breakpoint as text message in the debugger's console tab. This option is useful for following the code's progress without having to suspend the program's execution (deselect the **Suspend** VM **execution** option.)

The actual message text is determined by the debugger; it says which breakpoint was reached, at what line number of which class. For more control of the message, see the following option, which lets you log an arbitrary expression to the console.

Logging an expression to the console

This option lets you evaluate an expression in the breakpoint's context and display its value to the debugging console. Like the **Log message to console** option, this feature lets you obtain information about your running application without having to suspend its execution. This is an excellent alternative to inserting a bunch of `print` statements into your programs.

To enable this feature, select the checkbox and enter any valid Java expression into the option field. When the breakpoint is reached, this expression is evaluated, and the results, along with the original expression, are displayed in the console. If your expression evaluates to an object, the console shows the output of its `toString()` method.

6.3 *Debugging an application*

Now that you have a handle on breakpoints, we can look at how to analyze your application's data in the debugger. As we mentioned earlier, the general procedure for debugging is to set breakpoints in your code to suspend the VM at some point of interest, and then use the debugger to trace the application's program flow and examine the state of application data.

6.3.1 *Executing an application under the debugger*

Assuming you've met the criteria covered earlier in this chapter with regard to compiling with debugging symbols on and so forth, you should be ready to debug the application.

Selecting a runtime configuration

Executing an application in the debugger is similar to running your program from IDEA. As their name applies, the Run/Debug configurations covered in chapter 5 apply to both running and debugging your application. To debug an application, select its runtime configuration entry in the main toolbar, and do one of the following to launch it in the debugger:

- Click the **Debug** icon on the main toolbar.
- Select **Run | Debug**.
- Press **Shift+F9**.

Any of these actions will run your application and open the **Debug** tool window, as shown in figure 6.3. In the figure, the application being debugged has been suspended by a breakpoint. If you haven't defined any breakpoints, or you haven't hit them yet, the debugger still appears, but it's empty except for a message assuring you that your program is running. If you've enabled the **Make Module before running/debugging/reloading** option or have linked Ant targets to the build process, these actions take place before the application is launched.

Launching the debugger quickly

Alternatively, you can right-click inside the source code editor and select the **Debug** menu option to begin debugging the currently loaded class. If there isn't a matching Run/Debug configuration for the class, a temporary one is created for you, using the default settings specified in your project configuration. Of course, this option is available only if the class has a `main()` method.

Figure 6.3 The Debug window gives you insight into what's happening inside your application.

The Debug window

We'll cover the details of each area of the **Debug** window as we go along, but we want to introduce its basic layout. The tabs across the top perform the following functions:

- **Console** displays program input and output, courtesy of standard input and output streams. This tab isn't available if you're debugging an application remotely.
- **Threads** lets you view and navigate into all of your application's threads.
- **Frame** gives a view of the currently selected stack frame.
- **Watches** shows a list of expressions you're watching, evaluated under the currently selected stack frame.

Along the left is the debugger's toolbar, full of icons primarily used to step through the program. These actions are also available through the **Run** menu, if you prefer. We'll cover the meaning of these in a bit. You'll probably spend most of your time in the **Frame** tab, examining runtime values. We'll discuss how that works, and how to interpret the results, in section 6.4.

Suspending program execution

Once you launch your program in the debugger, IDEA hands over control of its execution to you. The execution options available in the debugger are summarized in table 6.2. Before you can begin stepping through your running application, the program must be suspended. There are two ways to suspend program

Table 6.2   The Debug tool window provides several buttons that are used to control program execution.

Icon	Default shortcut	Description
	Ctrl+F5	**Rerun Debugger**. Launches the program in the debugger again. Available when your application has stopped and you haven't closed the **Debug** window.
	F9	**Resume Program**. Continues running the program following a suspension in execution. The program will continue to run until it hits another breakpoint, exits, or is paused.
		Pause Program. Suspends program execution immediately, without the need for a breakpoint.
	Ctrl+F2	**Stop Program**. Causes the program to exit. If desired, you can restart the program by clicking the **Rerun** action.
	Ctrl+Shift+F4	**Close Debug Window**. If the program is still running in the debugger, you'll be warned, and you'll have the option to cancel your action.

execution. The first, by using a breakpoint, is the most common. The second is to click the debugger's **Pause Program** button or select the **Run | Pause Program** menu item.

Both approaches have the same end result, although if you suspend execution with a breakpoint, the debugger can more easily give you an appropriate reference point—especially in multithreaded applications where you may otherwise end up looking at the inside of a background event-handling thread.

Once suspended, the program remains idle until you use a stepping action to advance the execution (we'll get to that later) or click **Resume Program** to execute until the next breakpoint is encountered. Until then, you can take all the time you need to examine the state of things and think about the problem at hand. (You can even go eat breakfast, if you want; rest assured that your bug will be waiting for you when you get back.)

Stopping program execution

Beyond suspending execution, IDEA also lets you stop a program running in the debugger at any time. Perhaps you found the bug, or maybe you're giving up on the whole thing. Whatever the case, if you want to stop the program, click the **Stop** icon or press **Ctrl+F2**. Note that you're stopping the program, not just the debugger, unless you're debugging a remote application as described in the next section.

Once stopped, you lose any debugging information visible in the **Debug** window—there's no going back. You can click the **Rerun Debugger** icon to rerun your application in the debugger. If you've made code changes and your configuration profile specifies that the program should be rebuilt before debugging, it will be.

6.3.2 Debugging an application on a remote server

The debugger isn't limited to debugging only applications IDEA has launched for you. The JPDA technology utilized by IDEA allows it to exchange debugging information with an application running on a remote server, or another VM on the local machine, for that matter. This is particularly handy for debugging J2EE applications running on servers not directly supported by IDEA, as you'll learn in chapter 11. Remote debugging is also good for distributed applications using JINI or RMI, and for debugging applications running within a test environment that is different than your development workstation. In this model, IDEA doesn't start the application; it expects the application to already be running in order for the debugger to connect to its debug port.

Creating a remote debugging configuration profile

To debug a remote application, you still need to set up a Run/Debug configuration for your application; but instead of the **Application** entry, create a **Remote** entry. From the **Run/Debug** drop-down in the main toolbar, select **Edit Configurations** to bring up the **Run/Debug Configurations** dialog, and then click the **Remote** tab, as shown in figure 6.4.

Launching the remote application with debugging enabled

To debug an application remotely, you must launch your application with remote debugging enabled, which is accomplished through the use of JVM arguments. IDEA conveniently shows you the arguments that should be passed to the JVM based on the entries you specify in the **Run/Debug Configurations** panel. You can select and copy these options to the clipboard if you like. Your JVM may have additional settings you can specify to control the debugging information; refer to its documentation for details.

If your application is running under a Java application server, you must make sure the application server is being run with the appropriate debugging settings. Most application servers provide the ability to add arguments to the Java executable launch sequence by editing a configuration file or setting an environment variable. Refer to your server's documentation for more details.

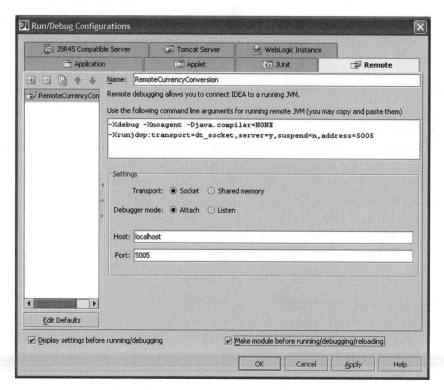

Figure 6.4   IDEA's support for the JPDA debugging architecture lets you debug not only local applications but remote applications as well.

TIP   If speed isn't critical during the development process, you may want to run your application server with debugging enabled at all times. This lets you quickly connect to it with the debugger as problems are encountered. However, you almost certainly don't want to run your production servers with debugging enabled, because doing so will reduce performance as well as introduce a potential security risk.

Debugging via socket connection

To use network sockets as the communication mechanism between the application and the debugger (the default mode of operation), select **Socket** as your transport on the **Remote** tab of the **Run/Debug Configurations** dialog. Enter the hostname or IP address of the host on which your application is running. It doesn't have to be running at this stage, but it must be running before you can attach the debugger to it. In the **Port** field, enter the port number to which the remote application is sending debugging information. The number entered here is arbitrary, but there must be nothing else running on the port, including other Java applications with debugging enabled.

> **WARNING** Don't confuse the debugging port number with your application server's port number. The debugging port number in the **Run/Debug Configurations** window is the port number the debugger uses to communicate with the application. This number should be the same as the one specified through the -Xrunjdwp switch when you launch the server. This has nothing to do with the port number on which your application server is handling HTTP requests (such as 80 or 8080).

Debugging via shared memory

Windows users have the option of using shared memory, rather than a socket, for communication between the application and the debugger. If you select this option on the **Remote** tab of the **Run/Debug Configurations** dialog, you'll be asked to enter the name of the shared memory segment as specified when you launched your application. In theory, there is a speed advantage to communicating in this manner, but your mileage may vary. Note that the shared memory transport option only works when you're debugging an application running on the same machine as IDEA.

Connecting to a remote application for debugging

Just as you would when debugging a local application, select the Run/Debug configuration you've created for your remote debugging session on the **Remote** tab of the **Run/Debug Configurations** dialog and click the **Debug** icon on the main toolbar or press **Shift+F9**. The debugger will attempt to attach itself to the application using the settings specified in the configuration. If it's unable to do so for any reason, such as if the program isn't running, you'll be dutifully informed.

Setting up IDEA as a debugging server

Rather than have IDEA connect to your process, you can flip things around and have the application contact IDEA when something goes wrong. To do this, select **Listen**, rather than **Attach**, as the debugger mode on the **Remote** tab of the **Run/Debug Configurations** dialog, and pass the required VM parameters when launching your application. When the condition you've set up (such as an uncaught exception) occurs on the remote application, it will attempt to contact IDEA and establish a debugging session.

Note that you still have to start a debug session before IDEA begins listening for debug requests. IDEA is passive in this mode, so you don't need to specify a hostname. If you're trying to debug an application that is running on several servers simultaneously (as in a web application cluster), this mode may prove useful, because you can't predict which server your code will execute on. Another advantage of this model is that in the latest versions of Java, the VM is smart enough to run at full speed until the exception is thrown, which can speed up debugging in a performance-critical environment. Otherwise, you should probably stick with the default **Attach** mode of operation.

Disconnecting from a remote application

When you're finished with your debugging session, click the **Stop** icon or press **Ctrl+F2** to disconnect from the remote application. You're given the option to terminate the remote program as well, if you're finished with it. However, if the remote application exits on its own for some reason, the debugger will automatically disconnect.

6.3.3 *Stepping through the program*

Once you hit a breakpoint or otherwise suspend the program, the **Debug** window becomes active and you're officially debugging. From this point, you control the program flow. You decide how and when the next line is executed. You also get to examine the stack and the current values of any variables in the execution scope. Often you can solve problems by just observing the program flow (for example, when it starts going into a code block headed by the comment `This should never happen`). Stepping actions are available through both the **Run** menu and the **Debug** window's toolbar.

The stepping actions are summarized in table 6.3. You use these actions to advance the current execution point one line at a time, with the option of skipping over methods you aren't interested in. Let's look at each action's function in more detail.

Table 6.3 The stepping actions allow you to run through the program at your own pace, in order to trace its execution path.

Icon	Default shortcut	Description
⬚	F8	**Step Over**. Runs until the next line in this method or file, skipping the methods referenced at the current execution point (if any).

continued on next page

Table 6.3 The stepping actions allow you to run through the program at your own pace, in order to trace its execution path. *(continued)*

Icon	Default shortcut	Description
	F7	**Step Into**. Steps into the method being referenced at the current execution point.
	Shift+F7	**Force Step Into**. Steps into the method being referenced at the current execution point, ignoring any filters or stepping restrictions specified in the debugging preferences.
	Shift+F8	**Step Out**. Resumes execution of the method currently being executed, suspending again after the method has exited.
	Alt+F9	**Run to Cursor**. Resumes the program until the execution point reaches the line at the current cursor location. No breakpoint is required.
		Pop Frame. Interrupts execution and returns to the initial point of method execution. In the process, it drops the current method frames from the stack.
		Suspend All Threads While Stepping. This verbosely titled option does exactly what it says it will; it suspends all the running threads in the application while you step through the breakpoints.
	Alt+F10	**Show Execution Point**. Highlights the current execution point in the editor, and shows the corresponding stack frame in the **Frame** tab.

 Mute Breakpoints, a new option in the **Debug** tool window, let you temporarily disable all the breakpoints in the project so that code execution can continue normally. Click it once to mute the breakpoints, and then click again to reenable them.

A similar (although more precise) mechanism for avoiding breakpoints is the **Force Step Over** action. This stepping option lets you step over any code that contains breakpoints without stopping.

Finding the current execution point

When you suspend execution, the source file (if available) associated with the current execution point is loaded into the editor automatically to give you a frame of reference. The current execution point (the next line to be executed) is marked with a solid blue bar, giving you an idea where you are in the program flow. If you visit other source files and want to return to this point, click the **Show Execution Point** icon (**Alt+F10**) to load the current source file into the editor.

Stepping into a method (F7)

One of the most basic stepping actions is **Step Into**, which advances the execution point to the next executable line of code. This lets you examine the program flow one line at a time. Each time you step to the next executable line, the current execution point is shown in the editor window, even if the next line calls a method, taking you into another class or source file. This is why this action is called **Step Into**—it steps *into* methods it encounters. If you aren't interested in tracing the program flow into the method, use the **Step Over** action. The option **Force Step Into (Shift+F7)** can be used to step into methods normally ignored by the debugger. By default, all synthetic methods and the core Java classes are skipped over during stepping.

The new version of IDEA also includes a **Skip Simple Getters** option. These methods are trivial and are typically stepped over manually in most debugging sessions. Having the debugger skip them automatically is a convenience that will save you time.

Stepping over a method call (F8)

The **Step Over** action advances the execution point just as **Step Into** does, but it doesn't drill down into method calls it encounters. It executes the next line in the current method or, when the method is completed, the next line in the current source file, jumping over method calls. It's important to understand that the code inside the stepped-over method call is still executed; you just aren't given the opportunity to trace the program through it. The debugging options discussed later in this chapter conveniently allow you to specify classes that should always be skipped over (for the project), saving you the trouble.

> **NOTE** If the method you intend to step over contains breakpoints, IDEA ignores the request to step over the method and shows the breakpoints specified. It does so to ensure that all breakpoints do their job in showing you the runtime information required to debug your application.

Force Step Over in IDEA 5, as mentioned previously, *does* ignore embedded breakpoints.

Stepping out of a method (F8) XE "stepping out" (Shift+F8)

Once you've stepped into a method for a closer look, the **Step Out** action lets you get back out. When you step out of a method, execution of the program resumes until the method exits. At that point, the program is suspended at the line immediately following the method call that got you into the method in the first place.

Running to the cursor location (Alt+F9)

The debugger provides a handy way to suspend the program at any point in your source file without requiring you to set up a line number breakpoint. While running under the debugger, place your cursor on the line at which you wish to suspend execution, and click the **Run to Cursor** icon or press **Alt+F9**. Program execution resumes, suspending immediately before executing the line you're on. This function follows the same rules as the line number breakpoint: You must place your cursor on an executable line of code, not a blank line or comment.

This can be a quick way to bypass uninteresting or long-running sequences of code that you encounter while tracing program execution. It's a great way to bypass long, iterative loops.

Backing out of the current frame of execution (Pop Frame)

The powerful **Pop Frame** feature lets you roll back the current frame of execution to the previous execution point. This is referred to *popping off* the current stack frame, as described later in this chapter. This effectively takes you back in the sequence of execution so you can rerun sequences of application logic.

6.3.4 Working with threads

Most Java applications utilize multithreading to some degree. Each thread operates independently and thus has its own stack frames. Because of this, IDEA allows you to examine each thread independently.

Accessing the threads list

The debugger shows your program's threads in two locations. The primary view of threads is through the **Threads** tab of the **Debug** window, as shown in figure 6.5. Each thread is shown along with its stack frames, optionally organized into their thread groups. From here, you can peek into whatever thread is of interest to you. The colors of the icons indicate the status of the threads and their thread groups. These icons are explained in table 6.4. Beside each thread instance is the thread's name (if any) and current status:

- *RUNNING*—The thread is active and running.
- *WAIT*—The thread is waiting for a monitor.
- *UNKNOWN*—The state of the thread can't be determined accurately.

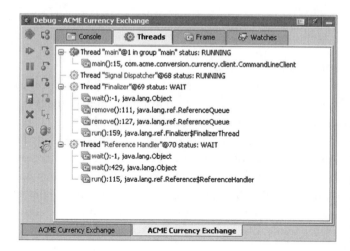

Figure 6.5
The Threads tab shows you the status of all of the threads in the system, optionally organized into thread groups. You can jump directly to a thread's stack frame from this view by way of the context menu called on the stack frame.

TIP If you're spawning your own threads, you'll probably want to give them meaningful names via the `Thread.setName()` method. That way, they're easier to locate in the debugger, because they appears as something like `DatabaseCleanupThread` rather than `Thread-7`.

Controlling which threads are suspended

When you use a breakpoint to suspend your program's execution, only the thread that triggered the breakpoint is suspended by default. Any other threads in the

Table 6.4 The icons in the Threads tab of the Debug window show both the kind of entity and, in the case of the threads themselves, their current active state.

Icon	Description
	A thread group
	The current thread group
	An active thread
	A suspended thread
	A frozen thread
	A thread at a breakpoint
	The current thread at a breakpoint

system continue to operate normally, doing their thing in the background. Stepping in this case only affects the suspended thread. For example, if you're debugging a web application, only the current request thread is suspended, allowing the server to continue to process requests on its other threads.

Sometimes, however, this behavior can lead to problems, confusion, or worse, because threads may have dependencies on each other that may negatively affect the system. The **Suspend All Threads While Stepping** option lets you simultaneously suspend all of the threads in the system any time a breakpoint is reached. Each time you step, all the threads continue, suspending again when the step is completed.

This is a good way to prevent background threads from affecting the state of the application you're trying to examine. We'll illustrate the usefulness of this feature with a true story: While debugging a web application, we kept finding ourselves logged out of the application by the time we finished tracing a request. Finally, we discovered that a background thread designed to prevent stale sessions was kicking us off the system after 5 minutes of inactivity! Suspending all the threads together fixed the problem, allowing us to debug in peace.

Suspending individual threads on demand

If you don't have the **Suspend All Threads While Stepping** option enabled, you can still suspend individual threads as needed. In the **Threads** tab of the **Debug** window, right-click an active thread and select the **Freeze** option from the context menu. The thread will now be suspended. Right-clicking a suspended thread gives you the option of resuming that thread independently of the rest. The only way to return this thread to its processing chores is to select the **Resume** option from the thread's context menu.

> **WARNING** Issuing collective **Resume** commands won't include individually suspended threads.

Exporting information about your threads

To obtain more information about your program's threads, select the **Export Threads** option from the **Run** menu or from the context menu in the **Threads** tab of the **Debug** window. This option creates a report on the status of all the threads; you can save the report to a text file, copy it to the clipboard, or view it onscreen. This is the same information you get when you invoke a thread dump from the VM by pressing **Ctrl+Break** on Windows systems or **Ctrl+** on Linux systems. Invoking a thread dump doesn't affect the JVM, and it will continue to run normally. Your program doesn't have to be suspended to create a thread dump; you don't even have to be running under the debugger.

Customizing Threads view

Expanding a thread shows its stack frames, if it has any, listed by the frame's method call. Right-click a stack frame reference and select **Show Frame** from the menu to view the current frame's detail in the **Frame** tab and see the source reference in the main editor window. In addition, you can use the **Customize View** dialog to control how these stack frames are displayed, via the context menu in the **Threads** tab of the **Debug** tool window. The following display options are available from this dialog:

- **Show line number** includes the line number of the method call.
- **Show class name** includes the name of the class containing the method.
- **Show source filename** includes the name of source file that contains the method.

Java threads can be organized into *thread groups*, collections of related threads that can be managed as a single unit. By default, IDEA doesn't show these threads groups, but you can easily change this by opening the **Customize View** dialog and selecting the **Show thread groups** option. Threads will now appear in a hierarchy of thread groups, allowing you to drill down into each group to access its member threads.

6.4   Viewing runtime data in the debugger

Being able to peek inside the VM and examine the values stored in your objects is often the key to finding out what's going wrong inside your code. As soon as you locate when and where things go south, you're well on your way to devising a solution. Toward that end, the debugger allows you to explore current runtime values and expressions and even change values or classes on the fly. You can only view these values while your program is suspended, however.

6.4.1   Understanding the Java call stack

When you examine a running application, you do so by glancing into the call stack. To understand why this is, and to use the debugger effectively, you must understand how the Java stack works. Like most languages, Java applications use a data structure known as a *call stack* to keep track of things while executing. The call stack holds a list of *stack frames*. A stack frame is all the data associated with a single method call. This frame holds all the data accessible within the scope of its method call, including its method parameters, local variables, and instance variables.

Each time a method is called, a new frame is added to the call stack. When that method returns, its frame is eliminated from the call stack, because it's no longer needed. When a Java program is started, the call stack contains only a single stack frame, belonging to the `main()` method of your executable class. As additional methods are called, new frames are added to the call stack. At any given time, there will probably be several frames on the stack, depending on the complexity of your code.

Examining the contents of the call stack

If you've ever thrown an exception and printed out its *stack trace* (and who hasn't), you're looking at the contents of the call stack at the time the exception occurred. Effectively, this gives you a history of the method calls that led to the exception. A called B, which called C, which called D, which threw a `NullPointerException`, for example.

Like that stack trace, the debugger lets you examine the contents of the call stack to see what called what when. In addition, it gives you access to the stack frames, which contain all the values available to that frame's method call. And unlike the stack trace, you can examine the call stack any time you trigger a breakpoint or manually suspend program execution. The **Frame** tab of the **Debug** window shows a view of the contents of the current, or topmost, stack frame. However, you can still examine the contents of other frames on the call stack.

Navigating through the call stack

At the top of the **Frame** tab in the **Debug** window are the call stack and thread selector, as shown in figure 6.6. The leftmost drop-down list represents the call stack; it lists each method currently on the call stack, as well as the class and line number they originated from. Changing the selection changes the current frame in the **Debug** window. By selecting previous frame entries, you can examine the contents of older frames to understand how things got to where they are now. As a convenience, you can also use the up and down arrow icons (or press **Ctrl+Alt+ Up** and **Ctrl+Alt+Down**) to navigate through the call stack sequentially.

Figure 6.6 The call stack component lets you select which frame of the call stack the debugger is examining and also look at the call stack of any thread in the VM.

To the right of the call stack is the thread selector. Changing the current thread also changes the call stack list, because each thread is assigned its own. Alternatively, you can select the thread you wish to inspect via the **Threads** tab to the same effect.

> **TIP** You can grab the divider between the frame and thread selectors to adjust the width of the two drop-down lists as needed to expose more information.

Popping off a stack frame to back up program execution

The **Run | Pop Frame** command (also available from the debugger's toolbar) interrupts program execution and moves the execution point back to the previous method call, dropping the current method and its descendants from the call stack. This in effect lets you move execution backward and repeat a series of method calls.

6.4.2 Inspecting a stack frame

An inspection view of your selected call stack appears in the main body of the **Frame** tab of the **Debug** window, as shown in figure 6.7. For each item in the list, you can see its name, type, and current value. The icons in this view, listed in table 6.5, let you quickly distinguish primitive values from object references and arrays. References are displayed hierarchically; you can inspect an object or array reference further by expanding its node in the tree. In this manner, you can access all the values that could affect the method's operation, including private instance variables of objects reachable by the method.

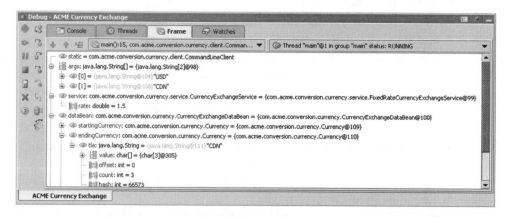

Figure 6.7 The debugger lets you examine the contents of each frame of the call stack.

Table 6.5 The icons in the Frame tab of the Debug tool window show what sort of data is active in the running application.

Icon	Meaning
	A primitive value, such as an `int` or a `char`.
	An array. You can expand it to view its contents.
	An object reference (except for arrays). Expandable to view its members, if any.

The new version of IDEA adds the ability to customize how objects are displayed in the debugger on a class-by-class basis, allowing you to assign an expression to display rather than relying solely on the object's `String` representation. For example, if an object represents a user, you may want to see users represented by their login name; or, for a cache entry object, its age and contents may be appropriate. IDEA refers to these as *type renderers*.

To create your own custom type renderers, bring up the **Debugger** settings panel and select the **Type Renderers** tab (see figure 6.8). This panel lists all the renderers you've defined and allows you to turn them on and off at any time using the checkbox next to their name. The order of the list determines which renderer is used in the case of ambiguity born of class inheritance. For each renderer, you specify a name, the object class for which it applies, and which expressions to use while rendering.

The first option determines how the object is displayed in the debugger. You can type in the expression you want to use to identify the object. In figure 6.9, we've created an expression that displays the user's full name by accessing the first and last name properties of the object. Note that you can use constants and string math as part of your renderer.

The second option is used when expanding the node. Normally, expanding a node in the debugger lists the object's member variables (using whatever renderer is appropriate for their object types). This option lets you override that behavior and select a single expression or a series of expressions to control the display. You may use this to limit the amount of information displayed or to be more precise in how the information is presented for example. In this example, we've elected to reflect only three of the object's properties and have used descriptive names rather than the member variable's name.

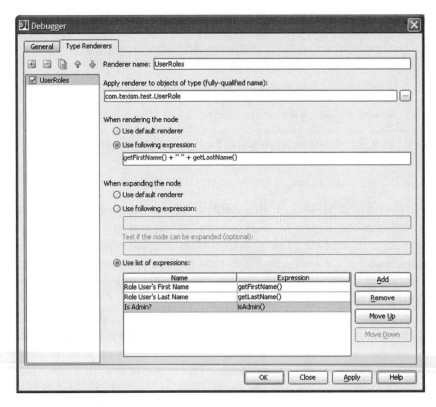

Figure 6.8 Type renderers let you specify how complex objects should be rendered in the Debugging window.

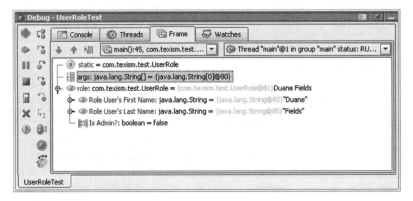

Figure 6.9 Using type renderers improves the readability of the Debug tool window.

When defining expressions, you can use IDEA's code-completion features to help you. All method calls and member variable access is relative to the object you're rendering.

Launching an inspection window

You can inspect any reference in its own window by right-clicking its icon and selecting the **Inspect** menu item. Doing so creates a separate window for that object reference, including all of its child references. An example is shown in figure 6.10.

Inspector windows are non-modal, and you can launch as many as you need. Any values that change in the main view are instantly visible in their corresponding inspector window. There is no difference in the two views; the inspector window just lets you focus on a particular

Figure 6.10 An inspector window lets you focus on the most interesting objects.

reference without all the clutter. This is particularly helpful if you need to examine two references in detail and there isn't enough screen real estate to view them both within the **Frame** tab's inspector view simultaneously.

Switching between hex and decimal views

By default, numeric values are shown in base 10 decimal. You can toggle the view by selecting the **Show as Hex** option from the context menu. A mark appears that indicates the viewing mode; it changes when you toggle the option. You must change the display type for each reference individually; there is no way to set hex mode for the entire view. All numeric values revert back to their decimal view at the start of the next debugging session. You can adjust the view for numeric arrays as well, allowing you to view all members of the array in the appropriate base. To do so, select the **View all as Hex** or **View all as Decimal** option from the context menu.

Viewing objects by their String value

Objects in the stack view are normally shown by their class name and instance ID. This is the fastest and tersest view possible, but not always the most useful. If you wish, you can have the debugger use an object's toString() method to generate the display name. To do so, right-click an object reference in the stack view, and select the **View toString()** option. Selecting it again turns off this option, reverting back to the default object view. You can also set the String value view to be the default view for object instances on a class or package basis, as described later in this chapter.

> **TIP** If a string value is too large to fit on a line in the stack frame view, it is truncated. You can view the full contents of the String by hovering your mouse pointer over it to display its contents in a tooltip window. Alternatively, right-click the value, select the **Copy Value** option to copy the value to the clipboard, and then paste into another text editor or a scratch file; you can then examine the contents of the value no matter how large it is.

Viewing the contents of an array

The debugger displays arrays as a tree of values. The top node represents the array itself, and its children are the contents of the array. As with other objects, you can further inspect each member of nonprimitive arrays. To show a subset of the array's members, right-click the array node and selecting the **Adjust Range** option, which lets you specify the first and last index you're interested in.

Peeking at variable values in the editor

Another handy way to inspect the value of references is through the editor. When you have a stack frame visible in the debugger, visiting the source code of any of the class allows you to see the value of any variable in a tooltip by hovering your mouse pointer over the variable reference in the source code. The value displayed is determined by the context of the current stack frame. If the current stack frame doesn't reference the class, you don't see a value of its members. The only exception is static members, which don't require a context.

Evaluating arbitrary expressions

Another handy feature of the debugger is its ability to evaluate arbitrary expressions in the context of the current frame. To access the expression evaluator, click the **Evaluate Expression** icon in the debugger's toolbar or select the **Run | Evaluate Expression** menu option (**Alt+F8**) to bring up the dialog shown in figure 6.11. Alternatively, you can select a reference in the **Frame** view, in the inspection window, or within the source code editor, and select **Evaluate Expression**

Figure 6.11
The expression evaluator lets you go beyond checking the current value of fields and variables; you can execute and evaluate the results of any valid Java statement in the context of the current stack frame.

from the right-click menu or with the **Alt+F8** shortcut. When launched this way, the selected expression is added to the expression field of the dialog automatically.

The **Expression Evaluator** window can accept any valid Java expression, as long as it can be properly evaluated in the context of the current stack frame. You can make method calls and perform arithmetic operations, boolean condition checks, and direct field references. The results of the expression are displayed in the **Result** area of the dialog, which behaves like the inspection window we looked at earlier. If the expression evaluates to an object, you can further inspect its members just as you can in the inspection window.

The expression evaluator remembers your expressions in the drop-down list until you exit IDEA. There is only one **Expression Evaluator** window, however, making it suited to quick, one-off evaluations. If you need to monitor the value of multiple expressions, or you want to keep an eye on the value of a particular expression throughout the debugging session, you should set up a *watch*, as described in the next section.

IDEA also has the facilities to debug arbitrary expressions. It's not in the critical path of development and is squarely in the realm of advanced features. You can consult IDEA's documentation for more information.

6.4.3 *Working with watches*

The **Watches** tab of the **Debug** window lets you evaluate any number of variables or expressions in the context of the current stack frame. The values of the expressions are updated with each step through the application but are only visible when the application is suspended. Unlike the **Expression Evaluator** window, you can view the value of multiple expressions simultaneously, and these expressions are persisted as part of the project. The number of configured watches is displayed in **Watches** tab.

Watched values are displayed in the watch view just as they are in the inspection window, and they're fully navigable. Expressions that can't be evaluated in the current context are displayed with question marks as the result.

You can add items to your watch list two ways. From the **Frame** tab, inspection window, or **Expression Evaluator** window, right-click an item and select **Add to Watches**. You can even add new watches while the debugger isn't running, by selecting items in the editor and calling **Add to Watches** from the context menu (they won't evaluate to anything until the debugger is running).

To remove a watch-list item, right-click the item and select **Remote Watch** or **Remove All Watches**. Alternatively, select the watch and click the **Delete** key. The right-click menu also provides an **Edit Watch** option that lets you change the expression represented by the watch list item.

6.4.4 Altering your program while debugging

The IDEA debugger has one more interesting feature worth noting: the ability to modify the running code in order to observe the resulting behavior, eliminating the need for recompiling the source code to test every theory.

Changing the runtime value of variables and fields

In the **Frame** view of the **Debug** window, right-click an item and select the **Set Value** option from the context menu. A text field appears in the **Frame** tab next to the desired item, so you can enter the new value. The value is now changed and will affect the program when you resume execution or continue stepping through the code. Note that you can only set primitive values and strings using this feature. To remove the text field from the **Frame** tab, select the text field and press the **Esc** key.

Hot swapping classes to test your fixes without leaving the debugger

One of the most powerful new features of the debugger in IDEA is support for swapping in new versions of classes while the program is running. This feature only works with applications running under JDK 1.4 or newer. To use the hot-swap feature during your debugging session, modify and recompile the classes you wish to swap in. If the debugger is running, IDEA suggests automatically reloading the changed classes, or it reloads them silently, depending on your current **Debugger** settings (described in the next section). Another way is to perform necessary modifications in your code and execute the **Run | Reload Changed Classes** command. Any classes that have changed since the beginning of the debugging session are recompiled by IDEA and automatically replace their old counterparts in the running program. This speeds the debugging process because it lets you try out your bug fixes immediately, rather than redeploying and executing the application.

There are limits to the type of changes you can make to a class that has been hot swapped. The exact requirements are VM dependent; but in general, the more independent the change, the more likely that it's supported. Changes to method signatures, interfaces, static members, and other elements that may be referenced by other classes may be off limits. For example, changing the algorithm behind a method may be supported, but removing a method completely may not. For simplicity's sake, if a change is made that alters the way *other classes use the changed class,* it may not be supported. If an incompatible change is detected, you'll see an error message displayed in the **Messages** tool window.

6.5 Configuring the debugger

Debugging properties are stored with your project and are accessible by selecting the **Debugger** control panel of the **IDE Settings** as shown in figure 6.12. These options control not only how the debugger runs, but also how it displays runtime information. You can use these settings to customize the settings to your liking and to increase the speed and efficiency of the debugging process.

6.5.1 Managing display preferences

IDEA provides a number of options for customizing the behavior and display of data values in the debugger. Under the **General** group in the **Debugger** window, you'll find these two settings:

- **Hide debug window on process termination**, if selected, makes IDEA automatically close the **Debug** tool window when the process you're debugging exits.
- **Value tooltips delay** specifies the delay (in ms) that you have to hover your mouse over a variable in the Editor window before IDEA shows you its current value through a tooltip.

The option **Reload classes after compilation** is used by IDEA's hot-swap debugging facility. This setting determines how IDEA reacts to compiling classes while the debugger is active. It determines whether the hot swap automatically reloads classes or asks you each time.

Figure 6.12 You can use the Debugger properties panel to customize the behavior of your debugger and to improve performance.

6.5.2 *Limiting the scope of debugging*

You can reduce the amount of code you have to step through while debugging by instructing the debugger to ignore classes and methods you don't expect to have problems. In IDEA, you can configure the debugger to automatically skip constructors, synthetic methods, and even entire branches of the class hierarchy.

Skipping constructors and synthetic methods

In the **Stepping** group of the **Debugger** window are options to skip constructors and synthetic methods. If they're enabled, the debugger always jumps over these types of methods, even if you choose the **Step Into** option on them while debugging.

Synthetic methods aren't present in the original source code; they're created automatically by the compiler. Synthetic methods include default, no-argument constructors and constructors for anonymous classes. Because they have no direct source reference, it's generally safe to skip over them.

Skipping over entire classes and packages

In the **Stepping** group in the **Debugger** window, you can create a list of classes and packages that you always want the debugger to skip over, by defining a series of simple filters. Beside each pattern is a checkbox that lets you enable or disable the filter without necessarily having to remove it from the system completely. Deselecting the option **Do not step into classes** disables the entire group of filters. By default, IDEA skips over all the classes included with the Java Runtime and those from JUnit.

6.5.3 *Customizing the data display view*

Inside the **Debugger** tool window, you can right-click anywhere in the data display region and select the **Customize View** option to further tweak your debugger preferences, as shown in an example of the frames options in figure 6.13.

Hiding null array elements

Selecting the **Hide null array elements** option in the **Customize View** window eliminates any array variable entries that aren't set from the data view. You'll still see the array variable, but if you drill down into the tree, only non-null index values are seen. This is a good way to limit the amount of data you have to weed

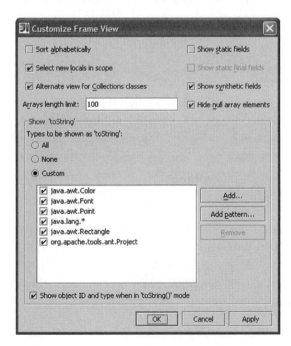

Figure 6.13
Use the Customize Frame View dialog to further adjust your debugging preferences.

through, and because it still shows you the index values of the non-null entries, you can easily tell what's going on. If all the values in the array are null, you see an information node stating this fact, rather than empty array entries in the **Frame** view.

Showing synthetic fields

Normally, the debugger hides any synthetic fields created by the compiler to manage things like anonymous inner classes. If you need to view these in the debugger, you can do so by enabling the **Show synthetic fields** option in the **Customize View** window.

Sorting the data view alphabetically

If the **Sort alphabetically** option is selected in the **Customize View** window, variables in the **Frame** view are listed alphabetically by name rather than by their declaration order. If the class you're debugging has references to a lot of variables, it may be easier to find the variable you're looking for by name, by enabling this option.

Limiting the length of arrays

The text field next to the option **Arrays length limit** in the **Customize View** window controls the maximum number of array elements shown in the debugger's display area. If an array has more than the number of values specified, only the entries up to the specified limit are shown.

Enabling toString() mode

In the **Debugger** tool window, you can right-click a value to display its `String` representation rather than an instance reference. Under the **Show toString()** group in the **Customize View** window, you can define a list of class filters that will automatically be viewed as `Strings` without the extra step. The option **Types to be shown as 'toString()'** enables or disables this behavior, and a checkbox by each pattern lets you temporarily enable or disable individual patterns.

To add a class name, click the **Add** button and select the appropriate class. You can begin typing the class name here to reduce the number of class options. To add a new pattern, click the **Add pattern** button and specify either a fully qualified class or a search pattern, using the asterisk as a wildcard match. For example, to view all the classes in the `java.lang` package via their `String` representations, add the filter pattern `java.lang.*` to the list.

Selecting new locals in scope

If the **Select new locals in scope** option is selected in the **Customize View** window, the **Frame** view automatically selects and highlights local variables as they're first encountered while stepping through your code. If you're sorting alphabetically, enabling this option will quickly alert you to the introduction of new variables.

Enabling the alternate view for collections

The debugger provides two different ways of viewing collection objects (such as Lists or Sets) in the **Frame** view. By default, the debugger displays a collection class as it does any other. If you drill down into the class in the **Frame** view, you can navigate its field and internal references. However, another view is available that, although more convenient, comes at the cost of performance.

The alternative view treats collections more like arrays, showing you the size of the collection and allowing you to easily see and examine its contents, much as you would an array variable. The **Alternate view for Collections classes** option in the **Customize View** window is used to switch between the two views.

6.5.4 *Improving the speed of the debugger*

Although the debugger is certainly useable, you must expect that your applications will inherently run somewhat slower in the debugger than in a production mode. In JDK 1.3, there were also noticeable speed differences in the debugging VM, but these have largely disappeared as of JDK 1.4.1. The speed decrease is primarily due to the extra overhead required by IDEA to process and evaluate the debugging information coming back and display it in the debugger. Here are a number of ways you can speed things up, should debugging prove too slow in your situation:

- *Turn off the alternate collections view.* The alternate collections view (which views collections as pseudoarrays) requires additional overhead, because it forces the debugger to evaluate the contents of any collection it encounters. This can be a problem particularly if you have a large number, or any number of very large collections.

- *Turn off the 'view as String' mode.* Likewise, forcing the debugger to call the toString() method for all your objects introduces extra work for the system. Try turning off this option or at least limiting the number of classes you use it option.

- *Suspend all threads while stepping.* Selecting the **Suspend All Threads While Stepping** option can be a productivity win, because the application suspends all the threads while you debug the application. It means the thread you're currently debugging is the only running thread. No other thread is affecting resources that may be required; all the energy of the application is helping you debug the current process. At the very least, no processing resources that you're not concerned with are being taken up in the background.

- *Avoid the use of method breakpoints whenever possible.* Method breakpoints are significantly slower than line number breakpoints and should be avoided when not required. Setting a line number breakpoint on the first line of the method is generally adequate if you're tracking method entries. Likewise, setting breakpoints on return statements is an equivalent substitute to tracking method exits.

- *Use the classic VM for debugging under JDK 1.3.* Under the **Launching** group in the **Debugger** dialog of the **IDE Settings** is the option **Force classic** VM. If your project is using JDK 1.3 or earlier, you'll almost certainly want to enable this option. In this release of the JDK, Sun introduced the Hotspot JVM, which significantly increases performance under normal operations but is a dog under the debugger. Enabling this option launches the VM with the `-classic` option, which should run quite a bit faster. This option isn't available if you're running JDK 1.4 or greater, because later versions of the JDK don't have this problem. This launching option doesn't apply to remote debugging sessions.

- *Use shared memory instead of socket access under Windows.* In the **Transport** group in the **Debugger** dialog of the **IDE Settings**, you can select your communication strategy, either **Socket** or **Shared memory**. Selecting the shared memory option tells IDEA to communicate with the debugger via a shared memory segment rather than via the default option of a local network socket and can provide a modest increase in performance. This option is available for IDEA users on the Windows platform only. Although this option only applies to local debugging sessions, you can use a similar option when setting up a Run/Debug configuration and launching your remote application to communicate via shared memory.

6.6 *Improving the quality of the ACME project*

If you've been following along with the ACME exercises, you may have noticed that we're suffering from a small bug. Running the command-line client tells you that the Canadian dollar is stronger than the US dollar! Obviously, there's some sort of logic bug in the code: The project compiles just fine, but the results don't make common sense. This is a case where using IDEA's debugger may help you discover where the erroneous code is hiding.

Open the `CommandLineClient` file, and click once on the gutter at the line inside the `main()` method that reads

```
if (args.length != 2 && args.length != 3) {
```

A red circle indicating a line breakpoint should appear in the gutter; this breakpoint will pause the execution of the program whenever the specified line is reached. Having placed the breakpoint successfully, select the Run/Debug configuration that runs a simple conversion from the drop-down control in the menu bar, and select the **Run | Debug** menu option (**Shift+F9**).

The breakpoint is quickly marked with a check (indicating its success as a valid breakpoint), and the running system comes to a stop as that line of code is reached. The Editor window shows the breakpointed line highlighted in blue, because this is where the current execution focus is found. In addition, the **Debug** tool window, usually docked to the bottom of the screen, shows the active frame and all its scoped variables. Feel free to explore this interface while the debugged program waits patiently.

To step through execution of the code, use the buttons on the left of the **Debug** tool window or the keyboard shortcuts. As noted in the text, **Step Into** lets you follow execution into a submethod, whereas **Step Over** lets the method return its result and keeps you at your current level on the stack.

Continue pressing **F8** (**Step Over**), watching the values of your variables as each step occurs. Note that the rate is being properly returned from the service, and the `oldAmount` is being parsed from the command line properly. It's the calculation of the `newAmount` that seems to be wrong. 5.00 dollars USD should not equate to 3.33 dollars CDN. The bug is in the formula: That line in `CommandLineClient` should set `newAmount` to `oldAmount * rate`, not `oldAmount * (1/rate)`. Repair the line, and rerun the configuration to see if the bug has been dispatched. Don't forget to rebuild/recompile before you test!

6.7 Summary

The software development process is responsible for producing both software and software bugs. Bugs are an unavoidable consequence. Creating a process to test, identify, find, and resolve the bugs in the software is a requirement for producing quality software, and that process needs to be backed by tools that can support it, or it will invariably fail.

IDEA's debugger is a sophisticated integration of the Java Platform Debugging Architecture and provides a rich feature set to help you be contextually aware of your software as it runs in many different environments. Standard Java applications, applets, remote application server sites, and several J2EE containers are all supported through the same simple interface.

Testing applications with JUnit

7

You could jokingly say that writing software doesn't create bugs, testing does. But if you ever intend to have an application used by anyone of consequence (a paying customer, for example), then the application must undergo some form of testing. Most applications also go through many changes and improvements. Testing becomes far more difficult the longer an application is in development, because you're not just testing new features—you have an obligation to maintain the old features, as well.

This area of continuing development is where automated unit testing comes into its own. Writing tests at the same time as the application code not only confirms the proper working of the application in the short term but also provides an automated means to confirm the application continues to work in the future.

JUnit (an open source project with excellent pedigree) has become a de facto standard in unit testing, and it's almost ubiquitous for unit testing in Java. IDEA has a very high degree of integration with JUnit. This integration provides the most productive means to write, manage and run unit tests without leaving the comfort of the IDE.

7.1 Testing applications with JUnit

Thorough, automated suites of unit tests are a cornerstone of the Extreme Programming movement and should be part of any large-scale development project. For the uninitiated, *unit tests* are used to programmatically verify the operation of code components, often down to the individual methods. By developing extensive unit tests for your code and running them often as part of the build and verification process, you can help reduce bugs and avoid regressions. IDEA encourages this practice through its integrated support for JUnit.

JUnit is a free unit-testing framework developed by superstars Kent Beck (of Extreme Programming fame) and Erich Gamma (master of design patterns). The package is built around a straightforward API that lets you create tests that verify your code's correct operation. You can learn the details of the framework and the JUnit API at http://www.junit.org. For the brave and impatient, we'll give a quick overview to get you started.

7.1.1 Understanding the JUnit philosophy

The benefit of using the JUnit framework is that it lets you write automated unit tests for your Java code so easily that you can't reasonably justify *not* doing so. The API is simple, readable, and—most important—painless.

Why you need automated unit tests

Automated unit testing is the easiest way we know to prevent regressions and to test those code nooks and crannies that are often overlooked during manual integration testing. As an added bonus, having code built on a solid foundation of unit tests can give you the confidence to explore design improvements, refactorings, new features, and other changes that you might otherwise deem too risky to pursue. If you can trust your unit tests, recertifying your code is as simple as rerunning your tests.

When to write unit tests

Everyone has their own opinion on testing, but most developers share a basic tenet: the earlier the better. Members of the Extreme Programming camp insist on having you write your tests first, before you begin coding the classes they're being designed to test. This approach has several advantages, such as giving you an idea of the type of operations that are required of the code and assuring the testability of your class. Tests are easy to write, but if you don't get in the habit of writing unit tests as you go, it's easy to fall behind. A common suggestion you'll hear is "Code a little, test a little."

Another good practice is to create a new unit test for each bug that is reported. Design the test to exploit the bug and reproduce its behavior. The unit test will of course fail until the bug is resolved, making it easy to know when you've fixed it. Just code until the test passes! This also ensures that the bug will never bite you again, as long as you continue running your unit tests.

When to run unit tests

You should run your unit tests frequently to stop bugs from creeping into your code. Ideally, every developer should run the full set of unit tests before each check-in (refer to chapter 8 for information on version control), to ensure that none of their changes have broken any of the existing code. You should also consider running unit tests on a nightly basis, perhaps as part of a nightly build process. Java build tools such as Ant fully integrate with JUnit, allowing you to easily automate not only the running of tests but the reporting of the results as well.

7.1.2 Exploring the JUnit API

JUnit tests are collections of methods designed to exercise all the possible operations your code is expected to perform. These testing methods are included in a Java class that is passed to a JUnit-aware application, which can then put them through their paces and report the results. A *test case* is a class that contains the testing code.

Test cases and test methods

All JUnit tests stem from the base class `junit.framework.TestCase`. To create your own test case, you extend this class. There are no required methods to implement, and there is no need to modify your existing code. What could be simpler? However, in order to test something, you must create at least one test method to exercise a portion of your code. Any test case can contain as many test methods as you require. Test methods should be fine grained, testing a single operation critical to the correct operation of your code. They should also be standalone and not require any special setup or be expected to run in any particular order. Not only does this make them easy to write, it also makes them easy to use. All that is required by the framework is that your test methods begin with the name `test` and adhere to the following method signature:

```
public void testSomething()
```

Test methods can also declare exceptions.

Beyond starting with the word `test`, it doesn't matter what you call your test, but you should probably name it something meaningful to help indicate its purpose—this name is used as a label when running and reporting on the results of the test. You're free to add other methods to the test class as needed to assist in testing.

How JUnit runs your tests

The reason for the naming restriction is that JUnit relies on Java's reflection mechanism to locate and run the individual test methods. When passed into an application that knows how to run JUnit tests (like IDEA), the test case's test methods can be determined on the fly. This means all you have to do to write new tests is create new methods and add them to a test case. No configuration files, no changes to your source code, no flaming hoops to jump through. You may notice that the test method doesn't return a boolean as you might expect. So how does a test pass? A test passes as long as it doesn't fail. And failing tests is the job of *assertions*.

Assertions

If you're familiar with JDK 1.4's `assert` keyword, be advised that it isn't used in the JUnit framework, but the concept is similar. Like the `assert` keyword, JUnit's assertion methods are designed to evaluate boolean pass/fail conditions. For example, a method may verify that a variable has a certain value, a list isn't empty, or that two objects that should be equivalent really are.

If any assertion fails, the test fails with a *failure,* an expected or tested-for condition; if any uncaught exception is thrown, the test fails with an *error,* an unexpected or untested-for condition. That's all there is to it. You could get by with a simple boolean test, but to make things easy, there are convenience methods for testing all sorts of common conditions. There are also methods that include a message parameter, which is reported back to the user when a failure occurs. Here are some of the assertion methods you're likely to use:

- `assertEquals(String message, int expected, int actual)`
- `assertTrue(String message, boolean condition)`
- `assertNotNull(Object object)`

If you look at the JUnit API, you'll see that there are assertion methods that accept `Objects`, `Strings`, and all the primitives as well. There are also negative equivalents, equality checks, and other combinations that make things simple for you, the busy developer.

A simple unit test example

Listing 7.1 shows an example test case so you can see these methods used in context. It's designed to test a simple encryption class with two methods, `encrypt()` and `decrypt()`. Although it isn't an exhaustive or complicated test case, it illustrates the intent of the unit-testing framework.

Listing 7.1 An example of a simple unit test

```
import junit.framework.*;

public class CryptTest extends TestCase {

  public void testEncrypt() {
    String plainText = "convoy sails for England tonight";
    String crypted = CryptUtil.encryptString(plainText);
    assertFalse("Encrypted value should not be equal to the"+
      " original", crypted.equals(plainText));
  }

  public void testDecrypt() {
    String plainText = "my password is elephant";
    String crypted = CryptUtil.encryptString(plainText);
    String decrypt = CryptUtil.decryptString(crypted);
    assertEquals("Decrypted value should be equal to the"+
      " original", plainText, decrypt);
  }
}
```

Test fixtures

The previous example is simple, but not all tests are so straightforward. For example, if a series of tests requires some amount of setup, you can override the setUp() method of TestCase. This method is called immediately before each test method, followed by a call to tearDown(), which can be overridden to perform any necessary cleanup. This shared setup code is known as a *test fixture*.

The benefit of using test fixtures is best illustrated with an example. Say you're testing code responsible for managing a message board or discussion forum. You've determined that a series of tests is required to verify that you can manipulate postings appropriately, such as changing the subject or author. Each of these operations can be tested by a single test method, but they all must act on an existing message. In this case, a test fixture is the best way to prepare the system for the test methods. The setUp() method is responsible for creating a new posting, and the tearDown() method is used to delete the test message from the system following each test method.

Test suites

Related test cases are grouped into logical collections known as *test suites*. When running your unit tests, you can run not only individual test cases, but test suites as well. Generally, you'll want to have a single test suite that relates all your unit tests together so you can run them in a single operation. Additional hierarchy is possible, because test suites can include other test suites. By combining groups of related tests into suites, you can avoid running the entire test suite if you just want to test one area of the code. For example, you may group all the security-related tests separately from your database tests, allowing you to spot test certain areas of your program.

Test runners

An application that knows how to interpret and run JUnit test cases is a *test runner*. Although JUnit ships with its own simple test runner, as does Ant, IDEA includes an integrated test runner with many more features. We'll discuss this in detail in the next section.

7.2 Adding test cases to your project

IDEA doesn't provide the ability to create new JUnit test case classes explicitly, but it's easy to add this capability through IDEA's file templates feature. As discussed in chapter 12, file templates allow you to create a starting point for new files created through the **Project** window. Using templates, you can start off with your basic class framework already defined, rather than an empty document.

7.2.1 *Creating a test case from a file template*

For our example template, we have followed the canonical JUnit test case structure and the optional constructor, as well as stubbing out the fixture methods. The complete text of our JUnit file template is shown in listing 7.2. Of course, you may prefer a slightly different layout, so feel free to customize it to your liking.

Listing 7.2 A file template for producing JUnit tests

```
#parse("File Header.java")
package ${PACKAGE_NAME};
import junit.framework.TestCase;

public class ${NAME} extends TestCase {
    public ${NAME}(String test) {
        super(test);
    }

    /**
     * The fixture set up called before every test method.
     */
    protected void setUp() throws Exception {
    }

    /**
     * The fixture clean up called after every test method.
     */
    protected void tearDown() throws Exception {
    }

    public void testSomething() throws Exception {
    }
}
```

As you can see, this template covers all the basic structure required by the JUnit API. All you have to do now is write your test methods, starting with adding some logic to the testSomething() stub, which as written doesn't accomplish a heck of a lot (but at least it always passes!).

7.2.2 *Adding the JUnit library to your Classpath*

IDEA ships with the latest version of the JUnit JAR file, but by default it isn't included in your project's Classpath. This causes IDEA to display import failure messages in the editor, and your project won't compile. To correct this, you must use the Project settings and add either a local copy of junit.jar (or the version at $IDEA_HOME/lib/junit.jar) to your Classpath. You may want to visit the JUnit website and download the latest release, its source code, and its API reference in order to create a reusable library, as described in chapter 4.

> **WARNING** IDEA's bundled JUnit library is built atop the latest release of JUnit (version 3.8.1 at the time of this writing). If you include an older version of the JUnit APIs in your Classpath, IDEA will be unable to execute tests.

As we mentioned in chapter 4, IDEA modules have two distinct types of source paths that you can define, one for production sources and one for test sources. These have distinct output paths as well. If you choose separate output paths, you'll be able to package or deploy your application without having to include your test classes. When you're running unit tests, IDEA will automatically include your test case output path in your Classpath.

From a technical standpoint, it doesn't matter where your test sources and classes live. However, we recommend that you always place your tests in their own source tree, and make use of IDEA's tests paths.

7.3 *Running test cases in IDEA*

IDEA's integration of JUnit makes it easy to run test cases directly from the IDE and provides a number of convenience features. You can run any test or suite of tests with a single click. Any resulting failures can be corrected by jumping straight to the source of the problem, because IDEA provides links in its test reports back into your source tree. IDEA also lets you debug your tests by stepping through the execution one line at a time using the debugger.

7.3.1 *Creating a Run/Debug configuration for your test*

There are a number of different ways to run your test cases from within IDEA, but the most common method is through the **Run** menu. As we discussed in chapter 5, the **Run** menu and the **Run/Debug Configurations** dialog are used to execute applications within IDEA. They're also used to set up configurations for unit testing. Here you select test cases (or suites of test cases) to run via the **JUnit** tab. The **Run/Debug Configurations** dialog is shown in figure 7.1.

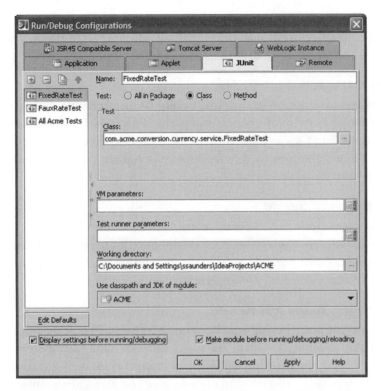

Figure 7.1 Use the Run/Debug Configurations panel to build one-click JUnit launch targets.

Selecting a test case to run

As with the other execution target types, the **JUnit** tab in the **Run/Debug Configurations** dialog lets you select a Java class that will become the target of this configuration. In this case, however, you are selecting a test case rather than an executable class. You can choose any test class in your Classpath—IDEA will even find classes for you and present an appropriately filtered list. Click the browse button next to the **Class** field to select the class by name, or navigate through your project tree. The list is filtered to include only JUnit tests—only classes that extend `junit.framework.TestCase` appear.

Select the test case you want to run from the class browser. You can name your test configuration whatever you wish; this is an arbitrary label for use in the **Run** menu. You also have the option to expand your selection to include all the test cases in a particular package or narrow it to a single method of your test. If you select the **Test Method** radio button option, an additional field appears, allowing you to choose which method to run from the selected test case. To select more than a single test method from a test case without running all of them, you must create your own test suite, as described in the JUnit documentation.

Changing the test's working directory

The **Working directory** option in the **Run/Debug Configurations** dialog lets you change the base directory for all relative file paths. This is useful if your test cases must read or write data files as part of the testing process. Before executing your tests, the test runner changes to this directory. By default, this directory is the same directory your project file is in.

Passing parameters to the VM

The VM **parameters** field in the **Run/Debug Configurations** dialog is used to pass system properties or VM options such as the maximum heap size. Any arguments specified here are passed to the JVM executing your tests, just as they would be when directly running an application.

Passing parameters to the test runner

IDEA's test runner application ultimately relies on the test-running application included with the JUnit framework. As such, you can pass parameters to the underlying test runner by entering them in the appropriate configuration field. However, since the other configuration options give you an easier avenue of controlling how the tests are run, there's not much benefit to be gained through extra parameters; but this option is provided in the **Run/Debug Configurations** dialog for the sake of completeness. Refer to the JUnit documentation for a list of current options.

Selecting the appropriate module

As you learned in chapter 4, IDEA manages most source and Classpath information at the module level. In the **Run/Debug Configurations** dialog, you'll therefore need to select the module to which the currently selected test case should run under if it exists in more than one module. This also determines the JDK used to execute the tests. An exception to this rule is when you're running all the tests in a given package.

Triggering a build automatically

The two checkbox options **Display settings before running/debugging** and **Make module before running/debugging/reloading** in the **Run/Debug Configurations** dialog behave exactly as they do for the other types of execution targets discussed in chapter 5. If enabled, the first option displays the setup dialog each time you run the test, giving you the option of tweaking the settings before execution. The second option causes IDEA to force a rebuild before running the test. Enabling this option lets you edit your tests and then run them without having to explicitly request a new build. On the other hand, you can disable this option if you're rerunning tests without code changes. Remember that these options are global, and they affect all your Run/Debug configurations, not just your unit tests!

7.3.2 *Running your unit test configuration*

The basic use of Run/Debug configurations was covered in chapter 5. Unlike application targets, which execute via their `main()` method, JUnit configurations pass the selected test class or classes to a test runner for processing—no `main()` method is required. The test runner locates and executes the tests and reports the results.

Running a selected Run/Debug configuration

Once your test target is configured, select it from the Run/Debug drop-down on the toolbar in the **Run/Debug Configurations** dialog, or from the **Run** menu, and then click the **Run** icon on the toolbar or press **Shift-F10**. IDEA understands that running a JUnit test means launching the test runner, rather than executing the class directly. JUnit tests can be distinguished from other entries in the **Run** list by their icon.

> **TIP** All tests run in the background, and you can execute multiple tests simultaneously if you wish. Each test gets its own tab in the **Run** tool window.

Defining temporary test targets

IDEA provides a convenient shortcut for creating and running test targets. When you select a package, class, or method in the project or structure windows, the right-click pop-up menu provides an option for running test cases for that selection, if there are any. If you've created a testing Run/Debug configuration, it's used. If not, a temporary target is created and added to the list of test configurations, and the test executes. Temporary targets are particularly handy when you're trying to debug a single test method. You can create a temporary target to run the method, using it until you correct the problem.

This shortcut works from the editor as well. Right-click inside the body of a test method from the editor, and select the **Run** option to run the test (or press **Ctrl+Shift+F10**). Clicking anywhere else inside the file allows you to execute the entire test case. See figure 7.2.

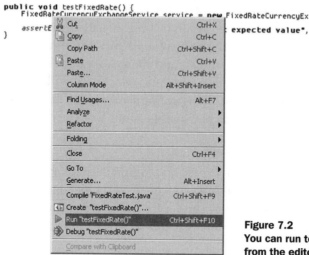

Figure 7.2
You can run temporary JUnit targets from the editor's context menu.

A Run/Debug configuration created in this manner is considered temporary, as described in chapter 5. It appears ghosted in the selection menu. To save it, select the corresponding **Save** option from the list under the **Run/Debug** drop-down. Even if you don't save it, you'll be able to tweak its behavior by selecting its entry in the **Run/Debug Configurations** dialog.

> **WARNING**   IDEA allows only a single temporary target to exist per project. If you create a second one, it will replace the first.

Debugging test cases

Not only does IDEA help you run your test cases, but it also helps you debug them. If you click the **Debug** icon instead of the **Run** icon in the toolbar in the **Run/Debug Configurations** dialog, your test cases execute in the debugger. This lets you set breakpoints and step through your code during execution, as described in chapter 6. You can set breakpoints in the test cases or in the application code the test cases call. Either way, this is a great technique to figure out why a test that ran fine last week suddenly blows up!

7.4 *Working with IDEA's JUnit test runner*

Each time you activate the **Run** or **Debug** command for your tests, IDEA invokes its test runner and opens a devoted tab in the **Run** tool window. IDEA's

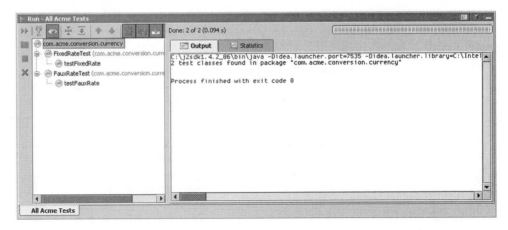

Figure 7.3 IDEA's JUnit test runner gives you complete access to test results and statistics.

test running can show you much more than just which tests passed and which failed. Through IDEA's JUnit test runner, you can also view any output or error messages your test cases produced, as well as how long they took to run and how much memory they used.

7.4.1 *Exploring the JUnit tool window*

When you run unit tests in IDEA, the test runner interface appears in a tab of the **Run** window, which pops up automatically when you begin the testing session. A typical example is shown in figure 7.3. Note that running applications and unit tests share the same tool window, but each target appears in its own tab.

The test runner toolbar

The **JUnit** tool window has a number of toolbar options. We'll discuss each of these in turn, and for your reference, they're shown in table 7.1.

Table 7.1 The JUnit toolbar affords you complete control over your JUnit execution.

Icon	Shortcut	Function
▶▶	Ctrl+F5	Rerun Test
▼		Hide Passed Tests
◉		Track Running Tests

continued on next page

Table 7.1 The JUnit toolbar affords you complete control over your JUnit execution. *(continued)*

Icon	Shortcut	Function
	Ctrl+Numpad(+)/Ctrl+Numpad(-)	Collapse All/Expand All
	Ctrl+Alt+Down, Ctrl+Alt+Up	Previous, Next Failed Test
		Select First Failed Test When Execution Finished
		Scroll to Stacktrace
		Auto Scroll to Source
		Open Source at Exception
	Ctrl+Break	Dump Threads
	Ctrl+F2	Stop
	Ctrl+Shift+F4	Close

The test tree structure

The left pane of the test runner window includes a tree structure that represents all the tests present in the current test configuration. The *root*—the topmost element of the tree—represents the entry point you selected to run; this may be a package, a test suite, or test case. If you're running an individual method, an implicit test suite is created for you. If you've nested suites of tests together, then additional levels of hierarchy are present. Because you're free to create suites of suites and so on, there is no limit to the levels of hierarchy you can create. In all cases, the innermost elements (the *leaf nodes*) are the individual tests, which come from your test methods. Each test is represented by an icon, which represents its current state. The meanings of these icons are summarized in table 7.2.

Table 7.2 The test tree keeps track of the state of all your tests.

Icon	Description
	Test Error
	Test Failed
	Test in Progress (animated)
	Test Passed
	Test Paused
	Test Terminated
	Test Not Run

Navigating through the test tree

As with other tool windows, the **Collapse All** and **Expand All** icons control the appearance of the test tree. Expanding all the entries lets you get to all the tests, whereas collapsing them limits the list to your top-level test cases or suites. These options are unavailable if only a single test case is involved, because there is only one level of hierarchy to deal with. Otherwise, you can use the tree controls to expand and contract individual nodes of the tree as desired.

You can achieve a similar navigation through the keyboard via the left and right arrow keys. Pressing the left arrow collapses the current node, and the right arrow expands it. You can visit each node in the tree by continually pressing the right arrow key until you've traversed all the entries. The up and down arrows similarly allow you to move between the individual tests, test cases, and test suites.

7.4.2 Monitoring testing progress

Once you begin testing, a message at the top of the **JUnit** window appears, showing the total number of tests being run in this session. After the tests have been run, the message indicates the number of failures (if any) and the total amount of time elapsed. All tests are run sequentially, one after the other. Tests are never run in parallel, ensuring that your tests don't interfere with each other. Keep in mind that the order in which tests are run is never guaranteed.

Tracking completion with the testing progress bar

The testing progress bar at the top of the **JUnit** window shows the percentage of tests that have been executed so far. This bar updates continuously through the testing process, as each test is completed, and represents the relative percentage of completion. The color of the bar indicates the current pass/fail status of your testing session. The bar's segments appear green if all your tests have completed successfully so far or red if any errors or failures were encountered.

This bar tracks progress across all the tests being run in this session, not just those that belong to the current test case or test suite. Also note that the test progress bar indicates the relative number of tests remaining, but not necessarily the amount of time left, because each test will take a different amount of time to complete.

Watching the currently running test

If you enable the **Track Running Test** option in the toolbar in the **JUnit** window, the test runner selects each test case as it's running, allowing you to monitor its output or runtime statistics as they're generated. When one test completes, the test runner automatically selects the next one.

7.4.3 *Managing the testing session*

IDEA lets you manage the currently running test session, just as it does when running other applications. You can stop or rerun tests if necessary. If you take no action, the test runner runs along happily on its own until all the tests have finished running.

Aborting a test in progress

You can end your testing session at any time by clicking the **Stop** button in the **JUnit** window (or pressing **Ctrl+F2**). Doing so shuts down the VM immediately, terminating any tests that are currently in progress. The icons of the tests tell you which tests completed, which were terminated, and which were never run, as shown in table 7.2. Note, however, that clicking **Stop** stops the entire testing session, not just the currently running test.

Running your tests again

You can easily rerun your testing session without having to leave the **JUnit** window. If you click the **Rerun** icon (**Ctrl+F5**), all the current tests are run again using the same settings as in the initial run. If enabled in your test configuration setup, your project is recompiled as needed before the tests are run. The new test results replace the old results unless you've locked down the current tab by selecting the **Pin Tab** option on the **Tab** context menu.

Dumping thread information to the output window

As in the debugger, while a test is running, you can ask the VM to give you some insight into thread activity. Clicking the **Dump Threads** icon in the **JUnit** window outputs the state of all your threads to the JUnit output stream. This operation doesn't affect your running tests and doesn't stop the testing process. You can view the results in the **Output** tab (along with the rest of your test output) by selecting the topmost test from the test tree.

7.4.4 *Analyzing test results*

When it's all said and done, you'll want to review the results of your tests and, if there were any failures, find out why they happened. When your tests have been run, a message at the top of the window summarizes the number of failures, if any, as well as the number of tests run.

Difference between errors and failures

As far as JUnit is concerned, encountering a runtime error or throwing an uncaught exception inside a test is enough to fail a test. IDEA, however, differentiates between these types of errors and a test method failing an assertion check. As shown in table 7.2, different icons are assigned to differentiate these two distinct conditions and highlight the errors. Errors include runtime exceptions, declared exceptions, and other problems: for instance, if a test case's class can't be found or can't execute for some reason. In figure 7.4, you see a number of failed test cases. In the **Output** window, it's easy to spot the problem—the rate returned by the fixed rate service wasn't the rate that was expected.

This distinction between errors and failures can be important when you're designing test cases. To take advantage of it, we suggest that you design your test cases such that exceptions are thrown only when a problem that prevents running of the test is encountered, and that a legitimate failure is the result of unsuccessful assertion. This strategy will allow you to more easily spot tests that can't run properly due to configuration problems or other issues rather than a true bug in your code.

Hiding the results of successful tests

Enabling the **Hide Passed Tests** option on the toolbar in the **JUnit** window alters the test tree to show only the tests that failed or encountered errors, thus allowing you to concentrate on the problems. This button is a toggle; you can toggle the

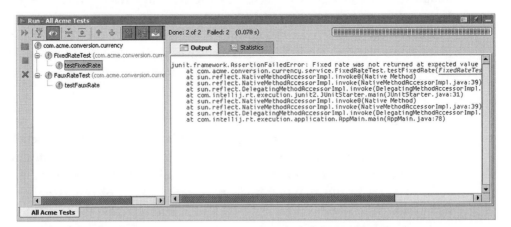

Figure 7.4 The JUnit tool window shows you the output from tests encountering both failures and errors as you select them. Failures are distinguished from errors by their icons in the test tree.

view of passed test cases on or off at any time. If a test case or suite contained no failing tests, it's hidden as well.

Navigating through the failed tests

Doubtless you'll encounter failed tests. Using the **Previous** and **Next Failure** arrows (or **Ctrl+Alt+Up** and **Ctrl+Alt+Down**, respectively) you can easily navigate through these failures. Each time you move forward or backward through the list, the next failed test is selected in the test tree. To automatically select the first failure upon completion of your tests, enable the **Select First Failed Test** option from the **JUnit** window's toolbar. You may also determine your starting point by clicking any test in the tree.

Reviewing test cases

In order to learn why a test failed, you need to understand the steps it was taking by reviewing the source code behind it. Double-clicking any test case in the tree (failed or not) takes you straight to that test's source code in the editor window. By backtracking into the source code behind the test as you review the test output messages, you should be able to spot the problem.

> **TIP**   Don't overlook the possibility that your bug might be in the test itself, rather than in the code you're testing!

Similarly, you can right-click a test in the tree and select either the **Jump to Source (F4)** or **Show Source (Ctrl+Enter)** option to review the test's source code. The difference between the two options is that **Jump to Source** moves your focus to the editor window, while **Show Source** leaves you in the **JUnit** window. You can also use the **Autoscroll to Source** toolbar button to keep the source window matching the current selection in the **JUnit** tool window.

Rerunning failed tests

You also have the option of running an individual test again by right-clicking its entry in the test tree and selecting the appropriate run option. Suites and test cases can also be run this way and will execute all the tests below them as well. If you run a test in this manner, it clears the current set of results unless you've locked down the results tab by right-clicking it and selecting the **Pin Tab** option.

Unfortunately, you're limited to running individual tests, test cases, or suites. It isn't possible to run ad hoc collections of tests (for example, all the failing tests) without manually defining a test suite using the JUnit API.

Examining test error messages and output

In the **Output** tab of the **JUnit** window, you can examine the runtime output generated by each test. This includes any output sent to the standard output stream as well as standard error (which is displayed in red text). If any exceptions were thrown, or if a test failed an assertion, this output is displayed here as well. This tab is also active while the tests are running, allowing you to monitor your tests' progress. If you have a stack trace in your test's output, any reachable source code reference is hot-linked to your editor, allowing you to quickly view or edit the source code. In the case of an assertion failure where a message was specified in the test, this message is shown along with a stack trace.

IDEA conveniently isolates each test's output. Clicking an individual test in the tree shows only the output stemming from the selected test. As you might expect, selecting any node in the test hierarchy includes the output of all the tests below it.

Tracking the time and memory usage of each test

The **Statistics** tab in the **JUnit** window shows how much time it took to run each test case and how much memory was consumed during its run. You can view test statistics summarized up to the suite or test case level by selecting the appropriate level of hierarchy in the test case tree. Here's what the columns mean:

- **Time elapsed**—The number of seconds it took to run this test.
- **Usage Delta**—The amount of memory apparently consumed during this test.
- **Usage Before**—The amount of memory in use at the start of the test.
- **Usage After**—The amount of memory in use after the test has been completed.
- **Results**—A summary of test results. For individual tests, this column shows a pass or fail; but for suites and test cases, it shows the number of passed and failed tests.

Take these statistics with a grain of salt—the timing and memory usage data are collected only to give you an approximate gauge of test case performance. Many things can affect the accuracy of this data; for example, if the garbage collector runs during a test case execution, the amount of memory shown in the statistics is wrong. Nevertheless, the **Statistics** view is a good way to keep an eye on the general state of things, as shown in figure 7.5. For example, if your unit tests now take twice as long, you may want to investigate. Perhaps there are just more tests than before, but a recent change may have drastically affected system performance.

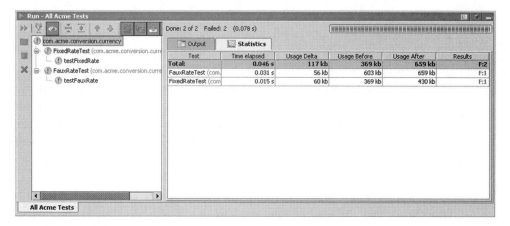

Figure 7.5 **The Statistics tabs can show you how much memory was consumed by each test as well as how long it took to run each one.**

Running tests with other test runners

The test runner built into IDEA is powerful and flexible. However, if you're nostalgic, you can use the classic test runners included with the JUnit framework. (Note, however, that you'll lose many of IDEA's JUnit integration features.) To do so, add a `main()` method, as shown in the following code, and run the class as a normal Run/Debug configuration target instead of a JUnit configuration:

```
public static void main(String[] args) {
    TestRunner testRunner = TestRunner();
    testRunner.run(StringUtilsTest.class);
}
```

Two test runners are included with the standard JUnit distribution: one in the `junit.swingui` package that creates a graphical interface, and another, text-only version in `junit.textui`. Import the appropriate version into your code. You can also use this technique to run other, third-party test runners if you wish.

The text-only version runs your JUnit tests in a standard IDEA **Run** window. A simple test summary report is shown in figure 7.6, along with a list of failures and their accompanying stack traces. Any errors are hot-linked back to the source of the failure inside your test case. In this example, you can see that a failure occurred inside the `testFixedRate()` method. Any output produced by the test cases is also displayed in this window, as are your assert failure messages.

The graphical test runner, shown in figure 7.7, is a little fancier than the text version, providing an alternate view of your test execution results. As shown, you

```
Run - Fixed Test
C:\j2sdk1.4.2_86\bin\java -Didea.launcher.port=7543 -Didea.launcher.library=C:\IntelliJ-IDEA-4.5\bin\breakgen.dll
.F
Time: 0.015
There was 1 failure:
1) testFixedRate(com.acme.conversion.currency.service.FixedRateTest)junit.framework.AssertionFailedError: Fixed r
    at com.acme.conversion.currency.service.FixedRateTest.testFixedRate(FixedRateTest.java:10)
    at sun.reflect.NativeMethodAccessorImpl.invoke0(Native Method)
    at sun.reflect.NativeMethodAccessorImpl.invoke(NativeMethodAccessorImpl.java:39)
    at sun.reflect.DelegatingMethodAccessorImpl.invoke(DelegatingMethodAccessorImpl.java:25)
    at com.acme.conversion.currency.service.FixedRateTest.main(FixedRateTest.java:15)
    at sun.reflect.NativeMethodAccessorImpl.invoke0(Native Method)
    at sun.reflect.NativeMethodAccessorImpl.invoke(NativeMethodAccessorImpl.java:39)
    at sun.reflect.DelegatingMethodAccessorImpl.invoke(DelegatingMethodAccessorImpl.java:25)
    at com.intellij.rt.execution.application.AppMain.main(AppMain.java:78)

FAILURES!!!
Tests run: 1,  Failures: 1,  Errors: 0

Process finished with exit code 0
```

Fixed Test

Figure 7.6   The textual test runner included with JUnit is simple, fast, and efficient.

can browse the list of test executions and failures as well as review summary information. All this information and more is available through IDEA's test runner, however, with better integration with the editor.

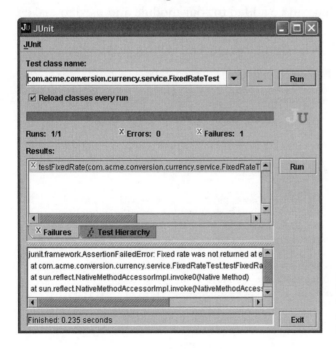

Figure 7.7
The graphical test runner included with the JUnit framework offers only basic options and no direct integration with IDEA.

Running unit tests through Ant

If your project calls JUnit through Ant, you should be able to run the same unit tests with IDEA. However, it's also possible to run your test cases through Ant directly, because it includes its own JUnit test runner (part of Ant's optional package, but included with IDEA).

When you execute test cases through Ant, the results are displayed in the Ant output window along with other build output. Any source code references present in the test output are hot-linked to the editor, but you won't get the GUI or other features of the IDEA test runner when running this way. Refer to the Ant documentation for details on creating JUnit targets in Ant.

7.5 *Improving the quality of the ACME project*

In the last chapter, you used IDEA's debugging features to identify a flaw in the ACME project. By implementing unit tests (and running them regularly), you can ensure that bugs like those don't creep in. Listing 7.3 shows a sample JUnit test, just for illustration, that can be added to your module and used to make sure the fixed-rate currency exchange service always returns the expected rate. Try adding it and running it with IDEA using the steps explained in this chapter.

> **Listing 7.3 JUnit test case that ensures `FixedRateCurrencyExchangeService` returns the correct rate**

```
package com.acme.conversion.currency.service;

import junit.framework.TestCase;

public class FixedRateTest extends TestCase {
    /**
     * To test the fixed rate, we need to do the following:
     * 1) Get an instance of the FixedRateCurrencyExchangeService
     * 2) From it, request its rate
     * 3) Compare that rate with the expected value, which is 1.5
     */
    public void testFixedRate() {
        FixedRateCurrencyExchangeService service =
            new FixedRateCurrencyExchangeService();

        assertEquals("Fixed rate was not returned at " +
            "expected value",
            1.5d, service.getRate(), 0.01d);
    }
}
```

7.6 *Summary*

IDEA has very close and natural support for JUnit, a technology for automated unit testing that's quickly and pervasively being adopted by the industry. Automated unit testing is a common-sense practice to ensure software quality, and it's a cornerstone practice that underpins the agile software development movement and the goal of continuous integration. Continuous integration invites many changes early and often. Unit testing with IDEA and its JUnit support provides the easiest means for you to write, manage, and run these unit tests, and to interpret the results of their output so that bugs are identified and fixed. As an application moves forward, this is the easiest way to keep abreast of continual changes.

Using version control

8

All real-world development projects rely on a version control system to keep track of source code changes. Using a version control system ensures that you can always back out ill-conceived changes, maintain different sets of revisions between customers, and prevent developers from overwriting each other's changes. If you've been developing professionally for any length of time, you're no doubt familiar with using a version control system to manage your source tree. IDEA has built-in support for a number of different version control systems, allowing you to integrate source management seamlessly into your development process. From within IDEA, you can check out projects, commit changes, view differences, and perform other common tasks. The version control system is even tied in with the refactoring process; as you rename classes or packages, the source code repository is likewise updated.

Probably the most popular version control system is the Concurrent Versioning System (CVS), an open source product used by millions of developers for both open source and commercial products. It has been available for a long time, and for most platforms. Although it isn't as powerful as some of the commercial products, it's more than adequate for most projects and has the advantages of simplicity and low cost going for it. This chapter will focus primarily on using CVS for version control, but the principals and procedures discussed apply equally, with few differences, to the other version control systems supported by IDEA.

8.1 Configuring your project for version control

Still using command-line CVS alongside IDEA? We've known many a WinCVS user who has been hesitant to switch over to using their IDE as their version control client. Why bother? *Convenience*. In IDEA, CVS support is seamless: When you create a new file or rename a class, the change is ready to commit into the repository. You can review your changes and commit your files with just a few clicks, without leaving the IDE. We think you'll find it well worth investigating.

> **TIP**   This chapter touches on some basics of version control, but for a more in-depth look at the main concepts, specific commands, and common terminology relating to the CVS system, visit the CVS documentation at http://www.cvshome.org.

8.1.1 Understanding version control basics

If you've never used a version control system before, it's easy to get tripped up by the concept. The full details of using the various version control systems supported by IDEA are too extensive for our discussion, but this section will introduce you to the basic concepts required for a fundamental understanding. If you're new to the idea of version control, we encourage you to explore it further: It's a critical component of any professional software development project.

Version control systems are designed to manage your project's source code to provide an accurate accounting of all the changes made to it. Using this information, the version control system lets you revisit older revisions of your code and analyze the differences between them. Doing so ensures that you can reverse any changes that turn out to be bad ideas and retrieve any code you may lose to file deletion. Most systems also allow you to maintain multiple concurrent versions of a project that diverge at a common version in the past. This is known as *branching* the code. You might do this to create a new version of the software with additional features that you don't want to be included in the main distribution. A summary of some of the version control terminology you'll encounter is shown in table 8.1.

Table 8.1 A brief glossary of version control terminology

Term	Meaning
Repository	The centralized location where all the master copies of your project's files are kept, along with their revision histories.
Working directory	The developer's local copy of the source code stored in the repository.
Check out	How you obtain a local copy of your project's files from the repository in order to make your changes. Each member of the project checks out their own copy of the project into their own working directory.
Check in	The process of sending any modified project files back to the repository. Checking in your changes is also known as *committing* your files.
Revision	A snapshot of your file that is created each time you check in your changes. This lets you return to older versions of the file if necessary.
Update	How you synchronize your copy of the project files with the most recent versions in the repository, ensuring that you pick up any changes checked in by other members of the team.
Roll back	To Revert a file back to an earlier revision of itself.

All of your source code is stored in a central location called a *repository*. This is usually located on a central server, and it holds not only the source code itself but a database of all the changes made to it, including who made them and when. The source code repository is usually backed up on a regular basis.

When developers want to work on a source file, they must first check it out from the repository. The developers' local copy is known as their *working directory*.

Depending on your version control software, only one developer at a time may be allowed to work on any particular file. Either way, your version control system makes sure that no developer can accidentally overwrite changes made by another developer. When developers are done with their changes, they commit them to the repository, and the version control system increments the version number of that file. If they decide they don't want to keep the changes, they can throw them away.

The centralized management and historical record keeping offered by a version control system let you tinker with a working program without fear of doing irreparable harm to it. Even if you commit a change that you later regret, you can always back out the change by rolling back to a previous revision level. When you're working with a team of developers, a version control system provides a safety net to ensure that no changes are lost as changes come, builds are made, and software is released. A version control system is an essential ingredient in managing a successful project of any complexity.

8.1.2 *Enabling version control support in IDEA*

Aside from a few global values, version control is configured on a project-by-project basis, allowing you to specify different settings for each project or to turn off version control on projects where it isn't required. This means you can use SourceSafe for one project and CVS for another. By default, new projects have version control support disabled unless you've changed your default project properties. To enable it, bring up the **Settings** dialog and select the **Version Control** option. In this panel, you can specify the type of version control system you're using for the current project and configure its options, as shown for CVS in figure 8.1. Using the **Template Project** settings described in chapter 4, you can configure a default set of version control system options for all new projects.

IDEA 5   IDEA 5.0 can now handle situations in which one of your project's modules uses a different type of version control system than the project itself. Under the project's **Paths** settings, select the module in question and then its **Version Control** tab. Here you can use the project's version control settings (the default) or specify one of the other version control systems supported by IDEA.

Although the interfaces shown in this chapter may look slightly different in IDEA 5.0, the general functionality is the same.

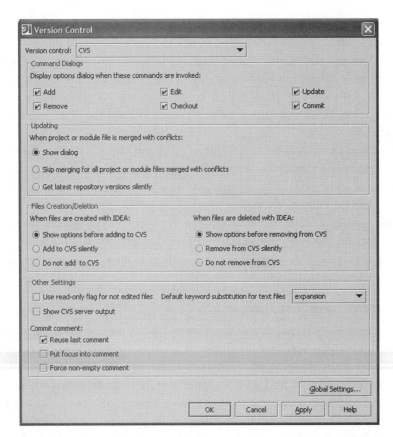

Figure 8.1 This is the version control configuration panel with CVS selected as the version control system of choice. The options change as the version control system changes, because each supports its own set of options.

Select the version control system you're using from the **Version control** drop-down list in the **Version Control** dialog. Each version control system has its own configuration settings. IDEA also understands that some of you are comfortable using your existing version control client and aren't ready to change. Nothing in IDEA requires you to use its version control system integration features; it will happily run outside of your client. Just disable integration in the **Version Control** settings panel and use your client normally. IDEA supports the following version control systems:

- CVS, an open source version control system
- Visual SourceSafe, from Microsoft

- StarTeam, from Borland
- Perforce (implemented as a plugin)
- Various other systems, through third-party plugins

IDEA 5 IDEA has always featured some level of support for Perforce, and plugins were available, but now native support is included as part of IDEA version 5.0. As with other systems, support is largely transparent, with the exception of the Perforce-specific options configured through the **Version Control** settings panel. These options allow you to specify the configuration settings necessary to connect to your Perforce server, and how you would like to enable automatic checkouts, adds, and so forth. This settings panel also lets you switch from using the native Perforce API to direct calls to the external Perforce executable (which may be necessary if you aren't running Windows).

Also now supported by IDEA is Subversion, the popular open source replacement to CVS. Subversion is quickly gaining popularity in the development community. If you're checking out a project for the first time, you need to know the URL for accessing your Subversion repository. IDEA supports all the popular protocols, including SVN and HTTP. Because version control in IDEA works largely the same regardless of which system you're using, the only other new element is the Subversion-specific version control settings. These are displayed when you select Subversion as your project's version control system.

8.1.3 *Configuring IDEA to use CVS*

IDEA includes integrated support for CVS, so no external client is required. CVS configuration information is stored both globally (for settings such as your CVS repositories and passwords) and on a per-project basis.

Understanding command dialog options

The checkboxes at the top of the **Version Control** panel give you the option of allowing IDEA to prompt you for additional arguments to CVS each time you perform various actions. For each action, a checkbox indicates that IDEA will present you with an option dialog with options specific to the type of action you're requesting. If these options are disabled, IDEA uses the default or the previously used options for each command.

For example, if you enable the command dialog option for the Commit action, IDEA will ask you to provide explanatory text for each set of changes you commit to the repository; this information is stored in CVS history. It's always a good idea to briefly explain the purpose behind the change and include additional information such as a bug number reference or customer change request. Doing so helps future developers (and maybe even yourself) understand the intent of the change. If you deselect the **Commit** check box, IDEA assumes you have nothing to say and doesn't ask you for comments or other options with your check-ins. This option is overridden by the **Force non-empty comment** option. If this is selected, IDEA will prompt for a commit comment if the most recent one was empty.

Configuring file creation and deletion options

The file creation and deletion options in the **Version Control** panel determine how IDEA deals with files you create or delete as you're working on your project. Using these options, it's possible to have IDEA automatically make the necessary calls to CVS when you rename, move, or delete files in IDEA. This is true for both explicit actions you perform (such as creating a new class) and side effects of refactoring or other operations.

There are three possible selections for both addition and deletion: You can have IDEA prompt you (with options, including the ability to cancel the operation), perform the operation silently without asking, or make no changes, in which case you have to go back and issue the appropriate CVS commands manually. These options differ from the command dialog options already discussed in that the command dialog options apply only to those cases where you explicitly invoke a CVS command, such as Add or Remove, on a file. Remember that until you commit your changes, the files aren't added or removed from the repository.

Working with other settings

The option **Use read-only flag for non edited files** in the **Version Control** panel forces all files to be checked out from the server as read only, unless you've already modified them. IDEA sets nonmodified files to read-only after each checkout, update, or commit.

The option **Show** CVS **server output** is primarily used for debugging; it logs all communications with the CVS server, giving you more information about what is going on. The output appears in the CVS message window.

Using comment commit options

Several options at the bottom of the in the **Version Control** panel control how IDEA handles comments for commit operations, assuming you've enabled the command dialog option for the Commit action as described earlier. The **Reuse**

last comment option remembers your previous commit comment and makes it the default for subsequent commits. You can always override the comment, of course—IDEA even selects the comment, allowing you to easily type over it. The option **Put focus into comment** places the cursor inside the comment box each time comments are requested, saving you the trouble of doing it yourself. The third option, **Force non-empty comment**, warns you with a confirmation dialog if you attempt to check in a file without comments attached.

Setting the default keyword substitution mode

The **Default keyword substitution for text files** option in the in the **Version Control** panel is designed for advanced CVS users. It controls how CVS handles different types of files that are checked in to the repository. Here are the choices:

- **Binary**—Corresponds to the command-line option -kb
- **Compression**—Corresponds to the command-line option -kk
- **Expansion**—Corresponds to the command-line option -kkv
- **Expansion locker**—Corresponds to the command-line option -kkvl
- **Replacement**—Corresponds to the command-line option -kv
- **No substitution**—Corresponds to the command-line option -ko

If you aren't familiar with keyword substitution in CVS, you probably won't need to touch this option.

Configuring your project to use a CVS repository

IDEA maintains a list of CVS *Roots*, which are references to configured CVS repository connections. Before you can enjoy the benefits of CVS integration in IDEA, you must configure a CVS **Root** entry that corresponds to your CVS repository account. When you specify CVS as the version control system for your current project, the CVS menu becomes available on the main menu bar and its **Configure** CVS **Roots** command is enabled. This command is the principal way to maintain your list of CVS Roots (although, like many of IDEA's configuration panels, you can often reach it in the middle of an operation and configure it on the fly).

IDEA 5 In IDEA 5.0, the specific version control system menu (such as CVS) has been moved. On the main menu bar is a general **Version Control** menu, and the selected version control system is shown as a submenu.

If your project is already associated with a CVS repository—for example, if you've been using the CVS command line or GUI interface to manage version control for an existing project—configuring your project for CVS integration should be as easy as enabling CVS integration in the **Version Control** configuration panel. IDEA can read the CVS configuration files stored in your project's path and use that information to connect with the appropriate CVS repository.

If you're configuring a new, empty IDEA project to work on an existing code base in a CVS repository, you can use the **File | Check Out from** CVS command to perform the initial checkout of the source files to your local working directory. Conversely, if you have a code base on your local file system that has not yet been put into the CVS repository for version control, you can use the **File | Import into** CVS command to import it. The first step in both of these processes is to select the CVS Root to which the operation applies (or add and configure it, if it doesn't exist on IDEA's CVS Roots list yet), as shown in figure 8.2.

The CVS Root includes the repository path and the connection method. If the connection method is *local,* then the repository path is the only information

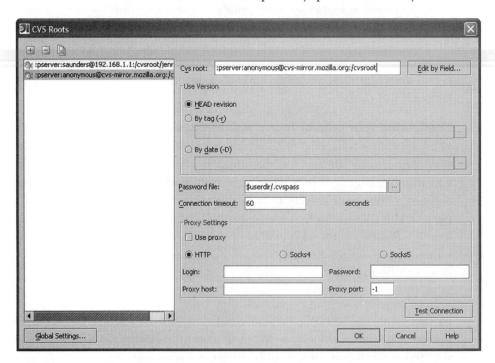

Figure 8.2   The CVS Roots window lets you configure references to all the CVS repositories you work with.

required (however, an external CVS client must be installed); in every other case, the method refers to a remote repository, and you need to specify the host, port (if not the default CVS port), and username in order to connect. If you know the CVS Root for your repository, you may enter it directly in the field provided. Click the **Edit by Field** button to enter the various component parts of the CVS Root individually. IDEA will build the CVS Root for you.

To check out a specific branch of the tree, you may specify it in the entry. Otherwise, select the **HEAD revision** option to check out the latest version. The version information is stored in the repository reference, allowing you to define multiple references of the same repository with different revisions. Details on how IDEA handles branching and concurrent versions will be presented later in this chapter.

Depending on the type of authentication used by your CVS repository, you'll have several different possible sets of security options. For example, if you're using the pserver style of authentication (as shown in the example in figure 8.2), you're asked to enter your password when you first attempt to connect to the server. The option **Password file** specifies the path to the file in which IDEA stores a copy of the password you use to access the CVS server. By caching a copy of your password (it's stored in an encrypted format), IDEA avoids having to ask you to enter it each time you access files under source code control. This authentication mechanism is somewhat simplistic, however, so most companies are moving away from it in favor of the secure shell protocol (SSH). This is common when working across the Internet, because the normal CVS communications mechanism is unencrypted.

Testing your configuration settings

When you think your CVS Root is configured properly, click the **Test Connection** button in the CVS **Roots** window to be sure. IDEA will attempt to connect to the currently selected CVS repository using the configuration and authentication settings you've specified and verify that it's able to communicate successfully with the server. If it can't, it will try to give you an idea of what the problem is, be it a bad password or invalid server name. You should always verify your settings before wrapping up your CVS configuration.

Configuring global properties

You can tweak additional CVS settings by clicking the **Global Settings** button in the **Version Control** panel to open the dialog shown in figure 8.3. In addition to letting you enter the location for storing your password and the connection timeout, it provides two additional important options. The first option, **Use UTF-8**

Figure 8.3
A few options that globally affect the operation of CVS can be edited here.

encoding, is most useful to developers whose CVS repository uses this style of encoding. The next option, **Use gzip compression**, is handy for users operating over slow connections such as dialup or VPN. It uses the gzip compression scheme to compress the stream of data going to and from the CVS server to improve the speed of the connection. Unless you have a really old, slow computer, you should enable this option for best performance.

8.1.4 *Configuring other types of version control systems*

IDEA includes support for a number of different commercial version control systems. This chapter focuses on CVS, but the concept and the ideas behind many of the examples apply equally to these other systems. Although each system has differences in features, capabilities, and practices, the core integration with IDEA is essentially the same.

Setting up Visual SourceSafe integration

The basic configuration settings for Visual SourceSafe (VSS) are shown in figure 8.4. To use IDEA with VSS, you must have installed the VSS client on your machine. Specify the path to the client in the appropriate field. Your configuration file may be on your local machine or shared through a network server. If it's stored remotely, you may enter the UNC path. Once you've specified your client and configuration file settings, enter your VSS username and password into the fields provided. You should enter the same access information here that you would normally use in the VSS client.

Next, create a working directory entry for each VSS project you'll be working with. Note that you only need to enter the VSS projects for the current IDEA project here; remember that IDEA has separate version control support settings for each IDEA project. Specify the VSS directory relative to the repository root, which is represented by a dollar sign. For each entry, specify the full path to your local working directory, which should be part of the current IDEA project. The general configuration settings are shown in figure 8.4.

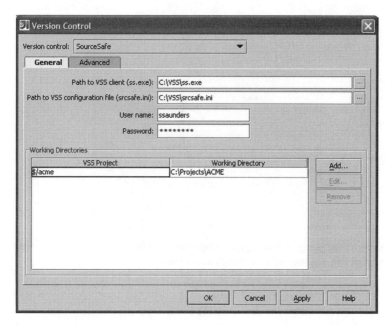

Figure 8.4   These are the general version control configuration settings for Visual SourceSafe.

VSS has a number of additional settings that you can specify by clicking the **Advanced** tab of the **Version Control** settings dialog. The first group of checkboxes let you specify whether you see an options dialog when performing various VCS commands, such as checking in, checking out, adding new files, and so on. The specific options appearing in the options dialog are different for each action. You should leave these checkboxes enabled until you've seen the options dialogs and you're satisfied with their default options. The other controls on the **Advanced** tab let you tweak the way IDEA handles comments in VSS; they're similar to the equivalent CVS options described earlier.

Setting up StarTeam integration

To use StarTeam with IDEA, you need to obtain a copy of the starteam-sdk.jar file; it's included with the StarTeam SDK, available through www.borland.com/starteam. This library lets IDEA communicate with your StarTeam database and integrate it with IDEA's version control features. Copy the library from the SDK's lib folder into the lib folder under your IDEA installation. You must restart IDEA for it to find the library; next time, you'll be able to specify your StarTeam settings as shown in figure 8.5.

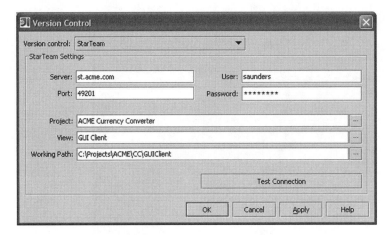

Figure 8.5   The StarTeam configuration panel contains the details necessary to connect and interact with the StarTeam server.

Because StarTeam doesn't have the equivalent concept of a CVS Root, you enter the properties used to connect to the StarTeam server on the **Version Control** configuration panel. These include server, port, username, and password. Select a project, view, and working directory either by typing them in or by using the ellipsis buttons to browse the list of available options for each. Use the **Test Connection** button to verify that your settings are correct and that IDEA can connect with the StarTeam server.

Although the StarTeam integration plugin is an excellent tool, some features of StarTeam aren't handled within the plugin. These advanced features must be managed with the dedicated StarTeam client application.

Using version control system plugins

As with other areas of the product, IDEA has designed a modular system that lets third-party developers extend the functionality of IDEA through plugins. One possible use of these plugins is to provide integrated support for other version control systems. You can check with your VCS vendor and in the IDEA Plugin Manager for information on any plugins that support your VCS of choice. Once they're installed, you should be able to select and configure your settings with the general **IDE Settings** window, either on the **Version Control** configuration panel or on a new configuration panel added by the plugin.

8.2 Working with files under CVS

Once you've enabled CVS support, a new CVS menu is added to the main menu and the context menu of the editor and **Project** browser windows. You'll use the CVS client in the examples for the remainder of the chapter. It's the most widely used version control system, and it's applicable for every platform. Each type of version control system may support slightly different options, but their operation is more or less the same.

8.2.1 Retrieving files from the repository

After you enable CVS support, IDEA lets you create new modules from CVS, check out existing ones, or automatically detect and configure IDEA to use an existing working directory.

Browsing the contents of your repository

You can use the **File | Browse CVS Repository** command to explore the contents of a CVS repository. You're prompted to select your repository from among the CVS Roots you've configured, and you're presented with a browser tool window like the one shown in figure 8.6. You can expand the nodes of the tree to explore all the files in the repository. To view any file, double-click it; it will be loaded into the editor. The editor tab is locked, because you're accessing a read-only view of the file. You can also access an annotated view of the source code or review the revision history of any file, both of which will be discussed later in this chapter. To check out the file or an entire folder, right-click the item in question and select the **Check Out** item from the context menu; or, use the **Checkout** command described next.

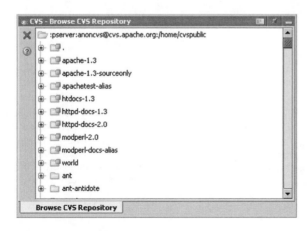

Figure 8.6
The Browse CVS Repository window

TIP   A folder with the little box icon denotes a CVS directory that has been designated as an official *module* (or *project*) by the CVS administrator. These folders are supposed to represent actual projects, as opposed to directories for organizational purposes. In practice, however, many administrators ignore this fact. IDEA (like other CVS clients) also ignores the distinction—you can check out any folder you like.

Checking out a module from the repository

If you want to work on source code that already exists in the repository, you can do so by using the **File | Check Out from** CVS command. It launches the checkout wizard, which walks you through these steps to check out a local copy of the project:

1. Select a CVS repository from the list of CVS Roots you've already configured (or configure a new CVS Root on the fly).

2. Browse the selected repository, and choose the elements to be checked out.

3. Select the local directory where the working copy of the repository files should be created.

4. Confirm your selection, and begin the checkout process.

If you select a single element to check out, the final step (shown in figure 8.7) of the process gives you the option of including the module name as part of the local project path. This is handy for keeping modules separate when you're working on multiple modules stored on the same repository.

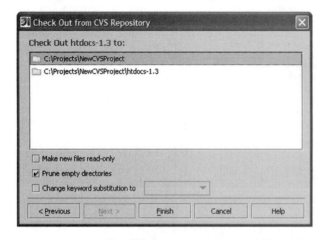

Figure 8.7
If you select a single module to be checked out from a CVS repository, IDEA gives you the option of making that module's name part of the working directory's path.

TIP   The global CVS options found on the **File** menu (such as **Check Out from** CVS) are accessible even when no project is open in IDEA. This is useful when your project definition file is stored in CVS and shared among your development team. You can start IDEA, check out the project (including the project file), and then open the IDEA project you've just checked out.

IDEA doesn't automatically open the project you just checked out into IDEA, even if it contains an IDEA project file. You still need to choose the **File | Open Project** command, browse to the IPR file, and open it. If you've checked out a CVS module for which no IDEA project exists, you must set up a new IDEA project as described in chapter 4 and enable CVS integration for the project. As described later, IDEA automatically retrieves CVS configuration information regarding the project from the working directory created during checkout.

TIP   You can hold down the **Ctrl** key to select or deselect individual files and folders from the repository during the checkout process, even those from different folders.

Creating a new CVS module from scratch

IDEA lets you add a new module to your repository, provided you have permission to do so from the CVS administrator. To do so, select the **File | Import into** CVS command to launch the import wizard. The wizard steps you through the process of importing (copying) a folder from your local file system into the CVS repository, summarized here:

1   Select the directory on the CVS server where your folder should be imported. You can select the repository itself to create a new folder at the root level, if appropriate.

2   Select a local directory to import into the repository. All files beneath the selected folder will be imported into CVS. You also have an opportunity to exclude/include specific files from the import by clicking the plus and minus icons and selecting the files.

3   Select the keyword expansion mode to use for each extension. Refer back to the beginning of this chapter for an explanation of the keyword expansion settings, or select the defaults (which are appropriate for most situations).

4   Specify the name of the new module and import settings, and begin the import process.

In the final step, shown in figure 8.8, specify these import settings:

- **Name in repository** specifies the name of the new module in the CVS repository and identifies the project.

- **Vendor** is an arbitrary tag used to describe the owner of the code being imported (it follows standard CVS tag naming requirements: no spaces, must begin with a letter, and so forth). A company name is a typical example.

- **Release tag** is a tag used to identify the initial version of all of the files being checked in. By convention, most people use `init` or `start` for the first tag name.

- **Log message** is a message associated with the import, synonymous with the message you include when committing changes to a repository.

The option **Checkout after import** is convenient if you want to begin using the newly created CVS module immediately. When this option is enabled, IDEA automatically converts your import directory into a working directory by performing a checkout of the new module immediately. If the directory you imported isn't part of the current project, you still need to set up a new project as explained in the previous section. The option to **Make checked out files read-only** locks all the files initially, if you prefer to use CVS in that fashion.

> **TIP** When you're importing new files into CVS, you generally shouldn't import files that can be regenerated by the build process, such as class files, build logs, and so forth. To make sure these aren't imported, delete them before beginning the import process.

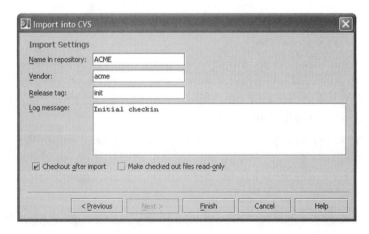

Figure 8.8
The final step in importing a local code base into CVS involves setting a few CVS module configuration options.

Using an existing working directory

Under CVS, each directory in your local working directory (including the root folder) contains a special directory named CVS that holds files used by the CVS client to keep track of state information such as the version numbers of the files you've checked out, files you've added, and the address of the repository they came from. If you have an existing working directory that is in your IDEA project's source path, and you've enabled CVS for your project, IDEA autodetects these CVS control folders and begins using version control for those files immediately. No additional configuration is required.

8.2.2 *Working with files under CVS control*

Of course, life isn't all updates and bug fixes. Sometimes you add new code to the system or remove old classes from the source tree. This is a nice aspect of utilizing IDEA's integrated version control system support over a stand-alone client, especially when you consider IDEA's refactoring capabilities.

Adding new files and directories

IDEA automatically attempts to add new files and directories that you create from within the editor to the CVS repository. If you're creating a new file and don't wish to add it to the repository, click **Cancel** when prompted (unless you've turned off dialogs for the **Add** command). If the file was created outside of IDEA, you must add it manually by right-clicking the file (you can select several files if you wish) and selecting **CVS | Add File**. Newly added files aren't committed immediately; they remain in limbo until you're ready to commit other changes. That's why CVS refers to adding a file as *scheduling a file for addition*. Directories, on the other hand, are added to the repository immediately under CVS.

> **TIP** IDEA lets you perform additions and deletions of an entire folder structure, recursively. Select a folder to add or delete, and it, along with all of its children, will be added to or deleted from the repository. This is a big time saver for importing new code into an existing module. If you're creating a new CVS module, however, the **Import into** CVS command is a better fit because it lets you create a new directory and add files in a single step.

Removing a file from the repository

You can remove files from the repository when they're no longer needed. You can also delete files that you've added to the repository but not yet committed. If you change your mind about a file before committing it, you can delete the file, and it will be as if it never existed: Right-click the file, and select the **Delete** option. In the case of Java files, you can use the **Refactor | Safe Delete** option, as discussed in chapter 9, to verify that you're removing an unused class. Upon issuing the delete request, IDEA asks if you wish to delete the file from CVS as well, as shown in figure 8.9. If you select the option to no longer show the dialog, the option you select (**Delete** or **Don't Delete**) becomes the default behavior for IDEA. You can later reset this setting in the CVS configuration panel.

The file is deleted from your working directory and from CVS as well if requested. Just like when you add a file, the file isn't removed from the repository until you commit your changes. You can un-remove the file using IDEA's rollback feature, discussed later in this chapter. When you commit your removals, the file is removed from the repository.

Of course, files in CVS are never really deleted—they're moved into a hidden archive folder called *Attic* and marked as deleted in the latest version. That way, older revisions of the source tree still have access to them. Note, however, that CVS doesn't let you delete directories; you're stuck with them. You can make them disappear from your workspace by using the **Prune Empty Directories** option when checking out your project from CVS.

Renaming, moving, and copying files

First the bad news: CVS doesn't provide rename or move facilities. If you're using the command-line client, you have to manually copy the file to its new location or name, add the new file to CVS, and remove the old file from CVS. Luckily, integration of CVS with IDEA's refactoring features relieves you from the underlying machinations. By using, for example, the **Refactor | Rename** refactoring, IDEA executes any and all CVS operations required to perform the requested refactoring. You can even use the **Undo** command to revert this change. When you commit your project, the removal and addition are recorded. If you've renamed a Java class (which results in the renaming of a Java file), IDEA's refactoring facility automatically corrects all the code references for you as well. The refactoring commands **Move** and **Copy** work the same way.

Figure 8.9
IDEA automatically deletes files from CVS, as well as the file system.

WARNING Unfortunately, as a side effect of the way CVS tracks changes, a file's version number and past history don't travel with it when it's moved or renamed. This is a fact of life with CVS. You must go back to the original filename to find any historical record before the changeover.

Keeping your files up to date

Working directories need to be kept synchronized with the latest changes in the central repository in order to avoid conflicts when you check in your personal work. Very often, this update is the first action taken in the morning by developers before they work on the code base. In IDEA, you can perform an update by selecting **CVS | Update Project** (or **Ctrl+T**) to update all the files in the project. Alternatively, select **CVS | Update** from a file's context menu to update the currently opened file in the editor, or choose the same command from an element on the **Project** tool window to update that selected hierarchy.

Updating files in an existing working directory is similar to performing your initial checkout, but you don't need to specify a CVS Root because IDEA determines it through the CVS control files present in your working directory. You'll see an options panel as shown in figure 8.10. For files, you can disable the dialog for update actions.

In this panel, you specify options related to how IDEA should handle the update. These are the familiar command-line CVS options passed to the CVS

Figure 8.10
When you perform a CVS update within IDEA, several options are configurable.

server. Next to each option is the corresponding command-line option. Here's a brief description of the options:

- **Merge with** merges the files in your working directory with those from a particular revision or branch.

- **By tag** and **By date** let you update your files to a particular tag or date. These options are mutually exclusive. Click the **Browse** button next to the branch option to select from a list of existing branches and tags. The **Default** option checks out the latest version of files (sometimes called the *trunk* or the *main line*).

- **Reset sticky data** returns a file to its default behavior of dealing with the trunk. In CVS, when you check out a particular version or branch of a file, this revision level is *sticky*, meaning it applies to all future commands (commits, updates, and so forth) as well.

- **Prune empty directories**, if enabled, removes from your working directory any directories that are present in the CVS module but don't contain any files.

- **Create new directories** creates directories in the CVS module that are missing from your working directory.

- **Clean copy** throws out any changes that you've made and reverts all the files in the update to their latest repository version.

- **Change keyword substitution** lets you change how CVS keyword expansion works.

The final option, **Do not show this dialog in the future**, is an IDEA option. It corresponds to the option in the **Version Control** configuration panel that lets you disable the dialog for update actions. If you disable it on this panel, you must go back to the **Version Control** configuration panel to turn it back on. Click **OK** to begin the update. Once it's complete, you'll see the results of the update in the CVS message tool window, as shown in figure 8.11.

The CVS window lists all the files affected by the update, along with summary information. You can right-click any file to load it into the editor or review its changes and history (as we'll discuss later in this chapter). The option **Group By Package** organizes files by their Java package names, giving you a more Java-centric view of the changes. The results window categorizes the modified files as follows:

- **Updated from server**—Files in your working directory that have been updated to a newer version

- **Added**—Files added to your working directory either because they were recently added to the CVS module or because you've picked up new directories not present in your working directory before the update
- **Deleted**—Files that have been removed from the repository and, consequently, your working directory
- **Modified**—Files that have been locally modified in your working directory
- **Merged**—Files that have been locally modified as well as updated on the server, and that CVS has successfully merged the changes into your local file
- **Merged with Conflicts**—Files that have been locally modified as well as updated on the server in such a way that CVS can't accurately merge the two sets of changes
- **Not in repository**—Files in your working directory that aren't under source control and that have not been explicitly added to the list of ignored files

Viewing the status of your project

You can use the **CVS | Check Project Status** command to see the files that have been added, removed, or modified by yourself and others. This view looks like the **Update** window we just discussed, but it obtains the information without modifying any of your local files (if you're familiar with CVS, this is like issuing the `cvs -nq update` command). Similarly, you can right-click a file in the project view or through the editor's context menu and select **CVS | Show Status** to review the status of just the selected file.

Figure 8.11 Output from the CVS update process is displayed in a tool window, making it easy to review for pertinent information.

8.2.3 *Committing your changes*

When you're finished making changes, you should commit them to the repository for safekeeping. Each time you commit your changes, the version control system increments the revision number.

To commit a single file, right-click, and select **CVS | Commit** to bring up the **Commit File** dialog (assuming you haven't turned it off). You're prompted for a log message, as shown in figure 8.12, which is stored in the repository's log to indicate the purpose of the changes. The option to not show this dialog in the future turns off the dialog and uses the last specified options for future commits. This is equivalent to deselecting the **Commit**

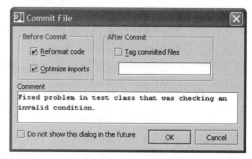

Figure 8.12 When committing a file to CVS within IDEA, you have the option of running a last-minute code reformat and import optimization.

command in the **Version Control** configuration panel we reviewed earlier. Click **OK** to commit your file. There's a chance that someone has already committed changes to this file since the last time you updated your copy, especially if you don't update often; if there is a conflict, you'll get an error message requiring you to perform an update before committing your changes.

The two options **Reformat code** and **Optimize imports** make it easy to keep your code clean and conformant. If the reformatting option is enabled, IDEA uses its code-formatting tool (**Tools | Reformat Code, Ctrl+Alt+L**) to normalize your code layout according to your current code style settings, as discussed in chapter 12. Likewise, you can optimize your list of imported packages, just as if you'd executed the **Tools | Optimize Imports (Ctrl+Alt+O)** command prior to check in.

IDEA 5 The **Reformat Code** and **Optimize Imports** commands were moved from the **Tools** menu to the **Code** menu in IDEA 5.0.

Similarly, you can commit changes to several files at once by **Ctrl**-selecting them from the project or source browser. Or, you can commit an entire directory at once; IDEA recursively commits its contents in one easy step. In most cases, however, it's simpler to use the **Commit Project** command, discussed later.

Tracking changes within your project

IDEA has a unique feature called the File View that lets you easily keep track of the files managed by source control. Select **Version Control | Show File View**, and a tool window opens that has a checkbox for each files state as managed by CVS. Select the states you're interested in, and IDEA filters the view of the project structure to show only those files. For example, to see all the modified files only, select the **Modified** option and deselect the others. The view of the project beneath the options will update with only those folders in the project that contain modified files. You can do the same for all the states managed within the version control system.

> **TIP** For CVS environments, a handy state to filter the project by is **Merged with conflicts**. Selecting this option alone shows you the files you're working on that had an update from another developer, meaning the merge couldn't be done automatically. These files always need attention, and this technique is by far the easiest way to find them.

Committing changes to your project

The previous technique is fine for committing a single file (or set of files), but more often than not you have several different changes that need to be committed. IDEA provides the **Commit Project** command to do just that. It's also a good way to see what's changed in the tree, even if you aren't yet prepared to commit your changes. Select **CVS | Commit Project** (**Ctrl+K**) to bring up a view of changes made across the project, as shown in figure 8.13.

The total number of modified files is shown in the lower-left corner of the **Commit Directory** dialog. This list shows all the files that will be affected by a commit, colored to indicate their status. The one status you may not be familiar with is *Unknown*, which indicates that a file in the working directory isn't under CVS control; this may be OK, or it may mean you forgot to add it to CVS. If you need to add it now, right-click the file and select the **Add to** CVS option. If you don't want the file to be under version control and wish to ignore its presence, right-click the file and select the **Ignore** option. This information is stored with your project. (IDEA uses the .cvsignore facility in CVS to hide these files.) Alternatively, toggle off the **Show unknown** option to hide all unknown files.

> **TIP** Want to edit your .cvsignore files in IDEA? Register .cvsignore as a file extension for text files. IDEA will help you do this the first time you double-click a .cvsignore file.

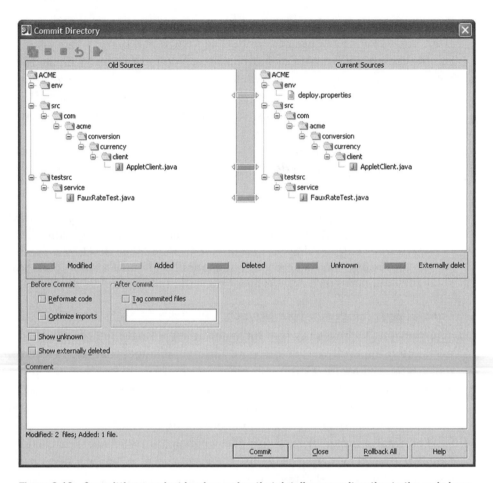

Figure 8.13 Committing a project invokes a view that details every alteration to the code base.

To commit all modified files, type your comments into the **Comment** field and click **Commit**. You can add files to and remove files from the commit by selecting them and clicking the **Include** and **Exclude** buttons in the toolbar at the top of the dialog or pressing **Insert** and **Delete**, respectively. Files that have been excluded appear ghosted and aren't committed to the repository. The modified files count changes to indicate the number of modified files that will be committed.

You can use the **Rollback Local Changes** icon in the toolbar (and the right-click context menu) to back out any changes made to the selected file since the last update. Rollback throws out all your changes, which means the file is longer be modified and disappears from the commit screen.

Files marked as externally deleted are files that are missing from your working directory but that IDEA wasn't responsible for deleting. This happens when you delete the files from outside IDEA through the command line, the file explorer, or another application. The option **Show externally deleted** lets you toggle the display of these items off and on.

Finally, the **Show Changes** command lets you view the line-by-line changes you're committing. This is discussed in the next section.

8.2.4 *Working with branches and tags*

CVS derives its name (Concurrent Versioning System) from the fact that it lets you maintain multiple simultaneous versions of your project through the uses of branches and tags. A *tag* is a symbolic name assigned to the current version of all the files in your project at a given point in time, generally a release or major milestone. From then on, you can always retrieve a copy of your project the way it was at that instant in time. A *branch* is a special type of tag that lets you fork off a separate line of changes to your code, which varies independently of the trunk. Typically, this feature is used to build minor updates to the shipping release of the project without having to include all the changes already made on the trunk.

Full instructions on using branches and tags are beyond the scope of this book, but we'll explain how IDEA lets you use them.

Creating a tag

Creating a tag is relatively straightforward: Use the **CVS | Create Tag** command to bring up the tag creation dialog. IDEA prompts for a valid CVS tag name. If you want to replace an existing tag (or review your old tags), click the **Browse** button to see the list of tags already present in the repository. An option is provided that lets you replace all existing instances of the tag, if any are present. The other option, **Switch to this tag**, updates your working directory to the specified tag.

Deleting a tag

Deleting a tag is equally straightforward: Select **CVS | Delete Tag**, choosing the tag you wish to delete from the provided list. When you delete a tag, all you're doing is removing the symbolic reference that links all the file versions under one tag name. Files aren't deleted or modified in any way when you remove a tag.

Creating a branch

Creating a branch operates almost the same as creating a tag, primarily because under CVS a branch is a special type of tag. Use **CVS | Create Branch** to bring up the branch creation dialog, which looks exactly like the tag creation dialog. As before, you have the option of switching to the branch once it's created, allowing you to begin working on that branch. It's good practice to include the word *branch* in your branch tag's name to distinguish it from regular tags.

> **TIP** You should always create a tag to identify the root of the branch you're creating. Doing so gives you an easy point of reference for viewing and merging back into the trunk the changes made along the branch.

Working on a branch

If you need to work on a branch—to fix bugs on an earlier release of your product, for example—you must update your working directory to work under that branch's context. Using the **CVS | Update Project** command, select the branch tag you want to work on from the **Use Version** option group (the second option, **By tag**). Note that CVS doesn't distinguish between branches and tags when performing an update, so both appear in the list. You can also create a separate project for the branch version, if you find you're switching between the trunk and the branch often. In this case, you can specify the branch at checkout time.

Once you check out or update your working directory against a branch, all future commits will be applied to that branch rather than the trunk. This is because of something CVS calls the *sticky* tag. Updating to a branch is a sticky operation: The branch name is automatically included as an option when committing your files to make sure all changes are applied to the branch. To go back to working on the trunk, you need to perform an update and select the **Reset sticky data** option from the **Update** dialog. Doing so removes the sticky tag from your working directory and performs all operations against the default version, which is the trunk.

Merging files between branches

In many cases, you should merge changes made on a branch back into the trunk. After all, a bug fix against an earlier version could very well apply to its descendants. You can make the change manually in both the branch and the trunk, but it's often easier and less error prone to use the CVS merge function.

You perform a merge through the **Update** dialog, either for an individual file or for the entire project. To perform a merge, select one or two early tags or branches in the **Branch Merging** options at the top of the **Commit Directory** dialog. If you select a single branch to merge against, CVS applies the differences between the latest files on the branch (the tip of the branch) and your local files. If you select two versions or branches, CVS applies the differences between those two versions to your local files. If there are conflicts, IDEA provides a handy merge tool (discussed later in this chapter) to assist in setting things straight.

8.2.5 *Viewing change history*

An important benefit of using a version control system is the ability to see changes made to a file between versions. This is often an important debugging tool, because "What's changed?" is often the first question asked when something that used to work fine suddenly doesn't.

The **CVS | Show History (Alt+H)** command reviews previous versions of the selected file. This brings up the history browser shown in figure 8.14. For each version, you can see the date it was created, the author, and any comments added when they committed the file. The columns can be sorted by clicking the headings. Throughout this section, we'll highlight the actions you can perform from the History view.

The line marked with bold font denotes the version with which you've last synchronized (updated or committed), and it isn't always the topmost version available in the repository. So, this view lets you be aware of how close or far you are from the most recent repository state.

Viewing the change history of a selection

A variation of the **Show History** command, **Show History for Selection** lets you inspect the changes made to a given selection of code over time. It combines the version history list with IDEA's diff viewer, giving you an easy way to review how previous revisions of a file affected the currently selected block of code, as shown in figure 8.15.

Version ▲	Branches	Date	Author	Commit M...	State	Tag
1.2		**30/01/05 6:46 AM**	**saunders**	**no message**	**Exp**	
1.1.1.1		21/01/05 7:22 PM	saunders	no message	Exp	init
1.1	1.1.1	02/01/05 10:44 AM	saunders	Initial revision	Exp	

Commit Message:

History for FauxRateTest.java

Figure 8.14 The History view in the CVS tool window gives an overview of all the changes made to a file since its creation.

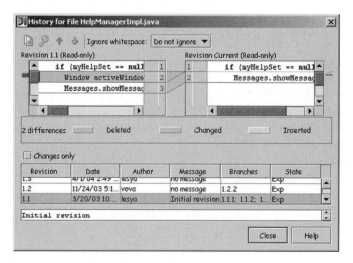

Figure 8.15   IDEA's Show History for Selection command allows you to review the changes to a given block of code over time.

Highlighting changes in the editor

As you make changes to a file under version control in the editor, change bars appear in the gutter next to the modified lines, as shown in figure 8.16. By default, areas in blue have been altered, areas in green have been inserted, and areas in grey have been deleted. If you click one of these change markers, a pop-up menu provides access to a few of the most useful CVS operations, listed in table 8.2 (you can see them in action in figure 8.16).

Changes are also indicated in the error stripe on the right-hand side of the editor, making it easy to spot them anywhere in the file, no matter what portion of it you're currently viewing. Clicking the indicator in the error stripe takes you to the change. When you commit a file, these change bars disappear, because they reflect changes made to the version last updated from the repository. You can modify the color of the change indicators in the error stripe through your **Colors & Fonts** settings.

Table 8.2 The options accessible from the change bars provide a quick and easy way to survey your changes.

Icon	Description
⬆	Go to previous change
⬇	Go to next change
🔄	Roll back changes
🔺	Show differences

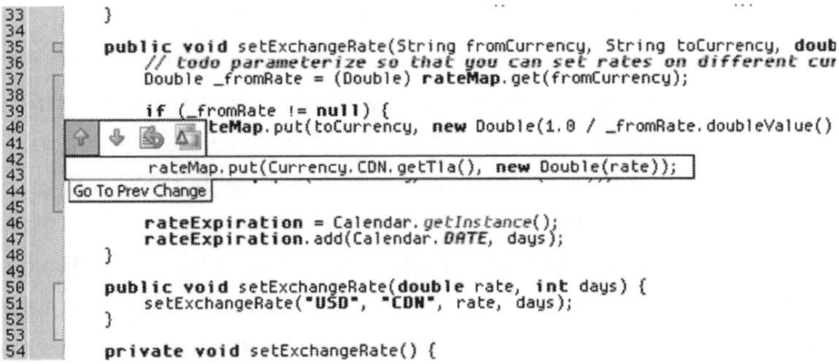

```
33        }
34
35    □   public void setExchangeRate(String fromCurrency, String toCurrency, doub
36            // todo parameterize so that you can set rates on different cur
37            Double _fromRate = (Double) rateMap.get(fromCurrency);
38
39            if (_fromRate != null) {
40    ⇧ ⬇ 🔖 ⚠  teMap.put(toCurrency, new Double(1.0 / _fromRate.doubleValue()
41
42            rateMap.put(Currency.CDN.getTla(), new Double(rate));
43
44  Go To Prev Change
45
46            rateExpiration = Calendar.getInstance();
47            rateExpiration.add(Calendar.DATE, days);
48        }
49
50        public void setExchangeRate(double rate, int days) {
51            setExchangeRate("USD", "CDN", rate, days);
52        }
53
54        private void setExchangeRate() {
```

Figure 8.16 Change bars are another way of recognizing what lines of a file have been altered.

Viewing an older revision of the file

If you want to examine an older revision of a file, double-click its entry in the **History** view. Doing so fetches the older version of the file into the editor. The name of the file also includes the version number, to prevent confusion; and the file is locked so you can't accidentally edit an older revision, believing it to be current.

Reverting a file to a previous version

You can use the version history list to revert a file back to a previous version. To do so, select the version you'd like to restore, and then click the **Get** icon in the history toolbar. The older version of the file is loaded into the editor, replacing the current contents of the file. If the file has modifications that haven't been committed yet, you're warned that those changes will be lost as the file is overwritten. When you commit the file back to the repository, it's assigned the next version number.

It's important to understand that you can't really go back to a previous version per se; rather, you can replace the current contents of the file with a copy of an older version of the file. You must re-commit the file to bring the repository up to date. Your newly committed file gets a new version number, but the contents of the file are identical to the earlier version you copied the content from. It's usually a good idea to note this in your commit message with an explanation of the rollback—something like "Reverted back to version 1.33 because the changes were causing serious performance issues."

> **TIP** If you want to throw out your local modifications, you can use the **CVS | Rollback Local Changes** command. It discards any edits since the most recent **Update** or **Commit** command.

Viewing the differences between two versions of a file

Through the **History** view, you can view the differences between the version listed and the source you're working on by selecting the version number and clicking the **Compare with Local** button in the **History** window to launch the diff tool. A *diff tool* is an application that lets you visually inspect each line that was added, removed, or modified in one file relative to another version of the file. This is commonly known as viewing *a diff*. IDEA ships with an excellent diff viewer, but you can configure your **General Settings** to use an external one if you like. Either way, you can view the difference between one version and another from many different locations within the IDEA:

- The History list
- The **Commit Project** screen
- The Project tool window's **CVS | Compare with** context menu
- The editor's **CVS | Compare with** context menu

To examine the changes between two arbitrary versions of the file, bring up the version history list, and then hold down the **Ctrl** key and select two different versions. The **Compare** button views the differences between the two selected versions. Note that you don't need to select sequential versions: IDEA can handle viewing the differences between any two versions of the file. Otherwise, the **Compare with Latest Repository Version** command, available from the CVS menu, shows you the modifications you've made to the file, compared to the latest version from the repository.

Using IDEA's diff viewer

When you request the differences between two versions, IDEA launches its diff viewer. The diff viewer features two panes: The older of the two files is shown on the left, and the newer on the right. The content of each file is shown in its respective frame, separated by a margin, which shows the line numbers for each file. You can adjust the size of the panes by left-clicking in the gutter area between them and dragging left or right. Any differences between the two versions of the files you're examining are highlighted with color-coded status indicators, as shown in figure 8.17. The colored callouts show the type of change that was made. Each change is mapped back to the appropriate line in the older file, showing you exactly how the file was affected.

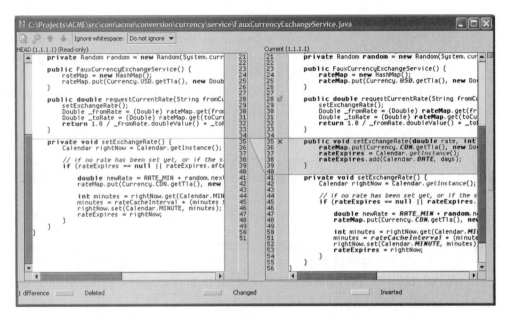

Figure 8.17 IDEA's internal diff tool is an excellent utility for reviewing file differences.

Navigating through the changes

Like the editor, the diff viewer features change marks in the right and left borders of the view that allow you to see all the changes in the file at a glance. You can click a change mark to move your cursor to that change, or you can scroll down through the file to review the changes. Scrolling between the two views is linked, making it easy to examine changes across the entire file; but for larger files, scrolling through all the changes may not be the fastest way of navigating. You can use the **Next Change** and **Previous Change** buttons on the toolbar (**F7** and **Shift+F7**) to jump from one change to the next.

The diff viewer also features its own version of the **Find** tool, which works just like the **Search | Find** command. Click the **Find** icon (or press **Ctrl+F5**), and enter your search terms. The **Find** command will search whichever panel is currently selected.

Copying over code from a previous version

To revert an entire file to an older version, you can use the **History** view to overwrite the current file with the contents of the older one, as discussed earlier. If, instead, you want to get a portion of the older version—for example, a single method—you can do so through the diff viewer. If you right-click over a change in either file and choose the **Select Change** option from the context menu, the affected code is automatically selected. By using the **Copy** icon in the difference viewer toolbar, you can copy the selected code into the clipboard for future use when you're back in the editor. You can also edit the current version of the file directly from the diff tool. Specifics of merging changes are described later in this chapter.

Ignoring whitespace

Often, minor changes or reformatting introduce new whitespace into a file. Extra whitespace won't affect the operation of the code, so IDEA provides a way to ignore these differences, allowing you to concentrate on the important changes. At the top of IDEA's diff viewer, you can control how it deals with whitespace by selecting one of these options:

- **Do not ignore**—Whitespace is important; highlight any changes.
- **Leading and trailing**—Ignore differences in whitespace if they appear at the beginning or end of the line only.
- **All**—Ignore all whitespace, wherever it occurs on the line.

Viewing the differences between files

In addition to viewing the differences between two versions of the same file, you can use the diff tool to examine the differences between two completely different files. To view the differences between any two files, select the first file from the project or source code views, and then hold down the **Ctrl** key and right-click the second file. From the context menu, select the **Compare Two Files** option to bring up the diff viewer with the first file on the left and the second on the right. This is a good way to spot differences between configuration files, output logs, DTDs, and so on.

> **TIP** Sometimes it's useful to compare two arbitrary blocks of code—say, two methods in different classes. IDEA gives you the ability to launch the diff between the current selection and the contents of your clipboard. To do so, copy the first block of code into the clipboard, make a selection in the editor, and select **Compare with Clipboard** from the context menu. The initial selection doesn't even have to come from another file within IDEA: You can copy it from another editor, your shell, or a web page.

Merging changes between versions

When you're using the diff viewer on a file that you have permission to edit, the file is editable inside the diff viewer. You can even copy and paste code from the older version, but there's an easier way to merge changes between versions.

IDEA provides a handy feature that lets you merge individual changes to the file. Alongside each change block is a chevron symbol (») for any changes or deletions or an X for any content added to the current version that wasn't present in the older one. Clicking either symbol applies its change to the current version of the file. Clicking the X removes the addition from the new version, and clicking the chevron merges in the new or modified code.

Resolving conflicts during merges

When you're working with multiple developers on the same project, conflicts may arise when one developer commits changes to a file that you're actively working on. When you attempt to commit your changes, CVS will require you to update your copy to include the most recent changes. In most cases, CVS can gracefully handle merging the changes into the modified file, but conflicts can arise in situations where both sets of changes affect the same lines of code. Conflicts also arise when merging changes between the branch and the trunk. When there are conflicts, you can use the CVS **Merge** tool shown in figure 8.18 to resolve them. Select the **Merge** option from the context menu of any item with conflicts listed in the CVS status window.

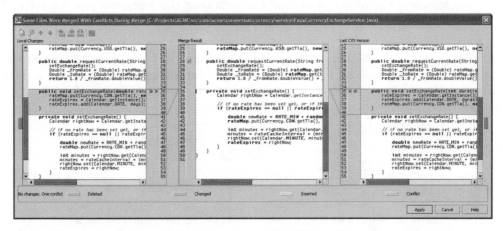

Figure 8.18   IDEA's Merge tool lets you review merge conflicts and decide on how they should be resolved.

The **Merge** tool is like a three-panel version of the diff tool you've already seen. On the left is your local copy of the file before the merge, in a read-only editor pane. On the right is the version that is checked in to CVS, also read-only. In the middle is the merge result: an editable file that will become your local file when you complete the merge. It starts with the contents of the file before you began making any local changes.

Using the change tools previously discussed, you can apply changes from either the left or right pane into the merge results file in the center. The **Apply all non-conflicting changes** button on the toolbar lets you automatically accept any changes that don't conflict with each other, allowing you to concentrate on the conflicts. For each remaining conflict, you can decide to either take your changes, take the other developer's changes, or edit the merge result file by hand where neither set of changes can be applied verbatim.

Auditing changes

You can certainly track down who was responsible for checking in any particular line of code by examining each revision of the file, but there is an easier way. The **CVS | Annotate** command shows an annotated listing of the file. In the gutter beside each line, you can see the version in which each line originated, the user ID of the person who committed that line, and the date that version was committed. An example is shown in figure 8.19. You can access annotated views of older revisions of the file by bringing up the file's history view (**CVS | Show History**), selecting the old version, and then clicking the **Annotate** icon or selecting the **Annotate** option from its context menu.

> **NOTE** This option is sometimes known as the *blame tool*, since it provides a convenient way to audit changes and discover exactly whom to blame for problem in any given line of code.

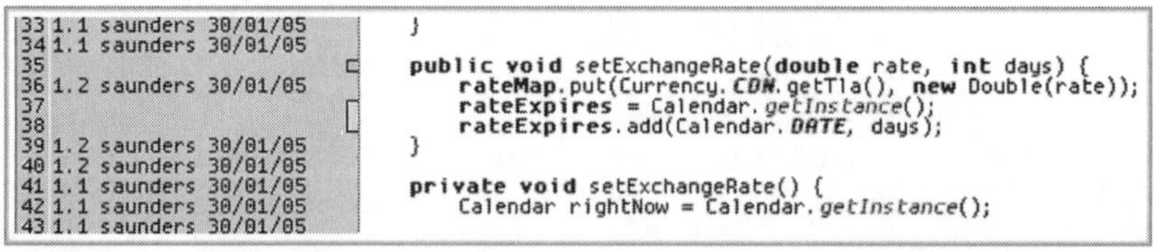

```
33 1.1 saunders 30/01/05        }
34 1.1 saunders 30/01/05
35                              public void setExchangeRate(double rate, int days) {
36 1.2 saunders 30/01/05            rateMap.put(Currency.CDN.getT1a(), new Double(rate));
37                                  rateExpires = Calendar.getInstance();
38                                  rateExpires.add(Calendar.DATE, days);
39 1.2 saunders 30/01/05        }
40 1.2 saunders 30/01/05
41 1.1 saunders 30/01/05        private void setExchangeRate() {
42 1.1 saunders 30/01/05            Calendar rightNow = Calendar.getInstance();
43 1.1 saunders 30/01/05
```

Figure 8.19 The CVS Annotate command shows you, for every line in the file, when it was last updated and who performed the commit operation.

8.3 *Using IDEA's Local History*

One limitation of CVS and other version control systems is that they can only track changes between committed versions of your code. If you try several different implementations on your own machine before finally committing one, there's no way to track these incremental differences should you change your mind. A similar problem occurs when you make that one last change before committing, only to find you've broken something else in the process. The undo mechanism can only go so far back, and it won't survive exiting IDEA or an unexpected crash. This is where the IDEA's Local History saves the day.

8.3.1 *Understanding IDEA's Local History*

IDEA augments its support for popular version control systems with something it calls the *Local History*. Local History is basically a personal, real-time version control system that operates alongside your traditional version control system. The Local History automatically tracks any changes to your code as you edit, compile, and test—allowing you to restore or refer back to changes you've made along the way.

How Local History differs from your normal version control system

Local History wasn't designed to replace your primary version control system—it doesn't support shared access, and it doesn't store changes forever (just a few days by default). Rather, it was designed as a companion to your existing version control system. Use of another system isn't required, however; you're free to use Local History by itself. Just note the limitations discussed in this chapter.

Enabling Local History

To turn on Local History, open IDE Settings and select the **Local History** control panel, as shown in figure 8.20. Select the **Enable Local History** checkbox to turn it on. Under **History**, enter the number of days for changes you want to keep. The more days you allow, the larger the cache IDEA must keep on your

Figure 8.20 The Local History configuration settings alter the behavior of your own personal version control system.

disk. The ideal number depends on many factors, such as the size of your source tree and the number of changes you make. Keep in mind that changes made in the distant past won't be that helpful, so a small number generally works best here.

8.3.2 How IDEA tracks your changes

Change-tracking in the local history is event based rather than character based. It doesn't store every keystroke like an undo facility—instead, it creates labels to identify sets of changes to the tree. When you roll back changes or view differences, they will be between two different labels. Labels in local history are analogous to individual versions in a normal version control system or tags in CVS. For example, in CVS, you may see version 1.3 and 1.4 of a file, whereas in the local history you may have the labels *before name change refactoring* and *after name change refactoring*.

Automatically labeling the source tree

Certain events, such as saving a file, building your project, and refactoring, automatically create Local History version labels. You can control IDEA's automatic labeling behavior via the **Local History** control panel. All of this happens automatically, with no special actions required on your behalf. The auto label scheme is designed to provide a series of fallback steps along logical milestones you're likely to encounter while coding. You're basically putting a stake in the ground so that if something bad happens, you know you can get back to a working point. IDEA also creates a version history each time the file is saved, including when you deactivate the window, if you've enabled that option.

Creating your own labels

Although IDEA's automatic labeling generally creates an appropriate version for rollbacks, we like to create our own version labels before attempting something risky. This allows us to create a more descriptive label, ensuring that we can quickly find our way back to a working version. To add your own label, select **Add Label** from the **Tools | Local History** submenu (also available from the context menu), and specify a meaningful description like *just before attempting that pooling strategy.*

Tracking external changes

If you add, remove, or modify files outside of IDEA, it has no way to track the change you made to them. It will, however, add a new version label as soon as it recognizes that file has changed. The new version of the file is labeled *Added externally* or something to that effect. You're able to see the before and after versions of this change.

8.3.3 *Exploring your Local History*

As with the other version control systems, you can view your local version history in IDEA's excellent diff viewer, which highlights changes graphically, as shown in figure 8.21.

Viewing an individual file's history

You can view a file's Local History by selecting the **Tools | Local History | Show History** command or by right-clicking in the editor and selecting the same. Each version of the file is listed with an optional history label and a date/time stamp. You can explore changes associated with each version by selecting its history row. Right-clicking a row lets you rollback to the specified version, even if the change affects multiple files used throughout the project, such as renaming a method. Other options, such as ignoring whitespace, function just as they did in the CVS diff viewer.

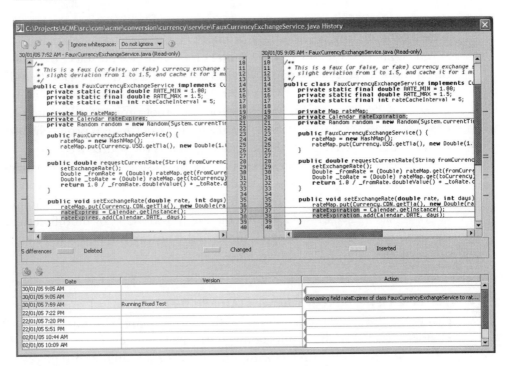

Figure 8.21 The Show History view of your Local History gives insight into the coarse-grained alterations made to your files.

Viewing the history of the current selection

The Local History system can also show you the history for an arbitrary block of code. Highlight an area of code, and then select the **Tools | Local History | Show History for Selection** command. The history view appears but only shows changes that affect the current selection. This makes it easy to focus on a selection portion of the code without being distracted by the changes to the rest of the file. Other than that, both history views work the same. This works much the same as the CVS command **Show History for Selection**.

Rolling back your changes

Rolling back changes from the **Local History** view works just as it does with CVS. Select the version you'd like to revert back to from those listed, and select **Rollback** from the context menu or click the button on the toolbar. Unlike CVS, Local History doesn't require communication back to a central server to update your source tree.

Viewing the history of the entire project

If you right-click a folder in your **Project** tool window and select the **Local History | Show History** command, you can access a more holistic view that displays the files that have changed rather than the contents of a single file, demonstrated in figure 8.22. Execute this command on your root project folder, and you'll see changes across the entire project. We like to think of this as a project history view, because it gives you a good view of changes across the source tree.

The project history view works just like the history view for individual files. Rather than viewing the lines of a file that have changed, however, you're viewing how the source tree has changed at the file and directory level. You can see where versions have introduced new files, removed them, or modified them. You can explore file changes, navigate through the history list, and roll back to previous versions.

 The new **View | Recent Changes** (**Alt+Shift+C**) command summarizes recent changes to the project in a pop-up list that lets you quickly jump into your **Local History** view to see the results of any particular changes. Each relevant change, such as adding a file, a refactoring operation, or a search and replace, is listed along with its time and date. Select one to bring up that change in the **Local History** view.

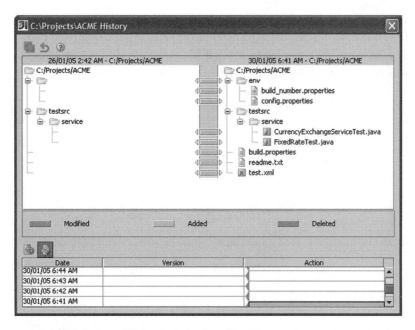

Figure 8.22 Showing the history of the entire project directory can give you a broad understanding of how your code is evolving.

8.4 *Summary*

On the surface, the benefits of version control exist at the management layer. There's safety in making sure you never lose your intellectual property through rogue deletions or poor organization. There's also support for team development, with automatic conflict resolution. There's accountability, with the infrastructure for determining who made changes, when they made them, and why they did so. The benefits for a professional development effort are significant. And, in an ideal world, the addition of a version control system would be natural and non-intrusive.

Dig a little deeper, and you'll find that version control has a huge benefit to the software project's developers: It gives you a warehouse of historical data on the lifecycle of your code. By tracking the history and development of the system, and being able to see the fine-grained comments left by you and other developers as you made changes, you can appreciate how to better drive the system forward.

IDEA has implemented support for a few version control systems, provided an extensible mechanism for users to integrate others, and supplied a home-grown local version control system that tracks changes at an arguably more useful level. The system is non-intrusive—meaning that many of IDEA's features, such as refactoring, perform the required version control system commands invisibly—and its information is conveyed through a series of color-coded and symbolic screen artifacts, making it intuitive and dependable.

Analyzing and refactoring applications

Regular analysis of your code will improve the maintainability and clarity of your source tree. Historically, however, the problem with any sort of design maintenance phase has been its negative impact on the development cycle, in terms of both time and accuracy. Having to manually update code structures and correct all the affected references not only takes time, but also is prone to errors. With IDEA, refactoring your program's design is a snap.

9.1 Analyzing your code

Whether during debugging, architectural review, or design improvement, code analysis is easier when you use IDEA's analysis tools. IDEA can help you understand your code's structure and the relationship between your classes. In this section, we'll discuss how to track down your dependencies, use the structure view to look through your code, and work through the code hierarchy.

9.1.1 Tracking down dependencies

An important part of understanding your code is having the knowledge of *what depends on what*. Where is this method being called from? What classes are using this constant? IDEA has a number of features that help answer these questions and track down how and where your code is being used.

Finding all usages of a class, method, field, or parameter

The **Search | Find Usages (Alt+F7)** and **Search | Find Usages in File (Ctrl+F7)** commands locate all the references to the current class, method, field, variable, or parameter. The difference between the two commands is that **Find Usages** searches the entire project, whereas **Find Usages in File** is limited to searching the file you're currently editing. Both commands are also available from the context menu in the editor.

Depending on whether you're searching usages on a class, method, field, or parameter, there are a number of different search options to select from the search dialog, as shown in figure 9.1. The exact options available depend on the type of symbol you're searching on and whether it's part of a library or local module. Here's what the options do:

- **Skip results tab with one usage** takes effect when only a single reference to your current symbol exists. In this case, your cursor moves immediately to that usage rather than displaying the sole usage in the results list.

- **Open in new tab** displays the results of the usage search in its own tab of the results window rather than overwriting the existing results, preserving both sets of results.

- The **Find** group lets you constrain the search to subset of usages. For classes and interfaces, you can specify any usage of the class, or just usages of fields, methods, and so forth. For interfaces and superclasses, you can search for implementations and derived classes.

- **Search in non-java files** searches for a literal reference (as far as IDEA can tell) to the class outside of source files, such as in an XML configuration file or tag library.

- **Scope** lets you define exactly where the searching will take place among external libraries and project files. The ellipsis button (**...**) to the right of the option lets you configure common scope options for quick selection and reuse in the future.

The results of a search are displayed in a **Find** tool window, just as you'd see when searching for matching text (See figure 9.2). Clicking any entry in the window or using the **Next** and **Previous** controls (**Ctrl+Alt+Down/Ctrl+Alt+Up**) lets you navigate through the usages. Using the **Find** window is covered in detail in chapter 2.

Highlighting usages in the current file

Another search option, **Search | Highlight Usages in File** (**Ctrl+Shift+F7**), is similar to the **Find** usages in the **File** command. In this case, however, the current symbol is highlighted throughout the current file, providing a visual indication of where it's being used. The highlighting also helps you quickly identify the type of use: They're color-coded by whether the symbol is used for write or read access.

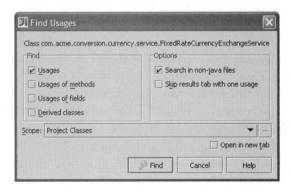

Figure 9.1
The Find Usages operation is sophisticated enough to search for contextual references. This figure shows Find Usages being applied to a class; you can narrow a find to a specific usage context, such as "find all classes that are derived from this class" or "find all places where methods in this class get called."

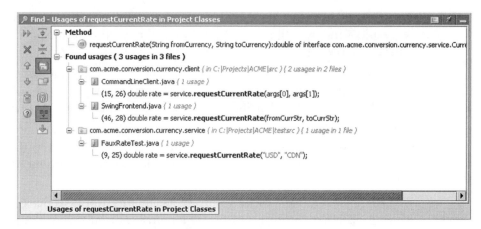

Figure 9.2 The Find Usages operation uses IDEA's intelligent understanding of the interconnections in your code to quickly and definitively show you where your code artifacts are being referenced. This is much more powerful than a simplistic substring search.

In addition, stripes of the same color appear in the marker bar, giving you a feel for the total number and locations of the usages. As with other stripe marks, clicking one navigates you to the usage. Another easy way to navigate the usages is to press **F3/Shift+F3** to move to the next or previous usage, respectively. To clear the highlighting, press **Escape**. You can control the color of the highlighting through your **Colors and Fonts** settings.

9.1.2 *Exploring code with the Structure view*

The **Structure** view provides a convenient view of the Java file currently loaded in the editor, broken down into its methods, fields, and other components. This view lets you examine and navigate through the source file structure rather than just look at the source code behind it.

Accessing the Structure window

Clicking the **Structure** tool window icon or pressing **Alt+7** accesses the **Structure** tool window (see figure 9.3). The **Structure** window always reflects the class or interface loaded into the current editor tab. As you move between files or switch tabs, the **Structure** view changes accordingly. For this reason, a common practice is to dock and pin the **Structure** window in place, creating an additional pane in IDEA's workspace for navigating among the members of the current class. The tool window has a number of options for controlling how the structure

Figure 9.3
The Structure tool window allows you to both view and control your Java code as a tree consisting of method, field, and property nodes.

information is presented (see chapter 2 for a review of working with tool windows if you aren't sure on how to create this multi-pane interface):

- **Sort Alphabetically** lists members alphabetically by name rather than in the order they're defined in the class. Any grouping options specified are honored, and the sorting applies within the group.

- **Sort by Visibility** sorts the list by accessibility (public, private, protected, and so forth). Methods and fields are listed in order of most public to least public, pushing all the private members to the bottom of the list.

- **Group Methods by Defining Type** organizes methods by the class from which they were inherited or the interface that required them. Each group appears in a little collapsible tree node.

- **Show Properties** toggles display of JavaBeans style properties. This option is discussed in more detail later.

- **Show Fields** toggles display of fields from the list.

- **Show Inherited Members** toggles display of members inherited from the base class. This option is discussed in more detail later.

- **Show Non-Public Members**, if disabled, removes all private, protected, and package visible methods and fields from the list, showing only the public API for the class.

- **Autoscroll to Source,** when enabled, causes single-clicking or selecting an item in the list with the keyboard to take you to that item's definition in the editor. (Double-clicking an item always takes you there, even if this option is disabled.)

- **Autoscroll from Source**, when enabled, scrolls the **Structure** view to select whatever method you're editing in the editor.

Viewing properties

The **Show Properties** button on the **Structure** view's toolbar lets you view your class's properties, as seen through the JavaBean API. Any methods that follow the JavaBean getter/setter conventions appear as properties when the class is accessed via reflection in a JavaBean-aware container such as a JSP. For each property, the name and type are shown under a property icon, along with its supporting access methods. This mode is useful if you're working with JSP tag libraries, EJBs, Swing components, or other types of Java classes that rely on the JavaBean naming conventions to define properties. It can help you see the class as a clear picture of what properties are available.

Viewing inherited members

Unless you enable the **Show Inherited Members** option on the **Structure** view's toolbar, each class shows only the methods, fields, and other symbols explicitly defined by it. Any inherited methods or fields don't appear in the structure view. When this option is enabled, you see a more complete picture of the class; any inherited fields or methods appear in a lighter color font with the name of their originating class shown in parenthesis.

9.1.3 Exploring the code hierarchy

As with all object-oriented languages, Java code isn't typically flat. Through Java's support for inheritance and interfaces, hierarchies are created to take advantage of the efficiencies of object-oriented design. IDEA makes it easy to analyze and navigate your code's hierarchies through the **Hierarchy** window.

Looking at class and interface hierarchies

You can visually inspect a class or interface's inheritance tree by executing the **View | Type Hierarchy** command (**Ctrl+H**). The hierarchy of the class you're editing is displayed in the Hierarchy window, which by default slides out of the right window bar (see figure 9.4).

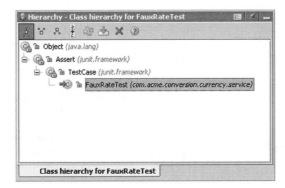

Figure 9.4
The Hierarchy tool window provides a view into the different hierarchies a class participates in, including its inheritance tree, as shown here.

WARNING   Unlike the **Structure** view, the **Hierarchy** window isn't updated automatically as you move between files or change tabs in the editor. It's similar to the **Find** window, displaying a static set of results that are updated only when you execute one of the hierarchy commands or click the **Hierarchy** toolbar's refresh button.

The **Hierarchy** window shows the class hierarchy all the way up to the `Object` class, which is the root of all Java objects. The default view is one of three different views of the type hierarchy that are available. You can change the view by clicking one of the first three icons of the **Hierarchy** toolbar. Each view is mutually exclusive:

- **Class Hierarchy**, the default view for classes, traces the lineage of the current class back to the `Object` class, which forms the root of the results tree. This view lets you see the chain of inheritance for the current class. This mode isn't available when you're examining interfaces.

- **Supertypes Hierarchy** shows the hierarchy of each supertype of the current class. In this view, the current class forms the root of a list of all the classes and interfaces from which it's descended. You can view each ancestral class's ancestors as well.

- **Subtypes Hierarchy** shows all the classes than extend the selected class or implement the selected interface.

Inspecting method hierarchies

The method hierarchy view is a feature related to viewing the class hierarchy. This view lets you explore the inheritance chain of methods, just as you can do for classes and interfaces. When you extend a class in Java, you can override the methods of the parent class in order to provide new or altered behavior, or, in the case of abstract methods, implement methods not provided fully by the base

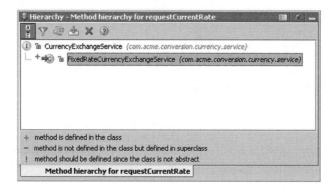

Figure 9.5
The view into hierarchy of a method is more insightful, because the Hierarchy tool window denotes where the method has been defined, overridden, and inherited using graphic icons.

class. The **View | Method Hierarchy** (**Ctrl+Shift+H**) command lets you view the chain of inheritance for the selected method, with special insight into which ancestral classes are providing implementations.

Figure 9.5 shows a view of the requestCurrentRate() method from the FixedRateCurrencyExchangeService class. You can see the inheritance chain for the selected method's class, similar to the view you saw earlier of a class hierarchy. In this view, however, a symbol next to an ancestral class indicates whether that class has implemented the method. There are three symbols:

- A **plus sign (+)** indicates that the method is implemented in the class.

- A **minus sign (–)** indicates that the method isn't implemented in the class.

- An **exclamation mark (!)** indicates that the method isn't defined, but it should be because it's required by the interface or an abstract method of its superclass.

In this example, you can see that the requestCurrentRate() method is originally defined by the CurrencyExchangeService interface and implemented in the FixedRateCurrencyExchangeService class. As with other views of this type, you can use the view as a navigation shortcut (with **Autoscroll to Source** enabled, click the class to view it in the editor, or press **F4**). Other common operations are available through the context menu.

Viewing call hierarchy

The **View | Call Hierarchy** (**Ctrl+Alt+H**) command is probably the most complex of the structure-oriented views. It's used to trace the usage of the currently selected method by exploring its calling hierarchy. Like the **Find Usages** command, the call hierarchy displays a list of all the calls being made to the method.

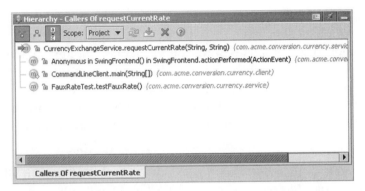

Figure 9.6 The method call hierarchy isn't truly a hierarchy; rather, it's a cross-cut of an intricate web of interconnections displayed in a hierarchical fashion. It's arguably more useful than the **Find Usages** operation, because it lets you traverse multiple levels through any usage of the method instead of tracing just one.

This view, however, also includes a recursive list of all code paths that can be used to reach the method.

Take, for example, the `requestCurrentRate()` method shown in figure 9.6, which requests the current exchange rate between two currencies from a currency exchange service. As you can see, it's called from three other methods: within two different client applications (one a command line, one a Swing GUI interface) and within a unit test class. At first glance, this information isn't any more helpful than the **Find Usages** command; but if you drill down further, you can see where each of those referenced methods is called.

This view is a great way to analyze how and where a method is being used in preparation for refactoring or reorganization of your code. The **Scope** option in the toolbar lets you limit the scope of the usages searched to the entire project, the current class, or everything (including libraries).

WARNING   If you have a very large source tree, don't be surprised if IDEA needs a few moments to track down all the call paths!

9.2 *Locating potential problems with the code inspector*

In chapters 2 and 3, you learned a lot about IDEA's ability to spot Java syntax problems as you type. This feature helps you handle almost all compilation problems as they arise. In chapter 6, you learned how to use the debugger to hunt down errors of logic. However, there is one other type of problems that we haven't talked about yet—problems with your program's design or structure. IDEA's code inspector feature will help you with that. It can spot something as simple as the usage of a deprecated method or more subtle issues like unused method parameters or fields and methods that could have weaker access declarations. IDEA provides more than 200 code inspections for this purpose.

 IDEA 5.0 includes more than 540 code inspections. We won't list them all here, but be warned that IDEA has *many* new ways to find problems with your code. Are you ready?

The IDEA inspector is unique in that it can actually be run either through the main IDEA interface or outside IDEA as a command-line application. Either way, you'll actually review the results in IDEA.

9.2.1 *Launching the inspector*

You launch the inspector from **Analyze | Inspect Code** or through the **Project** and **Commander** windows' context menus. When you select it from the main menu, you're requesting an inspection of the editor's current class or the entire project (IDEA asks you which). When you select it from the **Project** window, you can choose to inspect multiple files, packages, or the entire source tree. When the inspector launches, you see the **Inspect** dialog shown in figure 9.7, where you tell the inspector the type of problems you would like it to search for and report on.

Managing inspection profiles

Once you've created a configuration, you can save these settings as an inspection profile. Creating an inspection profile lets you rerun the tests without having to go through the configuration process again. You can save several inspection profiles—perhaps a quick test and a more thorough test. Use the controls at the top of the **Inspect** dialog to create, remove, and save your settings as an inspection profile.

Launching the inspector from the command line

You can also launch the inspector from the command line, which lets you use it outside of IDEA—perhaps as part of an automated build process. If you have a particularly big source tree, inspection can take a while, so moving it offline is

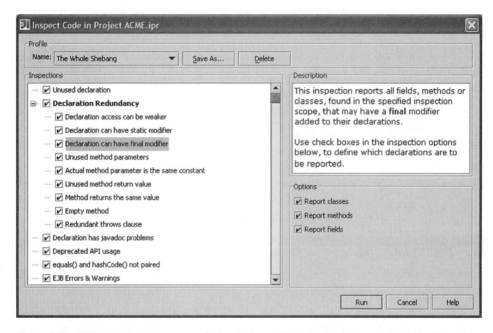

Figure 9.7 IDEA's inspector is aware of a host of conditions it considers questionable. From this screen, you can specify which inspections to run.

nice. The results are stored in an XML file that you can view with IDEA by selecting **Analyze | View Offline Inspection Results**.

To start the inspector from the command line, you use either the inspection.exe (on Windows) or inspection shell script (on UNIX and Mac), located under the IDEA_HOME\bin directory. The script takes the following arguments:

- **Project file path** is the path to the .IPR file of the project you want to inspect.

- **Inspection profile path** is the path to the inspection profile to use. Inspection profiles are saved under the inspection directory of your IDEA settings.

- **Output path** specifies the file where you want to store the results (the result is an XML file).

- Two **Options** are available: The -d <directory> option lets you limit the inspection to a certain directory rather than the entire project. The -v <verbosity level> option lets you control the amount of output generated (0 for quiet, 1 for normal, and 2 for extra noisy).

For example:

```
inspection.exe myProject.ipr
    c:\idea\config\inspection\offline_profile.xml
result.xml -v2
```

You can use offline code inspections for a number of different purposes, many of which we hope will become more evident as you learn more about their capabilities. For example, you might run the inspector every night to look for missing JavaDoc code.

> **TIP**   You can easily create an Ant task to run the code inspector, just as you would to run any other application through Ant. Just remember to add the IDEA JARs to the Classpath.

9.2.2 *Specifying inspections to perform*

IDEA's code inspector can detect and alert you to a wide variety of problems. Many of these problems are design related; these should be treated as warnings, because they may not affect the actual operation of your programs. However, other conditions detected by IDEA could point to real problems. Each of the inspection types can be selected independently, and many of them contain additional options that fine-tune the analysis to your liking. All of these inspections are well documented in the inspection dialog, but we'll discuss some of the most interesting ones.

Unused declarations

The **Unused declaration** inspection finds methods, fields, and classes that apparently aren't referenced from anywhere in your project. We say "apparently" because although IDEA can identify direct code references from both Java sources and JSP files, the inspector can't spot usages that involve reflection; so, be on your toes before you start deleting declarations.

It's also important that you set the entry point options associated with this inspection. An *entry point* defines the start of a code path and gives IDEA some insight into how the code will ultimately be run. You can tell IDEA to use a number of different types of entry points such as servlets, applets, and unit tests. IDEA uses the code paths specified with entry points to determine the actual usage. If a method is never called during the course of one of these code paths, IDEA considers it unused, even if it's called by other methods. When examining the results of a code inspection, you can specify more specific entry points to refine the analysis.

Declaration redundancy

The **Declaration Redundancy** group of inspections examines field and method declarations for potential problems. It points out methods whose return values are never used or that declare impossible exceptions. It also looks for optimizations—for instance, fields, methods, and parameters that could be declared final. Fields and methods that are declared as final enjoy a slight runtime speed advantage because the VM doesn't have to check for overriding values in a subclass.

Local code

The **Local Code Analysis** group of inspections look for problems in the expected code execution. For example, if you retrieve an item from a collection and cast it to type Object, this is considered a redundant cast because the item is already of type Object. Other inspections in this group include finding unused assignments, potential null pointer problems, and conditions that are always constant.

JavaDoc problems

The **Declaration has javadoc problems** option alerts you to the presence of bad or missing JavaDoc comments. The options for this inspection allow you to fine-tune the check to include only the type of tags you require and the scope within each type of element that requires JavaDoc.

Locating deprecated API usages

The **Deprecated API usage** inspection performs the same sort of deprecation checks that your compiler would. Any attempt to use a deprecated symbol (such as a method or constant) is flagged for inspection. In general, you should avoid using deprecated code. Most of the time, the reason for the deprecation and suggested alternatives can be found in the JavaDoc of the deprecated symbol.

Unpaired equals/hash code methods

Many developers either aren't aware of or forget about the following Java rule: A class must always implement the `equals()` and `hashCode()` methods together to ensure that the object is handled correctly when placed into a collection. The **equals() and hashCode() not parsed** test locates instances where a class overrides one of these methods but not the other. You can use IDEA's code generation facility to create these methods for you, as discussed in chapter 3.

Probable bugs

The inspections within the **Probable Bugs** inspection group make IDEA search for many types of common programming problems. Some of the items within this group are idiosyncratic bugs that come out of the Java platform itself; like using == where you should have used Object.equals(). Other bugs are definitely the programmer's fault: infinite recursion, statements with empty bodies, and switch blocks that fall through. They're all part of the powerful way IDEA can help improve the quality of your programming logic.

9.2.3 *Viewing the inspection results*

When the inspection is complete, or if you've performed your inspection offline and loaded the inspection results by running **Analyze | View Offline Inspection Results**, the results are displayed in the **Inspection** window, as shown in figure 9.8.

Each inspection group that yields problems is shown in the tree on the left side of the **Inspection** window; click the nodes of the tree to review the results of the inspection. The pane on the right explains the problem and may offer a solution. The problem summary also includes a link to the source of the problem, allowing you to inspect the source code more fully.

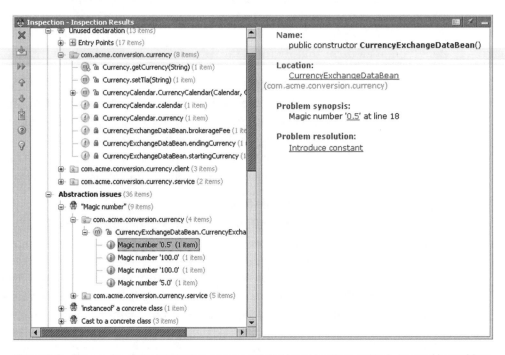

Figure 9.8 The results of the inspection process are displayed in a tree control, grouped by problem area, and summarized in the right-hand pane. Many of the problems have suggested resolutions that can be automatically applied, much like intention actions.

Allowing the inspector to fix problems for you

IDEA can fix many of the problems it finds for you automatically. When it can do so, it provides an entry in the **Problem resolution** field in the inspection report. In some situations, there may be multiple recommendations, allowing you to pick the most appropriate one. In figure 9.8, IDEA suggests removing a *magic number*—a literal numeric constant, compiled directly into the code—and replacing it with a constant stored in a class variable. The fact that this recommendation is hyperlinked tells you that IDEA will take care of the problem if you click the recommendation. If no hyperlink is present, you must fix the problem by hand.

9.3 *Other advanced code analysis features*

Automated analysis is well suited for the class of problems that are common and easy to identify. If you look at the list of code inspections performed by IDEA, you'll see common performance problems, common encapsulation issues, common security violations, and so on. Other problems—such as replacing an inefficient code structure throughout a project, or finding functionality that's been duplicated in more than one place—are more complex and typically need to be addressed manually. In addition to the automated features already discussed, IDEA provides several features to aid your manual code and design review process.

9.3.1 *Using Structural Search and Replace*

With IDEA 4.5, JetBrains provided a powerful new feature known as Structural Search and Replace (SSR). Essentially, SSR performs the same type of operations as the textual search and replace feature, but it takes advantage of IDEA's intelligent knowledge of Java syntax, code structure, and code dependencies. Architecturally, it combines elements of **Find Usages**, IDEA's refactoring operations, and live templates into a generic code analysis and refactoring tool.

This tool aims to solve the textual search's inability to restrict the scope of a search or replace operation effectively. Rather than relying solely on text matching, SSR lets you specify search conditions within the context of your code, from something as simple as restricting a search to a certain type of element (such as a class name or method declaration) to something as complex as a multiline code pattern.

To access the SSR panel shown in figure 9.9, select the **Search | Search Structurally** command (**Ctrl+Shift+S**). The text box at the top of the window is where you specify the code structure being sought. If this were a regular search

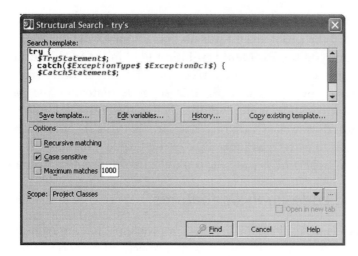

Figure 9.9
The Structural Search and Replace command lets you perform search and replace operations on logical structures of code. It's effectively a template-based Java-aware search and replace.

operation, you'd type the word or phrase you're searching for; here, however, you specify a fragment that describes the code. This is called a *search template*.

Below the **Search template** text box are a number of options and settings:

- **Save template** allows you to save the current search template for later reuse via the **Copy existing template** button.

- **Edit variables** lets you edit variable references within the search template.

- **History** accesses a list of recent searches so you can reapply them.

- **Copy existing template** accesses a library of dozens of search templates bundled with IDEA, or templates you've saved yourself through the **Save template** button.

- **Recursive matching** enables a structural search in the search results, recursively. For example, if you search for classes, IDEA will also look for classes inside those it finds.

- **Case sensitive** determines whether two letters match if they differ only in case.

- **Maximum matches** limits the number of matches to the specified amount.

- **Scope** limits the search to certain subsets of files with the project.

Working with search templates

The essence of SSR lies in creating the search template. A search template works similarly to the live templates already discussed. It consists of code fragments with one or more template variables, which you define through the **Edit variables** button. A template should be one of these formed Java constructions:

- An expression, such as `new UserAccount()`
- A statement or sequence of statements, like `index = 0;`
- A class designator, like `class UserAccount implements Credentials {}`
- A line or block comment, such as `// this should never happen`

The power of templates lies in using variable references. Any code symbol—such as a method, parameter, or class name—can be replaced with a variable reference; this substitution also works on comments and `String` literals. Typically, you don't use explicit statements like the previous examples in your templates; rather, you use variable placeholders and then specify values for each variable you want to restrict in the search.

> **TIP** Many basic code structures are already written for you, in the form of templates. They serve both as useful structured searches and as examples for how to author your own templates. They're available through the **Copy existing template** button of the **Structural Search** dialog.

Working with variables

As in live templates, you specify variables by surrounding their name with $ symbols, such as `$search-class$` or `$returnType$`. The names themselves are arbitrary. As an example, this template represents a `try`/`catch` block:

```
try {
  $TryStatement$;
} catch($ExceptionType$ $ExceptionDcl$) {
  $CatchStatement$;
}
```

During the search, your template is compared with the source code syntactically rather than textually, using IDEA's internal understanding of Java code structure and syntax. This means that whitespace and formatting aren't considered significant; nor are semantically equivalent differences such as the order of class fields, methods, or references in an implements list.

Without specifying any constraints on the variable, IDEA matches anything for the variables and relies solely on the Java statement structures—in this case, the `try` and `catch` keywords. This example search finds all `try`/`catch` blocks in the project (or whatever scope you have specified). Again, exact layout doesn't matter. Taking the example a step further, let's say you're interested only in `try`/`catch`

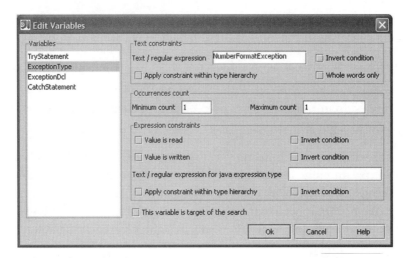

Figure 9.10   Editing variables of your structured search lets you apply more fine-grained search criteria.

blocks that catch number format exceptions. Click the **Edit variables** button to apply additional constraints to the $ExceptionType$ variable. This brings up the **Edit Variables** screen shown in figure 9.10.

All the variables referenced in your template are listed here, and you can apply additional constraints to any, all, or none of them. If no constraints are applied, a variable matches anything. To achieve the desired result of limiting the search to those dealing with NumberFormatExceptions, select the Exception-Type variable and add a text constraint so that only exceptions that match that class name are matched. Note that you can enter a fully qualified type or even a regular expression.

Applying variable constraints

Text constraints are relatively straightforward: Specify the text pattern to match against in the **Edit Variables** window. In the case of references to symbols such as class names, you can optionally fully qualify the reference. If you hold down the **Ctrl** key while placing the mouse over the symbol name, IDEA shows you the fully qualified name, if any. If your search contains any regular expression metacharacters such as parentheses, brackets, dollars signs, and so forth, you need to escape them with a single backslash (\). You can invert the match to a "don't match" by selecting the **Invert condition** option, or limit the match to those within word boundaries with **Whole words only**. The remaining option, **Apply**

constraint within type hierarchy, determines that the search should be also made within the class hierarchy of the type being matched. It has sense only when the variable's target is restricted to a particular type name.

The **Occurrences count** constraints dictate how many sequential elements (in a parameter, declaration or statement list) a variable can include and whether a variable is required to be present in a pattern. By default, both the minimum and maximum counts are set to 1, meaning only a single symbol should match the variable.

The **Expression constraints** allow you to apply semantic conditions to the search. For example, you can find all the instances where the symbol is read or written to. Other options in this group work in a similar way to those available for the text constraints.

The final option, **This variable is the target of the search**, lets you tell the search engine that the matches against the current variable are what you wanted reported in the search results. Otherwise, the default behavior of matches against the entire search template are in effect.

Replacing structurally

The command **Search | Replace Structurally** (**Ctrl+Shft+M**) expands the search capabilities by allowing you to perform replacements on the matches automatically. It adds a **Replacement template** field to the search interface in which you specify the replacement code to be generated (see figure 9.11). You can use any of the variables from the search template to design your replacement code. This lets you use SSR as a powerful refactoring tool.

Let's take as an example a refactoring operation where a class has changed from using static utility methods to a singleton pattern. For instance, the method `XmlUtils.removeNode()` has become `XmlUtils.getInstance().removeNode()`. To accomplish this replacement, you use the following search template

```
XmlUtils.$MethodCall$($Params$)
```

and this replacement template:

```
XmlUtils.getInstance().$MethodCall$($Params$)
```

For constraints, you also need to set the minimum count of the `$Params$` variable to 0, to account for methods with no arguments, and the maximum count to a huge value. Otherwise, with the default values of 1 and 1, you'll only match methods with single arguments. If necessary, you can use the fully qualified name of the target class in the search template, as well.

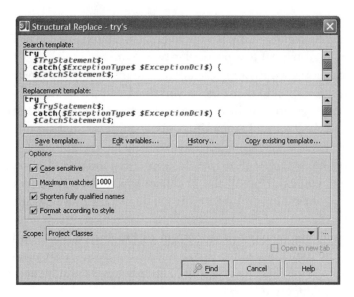

Figure 9.11   SSR lets you change one structural pattern with another.

In the **Structural Replace** dialog, the **Shorten fully qualified names** option, if enabled, uses the short name of any class references, automatically adding any necessary `import` statements to the replacement source code. The **Format according to style** option enables/disables automatic code formatting when the replacement text is generated.

9.3.2   *Analyzing dependencies*

One audit often performed on a software project is an analysis of dependencies in which your software participates. You may need to validate your design: Some software design metrics attribute one-way dependencies from highly abstract packages to specific implementation packages as a sign of good design. You may need to determine a canonical list of which third-party libraries are being referenced from within your project. You may be examining the relationship between the different modules in your project. This could be an arduous task, but IDEA 4.5 introduced a dependency analysis tool to help you find these dependencies.

To analyze the dependencies in your project, select **Analyze | Analyze Dependencies** from the main menu. Alternatively, right-click the subject of the analysis (package, class, and so on), and select the appropriate item from the context menu. In the editor and the **Project** and **Packages** tabs of the **Project** tool window, this menu item is found under **Analyze | Analyze Dependencies**; in the

Commander tool window and the **J2EE** tab of the **Project** tool window, it's not in a separate submenu.

The **Dependency Viewer** tool window provides a three-pane view into the results of the analysis, as shown in figure 9.12.

The upper-left pane, the **Analyzed Code** window, contains a tree view of your project's files. Selecting an entry on that tree (such as a specific package or a class) populates the upper-right pane, the **Parent Code** window, with a tree that represents the classes on which your selection depends. These dependencies include not only other classes in the project but also any classes in libraries and in your test sources, if the corresponding view filter is enabled.

The bottom pane, the **Usage** window, is populated when you select an entry in the **Parent Code** window. Much like the **Find** tool window, the **Usage** window shows a tree view of the lines in the **Analyzed Code** selection that explicitly refer to your **Parent Code** selection. For example, if you analyze the dependencies in your project and select the FixedRateCurrencyExchangeService in the **Analyzed Code** window, you can see in the **Parent Code** window that it depends on the CurrencyExchangeService interface. When you select the CurrencyExchange-Service interface from the **Parent Code** window, the **Usage** window shows all the lines in FixedRateCurrencyService that refer to CurrencyExchangeService. In this

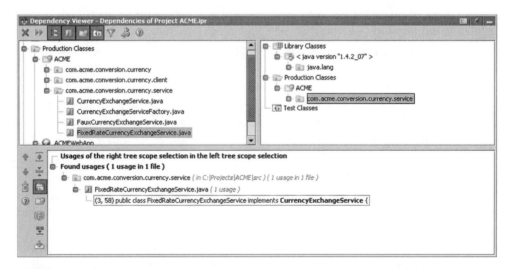

Figure 9.12 The Dependency Viewer tool window is used to explore the network of interdependencies within your body of code.

illustration, the line found is the class declaration, because the class implements that interface.

IDEA 5 Several new types of dependency analysis have been added in IDEA 5.0. You can find them under the **Analyze** menu. They all do basically the same thing: determine the relationships between parts of your project. These analyses can operate on a single class, a single module, a set of modules, or the project as a whole, referred to as a *scope*:

- **Analyze Backward Dependencies** determines what other classes or modules depend on the selected scope.

- **Analyze Cyclic Dependencies** finds any circular relationships between the packages of the selected scope.

- **Analyze Module Dependencies** shows all modules of the selected scope and their dependencies. It also detects and visually presents all found cyclic dependencies for the shown modules.

9.3.3 *Locating duplicate code*

A common and insidious problem with many software projects is duplicated code (sometimes referred to as *copy and paste programming*). By including duplicate code in your project, you make your project less maintainable. Issues that need to be addressed in the original copied code must be addressed in more than one place, and forgetting a single instance usually means you've introduced a bug.

IDEA 4.5 can analyze a specific file (or your entire project) and report on blocks of code that are repetitive. To start a search for duplicates, select **Analyze | Locate Duplicates**. Alternatively, you can choose the same command from the context menu by right-clicking a class (in the editor) or from a class, package, or module in the **Project** view.

If a file is selected when the command is issued, you're prompted to specify the scope of the code duplication analysis—either the selected file or the entire project.

The **Code Duplication Analysis Settings** dialog appears, allowing you to specify preferences for the requested analysis. The **Anonymize** options control whether code must be an identical match in order to be considered a duplicate. For example, if two methods are identical but use different local variable names, they're considered duplicates if **Anonymize Local Variables** is enabled. **Do not**

show duplicates simpler than sets the threshold size for a Java construct to be considered during this analysis: 10 is the default and the minimum. (You don't want every if statement to be reported as a duplicate of every other if statement just because they share the same syntax. A construct needs to be a certain complexity, a certain *size,* before the analysis process considers it.)

Anonymize uncommon subexpressions simpler than sets the threshold size for considering subelements within Java constructs. For example, let's say you have two large methods in your code that are identical except for a few lines. With this setting at 0, the methods are considered sufficiently different and not duplicates; with this setting at a higher value, the analysis may find the methods to be duplicates, but with an *uncommon subexpression.*

If the **Visible from outside of the scope only** option is selected, the analysis checks whether the discarded subelement is valid outside the current construct. If the subelement is senseless, it can't be discarded and is considered nonduplicated.

9.4 *Improving code design through refactoring*

Many professional developers are familiar with the concept of refactoring their code. For the uninitiated, *refactoring* is the process of updating and improving the internal design of software without changing its functionality. For example, you may decide that a method inside an existing class should be pulled up into an abstract class, allowing it to be reused across other classes. In this case, the new code doesn't behave differently, but it now has a cleaner, more reusable structure. IDEA can quickly and easily track down and correct the affected code references automatically, even those within JSP code. Not only do IDEA's automated features ease the refactoring process, but they also encourage you to refactor more often—leading to better software design.

9.4.1 *Performing a refactoring*

Performing a refactoring in IDEA is easy. Although each refactoring operation has its own settings and options, the basic procedure is always the same.

How refactoring works

Although you can manually change the name of local variables easily enough, the real benefits of a rename refactoring over manual manipulation are revealed when you need to rename things on a larger scale, such as a class, package, or widely used public method. In these circumstances, IDEA performs a number of important tasks:

- Checks for name collisions in the current scope.

- Verifies that the new name is syntactically legal.

- If a class or package is being renamed, creates the new files and directories needed, and deletes the old ones.

- Informs the version control system of any files that have been added or removed from the source tree because of the name change.

- Corrects all direct code references to the symbol so that they're using the new name. This includes JSP scriptlets and bean property references.

- Corrects any indirect references found in `String`s or non-Java configuration files, such as when you're using reflection to invoke a class by name.

- Corrects JavaDoc annotations that reference any code symbols that have moved or renamed.

- If a class or a package has been renamed, corrects the `import` statements.

Previewing your changes

All the refactoring functions in IDEA allow you to preview their effects before they're performed, as shown in figure 9.13. This a good way to understand the scope and effect of the changes IDEA is planning, and it also offers a way to fine-tune the refactoring to your liking.

Navigate through the usage tree to examine IDEA's refactoring plan and decide if everything looks good. Pay careful attention to any changes to comments,

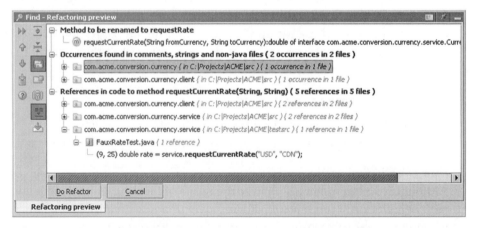

Figure 9.13 Before any refactoring is executed, the summary of its potential operation is outlined in a preview tool window. This gives you the opportunity to cancel at the last second or exclude usages from the operation.

Strings, or non-Java files in the list, because they may not be changes you wish to make. The preview window's toolbar lets you control various aspects of the preview's display to help you in your search, as described in table 9.1.

Table 9.1 The refactoring preview tool window contains a set of controls that help you review and investigate the ramifications of the refactoring before the changes take place.

Icon	Name	Meaning
▶▶	Rerun Search	Performs the search for usages again, taking into account any code changes you've made since requesting the refactoring. You can make code changes while in the preview and then rerun the usages search and complete the refactoring.
⬇ ⬆	Next /Previous Occurrence	Navigates the editor to the next and previous usages in the list, respectively. The shortcuts are **Ctrl+Alt+Down** and **Ctrl+Alt+Up**. This is a good way to review each change in context, if you need to do so.
🖺	Export to Text File	Saves all this information to a text file.
❓	Help	Accesses the help system.
⬍ ⬍	Expand All, Collapse All	Expands or collapses the usages tree, respectively.
🗐	Group by Packages	Adds the containing packages to the results hierarchy, and groups all references originating from within the package.
🗐	Group by Method	Adds the containing method to the results hierarchy, and groups all references originating from within the method.
≡⬇	Merge Duplicated Lines	If enabled, removes any duplicate references from the list.
⬇	Autoscroll to Source	If enabled, selecting an entry in the results list causes the editor to navigate to that reference. This is a good way to inspect changes within the context of their source: Enable this option, and then click the usages you want to review further.
◂◇	Show Read Access	Indicates the read access to the variable at the corresponding location.
▸◇	Show Write Access	Indicates the write access to the variable at the corresponding location.

If IDEA is planning to change a reference that you prefer to be unchanged, right-click the reference and select **Exclude** from the context menu (or press the **Delete** key) to hide the reference from IDEA. It's shown as struck out to signify its exclusion. You can re-include the reference in the refactoring by right-clicking and selecting **Include** or pressing the **Insert** key. If, on the other hand, your review of the proposed change causes you to rethink your decision, click **Cancel** to abort the refactoring. To execute the refactoring, click **Do Refactor**.

Undoing your changes

So you've just done a massive refactoring, and you realize that you didn't know the code as well as you thought you did and what you've done has made things worse. Before you panic, rest assured that IDEA's compound undo mechanism supports its refactoring features. Press **Ctrl+Z** or select **Edit | Undo** to back out the refactoring changes and restore the code to its previous state.

9.4.2 *Renaming code symbols to improve readability*

At first glance, you may not think that the seemingly simple act of renaming a code symbol would fall under the jurisdiction of refactoring, but consider the implications. Assigning appropriate and meaningful names to your classes, variables, and constants is the first step in creating readable code. Moreover, creating understandable code is the first step in building a maintainable system. IDEA allows you to rename any of your Java code's symbols, including the following:

- Packages
- Classes
- Methods
- Fields (instance and static class variables)
- Local variables
- Method parameters
- Non-Java files

Renaming a code symbol through the refactoring system is easy. Start by placing the cursor on the symbol you wish to rename. You can rename a symbol from any reference point in any file, not just its declaration; thus, you don't have to go to a method's declaration, or even its containing class, to rename it—you can rename it directly from within a calling class. Either way, the operation is the same. You can even call the **Refactor | Rename** command from within the **Project** view by selecting the file or package you wish to rename.

Once you've selected the symbol you wish to rename, select **Refactor | Rename** from the menu or press **Shift+F6** to activate the **Rename** dialog, as shown in figure 9.14. Alternatively, you can right-click a symbol in the editor or in any of IDEA's tool windows, including the **Project** and **Structure** views, and select

Figure 9.14 Renaming a symbol is one of the most fundamental and commonly used refactorings. It's hard to believe how difficult this task is in a nonintelligent editor.

Refactor | Rename from the context menu. The process is the same regardless of the type of symbol you're renaming.

The **Rename** dialog summarizes your selection and asks you to specify the new name for the symbol. When you're renaming a field, parameter, or local variable, the drop-down box lists IDEA's suggestions for the new name: combinations gleaned from the symbol's usage and type. If one of these is acceptable, select it. Otherwise, enter your new name.

Two checkbox options are available in this dialog:

- **Search in comments and strings**—If deselected, only Java code references to the symbol (including those within JSP pages) are changed. If selected, IDEA also finds and changes references to the symbol within code comments, String references, and non-Java files (like XML). Be careful when using this option, because IDEA can only guess these types of usages; you may want to enable the preview before the refactoring takes place.

- **Preview usages to be changed**—If enabled, IDEA shows you all the changes it plans to make to your source tree because of the renaming, giving you a chance to tweak the refactor or abort the operation.

When you're ready to issue the rename, click **OK**. If you haven't requested a preview, IDEA makes all the necessary changes to your files. If you've requested a preview, you'll see the preview window as shown earlier.

9.4.3 *Refactoring to improve class or package organization*

It's also possible to delete, copy, and move classes, methods, and other elements in IDEA to improve the organization of your code. For instance, you can delete a method or class you're no longer using, or move a class from one package to another. These operations are more than simple cut-and-paste or file-movement operations; they're full-fledged refactoring operations that make all the necessary adjustments to your project's source code.

Deleting unused classes and symbols safely

You don't want to delete a method or other symbol that is being used by another part of your program. Although you could certainly use the **Find Usages** command as a way to ensure that something is as useless as you think, IDEA makes it easy with the **Safe Delete** command. **Safe Delete** automatically performs a usage check for you, proceeding with the deletion only if the symbol really is unused (or you accept the warning and delete it anyhow).

You execute a **Safe Delete** refactoring by placing your cursor on the doomed symbol inside the editor and pressing **Alt+Delete**, executing the **Refactor | Safe Delete** command from the main menu, or right-clicking the symbol and selecting the **Refactor | Safe Delete** option. You can also delete packages and classes through the **Project**, **Structure**, and **Commander** windows.

Once you request the deletion, IDEA checks for existing usages (see figure 9.15); if any are found, it presents a warning dialog and gives you a chance to see the usages. The usages view works the same as the **Find** tool window; this includes giving you the ability to exclude individual references from the deletion operation. Generally, you use the results to track down all the references, examine or modify them, and then make the decision to proceed with the deletion. If you click the **Ignore** button under the list of detected usages, IDEA performs the deletion regardless of usages, leaving you to clean up your own mess. Alternatively, you can choose to cancel the entire operation. If you perform a delete on a class or file and are using a version control system, IDEA performs the necessary operations to record the deletion. (See chapter 8.)

Figure 9.15   Safe Delete makes sure you don't delete something you shouldn't by finding all its usages.

> **TIP**   When you're deleting a field variable with corresponding access methods, IDEA gives you the option of deleting the access methods as well.

Creating new classes by copying existing ones

You can use the **Copy** refactoring to copy a class (or an entire package). This is often a good way to create a new class using an old one as a starting point. You can only perform the **Copy** refactoring on a class, file, package, or directory. (It doesn't make any sense to copy a method or variable.) To initiate a copy operation, use the **Refactor | Copy** command (**F5**) on the file/class or directory/package you want to copy. If you're editing a file and select this operation from the **Refactor** or context menu in the editor, the class file you're editing is copied.

When you copy a file or directory containing something other than Java code, a copy is just that—a simple copy operation, during which you're prompted to select a name for the copy. When you copy a class or package, however, something much more interesting happens. When you select the name for the new class or package, IDEA automatically makes the necessary adjustments to the source files, including changing the class and package declarations and changing the import statements as required.

You're even free to copy classes across package boundaries. If you do, and the original class uses other classes from its package, they're imported into the new class appropriately. IDEA watches for situations that would make the copy operation illegal. For example, if the source class accesses package local methods, these aren't accessible to the new class, and IDEA isn't shy about telling you so.

> **TIP** You can use the **Cut**, **Copy**, and **Paste** clipboard operations as shortcuts to the copy and move refactoring operations. Select the class or package to refactor in the **Project** window, and then use the appropriate clipboard command on it. A **Copy** and **Paste** works like the **Copy** refactoring, and a **Cut** and **Paste** works like the **Move** refactoring.

Moving classes between packages

Moving classes, files, packages, and directories works just like the **Copy** and **Delete** operations. It's the logical equivalent of performing a copy of an item and then deleting the original. To move something, select the item (or items) to move, and then execute the **Refactor | Move** command either from the main menu or through the context menu (or press **F6**). When prompted, provide the new name and destination package. The **Move** command is available from the context menus of the **Project**, **Commander**, and **Structure** windows, like the **Copy** and **Delete** commands. Once you enter the destination and accept the move operation, IDEA handles making all the necessary changes to the affected source files.

> **TIP** You can move or delete multiple files in one operation, but you can only copy files one at a time!

Moving static methods and fields to other classes

The **Move** command has another nifty trick up its sleeve. When you call it from within the editor, the command moves static members out of the class and into another class.

> **TIP** If you type in the name of a class that doesn't yet exist, IDEA will offer to create it for you.

When you execute the command, you're presented with a dialog like the one shown in figure 9.16. In the **To** field, enter the fully qualified name of the class that will receive the methods or static fields. You can use the class browser to select the destination class by clicking the browse button (**...**) next to the field. Then, select the methods or fields to move from the list of appropriate selections from the current class. You can use the **Visibility** options to modify the visibility of the members in their new location. The default value, **As is**, preserves the current visibility of each moved item.

IDEA 5 The **Move** refactoring for methods can now be used to move a method from one class to another even if the method isn't declared static. Previously, only static methods could be relocated like this. Note that you can't move constructors and methods that are part of the class hierarchy.

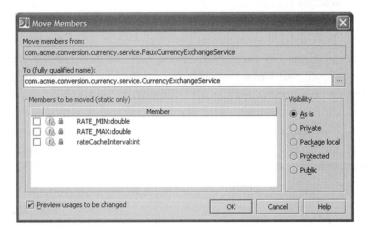

Figure 9.16
The Move refactoring does more than move files around; it also lets you move static methods and fields between classes.

Moving inner classes up

The **Move** refactoring has one final trick. You can use it to move an inner class to the upper level, where it's moved to its own file that IDEA creates for you. To activate this type of refactoring, put your cursor on the class definition line of the inner class you wish to move, and execute a **Move** refactoring. Doing so brings up yet another variation of the **Move** refactoring dialog, as shown in figure 9.17.

This refactoring also gives you the option of passing in a reference to the original containing class as a parameter to the new class's constructor. Any references to the original class instance are appropriately remapped if you select this option.

9.4.4 Working with fields, variables, and constants

Next we'll discuss refactoring operations that deal with manipulating fields, variables, and constants used in your project.

Converting literal values to a class constant

Have you ever had to work on someone else's code (or code you wrote yourself a long time ago) and encountered code similar to the following?

```
int delay = lastreboot * 3600000;
user.setRoleId(64);
```

Where did that `3600000` come from, and what does it mean? Is role ID 64 an administrator or a regular user? Sometimes numbers like these are referred to as *magic numbers*; they're magic in the sense that they must have importance and meaning—but, magically, that meaning has disappeared. Magic numbers make programs difficult to read, harder to maintain, and more likely to be buggy. For example, what if someone changes the numbers assigned to the roles IDs? Will role 64 still make sense? It's always a good idea to avoid magic numbers while programming, and IDEA offers a solution to this problem.

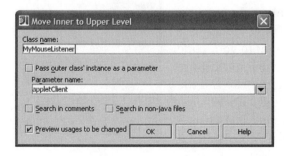

Figure 9.17
The Move refactoring can also refactor an inner class into an upper class.

You can use the command **Refactor | Introduce Constant** (**Ctrl+Alt+C**) to replace magic numbers with a reference to a named static final field. To create a constant, select an expression, number, String, or character, and execute the **Refactor** command. You'll see a dialog like that shown in figure 9.18.

In this box, you define the name and visibility for the constant you're about to create. IDEA suggests a name, but you'll probably want to make up your own. By convention, constants are named in all capital letters, using the underscore character as a word separator. Following this naming scheme immediately tells someone reading your code that the purpose of this field is to hold a constant value.

Figure 9.18   The Introduce Constant refactoring is used to remove magic numbers from your code.

The option **Replace all occurrences of expression** is particularly handy. If it's selected, IDEA replaces the selected expression with your new constant reference throughout the current file, rather than just the one selected occurrence. The number of occurrences that IDEA has found is shown in parentheses. After replacing them for you (if you accept the option), IDEA highlights the changes in the file, giving you a chance to quickly back out any inadvertent changes. For example, if you're using 64 in a method call and also in some math (32 + 64), IDEA can replace one or all of the values with the new constant.

Introducing a new field or local variable

Two other refactoring commands work like the **Introduce Constant** refactoring: **Introduce Variable** (**Ctrl+Alt+V**) and **Introduce Field** (**Ctrl+Alt+F**). Both of these commands are available through the **Refactor** menu. As with constants, these refactoring operations are used to replace an expression in your code with a reference to a symbol so that its purpose is clear. Select the expression and execute the command, and you're presented with a dialog similar to the one shown in figure 9.19, which is simplified quite a bit when introducing a variable rather than a field. As with converting constants, the name and type are requested;

Figure 9.19   The Introduce Field option is another commonly used refactoring.

but you must also select other options, including whether the field or variable should be final and where it should be initialized. The initialization option specifies the point at which the selected expression is assigned to the new field. The exact options available during the refactoring vary depending on the circumstances, and local variables don't have the initialization or visibility options.

You can also use this refactoring to assign the result of an operation that isn't being captured to a field or variable. For example, consider the following code fragment, realizing that the remove method of movieList returns the item removed:

```
movieList.remove(3);
```

Select the line, or place your cursor anywhere on it, and execute the **Introduce Variable** refactoring. After entering a new name, you end up with something like:

```
Movie removedMovie = movieList.remove(3);
```

This operation is so handy, we find ourselves using this refactoring frequently as a shortcut for creating and defining new variables, even when we know ahead of time that we'll need them. IDEA does most of the typing for us, and it even picks good variable names!

Another use of this refactoring is to convert existing fields to variables and variables to fields. When you place your cursor on a local variable reference and execute the **Introduce Field** refactoring, you promote the local variable to field status, making it accessible throughout the class. This is handy when working with Swing classes, where we find ourselves creating GUI components as local variables at first and then promoting them to field variables when we need to work with them further.

Converting direct field references to method calls

The command **Refactor | Encapsulate Fields** replaces all direct references to a field variable with appropriate access methods. You don't need to select a particular field; just make sure your cursor is positioned inside the class you wish to refactor. The refactoring dialog appears, as shown in figure 9.20.

The dialog lists all the fields in your selected class, along with some suggested names for the getter and setter methods the refactoring will generate. Select the fields you wish to encapsulate; you can modify the names of the methods if you wish. A number of refactoring options are available—note that they affect all the fields you're refactoring, not just the currently selected one:

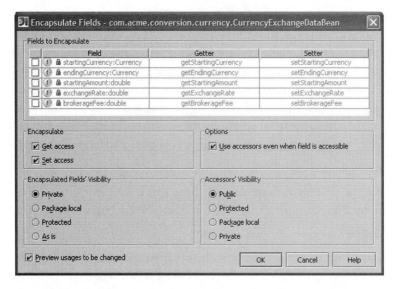

Figure 9.20 Finally, a tool that can help developers enforce proper encapsulation! The Encapsulate Fields refactoring protects all field variables behind an accessor/mutator layer.

- **Encapsulate**—Select the type of encapsulation you want to perform. You can encapsulate get requests and/or set requests. You must select at least one of these two options.

- **Options**—There is only one option, to use the accessors even when the field is available. If this is deselected, existing direct references that are still legal after any change in visibility to the field are left as direct references, not going through the accessor methods. Otherwise, all references go through the new accessors.

- **Encapsulated Fields' Visibility**—This option allows changing the field's visibility as part of the refactoring. For example, you can take a public field, encapsulate it behind public accessor methods, and change its visibility to private.

- **Accessors' Visibility**—This option sets the visibility of the accessor methods created as a result of the refactoring.

9.4.5 *Refactoring method calls to improve usability*

In addition to the already covered ability to rename methods, IDEA provides a number of refactoring operations for creating, modifying, and restructuring Java methods.

Changing a method's signature

The **Refactor | Change Signature** command (**Ctrl+F6**) is a particularly handy refactoring command. It lets you modify a method's signature in several ways, including reordering the parameters, adding or removing parameters, changing the return type, and more. Place your cursor on the method to refactor, and then issue the refactoring command to bring up the **Change Method Signature** dialog, as shown in figure 9.21.

Changing the name is easy; change the text in the **Name** field. This is equivalent to using the **Rename** refactoring we covered earlier, but it's provided here as a convenience. You have the option of leaving the current method alone and creating a new method that delegates to the method by selecting the option. You can also combine a name change with some of the other options available through this dialog. The method's visibility can be changed: Select a new option from the **Visibility** group. Be aware, however, that if you make a method more restricted, you may cut it off from existing code.

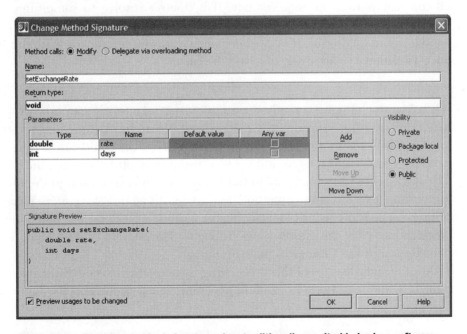

Figure 9.21 Changing method signatures has traditionally resulted in broken software builds, because developers have difficulty remembering every place a method is called. IDEA's intelligent refactoring makes changing the signature throughout the code base simplistic, up to and including specifying defaults for new arguments.

Changing the return type seems easy, but IDEA can't handle many changes of return type. You must fix many of them yourself. For instance, if you change a method's return type from a `boolean` to an `int`, there is no logical mapping between the two. As you make changes to your method, you can see a preview of the new method signature in the dialog. This gives you a good idea of what you're doing to the method and what the method will look like when you're done. Fortunately, this situation doesn't arise too often. If you're making such a drastic change, you're probably better off writing a new method from scratch.

As we alluded to earlier, you can easily add, remove, and reorder the method's parameters. Use the **Move Up** and **Move Down** buttons to reorganize them as you prefer. You can also change the name of the parameters by editing the **Name** entry in the **Parameters** table. If you add a new parameter, you need to specify a default value so that existing method calls have something to place in the calls. This can be a literal value such as an `int` or a `String`, or the name of a variable reference. Whatever you type here is placed verbatim in the existing method calls to fill the new parameter requirement. If it doesn't resolve to something in the caller's scope, you must go back and fix it; the same is true with setting or changing types. But be careful! It's possible to create invalid references. With the **Introduce Parameter** refactoring, this isn't the case.

 When you're changing a method signature, the refactoring can now propagate parameter additions through the method call hierarchy. Assume that you decide to add a new parameter to a method. Previously you could affect only direct method calls. Now, if the method is called from some other method, the parameter can be added automatically to that containing method, then to the methods that contain that containing method, and so on. It's a kind of recursive parameter addition. The same feature is available for method exceptions, as well. To enable propagation, click the appropriate **Propagate Parameters** or **Propagate Exceptions** button in the **Change Signature** dialog.

Another new feature of this refactoring is the ability to modify the exceptions thrown by the method. You can add and remove exceptions on the signature as part of the process.

Introducing a new parameter to a method

The **Introduce Parameter** refactoring takes a selected expression inside a method and converts it to a parameter. For example, suppose you have a method that takes a purchase price, calculates sales tax, and returns the new price. If the current implementation multiplies by 8% to figure the tax, and you'd like to make the tax rate a method parameter for added flexibility, select the 8% value and then execute **Refactor | Introduce Parameter** or press **Ctrl+Alt+P.** You're asked for a name, and IDEA corrects all the references.

Converting an instance method to a static method

You can use the command **Refactor | Make Method Static** to convert an instance method to a static one. This does more than just change the method signature. If the method you're converting references any fields or instance variables, these aren't available to a static method. Instead, they must be passed into the method as parameters. IDEA asks you to provide parameters for these references, as shown in figure 9.22. Alternatively, you're given the option of passing in the instance object itself as a parameter, in which case the method gets the values it needs directly from the instance.

When you're converting a static method to an instance method, you can now control the scope of the generated instance variables, making them private, public, and so on.

Creating a new method from a code block or an expression

The **Refactor | Extract Method** command (**Ctrl+Alt+M**) turns a selected block of code (or even an expression) into a method. The selected area is replaced by a call to the newly created method. The new method may become void or may return a value. It may also acquire parameters. This depends on the variables that

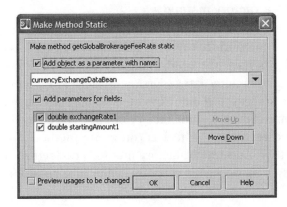

Figure 9.22
The Make Method Static refactoring has the added side effect of translating all internal class references into method parameters.

are assigned values or referenced in the selected block. If a variable or variables are used only in the block, they're converted into the new method parameters. If a variable is assigned inside the selection and used later in the code flow, this variable determines the return type of the method. If you have several such variables, IDEA prompts you about the impossibility of having multiple output values. If no variables are assigned in the block, the new method has the void return type.

IDEA does a good job of naming the new parameters, but you can specify your own names if you wish, and reorder the method parameters to your liking. You can disable any of the parameters, in which case IDEA provides its own local variable replacements with default values that probably aren't what you want. You must go into the code and initialize them to appropriate values.

Converting a local variable reference to a method call

This refactoring operation lets you extract a local variable's initialization expression into a method and then replace all references to the local variable with the new method call. To perform this operation, select the variable you wish to replace, and execute the **Refactor | Replace Temp with Query** command from the main menu. The resulting dialog is similar to that used during the **Extract Method** refactoring discussed earlier. You can choose a name for the method as well as the names and order of any parameters it requires.

Even though the end result may be more method invocations, the resulting changes make the code cleaner. The resulting difference in speed is negligible if the initialization is a simple expression or access method. If the initialization step is computationally expensive, however, it may be best to retain the local variable, in effect caching the results of the expensive operation. Besides, local variables live on the stack and are therefore the fastest way to access data in the VM.

Replacing a constructor with a factory method

This refactoring converts an existing class constructor to a static factory method. A *static factory method* is a static method that returns an instance of the class you wish to create. Factory methods have three advantages over constructors that make them worth considering as an alternative. First, you can name them whatever you want, so if you have several different ways of creating your object, you can give them distinctive names. Second, static factory methods don't have to be members of the class they're constructing. This lets you group methods for constructing related classes together. And finally, factory methods can return one of many different concrete classes by declaring a return value of a common base class. This lets you hide the implementation class from the client method, providing an additional level of abstraction.

To convert a constructor into a factory method, select the constructor's name, and choose **Refactor | Replace Constructor with Factory Method** from the menu. You're asked to specify a name and the class in which the new method should be created. IDEA even suggests names with prefixes like `create`, `new`, and `getInstance`. Another popular name for factory methods that perform an implicit conversion is `valueOf`. Once the refactoring is completed, the original constructor is removed, and references to it are replaced with references to the factory method.

Improving performance by inlining variables and methods

Inlining is a process of removing a method call or variable reference and replacing it with the body of the method being called or the value of the replaced variable. This change preserves the functionality of the code while avoiding the method call or variable reference. It's exactly the opposite of the **Extract Method** refactoring. This is usually done as a performance optimization or to remove a dependency between classes. You should use this refactoring sparingly: The speed benefits are very minor in most cases, and you'll break encapsulation by pulling code out of a centralized method and essentially copying it out to its usages.

To execute the command, select **Refactor | Inline** (**Ctrl+Alt+N**) after selecting either a local variable or a method to inline. For methods, you also have a couple of options:

- Inline all invocations and remove the method
- Inline a single invocation only and keep the method

> **TIP** If you try to delete a method that's in use, **Safe Delete** will complain. If you use the **Inline** refactoring first, however, you can remove the method with no loss of functionality.

9.4.6 Restructuring class hierarchies

IDEA provides a number of refactoring operations that are designed to help you change the structure of your code by introducing new superclasses and interfaces, as well as adjusting the relationship between classes, their ancestors, and their descendents. IDEA has a wealth of refactoring options and there isn't enough room in this book to cover all of them. We'll discuss some of the most powerful options, but it will be time well spent if you look up IDEA's latest refactorings.

Extracting an interface to introduce abstraction

The **Extract Interface** refactoring allows you to create a new interface using an existing class as a template. Execute **Refactor | Extract Interface** to bring up the refactoring dialog shown in figure 9.23. In this example, we're taking an existing class `FixedRateCurrencyExchangeService` and extracting a generic `Scalable` interface from it.

Begin by choosing one of two options: **Extract interface** or **Rename original**. In the first case, the new interface is created in the specified new location, and the current class contains its actual implementation. If you choose to rename the original class, the extracted interface obtains the current name and location, whereas the actual implementation is moved to the new location with the new name.

Then specify a name and package for the new interface. Select the methods (and constants, if any) that you wish to include in the new interface. The method signatures are copied over as is, but you can use the **Change Method Signature** refactoring command to fine-tune them later. Finally, select one of the JavaDoc options to tell IDEA what to do with any JavaDoc comments on the methods going into the new interface. Your choices are as follows:

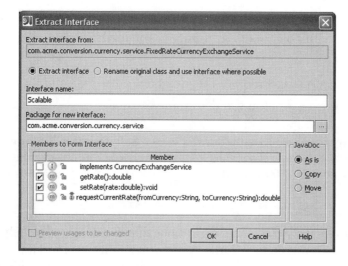

Figure 9.23
The Extract Interface refactoring lets you select a set of already-implemented methods in a class and use them to define a new interface.

- **As is**—No changes are made to the JavaDoc. If present in the class, it stays there, and the interface has no JavaDoc entries.

- **Copy**—Any JavaDoc found on the class methods is duplicated in the interface.

- **Move**—Any JavaDoc found on the class methods is deleted and moved into the interface.

Creating hierarchy by introducing a superclass

The **Extract Superclass** refactoring operation is very similar to the **Extract Interface** command discussed earlier. However, instead of creating a new interface, the refactoring creates a new base class for the current class. Any methods in the current class can be moved into the base class with their implementation intact or as abstract methods, leaving the implementation in the existing class.

Begin by executing the **Refactor | Extract Superclass** command; the **Extract Superclass** dialog appears, as shown in figure 9.24. In this example, you're creating a new base class for the FixedRateCurrencyExchangeService class from the previous example. If you want, you can then use the **Extract Interface** refactoring on the superclass to separate the interface from the base implementation class.

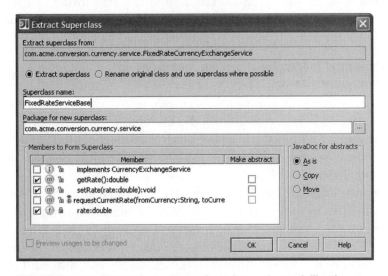

Figure 9.24 The Extract Superclass refactoring works much like the Extract Interface refactoring, except the former is usually used to define base classes as opposed to interfaces.

As before, choose whether you want to extract a new superclass or to rename the original class, and then select the methods you wish to define in the superclass. If you want the method to be abstract, select the checkbox next to the method name. In this case, the implementation remains in the existing class. If the box is left deselected, the implementation is moved into the new superclass. JavaDoc for concrete methods is moved along with the methods, but you need to tell IDEA how to handle the JavaDoc for abstract methods by selecting one of the JavaDoc options as in the **Extract Interface** refactoring.

When you click **OK**, IDEA attempts the refactoring and alerts you to any problems it encounters. When you move methods to the superclass, you need to be sure that you've resolved any dependencies between them. For example, if method A calls method B or uses field C, these must be moved as well. IDEA calls your attention to dependencies by highlighting any unselected members that are dependencies of selected ones. If you ignore them, you get an error message. You must keep the methods with the dependencies where they were or move the dependencies over them.

The refactoring creates or renames the new superclass for you and changes your existing class to extend it. Any non-abstract methods created in the superclass are removed from the original class. When the refactoring is complete, you're given the option to automatically find references to the existing class and replace them with reference to the more generic superclass type.

Rearranging method hierarchies: pulling members up and pushing members down

IDEA makes it easy to restructure your inheritance relationships by allowing you to move methods and fields up and down the hierarchy. This means you can go back to the example and move additional methods into the interface or supertype. Or, from the base class or interface, you can move them back down into the implementation classes.

The commands **Refactor | Pull Members Up** and **Refactor | Push Members Down** work similarly to the other hierarchical structure refactoring operations we've been examining. You specify which method to push or pull. When you're pushing members down from supertype classes, you can specify that the methods should not be removed from the superclass but made abstract instead. Likewise, when pulling up into a superclass, you can make the new methods abstract if you wish, just as you saw with **Extract Superclass**.

Converting an anonymous class into an inner class

The **Refactor | Convert Anonymous to Inner** command lets you take an anonymous class and change it to an inner class that can then be reused throughout its containing class. This situation occurs most frequently during Swing development, due to the large number of listeners, renderers, and other interfaces you implement for the benefit of a single button or other component. This refactoring is simple: Put your cursor on the anonymous class, and execute the refactoring. You're asked to specify a name for the new class and order any constructor parameters that are required. You also have the option of making the class static.

Replacing inheritance with delegation

As we discussed in chapter 3, IDEA can generate delegation methods for you, making it easy to proxy behavior between classes. The **Replace Inheritance with Delegation** refactoring concerns using delegation to provide behavior instead of inheritance. Rather than extend a class to gain access to its behavior, you can delegate some or all of the methods of a superclass to an instance of that superclass encapsulated into the current class. This enables you to extend some other class if you wish while retaining the behavior you rely on the original superclass to provide. During the refactoring, a new constructor for your class is created, accepting an instance of the superclass you wish to delegate to. You can also delegate to an instance of an interface that you no longer wish to implement directly. In this case, IDEA creates an inner class implementation of the interface for you, delegating the calls to its methods to the inner class.

Execute the **Refactor | Replace Inheritance with Delegation** command to access the refactoring dialog shown in figure 9.25. Select the superclass or interface to which you'd like to delegate. All the accessible methods of that class are listed in the **Delegate members** list. Next, specify the name of the field that will hold the delegate instance. The option **Generate getter for delegated component** should be selected if you want to access the superclass instance from outside the current class. If you're delegating to an interface, specify the name of the inner class that is implementing that interface. Select the methods to which you wish to delegate, and click **OK** to begin refactoring.

Generalizing class references

The command **Refactor | Use Interface Where Possible** finds places in the source code where it's possible to refer to the current class by its interface or one of its superclass types. This has the effect of creating a more general reference to the class. To use this refactoring, select the class you want to refactor, and execute

Figure 9.25
The Replace Inheritance with Delegation refactoring

the command. You're asked to pick which of the superclasses or interfaces you'd like to use.

9.4.7 *Migrating source code to new package or class names*

You probably won't use the migration tool much, but if and when you do need it, you'll be glad it's there. The migration tool is accessible from the **Tools | Migrate** command. It lets you define a series of rename operations in order to take source code developed with a package or class naming scheme and migrate to a new naming scheme.

The only migration included with IDEA is a good example of the type of thing you'll find yourself using this tool for. When Sun introduced the Swing components, they were placed in the package hierarchy com.sun.java.swing. However, by the time 1.1 came around, they were moved to javax.swing. This is a real problem if you've already written code against the old package.

To perform a migration, bring up the migration tool and select a migration from the list. When you click **Run**, IDEA performs a **Find Usages**-type command to locate all the code that needs to be changed. As with the **Refactoring Preview** window, you can choose to accept the changes or cancel. Once you proceed, you can still undo just as you can with a refactoring.

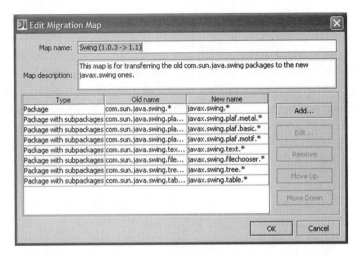

Figure 9.26 **The migration tool mimics refactoring in that it batch processes a series of files and changes all supplied package references.**

Creating a migration

Editing or creating a new migration is easy. Click **New** (or **Edit** on an existing migration) to bring up the **Edit Migration Map** window, shown in figure 9.26. For each package hierarchy or class you need to rename, click **Add** to create a new entry, specifying the appropriate **Old** and **New** names. For packages, you must enter each package, because the migration process isn't recursive and subpackages aren't included by default.

9.5 *Summary*

The Java compiler warns you about compile-time errors. Common sense makes you aware of runtime errors. But a developer sitting alone at a desk and architecting a solution to a problem typically has no feedback on the design until it's fully implemented and someone else can look at it. Common mistakes in design and implementation consume a diabolical amount of development time by requiring bug fixing at a later stage in the process. IDEA includes a configurable code-inspection facility that gives you a much-needed layer of feedback. It offers immediate benefit in the form of an inspection audit—and imagine the ROI when developers see their habitual mistakes outlined by the inspector and change their habits and processes to avoid those mistakes in the future.

Refactoring can also improve the overall design and architecture of a software system. For example, this modern-day best practice helps agile software development teams effectively deal with rapid requirements, scope, and direction changes. Although the refactorings themselves are well documented (with many thanks and praise to Martin Fowler et al.), implementing something as simple as a method rename is a time-consuming and error-prone task. The minds behind IDEA have used its intelligent understanding of the network of connections and relationships in your Java code to automate many of the core refactorings, which puts much of the power of agile software development within easy reach.

Developing Swing
applications

10

Creating graphical user interfaces (GUIs) for your applications in Java using Swing components is a necessary yet tedious task. The Swing component architecture may be very flexible and allow for very complex and powerful GUIs to be modeled, but implementing even a simple dialog can be a time-consuming process.

IDEA includes a GUI Designer that automates many of the monotonous aspects of GUI design in Java. By implementing an additional abstraction layer, IDEA lets you build dialogs or panels of GUI components more efficiently than writing pure Java Swing code. The abstraction layer lets you design your interface visually, use tools to simplify some of the more complex aspects of GUI design in Swing (such as layout managers), and bind underlying functionality in an on-the-fly and modular fashion.

To illustrate some of the points in this chapter, we'll use IDEA's GUI Designer to implement a snazzy GUI atop the ACME Currency Converter.

10.1 *Understanding the GUI Designer*

Central to IDEA's GUI Designer is the concept of a *form,* which is IDEA's abstraction of a Java Swing GUI. Because implementing GUIs by hand in Java is time-consuming and tedious, IDEA uses the concept of a form to improve efficiency. In the editor, a form is shown in WYSIWYG format, allowing direct manipulation through a point-and-click interface; on the disk, a form is stored as an XML file, containing metadata about the GUI and all its constituent components. You can easily implement all the GUIs in an application—a main screen interface, a simple About box, a Confirm Delete dialog, and so on—as forms.

10.1.1 *The GUI-building process*

Let's run through a quick overview of the typical process used to create GUI applications in IDEA. This chapter will cover each of the following steps in more detail, but it will be helpful for you to have a notion of the process in general. Regardless of the type and complexity of your specific interface, the steps required to build a GUI using IDEA's GUI Designer are the same:

1 *Create a form by populating it with GUI components.* Using the GUI Designer, visually lay out all the components for your interface. Place the components where they should generally appear, setting their approximate sizes and positions. This flexible design mode is called *XY Layout mode.*

2 *Customize the properties of your form.* You can edit labels and most visual text (such as the text shown on a button) directly in the design area. You can edit other properties using the Properties Inspector.

3   *Group components as necessary.* Grouping components allows them to be aligned and proportioned properly. It marks the transition from XY Layout mode into *grid layout mode*, where their size and position are controlled by the bounding grid.

4   *Preview your form, if desired.* Use the preview tool to test your user interface to see that it looks as intended.

5   *Bind your form and components to an application class.* Using the GUI Designer, bind your form to one of your application classes. Also bind each important component of your form to the instance variables within that class to give you a handle to them. You can bind to existing classes or let IDEA create them for you on the fly. Implement methods in that class that make the form functional.

6   *Compile and run your application.* During the compilation phase, IDEA uses the form object you've designed, as well as its bindings to your application classes, to generate the code required to build and lay out your interface. Forms don't become their own classes; they're more like templates used to generate the layout code within your application classes at compile time. You never have to see the generated code if you so choose.

TIP   These steps describe the ideal situation when you have a simple form and know exactly what it will contain. But in most real-world cases, you need to maintain your existing form, adding, modifying or moving its components. IDEA's GUI Designer lets you work on existing forms without breaking their layout so that you can easily introduce changes at any time.

10.1.2 *Working with the user interface*

Creating a new form or editing an existing one brings up the GUI Designer (see figure 10.1). It's divided into four main areas: the Components Tree view, the Properties Inspector, the GUI Designer toolbar, and the Form Workspace. You can resize the areas as desired, but you can't rearrange them or split them off into their own windows.

The Components Tree view is a hierarchical view of the current form. Each component in your form appears in the tree under its parent container. For a simple form, there may be only a single level of hierarchy. It isn't uncommon for complex interfaces to use many layers of nested containers of components to simplify layout. Clicking a component selects it in the design window.

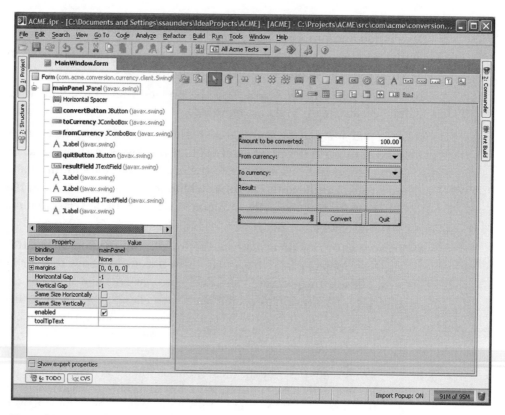

Figure 10.1 The GUI Designer lets you design GUIs in a visual manner instead of editing code by hand.

The Properties Inspector lets you review and modify properties of the currently selected container or component. Properties are used to control all sorts of settings, including the component's application binding, layout, alignment, and behavior. Each type of component has its own set of properties.

The GUI Designer toolbar is located at the top of the design panel, and contains selection and layout tools as well as a selection of components that you'll use to design your interface. Depending on your setup, your component palette may contain several different sets of components, each in its own tab.

The Form Workspace makes up the bulk of the GUI Designer; this is where you design and create your form. You use this area to lay out and visualize your interface. It contains an editable preview of your design.

10.2 *Working with forms*

Forms are stored as files in your project, just like Java files, images, HTML, and so forth. You can access them through either the project or source code views. Creating or editing a form invokes the GUI Designer, as shown in figure 10.1. The GUI Designer is just a different type of editor, so forms appear in the main editor window of IDEA in their own tab, just as Java classes and other files do.

10.2.1 *Creating a new form*

The files that represent GUI forms, although not Java classes themselves, live in the source tree of your module. Forms are stored on disk as files with the .form extension but are really XML files that contain all the information about your form (such as component definitions, and alignment and layout metadata). At some point, IDEA must generate Java code from that XML definition and then compile that generated source in order to run your GUI.

Creating a form is similar to creating a Java class. In the **Project** tool window, choose the package where the form should reside, and then right-click that package and select **New | GUI Form** from the context menu. You're prompted for a filename, and that form file is stored in that package. Like most other files, you can move, copy, rename, and delete forms as necessary, although you should never edit the XML in this file directly. These operations act like other refactorings; IDEA smartly manages all the necessary references.

> **TIP** If you need to create a simple dialog, the **New | Dialog** command automatically generates both the class and form stubs (including **OK** and **Cancel** buttons) and their respective handlers, if you so choose.

10.2.2 *Placing components into the workspace*

The next step in designing a user interface form is to add your components to the workspace and arrange them into a rough approximation of your desired layout.

Adding components to your design

To add a component to your form, first click an item from the component palette on the Designer's toolbar. It's highlighted to show that it's selected. Next, move your pointer into the design panel, and left-click to place the new component (note that you don't drag items from the palette bar—you click to select and then click to place them). When you're placing a component into your form, your mouse pointer changes to indicate a valid placement. You can only place components into the following areas:

- An empty area of the design window
- An empty container
- A container with no assigned layout
- An empty cell in a container with layout

TIP When you're placing container elements such as a JPanel, you can hold down the mouse button and drag the container out to the desired size, placing and sizing in a single step. You'll learn more about sizing later in the chapter.

Selecting components

To select a component, click it in the design view. For a container such as a JPanel, click anywhere inside the container. Once selected, the container or component is outlined in a series of resizing handles, as shown in figure 10.2. A small drag icon appears next to the selected element, providing a more convenient handle for moving the item. Clicking another component or clicking an empty area of the design view cancels your selection.

Figure 10.2 Selecting a component surrounds it in blue resizing handles.

You can also select an item by clicking its name in the component tree. Sometimes this can be more convenient if an interface is crowded with components. If a container is completely filled by components, this is the only way to select the container itself.

To select multiple components at once, hold down the **Ctrl** key while you select. To select a group of items, hold down the **Shift** key while dragging a selection box around them; all components completely within the selection box are selected.

TIP You can use the grow/shrink shortcuts from the text editor (**Ctrl+W** and **Ctrl+Shift+W**) to progressively expand and reduce the selection of components within a container.

Positioning components

To move a component, click anywhere in it and then, while keeping the mouse button down, move the component to its new location. The pointer changes to an icon to indicate valid landing sites. You can abort a move in progress by pressing the **Esc** key.

TIP   It can be difficult to get hold of a container whose contents fill it completely, because any attempt to select the container instead selects its contents. To move a container obscured by its contents, select the container from the form component tree, and then move your mouse over the container but don't click it! A move handle icon appears above and to the left of the component. Grab the handle with the mouse, and you can move the entire container and its contents.

10.2.3 Setting component properties

You can configure each component and container in your interface by using the Properties Inspector. This panel is used to configure and customize the behavior and appearance of the components in your interface. You can find properties automatically by IDEA through introspection; or properties can be *synthetic*, meaning that you supply properties such as a preferred width and height for a component.

NOTE   Properties are explored in greater depth in section 10.4.

Setting the values for each property is relatively straightforward, because each is manipulated by controls appropriate for its type. For example, *boolean* properties have a checkbox you use to set their value to true or false. If a property takes a literal text or numeric value, you can type the value into the field. IDEA validates your input to ensure you don't assign text to a numeric value or vice versa.

Some values use a select box that restricts your selection to a few distinct choices. For example, alignment properties allow you to choose from left, right, and center alignments. In most cases, these selections correspond to numeric constants in the Swing API; you can determine their exact meaning by reading the JavaDoc.

Values shown with several numbers in square brackets, such as margins and sizing properties, are composed of a set of two or more distinct values. A component's preferred size, for example, is expressed in terms of its height and width. The value in brackets shows each of the component values and can't be edited directly. To edit these values, you must expand the property to expose its subvalues, which you can edit directly.

The shaded properties listed at the top of the properties panel are specific to the IDEA GUI Designer. They're used to control the layout, alignment, and sizing of components. We discuss the use of these properties in detail later in this chapter.

By enabling the **Show expert properties** option at the bottom of the panel, you can reveal quite a few additional properties for each type of component. The properties that appear here depend on the type of component you're configuring. All of these properties correspond directly to setter methods in the component's class; details on their usage can be found in their JavaDocs.

10.2.4 *Laying out a form*

A significant part of designing a GUI in Java involves not only choosing the visual components but also controlling their layout, sizes, and relative positioning using containers (such as JPanels) and layout managers. This approach isn't always intuitive, and it represents some of the complexity that makes GUI design time-consuming. The GUI Designer in IDEA provides a facility for laying out forms quickly without getting bogged down by the underlying implementation details. In the Form Workspace, you visually lay out the components in an arrangement that roughly corresponds to the layout you desire. You then group the components together appropriately and fine-tune the layout to finalize the design.

When you're designing your GUI, the default layout for the components is called XY Layout. This type of layout uses absolute positioning, allowing you to arrange things where you want them. All components that aren't found within a container are considered to be in XY Layout. XY Layout is the convenience mechanism used by the GUI Designer to insulate you from Java's complex layout management, but it's only intended for initial design. IDEA won't let you run (or even preview) a form without a single top-level container, which implies that all components must be contained somehow. You wrap components in a container by selecting them and applying one of the grid layout options.

IDEA offers three types of grid layout: horizontal, vertical, and grid. The horizontal layout positions items along the X-axis (across the interface), and the vertical layout positions items along the Y-axis (up and down). The grid layout, on the other hand, defines a table in which each cell can hold a single component (which may be a container). In actuality, the horizontal and vertical layouts are special cases of the grid layout. A horizontal layout is a grid with a single row, whereas the vertical layout has a single column. Once the layout is applied, you're free to add and remove rows and columns as you see fit, effectively transforming the layout into one of the other types.

As you develop a form, it's likely that you'll need to remove a container, freeing up its components to be repositioned elsewhere. You can easily do so by selecting the container and using the **Break Layout** button in the toolbar. The containing grid layout is removed from the workspace, but its contents remain.

Modifying your layout

Once you've placed components inside a container by using one of the grid layouts, their size and positioning are controlled by the container's layout manager. The ongoing development of a form may require adjustment to the number of rows and columns that made up the grid, so special container controls appear in the Form Workspace (see table 10.1).

NOTE There are two basic approaches to modifying a UI in the GUI Designer:

- Breaking the grid, modifying components (adding, removing, moving), and joining them back into a grid
- Adding and removing columns and rows (without breaking the grid)

Arrange the components you wish to include in your interface into position. Select the components you wish to lay out together, and click one of the layout icons in the GUI Designer's toolbar to apply the layout. The selected components are added to a new JPanel container, and the selected layout is applied. If you've selected a grid layout, the designer attempts to apply appropriate layout constraints in order to approximate the initial arrangement of the components. For

Table 10.1 Special container controls used to fine-tune the configuration of your GUI containers

Icon	Control	Description
⊞	Drag handle	Indicates that the selected component can be moved; click and drag the handle or the component to do so
▼	Row/Column menu	Allows access to a menu of controls for row/column manipulation
◫	Insert column to left	Creates a new column, inserted to the left of the current column
◫	Insert column to right	Creates a new column, inserted to the right of the current column
◫	Split column	Splits the current column in two; any components in that column expand to span both new columns
▤	Insert row above	Creates a new row above the current row
▤	Insert row below	Creates a new row below the current row
▥	Split row	Splits the current row in two; any components in that row expand to span both new rows
✕	Delete row/column	Deletes an empty row/column from the layout

example, if one element is twice as big as elements below it, the designer causes the larger component to span two columns.

> **TIP** To apply a layout to all the components in the design area, you don't need to select them. Clicking one of the layout buttons applies the layout to all of them.

Nesting components to control the layout

Although the capabilities of the grid layout are good enough for simple interfaces, you'll find that with any complexity, you'll need more control over your layout options. To gain more control, subdivide your interface into several smaller panels, nesting them together to form complex arrangements. Use the grid layout of the topmost container to position your smaller panels. To group components, select all of the components that will make up your group, and then select a layout from the toolbar.

Creating the top-level container

Each layout you design must ultimately be part of a single container element that will eventually be placed into your application either as part of a larger interface or as the root content pane of a JWindow or JFrame. The top node of your component tree is this root element, and when you use the grid layout buttons, it defaults to a JPanel. The component toolbar also contains buttons for JScrollPane, JTabbedPane, and JSplitPane, all of which can also be used as root-level elements. All the components in your layout must be placed as children of a top-level container. Typically, the top-level container is bound to your form class and becomes the content pane of the JFrame displaying your application interface.

The most basic and common type of container is the JPanel. It's an empty panel that you can use to group any number of components, including other JPanels. You assign it whatever layout is appropriate for the components it holds. You can nest several JPanels together to create more complex interfaces.

The JScrollPane is a simple extension of the JPanel that automatically adds scrollbars to itself when required to view its contents. You can use a JScrollPane just like a JPanel: create it, arrange your items into it, and assign a layout.

The JSplitPane component creates a two-part container with either top and bottom or left and right sections divided by a resizable splitter bar. Each half of the JSplitPane is independent of the other and is its own container. Generally, you should add a JPanel to each side to hold any controls you need to place into it.

Although a tab pane appears visually complex, creating one with the GUI Designer is surprisingly simple. Unlike the other container components, which are designed to hold components, the JTabbedPane is designed to hold other containers, which in turn hold the components that make up each pane. To create a JTabbedPane, add it to your workspace. It begins life with no tabs and no content. To begin adding components, first create a new JPanel, and then drag and drop it into your JTabbedPane. Doing so adds the JPanel to the JTabbedPane and creates a new tab at the top of the pane (called the *tab region*). You can rename the tab by double-clicking it and entering a new name. Now you're free to add components to the newly created tab and set the layout as required. To create additional tabs, create new JPanels and drag them into the tab region of the JTabbedPane. To remove a tab, activate its JPanel on the tree view, and delete it.

Previewing your design

You can click the **Preview** button to build and run your form as a standalone dialog. In this dialog, you can see how your components look as well as how they handle resizing, text entry, and so forth.

10.3 Designing an ACME GUI

Let's create a GUI for the currency converter. Assuming you distribute the application as a standalone desktop application, you'd like to provide more than just a command-line interface. The GUI can be simplistic: a single form that a user fills out to provide the data for the conversion. This data includes the starting currency, the ending currency, and the amount of currency to be exchanged. You'll also need a control component to execute the conversion and a view component to show the results. In addition, most simple GUIs like this have a **Close** or **Finish** control component to shut down or leave the GUI.

10.3.1 Creating a new GUI form in IDEA

Navigate in the **Project** tool window to the `com.acme.conversion.currency.client` package. With that node selected, right-click, and choose **New | GUI Form** from the context menu. When prompted for the form name, enter `ACMEGUI` and click **OK**. A new GUI Designer tab opens in IDEA, ready for you to begin.

10.3.2 Manually creating the basic layout

The first step is to manually lay out the interface with all the components required. Let's use a JTextField for textual input (for simplicity), JComboBoxes

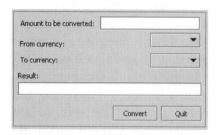

Figure 10.3 The components are laid out in the Form Workspace at a near approximation of where they should appear in the GUI.

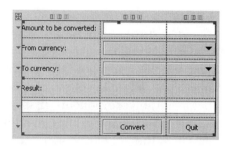

Figure 10.4 After you apply a grid layout, the components fall into cells (or sets of cells) that keep them aligned and constrained.

for the currency lists, JButtons for the **Convert** and **Quit** operations, and JLabels to explain the various components. In figure 10.3, the components are roughly in the desired arrangement.

10.3.3 Applying the grid layout

Click the grid layout button to automatically enclose the components in a JPanel, as shown in figure 10.4. As you can see, the items are placed into a grid layout with spacing appropriate to the original layout. The **Result** field spans three columns; the labels and input fields are aligned; and the action buttons are on the bottom, offset one column to the right (thanks to a horizontal spacer).

10.3.4 Setting component properties

Select the **Amount to be converted** text field, either by clicking it in the Form Workspace or by choosing its entry on the component tree view. Blue resize handles indicate that you've selected the correct field. Because this field only makes sense if you enter a number, let's set a default. Find the text entry in the Properties Inspector, and enter 100.00 in the value field. The Form Workspace changes to reflect the default value.

Also select the **Results** text field, and prevent users from typing anything in that field by setting its enabled property to false. That field is strictly for feedback from the software; there's no need for users to enter any data.

10.3.5 Touching up the final interface

Now that you have a clean, flexible layout, you're free to touch it up as needed. In this case, we added a margin of 11 pixels around the JPanel to give the interface a

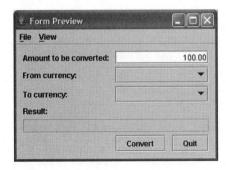

Figure 10.5
A preview of the dialog, which looks right but still has no functionality behind it.

cushion. To do this, select the top-level JPanel, and enter appropriate values into the `margin` fields using the Properties Inspector. The final dialog is shown in action in figure 10.5.

10.4 *Understanding properties*

Once you've created a basic layout for your form, you can use the Properties Inspector to fine-tune the alignment and other properties necessary to achieve the finished interface. The shaded properties at the top of the Properties Inspector are proprietary to IDEA; they're mainly used to control the layout of your user interface. Many of these properties appear only after you've added a layout to the component's container. We'll discuss each of them in turn throughout this chapter, but you can see a brief summary of their usage in table 10.2. Some properties (such as `margins`) are only available to container components.

Table 10.2 Many of the properties found in the Properties Inspector are used to control the layout of the containers and their components.

Property	Effect
binding	Specifies the instance variable to which this component is bound
border	Adds a decorative border around the container
margins	Creates padding between the container and its contents
Horizontal Gap	Specifies the amount of horizontal spacing between cells
Vertical Gap	Specifies the amount of vertical spacing between cells
Horizontal Size Policy	Determines how the component can be resized horizontally
Vertical Size Policy	Determines how the component can be resized vertically

continued on next page

Table 10.2   Many of the properties found in the Properties Inspector are used to control the layout of the containers and their components. *(continued)*

Property	Effect
`fill`	Determines if and how the component expands to fill its container
`anchor`	Controls the alignment of the component within its container or cell
`Row Span`	Allows the component to span multiple rows in a grid layout
`Column Span`	Allows the component to span multiple columns in a grid layout
`Minimum Size`	Specifies the smallest allowable size for the component
`Preferred Size`	Specifies the most appropriate size for the component
`Maximum Size`	Specifies the largest possible size for the component

10.4.1   *Spanning rows and columns*

If you're familiar with building tables in HTML, then you have a pretty good idea of how you can use the `Row Span` and `Column Span` properties to structure your layout. Unless you're building a tic-tac-toe game, you'll almost certainly have to use these properties to achieve the layout you desire. The `Row Span` property allows a component to occupy multiple adjacent rows. Likewise, the `Column Span` property causes a component to stretch itself across several columns.

These properties are set to initial values when you place your components in grid layout, and IDEA tries to replicate your XY Layout as best it can within a grid. You can edit the properties in the Properties Inspector to gain more fine-grained control over the GUI you're building.

To illustrate the point, figure 10.6 shows a variation on the ACME GUI. In this example, the JComboBoxes' `Column Span` property has been changed from 2 to 1, and those components have been moved one cell to the right.

10.4.2   *Setting an anchor point (cell alignment)*

When a component is placed into a layout cell, its position within that cell is determined by its `anchor` property. `anchor` can be set to any of the eight compass directions or to `center`. Figure 10.7 shows a JLabel positioned in each cell of a 3x3 grid layout, with a different anchor point for each. It's important to recognize that the anchor controls the placement of the component inside its cell, not its position in the overall container.

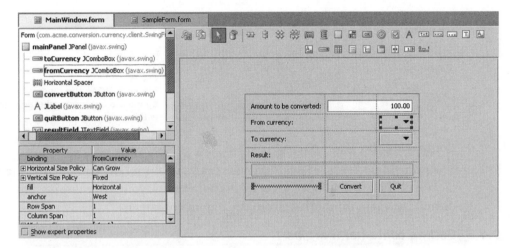

Figure 10.6 Changing the column span and the row span of components makes them take up more or less room on the grid. Notice the smaller combo boxes in this image (column span of 1 instead of 2).

10.4.3 *Using spacers to control layout*

On the Component palette, you'll find the horizontal and vertical spacer components (they look like springs). These are used to control spacing within your user interface. When placed in your layout, they grow to take up all the space remaining in their appropriate direction after you've sized the other components. If you insert more than one spacer in a given direction, they divide the remaining space equally among themselves. So, a horizontal spacer on both sides of a group of components forces the components to be centered.

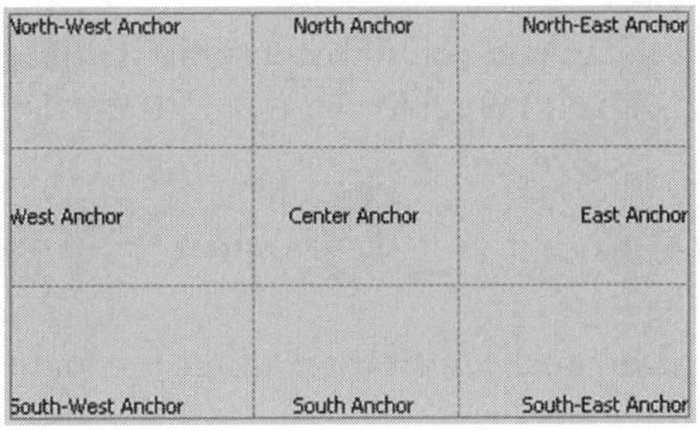

North-West Anchor	North Anchor	North-East Anchor
West Anchor	Center Anchor	East Anchor
South-West Anchor	South Anchor	South-East Anchor

Figure 10.7
Anchoring determines where the content appears within a component.

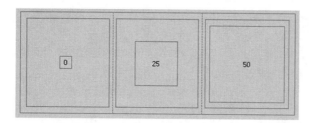

Figure 10.8
Margins define the range of empty space around the numbered label within a component.

10.4.4 Controlling the grid spacing

The properties Horizontal Gap and Vertical Gap control the amount of horizontal and vertical space between each cell in a container's layout. If a value is set to -1 (the default), the gap is inherited from the parent container.

10.4.5 Setting container margins

The margins property allows you to add empty space to the inside of a container element. Depending on how you look at it, you're either adding a margin around the contents of the container or adding padding to the container itself. You can independently specify margins for the top, bottom, left side, and right side. Values for the margin settings can't be negative.

In order to specify a margin, the container must be under layout control, and it can't be empty. Any margins you add to a container cause its contents to shift in position accordingly. Regardless of the overall size of the window, the margins you specify will be honored. In figure 10.8, three nested panels are placed in three equal columns. Only the margins around their contents differ, causing the contents to be constrained appropriately.

10.4.6 Setting sizing policies

The horizontal and vertical sizing policies control how the component responds to its parent container being resized. The acceptable values and their definitions are as follows:

- canShrink—This component's size can be reduced when the parent container is resized.

- canGrow—This component's size can be increased when the parent container is resized.

- wantGrow—This component's size can be increased when the parent container is resized. wantGrow has a higher priority then canGrow. Should the two collide, wantGrow is given priority when competing with other components' cells.

■ `fixed`—This component's size doesn't change when the parent container is resized. When no other sizing policy is selected, the `fixed` policy is in effect.

10.4.7 Setting fill policies

Each component under layout control has a property setting called `fill` that controls the directions, if any, in which the component should expand to fill its cell in the grid layout. This is best illustrated by the example shown in figure 10.9. This layout is a grid of four cells, equally distributed, with a button in each cell. A different fill mode has been specified for each button, as indicated by the buttons' names. A `fill` mode of `none` uses default values, typically as small as permitted.

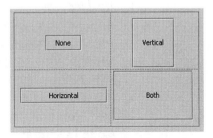

Figure 10.9 The `fill` property controls the behavior of components when they're added to the grid layout, defining how they react to the grid cell they're placed in.

10.4.8 Adding borders

You can add a decorative border to any JPanel or other container, including the root container of your interface. To do so, select the container and edit its `border` property. You must expand the property node, because there are two settings to specify: The `type` and `title` properties are set separately, meaning you can combine them for best effect. For example, you can combine an etched border with a title to get an etched style, titled border, and so forth. Titled borders are a good way to group related components together within a more complicated dialog. You can see an example of some of these combinations in figure 10.10.

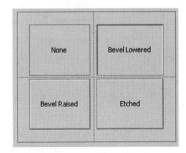

Figure 10.10 The GUI Designer uses simple properties to support borders, a common visual component to many complex GUI designs.

10.5 Adding functionality to forms

A form that has been designed and laid out may be pleasing to the eye, but if it isn't bound to an underlying Java class, it's useless. It has no business logic and no functionality behind it. Buttons click without effect, combination boxes stand empty, and so on. If the purpose of a GUI is to let the user interact with predefined valuable business logic, you need to integrate the GUI with back-end services. Let's run through a quick overview of the typical process used to add functionality to a GUI form in IDEA:

1   *Bind the form to a Java class, and bind its important components to fields of that class.* The GUI Designer depends on the fact that a Java class will underpin the form. You can bind the form to an existing class or create one on the fly; similarly, you can bind components to existing fields or create new ones as needed.

2   *Add a constructor to the form class.* If any fields in the form should be initialized, you can create a constructor in the Java class. You can use IDEA's **Code | Generate** command or press **Alt+Insert** to create this constructor.

3   *If necessary, define functional groups of components.* Some components (like radio buttons) are logically divided into groups. These group relationships need to be implemented in the constructor of the underlying Java class.

4   *Implement actions for all components that perform actions, such as JButtons.* The business logic that is called by interactions with the GUI must be connected by hand using the Swing event model.

5   *If desired, bind component fields to data from a JavaBean.* The GUI Designer has the ability to leverage the JavaBean framework and populate the GUI's state from bean data. If you're working with JavaBeans, you may wish to configure the GUI in this fashion.

6   *Implement initialization code that uses the form.* Provide a point of entry where the form can be run and tested.

10.5.1 Binding forms and their components

Once you're happy with your user interface's layout and behavior, you need to bind it to a class in order to use it as part of your application. After associating your form with its class, you then bind each of the components you wish to access programmatically to the field variables of your form class.

Binding the form to a class

To be useful, your form must be bound to a class that contains the methods and behavior that do whatever the form has been designed for. You can bind a form to any class: The class serves as a container for accessing the form and its components.

In the GUI Designer, select the **Form** root node from the component tree, and enter the fully qualified name of the class to which you wish to bind your form in the Properties Inspector; or, select it from your project by clicking the **Browse** button. If you type the name of a class that doesn't yet exist, IDEA will ask to create it for you by offering an intention action (described in detail in chapter 3).

> **TIP** Although there is no requirement around the naming of forms and the naming of their underlying classes—they can be vastly different, which is perfectly legitimate—the convention of giving them the same name (in the same package) can help eliminate confusion. You'll always remember that the functionality for `MainGUI.form` is found in `MainGUI.java`.

Binding individual components to field variables

In order to access the buttons, form fields, and other components in your form, you must bind each of them to a member variable of your form class. If you don't need to access a particular component (for example, if you never have to manipulate a label), there is no need to bind it.

To bind a component, select it in the GUI Designer, and click the `binding` entry in the Properties Inspector. Now you may either select an existing member variable from the list (the list is filtered to include only the appropriate types of field variables) or type in the name of field variable you'd like to use and let IDEA's intention actions create it for you.

> **TIP** When we're using the GUI Designer, we rarely create fields ahead of time. As soon as we realize we need to programmatically access a component, we edit the `bind` property of the component, type in an appropriate variable name, and let IDEA take over.

To display your form, you need to bind your top-level panel to a field in your form class. This panel is the panel you'll use to display your GUI.

10.5.2 Creating a constructor

You need a constructor (or you can let Java create an empty one for you if none is explicitly defined) for your form class so that it may be instantiated. You can initialize the fields of your form class either in the constructor or in their declaration. At compile time, IDEA automatically (and transparently) adds code to the constructor that will initialize the form and bind it to your class's field variables. This will happen ahead of any additional code you place into the constructor, allowing you to further customize the components within it.

Defining radio button groups

Some components require grouping in order to function. Mutually exclusive radio buttons, for example, need to know about the group they belong to so that the selection of one leads to the deselection of all other group members. Ten radio buttons on a GUI might belong to one large group, five sets of two, or some mix in between. This group relationship isn't visible or accessible in the Form Workspace of the GUI Designer; you should implement it in the form class's constructor, an example of which is shown in listing 10.1.

Listing 10.1 Defining a group of radio buttons in a form class's constructor

```
...
public class SearchGUI {
    private JRadioButton dirForward;
    private JRadioButton dirBackward;

    public SearchGUI() {
        ButtonGroup searchDirection = new ButtonGroup();
        searchDirection.add(dirForward);
        searchDirection.add(dirBackward);
...
```

Implementing actions

Some components exist on the GUI to take action. For example, the **Convert** button on the ACME GUI is responsible for collecting the data on the form, executing the business logic in the currency converter, and providing the results back to the user through the GUI. This work has to be done programmatically, and it's beyond the responsibility of the Form Workspace. It requires you to use the Swing event-handling model and is another good candidate for implementation in the form class's constructor.

To illustrate, imagine the simplistic GUI and use case that have been implemented in listing 10.2. The GUI has a text field, a button, and a label. The user types something in the text field and then clicks the button. The button's responsibility is to check whether the data in the field is an integer value, as opposed to textual or alphanumeric gibberish. The result of the test is shown in the label.

Listing 10.2 Defining the action for a "Check if this is an integer" button

```
...
checkButton.addActionListener(new ActionListener() {
    public void actionPerformed(ActionEvent e) {
        String datum = datumField.getText();
```

```
         boolean result = true;

         try {
           int integer = Integer.parseInt(datum);
         } catch (NumberFormatException e) {
             result = false;
         }

         if (result) {
             feedbackLabel.setText(datum + " is an integer");
         }
         else {
             feedbackLabel.setText(datum + " is not an integer");
         }
      }
   });
```

10.5.3 *Generating getter/setter methods for fields bound to data*

If you have a JavaBean class whose properties should be bound to controls on your GUI, you can integrate these properties by making changes to the underlying form class. For example, you may have a JavaBean with five `String` properties and a GUI with five text fields that are designed to show the bean's values and, if the user edits that data, set new values in the bean. You can accomplish this by editing the underlying form class, hooking in each of the getters and setters to draw from and persist to the bean. This pattern, however, is common enough in GUI implementation that the GUI Designer provides an additional control to handle the binding for you. It's called the Data Binding Wizard.

Once you've bound a form to an underlying form class, click the **Data Binding Wizard** button on the GUI Designer's toolbar. The wizard process prompts you to choose to bind to an existing bean or to create a new one. You're then prompted to select the property of the bean that should be bound to the GUI component. All integration work, imports, and so on are taken care of for you. Running the wizard on a component also allows you to sever the binding or reapply it to a different location.

10.5.4 *Invoking your form*

When you want to invoke your form class within your application, construct an instance of the class, place your form's top-level panel into a JFrame (just as you would normally do with a panel you created by hand), and invoke it. Listing 10.3 shows a typical example, using the `main()` method as a starting point.

Listing 10.3 A `main()` method that invokes the GUI

```
...
public static void main(String[] args) {
    MyForm form = new MyForm();
    JFrame frame = new JFrame("My Form");
    frame.setContentPane(form.mainPanel);
    frame.pack();
    frame.setResizable(false);
    frame.setDefaultCloseOperation(JFrame.DISPOSE_ON_CLOSE);
    frame.show();
}
...
```

Within your form class, you can access any of the components you've bound to fields within the class. You don't need to do any special initialization; by selecting them for binding, IDEA initializes them at the beginning of your class's constructor. You're free to hook up action listeners to your buttons, load initial data into JTables, or whatever other setup you require.

10.6 Adding functionality to the ACME GUI

Now that we've talked about the fundamentals of adding functionality, let's make the ACME GUI do what it's intended to do: perform a currency conversion. You've already laid out the GUI, so it's a matter of specifying the form class and adding functionality to it to bridge the gap between the currency conversion library and the interface.

10.6.1 Binding the ACME GUI to a form class

First, you need to bind the form to a new class. Select the root node of the tree—the one that represents the form as a whole—in the component tree view. Edit its `bind to class` property, and type in the value `com.acme.conversion.currency.client.ACMEGUI`. When you press **Enter** to accept this value, you'll notice that the form node on the component tree view is visually marked as having an error (by default, IDEA uses the wavy red underline that you've probably seen in open Java files). Click the form node of the component tree view once more, and you'll see the error: the class doesn't exist. You'll also see the light bulb icon that suggests an intention action. Open the light bulb, and select the **Create class** intention action option. The new form class is created for you.

The next step in the process is to bind all the important GUI components to fields in that new class. You can use intention actions to create them individually, or you can edit the file to add the references by hand and then pick their names from within the Properties Inspector. Opting for the former, select the JPanel on the component tree view, edit its `binding` property in the Properties Inspector to refer to the `mainPanel` field, and then use the intention action to create that field in the ACMEGUI class. Repeat those steps for the components listed in table 10.3.

Table 10.3 By binding your components to specific fields in your form class, they can be accessed and manipulated programmatically.

Field name	Component
amountField	JTextField where the user is expected to enter the amount of currency to convert
fromCurrency	JComboBox where the user is expected to select the currency at the beginning of the conversion
toCurrency	JComboBox where the user is expected to select the currency at the end of the conversion
resultField	JTextField where you intend to display results to the user
convertButton	JButton that the user uses to perform the conversion after all the data is collected
quitButton	JButton that the user uses to close the GUI and stop using the application

10.6.2 *Creating a constructor*

Now that the components are bound to the form class, you need to implement a constructor. This is made simple by IDEA's **Generate** functionality. Open the source file, select **Code | Generate** or press **Alt+Ins**, and select **Constructor** from the pop-up menu. Select the **Select None** button when prompted for fields to initialize through parameters. IDEA inserts a default, empty constructor.

The GUI needs some initialization, however. Two JComboBoxes need to be populated with the list of currencies the system is aware of. You need to populate those JComboBoxes in the class constructor so that they'll be properly filled with the correct data before the GUI is shown on the screen.

So far in the implementation, you haven't created a class to track which currencies are supported and which aren't—you've only been interested in USD and CDN. Listing 10.4 shows a simple class that you can programmatically query to return this list.

Listing 10.4 The `Currency.java` class

```
package com.acme.conversion.currency;

import java.util.HashSet;

public final class Currency {
    private static Set allCurrenciesSet;

    static {
        allCurrenciesSet = new HashSet();
        allCurrenciesSet.add("USD");
        allCurrenciesSet.add("CDN");
    }

    public static Iterator getCurrencies() {
        return allCurrenciesSet.iterator();
    }
}
```

Now, you can rely on the Currency class to provide a list of currencies you support. You can query the Currency class for its list of known currencies and then add a string into the JComboBoxes' option lists for each occurrence. Listing 10.5 shows the first version of the form class's constructor.

Listing 10.5 The `ACMEGUI.java` constructor, which populates the GUI's JComboBoxes

```
...
public ACMEGUI() {
    Iterator currencies = Currency.getCurrencies();
    while (currencies.hasNext()) {
        String currency = (String)currencies.next();
        fromCurrency.addItem(currency);
        toCurrency.addItem(currency);
    }
}
...
```

10.6.3 *Implementing the Convert functionality*

In addition to initializing the JComboBoxes with data, you need to add another significant piece of functionality: the power behind the **Convert** button. When this button is clicked, the GUI should collect the amount and the currencies from the form, use them as arguments to the currency conversion process, and then return the result of the conversion to the user in the **Results** field.

Swing's event model says that when a button is clicked, an ActionEvent is fired and passed through the queue of registered ActionListeners. In the constructor of the class, shown in listing 10.6, you implement this feature by defining an anonymous inner class of type ActionListener.

Listing 10.6 Implementation of the Convert button's functionality

```
...
convertButton.addActionListener(new ActionListener() {
    public void actionPerformed(ActionEvent e) {
        String fromCurrStr = (String)fromCurrency.getSelectedItem();
        String toCurrStr = (String)toCurrency.getSelectedItem();
        String amountStr = amountField.getText();

        DecimalFormat df = new DecimalFormat("0.00");
        try {
            double amount = Double.parseDouble(amountStr);
            CurrencyExchangeService service =
                    CurrencyExchangeServiceFactory.getService();
            double rate = service.requestCurrentRate
                (fromCurrStr, toCurrStr);

            resultField.setText(df.format(amount * rate));
        } catch (NumberFormatException e1) {
            resultField.setText(
                "The amount specified was not a valid number.");
        }
    }
});
...
```

10.6.4 *Providing an entry point*

Finally, you require an entry point: Somewhere in the system, a class has to be responsible for creating a new frame or window and placing the form in it for the user to see. This same class is typically responsible for proper disposal of the frame. You can implement that functionality in a main() method, as shown in listing 10.7.

Listing 10.7 main() method that gives a launching point for running the GUI

```
public static void main(String[] args) {
    ACMEGUI acmeGui = new ACMEGUI();
```

```
final JFrame frame = new JFrame("ACME Currency Converter");
frame.setContentPane(acmeGui.mainPanel);

acmeGui.quitButton.addActionListener(new ActionListener() {
    public void actionPerformed(ActionEvent e) {
        frame.dispose();
    }
});

frame.pack();
frame.setResizable(false);
frame.setDefaultCloseOperation(JFrame.DISPOSE_ON_CLOSE);
frame.show();
}
```

TIP   You may notice that both the `mainPanel` and the `quitButton` fields are referenced from this lifecycle code, and that this code doesn't necessarily have to reside in the same class. This means external classes may need to reference some of your components—those involved with the lifecycle of the GUI. In that case, you have the option of making `mainPanel` and `quitButton` nonprivate fields, or you can implement getters as a way of providing references.

10.7 *Building and running your form*

The XML-formatted .form file is the output of working with the GUI Designer, but that XML file can't be compiled the way Java is. During the build process, that file is read by IDEA, parsed and processed into a valid Java file, and then compiled into byte code like the rest of your source. That parsing and processing stage must take into account that your form is bound to another Java class and that the functionality of how the form should act is defined there. By making the design of the forms more efficient, the process of how they're eventually converted to byte code became necessarily more complex.

Luckily, most of this complexity is hidden from you and dealt with in the inner workings of the IDE. By default, the passage from the WYSIWYG Form Workspace to a working, testable application is handled seamlessly with a single command. If you're using IDEA to run build scripts, there's no change in process: **Build | Make Project** (or **Ctrl+F9**) or even **Build | Make Module** processes your form files. Once built, the classes can be run and tested just like any other classes.

10.7.1 *Generating the GUI to binary or source*

When you make your project, IDEA adds the necessary code to create and initialize the forms that make up your project with their respective classes. Normally this is all transparent to you. IDEA modifies your source code on the fly, compiling in the changes silently. If you wish, you can disable this behavior through the GUI Designer settings panel by switching the **Generate GUI to** option to Java source code. If you do this, you'll see the generated source code added to the form class in a method called `$$$setupUI$$$()`. A call to this method is also added to the constructor. However, you aren't allowed to edit this code or call the setup method yourself. This method is regenerated each time you build the project as the form XML file is processed.

Why would anyone want to generate Java source and compile the class by hand when IDEA's build system handles the process invisibly for you? The only reason to expose the generated source is to export the source code out of IDEA, to eliminate any dependence on IDEA. If you have a team of developers, some of whom don't use IDEA, you probably shouldn't store form files to define your user interfaces. If you do, only the developers using IDEA will be able to edit those GUIs. Any changes made to the `$$$setupUI$$$()` method by non-IDEA developers will be overridden the next time someone runs a **Make Project** command. In this situation, you could design your form in the GUI Designer, build it to Java source, and then refactor the content out of `$$$setupUI$$$()` into other methods, like the class constructor. You could then discard the original form file and treat the form class as if you'd written it by hand.

10.7.2 *Including the forms library*

When you create your user interface with IDEA's GUI builder, you're using IDEA's custom layout classes and must include them with your application in order for users to run it. When you build an application using the GUI Designer, IDEA automatically copies a few files into your output folder under the `com.intellij.uidesigner.core` package structure. That way, you can package up these classes along with your own to ensure you application runs outside of IDEA.

You can disable this behavior through the GUI Designer settings panel by deselecting the option to automatically copy the form classes to the output directory. If you do so, you still need to distribute the classes. These classes are included in a JAR file located in the redist folder (short for *redistributable*) of your IDEA installation. The name of the library is `forms_rt.jar`. Of course, you must also add it to the Classpath when running your application.

10.7.3 *Compiling with Ant*

Perhaps you're lucky enough to be working under agile methodologies and you have a test machine continuously integrating your code, syncing up to your source code repository and running a full build and test multiple times a day. The build is running as a series of Ant scripts. How can that process mimic IDEA's ability to process form XML files into byte code, if it isn't running a build from within the IDEA program itself?

IDEA includes, in its redistributable JARs, com.intellij.uiDesigner.ant. Javac2. This class is a custom Ant task that provides access to the form XML-to-Java process. If you include a few libraries in your Classpath and define this custom task, as in listing 10.8, an Ant process can handle GUI Designer forms easily.

> **Listing 10.8   Defining a custom Ant task and using it in lieu of the standard Javac task**

```
...
<path id="compile.classpath">
    ...
</path>

<path id="uiDesigner.classpath">
    <path refid="project.classpath"/>
    <pathelement location="C:\Intellij-IDEA-4.5\lib\bcel.jar"/>
    <pathelement location="C:\Intellij-IDEA-4.5\lib\jdom.jar"/>
    <pathelement location=
        "C:\Intellij-IDEA-4.5\redist\javac2.jar"/>
</path>

<taskdef name="javac2"
         classname="com.intellij.uiDesigner.ant.Javac2"
         classpathref="uiDesigner.classpath"/>

<target name="...">
    <javac2 srcdir="..." destdir="..."
        classpathref="compile.classpath" />
</target>
...
```

This example creates a custom task, javac2, which uses libraries shipped with IDEA. Then you use this new task as a replacement for the normal javac task, and it automatically compiles the .form files and performs the necessary binding operations.

10.8 *Summary*

IDEA has done an excellent job of making Swing GUI design and implementation more efficient. Implementing GUIs by hand is tedious work for developers skilled in those libraries and downright frustrating for those developers new to them. Other IDE vendors' previous attempts at solving this problem have resulted in graphical design workspaces crippled by poor performance, or a total inability to edit the generated code, or an attempt at a visual medium for defining functionality that wasn't sufficient for the needs of its audience.

IDEA avoids these pitfalls by providing an *enabling* technology: an abstraction layer atop the Swing code that lets you handle the tedious parts of the process quickly—fighting with layout managers and layers of containers to make the UI look right—without attempting to handle the parts in the process that need the full flexibility of the Java language—integration of the UI to functionality.

Finally, in courteous recognition of the need to work within a process that might not be IDEA-pervasive, the IDE doesn't demand that you design forms using this feature. You're free to build them by hand if you wish. And the GUI Designer tool can be used to generate a UI that is then refactored and reworked in such a way that the GUI Designer no longer needs to maintain it. IDEA's solution for the design and implementation of GUIs is a flexible and robust system that you'll find relatively easy to fit into your specific development needs.

11

Developing J2EE applications

In this chapter...

- Setting up web applications in your project using web modules
- Editing JSP files and servlets as part of a web application
- Setting up EJBs in your project using EJB modules
- Running and debugging J2EE applications within IDEA
- Working with web content in IDEA 5.0

IDEA provides extensive support to the J2EE architecture, including support for servlets, JavaServer Pages (JSPs), and Enterprise JavaBeans (EJBs). IDEA's support goes far beyond just recognizing JSP syntax and the Servlet API; it covers everything from initial creation and editing of source files and content to building, deploying, and real-time debugging of web applications.

IDEA has rich support for web applications embedded throughout all its tools and features. IDEA's web development support should appeal to servlet and JSP developers of any skill level, whether you're architecting a large-scale J2EE application or doing basic JSP markup.

To illustrate some of the points in this chapter, we'll extend the ACME Currency Converter by adding a simple web application front-end.

11.1 *Working with web applications*

Web applications are designed to run across a network and in the context of a web browser, and the J2EE platform provides a strong foundation on which to build these applications. Those based on the J2EE platform are typically implemented using the Java Servlet and JavaServer Pages APIs. In fact, a web application can be thought of as a collection of libraries, Java classes, JSP files, and other resources bundled together with a deployment descriptor that describes their use. Such an application can be deployed to any J2EE-compliant server in the form of a web application archive file (also known as a WAR file or a WAR). The format of the WAR file is part of the Java Servlet Specification; it's a standard JAR file with some additional requirements.

A WAR file defines a provider-independent way of combining HTML, JSPs, servlets, Java classes, and JARs into a single deployable package. This vendor neutrality is made possible through a standardized XML deployment descriptor that controls such elements as servlet names and URL mappings. Once created, the WAR file is deployed into an application server, which reads the deployment descriptors and makes the application available.

Exploring the full extent of the servlet and JSP technologies is beyond the scope of this book, and we're going to assume that you have some degree of familiarity with those technologies. The following material will focus on IDEA's support for the working with J2EE web applications.

11.1.1 *Understanding web modules*

Simply put, a *web module* is a specific type of IDEA module that is designed to contain a web application. By defining a web application inside a web module (as opposed to one of IDEA's generic Java modules), the IDE is better able to support your development with special features for that context.

You aren't required to work on web applications by defining them in a web module. If a deployable web application in a WAR file is defined as a deployment descriptor and a directory structure of Java sources, you could conceivably use IDEA to edit the files and then package the collection together into a web archive. IDEA, however, understands the structure and intent around the WAR file format and provides a web module that enhances web application support.

11.1.2 *Creating a new web module*

Let's extend the ACME currency conversion tool by adding a web application front end so that its functionality can be accessed by anyone with a web browser on the corporate intranet. The first step in this process is to create a new web module in your project, which can be accomplished by following these steps:

1   Select **File | New Module** from the main menu.

2   The first dialog in the **New Module** wizard appears and prompts you to select the type of module to create. Click the **Web Module** option, and then click **Next**.

3   The next dialog prompts you to select a module name and a module content root. Enter ACMEWebApp as the module name, and specify the module content root to be a sibling directory to the currency converter's Java module (for example, if the module you've been working on can be found in the C:\Projects\CurrencyConverter directory, make this module use the C:\Projects\ACMEWebApp directory). Click **Next**.

4   The next dialog prompts you to select the application server for which this web application is being written, but you don't have an application server configured yet! Not to worry—this step can be reconfigured at a later time, so defer the matter and click **Next**.

5   Specify the path and version of your web application's deployment descriptor, the web.xml file that defines how this web application should be deployed to a web application server. Because you're creating a new web module, IDEA suggests the WEB-INF/web.xml file relative to your module root. This default is appropriate, so click **Next** to continue.

6   You're prompted to specify a web resource directory. As the dialog suggests, a web resource directory contains web-specific resources like JSP files, additional deployment descriptors, and so on that you want to be

eventually located somewhere in a deployment directory. The default suggestion of *resources* is fine, so click **Next**.

7 The next dialog prompts you to specify the path for the web module's exploded directory. As the dialog suggests, an exploded directory is used for deployment of a web application to a web application server. It will serve as the deployment root. The contents of this directory will look exactly like the contents of a WAR discussed earlier. The default suggestion of *exploded* is fine, so click **Next**.

8 Specify a source directory for the web module. This is where the source files for any custom Java classes will reside. The default suggestion of *src* is fine, so click **Next** to continue.

9 The final dialog prompts you to specify an output directory where the compiled Java sources will reside. If you defined an exploded directory two steps ago, you'll notice that the suggested compiler output directory is exploded/WEB-INF/classes. The WEB-INF/classes directory is where all custom Java class files *must* reside for use by the web application, according to the Java Servlet Specification. Click **Finish** to finish the process.

If you look in your **Project** tool window, you'll notice that you now have two modules on your project tree. One represents the initial work you've done on the currency converter, and the other represents your new web application front end. Expanding the latter branch reveals the following set of directories: a resources directory (for HTML files, JSPs, image files, and other web resources); a src directory (for Java sources used by the web application); and a WEB-INF directory containing a web.xml file (your web application's deployment descriptor).

11.1.3 *Configuring a web module*

All modules in IDEA are managed through the **Paths** configuration window. You can access this window by selecting the **File | Settings** menu option and then choosing the first entry, **Paths**. The module list on the left side of the window lists two modules whose icons differ: one is a Java module, and the other is a web module. When you select the web module from that list, the tabbed panels on the right side of the window change to reflect web module settings.

The **Paths**, **Libraries**, **Dependencies**, **Order/Export**, and **Javadoc** tabs that you saw with Java modules are all still present and operate the same way, but the **Web Module Settings** and **J2EE Build Settings** tabs are new. These tabs contain controls and configuration settings that are contextually important to web applications but aren't for standard Java projects.

Controlling web module settings

The **Web Module Settings** tab of the **Paths** window, shown in figure 11.1, lets you control the structure and dependencies of the web application defined within.

The **Application Server** drop-down lets you specify the application server on which this web application should be run and debugged (you'll see how to configure application servers in IDEA later in this chapter). The **Deployment Descriptors** group lists the types, paths, and versions of the descriptors available in the module.

The **Modules and Libraries to Package** group shows a list of all modules and libraries that need to be packaged with this web application in order for it to function properly. This list is populated from the library dependencies marked in the **Libraries** tab and the module dependencies marked in the **Dependencies** tab. For example, if the ACME web module were to rely on a third-party library to handle user authentication, that library would have to be packaged somehow in the WAR in order for the web application to work properly. The table lets you specify

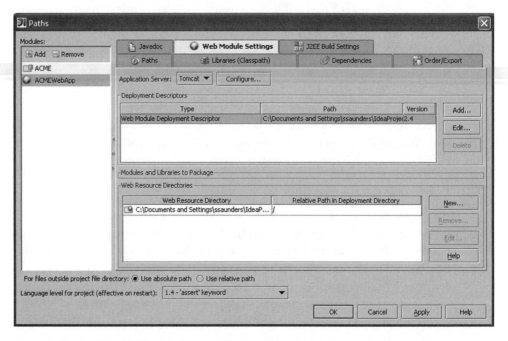

Figure 11.1 The Web Module Settings panel, accessible when you're configuring a web module in a project, lets you set the default application server, the deployment descriptors, the modules and libraries that need to be packaged along with this web application, and the resource directories.

the packaging method and the relative path where those libraries and modules can be found.

Packaging methods vary, depending on the type of material being packaged. For module dependencies, the following options are available:

- **Do not package**—Despite being marked as required, don't include the specified module's content in the final web application.

- **Copy module output to**—The output of the module (a collection of compiled Java classes) is copied to the specified directory, relative to the deployment root (usually /WEB-INF/classes, which is in the Classpath).

- JAR **module output and copy file to**—The output of the module is stored in a JAR archive and then copied to the specified directory, relative to the deployment root (usually /WEB-INF/lib, which is in the Classpath).

- JAR **module, link via manifest and copy to**—The output of the module is stored in a JAR archive and then copied to the specified directory, relative to the deployment root (defaults to /). A link to the JAR is added in the META-INF/manifest.mf file in the created web module.

For library dependencies or JARs, the following options are available:

- **Do not package**—Despite being marked as required, don't include this library in the final web application.

- **Copy files to**—This library is copied to the specified directory, relative to the deployment root (usually /WEB-INF/lib, which is in the Classpath).

- **Link via manifest and copy files to**—The library is copied to the specified directory, relative to the deployment root (defaults to /). A link to the library is added in the META-INF/manifest.mf file in the created web module.

The **Web Resource Directories** group specifies the location of web resources (such as HTML files, JSP files, image files, and so on) that are included in your web application. The group shows a table that maps directories on your local file system to relative paths in the deployed web application. Thus, if you specify that a directory is mapped to the relative root of the web application (/), the files in that directory are copied into the root of the deployment directory, also known as the *deployment root*.

Configuring J2EE Build Settings

The J2EE **Build Settings** tab of the **Paths** window, shown in figure 11.2, lets you control how your web application are built and deployed to the application server.

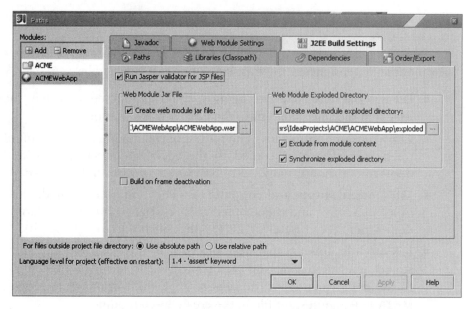

Figure 11.2 The J2EE Build Settings panel lets you set whether to use Jasper for JSP validation, options around the J2EE deployment (which can occur as a JAR or as an exploded directory), and whether to perform builds when the frame is deactivated.

Jasper, a JSP compiler that comes bundled with the Jakarta Tomcat servlet container, is fully integrated into IDEA. It's used to validate JSPs against the specification and report any errors found, ensuring a higher standard of quality and compliance in your code. If you enable the **Run Jasper validator for** JSP **files** checkbox, IDEA will run Jasper each time the web application is built. Alternatively, you can choose to not validate your JSPs or to selectively validate them by hand using the context menu when editing a JSP.

Web applications can be deployed to a web application server in two ways: as a WAR file (a single archive containing a directory structure) or as a simple directory structure that hasn't been packaged into an archive file. This latter format is referred to as an *exploded* WAR *file* (or exploded directory) because it represents the contents of a WAR if it was un-archived and expanded onto the file system. The J2EE **Build Settings** tab lets you specify which of these two deployable formats is produced when the IDE builds the web module.

> **WARNING**   You can tell IDEA to produce neither deployable format by disabling both checkboxes, but IDEA will be unable to deploy your web application to the web application server if you do so.

Because web applications are tested by using a web browser to visit their web application server, IDEA also allows automatic builds to take place, triggered by frame deactivation. Thus, when focus is diverted to another application (such as your web browser), IDEA immediately performs a build on the web application you were modifying if the **Build on frame deactivation** checkbox is enabled.

Handling the Classpath of a web application

Web applications, if they want to adhere to the ideal of being portable and deployable on existing web application servers, need a degree of self sufficiency. Although the standard Java libraries are provided by the container, any additional libraries that the web application relies on must be included in the web application. In the example of the ACME currency converter, the web application that you'll write shortly exposes the converter's functionality to the Web, but the web application is useless if it can't access the underlying code in the base ACME Java module. The classes defined in the base module need to be included in the web application's Classpath.

IDEA handles the Classpath through the mechanism of module dependencies and libraries. All the code known to the system falls into one of these two categories: It's either code that has been written as part of a module in the project (typically work in progress, code that is apt to change), or it's encapsulated in a library either as directories of class files or a set of JARs containing classes (typically release code, code unlikely to change). Instead of explicitly defining a Classpath for your web module, you control what classes are within the scope of your web application by configuring the module dependencies and libraries in the **Paths** configuration window.

When you're adding a module dependency or adding a library to a web application, you're also implicitly saying that the module's output and the library itself are included in the web application's WAR archive or exploded directory. You can see this by viewing the **Web Module Settings** tab of the **Paths** configuration window: The **Modules and Libraries to Package** group includes references to all the modules and libraries that this web module is dependent on. We discussed the specific options you can set in this group in this chapter in the section "Controlling web module settings."

11.1.4 Using the J2EE tab of the Project tool window

Once you've added a web module to your project, a new J2EE tab becomes accessible on the **Project** tool window (adding a J2EE module or an EJB module also enables this tab). This tab, shown in figure 11.3, lets you explore your project

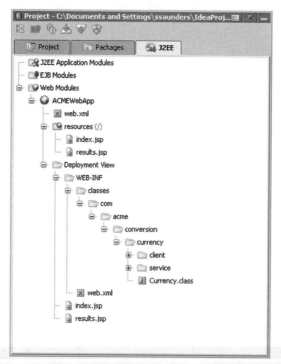

Figure 11.3
The J2EE tab of the Project tool window provides a new perspective into your project's J2EE, web, and EJB modules.

from the perspective of a J2EE application; it ignores plain Java modules and shows a tree-representation of your J2EE, web, and EJB modules. Nodes on the tree represent J2EE-specific elements, such as web applications, servlets, filters, EJBs, and so on.

For web modules, the J2EE tab contains a special branch entitled Deployment View. This view shows the structure your web application will have after it is deployed to a web application server.

We've referred several times to the web application deployment descriptor. According to the Java Servlet Specification, the deployment descriptor is responsible for conveying the elements and configuration information about the web application to the web application server. It specifies deployment settings such as what servlets are defined and how they're mapped to URLs, configuration settings for the servlet context, security roles and permissions, and the like.

The deployment descriptor is implemented as an XML file called web.xml that can be found in the WEB-INF directory of your web application. Because this is an XML file, you can open it and edit it directly like any other file in your project. But

IDEA's web modules provide a facility for editing deployment descriptors that you may find more intuitive than editing the XML directly—a property editor.

From the J2EE project tab, you can edit the web module node itself—not the web.xml file. Double-click the node directly under **Web Modules** to open the web module editor shown in figure 11.4. This interface lets you edit the most common properties of a web application's deployment descriptor.

11.1.5 *Working with servlets and filters*

A *servlet* is a Java-based web component that generates dynamic content by accepting a request and producing an appropriate response. To oversimplify, when a client makes a request to a servlet container, that request is inspected by the servlet container, and the request is routed to the appropriate servlet. The

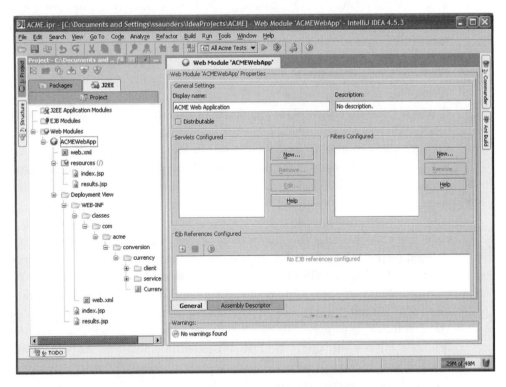

Figure 11.4 By editing the web module from the J2EE Project tool window tab, you're given an interface that lets you edit the web application's deployment descriptor without editing the XML directly.

chosen servlet is responsible for fulfilling the request and ultimately crafting a response that is returned to the client.

A *filter*, on the other hand, is a Java-based web component that can transform the content of a servlet request, response, or header information. It isn't responsible for crafting a response to a request but rather is intended to modify requests sent to, and responses sent from, servlets. Filters are often used to perform authentication, logging, encryption, tokenizing, event notification, and other data-manipulative or data-reactive responsibilities.

Because servlets are Java objects that implement the `Servlet` interface, and filters are Java objects that implement the `Filter` interface, you can work on both types of files using the full editing capabilities of the IDEA editor. All the features discussed that apply to editing plain Java objects also apply to editing servlets and filters. But because servlets and filters exist within the context of a web application, running and testing them is handled a bit differently. We'll discuss that specifically later in this chapter in section 11.4.

11.1.6 *Working with JavaServer Pages*

JavaServer Pages is a technology for building applications that use or generate dynamic content, typically HTML, XML, or one of their variants. Much like servlets, JavaServer Pages (JSPs) are responsible for handling a request and crafting an appropriate response; in fact, the JSP technology is built directly atop Java Servlet technology and gives web application developers a more convenient framework.

JSPs use a template framework. A JSP page that is intended to return an HTML page as a response to a client looks much like an HTML page with some dynamic content added through the use of JSP tags. The web application server is responsible for transforming the JSP into a servlet that produces the exact output defined by the JSP and then using that servlet to service incoming requests.

IDEA identifies JSP files by their file extension and enables special JSP editing features when you open a file with the appropriate extension. By default, the file extension .jsp and the extensions for JSP fragments (.jsf and .jspf) are recognized. You can make adjustments to this list—such as adding a new extension that represents a JSP file—through the **File Types** settings window. As with creating any new file, you need to provide the proper extension or IDEA will be unable to open files in the appropriate editor.

Using JSP syntax highlighting

IDEA supports syntax highlighting for JSPs. You can map different colors and styles to the types of JSP entities, including scriptlets, directives, actions, and comments.

In addition, any HTML in your JSP uses the color settings defined for HTML files. Likewise, scriptlets use the appropriate Java syntax font and foreground color options, but their background color is controlled through the JSP settings. Both sets of styles can be controlled through the **Colors and Fonts** settings window.

As you edit a JSP file, IDEA constantly checks the syntax of your JSP code for errors. Any errors or warnings it detects appear in the error stripe, as they do in the Java editor. In addition to checking Java syntax, the JSP editor also verifies that (to the best of its knowledge) you're using the JSP tags correctly. This includes making sure you've specified all the required attributes for each tag and that any references to local variables and JavaBeans are valid.

IDEA 5 The **Code | Reformat code** command (**Ctrl+Alt+L**) now has improved support for JSP files. For scriptlets, the Java code style settings are used; otherwise the HTML formatting settings from the **Global Code Style** settings come into play.

The structure view now supports JSP files as well. This gives you an easy way to view and navigate the elements in the page. JetBrains has stepped up its structure view in the new release, adding support for HTML, JavaScript, and CSS files.

Managing imports in JSP files

As in the Java editor, IDEA's JSP editor automatically resolves any new class references in your file and prompts you to import them. IDEA uses the import settings from your code style to determine how classes are automatically imported into your page. Of course, the JSP editor uses the JSP equivalent of the import statement, the import attribute of the page directive. All the imports are appended to the import list.

> **NOTE** Conversely, in IDEA 5.0, **Optimize Imports** works on JSPs imports. Just as it does in Java files, the **Code | Optimize Imports** command (**Ctrl+Alt+O**) throws out any unused import statements and organizes the remaining ones according to your code style selections.

Using JSP tag completion

IDEA's JSP editor understands the directives defined by the Servlet API. It puts this knowledge to good use by providing convenient completion of the commands and all their attributes and attribute values. Basic code completion (**Code | Complete Code | Basic**, or **Ctrl+Space**) and class name code completion (**Code |**

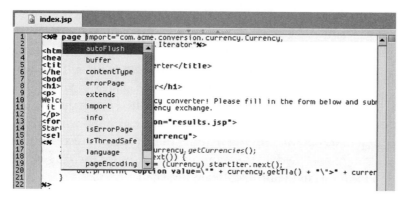

Figure 11.5 Code completion is enabled in JSPs, even completion of non-Java code. This figure shows an example of code-completing a JSP tag.

Complete Code | Class Name, or **Ctrl+Alt+Space**) are available when you're working with directives, their attributes, and their attribute values; SmartType code completion (**Code | Complete Code | SmartType**, or **Ctrl+Shift+Space**) is available in a scriptlet. As shown in figure 11.5, IDEA helps you select the attributes of any of the JSP commands. As you'll learn shortly, it also helps complete custom tags and references to JavaBeans.

> **TIP** When you're working with a JSP tag, you can use the **View | Parameter Info** command (**Ctrl+P**) to see an overview of the tag's attribute options. The list of supported attributes appears in a pop-up window. Attributes listed in bold are required, and optional elements are listed in a normal font. Any attributes already present in the tag are shown in gray.

JSP includes

IDEA recognizes relative file references in your JSPs. When you deploy a web application, remember that JSP URLs in it are relative to the context path of the application. So, when you include a file via the `<jsp:include>` tag, IDEA can use your web application root settings to verify the path reference for you. It even lets you edit the included file by using the **Go To | Declaration** (**Ctrl+B**) function when you're in the page attribute. In figure 11.6, IDEA is showing off its ability to complete the value of the page by finding all the JSP files in the specified directory.

Note, however, that this convenience only applies to path references in your JSP code, not references in HTML such as anchor tags, links, or image references. A web application can be deployed under any context (top-level path) on the

Figure 11.6
IDEA is aware of the context root of your web application and finds files accordingly.

application server, so there's no way for IDEA to determine with any certainty the validity of an HTML path. If IDEA is complaining about paths that you believe to be valid, chances are your web root is configured incorrectly.

 In IDEA 5.0, reference handling for all web content files is supported.

The new **Extract Include** refactoring lets you select a block of JSP code and extract it into an includable JSP fragment that can be reused across multiple pages. In its place, IDEA inserts the appropriate JSP tag to include the file. Conversely, the **Inline** refactoring does the opposite. Given an `include` tag, this refactoring replaces the tag with the contents of the included file.

Working with JavaBeans

Perhaps even more interesting than basic tag completion is the JSP editor's support for JavaBeans. JavaBeans are objects that are stored in the page, request, or user's session and made available to the `<jsp:getProperty>` and `<jsp:setProperty>` tags. They're placed there through custom tags or through the `<jsp:useBean>` tag.

The `<jsp:useBean>` tag fetches JavaBeans and places them into the page context so that they're available to scriptlets and other tags. When using this tag, you must specify the class of the JavaBean as well as the scope in which it can be found (or, rather, the scope it is placed into). For the `class` attribute, you may either type the fully qualified class name of the JavaBean you wish to make available to the JSP page or navigate down by using the basic completion mechanism and selecting the appropriate packages, as shown in figure 11.7. Keep in mind that the JSP Specification requires that class names be fully qualified. For the `scope` attribute,

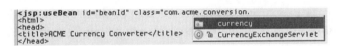

Figure 11.7 Completion of class names is restricted to the Classpath of the web application.

IDEA lets you select from the four scopes allowed by JSP: application, request, page, and session (request is the default).

Once a JavaBean is placed in scope, the editor can also perform completions when using the `<jsp:getProperty>` and `<jsp:setProperty>` tags. These tags require that you specify the reference name of the JavaBean you wish to access. The editor completes the name for you, allowing you to select from all the Java-Beans made available through JSP tags. If you use a name that isn't available in the current context, IDEA flags this as an error.

JavaBean properties are determined through a set of naming conventions (the familiar getter and setter methods). When you perform a code completion on the `property` attribute of either the `<jsp:getProperty>` or `<jsp:setProperty>` tag, IDEA uses these conventions to provide a list of valid property names. Additionally, you can visit the source behind these properties (if the code is in your project's source path) through the **Go To | Declaration** command **(Ctrl+B)**, and you can view their JavaDoc with **Ctrl+Q** (**View | Quick JavaDoc**).

IDEA 5 The JSP 2.0 expression language (EL) is fully supported by IDEA's code completion and validation features in version 5.0. But note that, because EL has dynamic nature, only statically known info is highlighted and completed.

Custom and third-party tag libraries

IDEA also has the ability to perform syntax checking and code completion on custom JSP tags. Support for standard JSP tags like `<jsp:getProperty>` and `<jsp:use-Bean>` is automatic, with no additional setup necessary. For custom tag libraries you've developed yourself, and for third-party libraries such as JSTL or Struts, you must take a few initial steps. For IDEA to provide completion and syntax checking on your tag libraries, it has to know where to find them.

First, your tag library's class files must be part of the module's Classpath. This is achieved either automatically (if you have the library's sources under the module sourcepath) or manually by adding the library's JAR file to the module `Libraries`.

IDEA must also be able to find your tag library descriptor (TLD), which can either be represented as a separate .tld file or be part of the JAR. Depending on your case, the necessary settings differ, but they all can be configured in the Web Module Settings tab of the Paths dialog (covered earlier in this chapter):

- In case of a separate .tld file, make sure that its containing folder is registered in the **Web Resource Directories** list and mapped to the /WEB-INF deployment directory or one of its subfolders.

- In case of a JAR, once it's added to the Classpath, IDEA resolves all references to the tag library and provides appropriate code completion and highlighting. But for the deployment purposes (to avoid possible runtime errors), you may need to specify packaging method and deployment path for that JAR in the **Modules and Libraries to Package** list.

- In rare cases, when you have the accompanying .tld file detached from its JAR, you need to configure references for file and JAR separately, as described earlier.

IDEA 5 IDEA 5.0 supports the new JSP 2.0 tag files format. This format makes it easy to add new tags without writing a line of Java code, mucking with the TLD, and so forth. IDEA can locate your tags through the direct reference to their containing folder in the `tagdir` attribute of the `taglib` directive. IDEA supports both the scriptlet-based .tag and XML .tagx formats. The editor assists you in including these through code completion and identifies invalid usage or syntax errors.

IDEA 5.0 fully supports the XML version of JSP files known as JSP *documents*, which have the file extension .jspx, including those features of the format new to JSP 2.0. In JSP documents, a JSP is represented as well-formed XML code, and any embedded HTML must be well-formed XHTML. When you're working in JSPX documents, you have both the benefits of IDEA's XML editing features as well as the Java code completion and other aspects of the traditional JSP editor. JSPX documents have their own file type designation and code style settings.

This TLD file, which describes the tags in the library and defines their attributes, can be located by IDEA through a variety of means defined in the JSP specification. We'll describe the most common ones momentarily.

When you use a tag library in JSP, you must specify the tag library's URI and its prefix on each JSP page in which you wish to use it. Both direct and indirect URI references can be used, as shown in the following examples:

```
<%@ taglib uri="my_descriptor.tld" prefix="descriptor" %>
```

IDEA looks for my_descriptor.tld file in all web resource directories that are mapped to the deployment directory /WEB-INF.

```
<%@ taglib uri="http://jakarta.apache.org/taglibs/mailer-1.1"
    prefix="mailer" %>
```

IDEA searches JARs from the module's Classpath for the .tld file containing the tag `<uri>http://jakarta.apache.org/taglibs/mailer-1.1<uri>`. In version 5.0 of IDEA, the search is also performed for separate .tld files in registered web resource directories.

```
<%@ taglib uri="taglibs-string.jar" prefix="string" %>
```

IDEA searches for taglibs-string.jar file in the module's Classpath and then looks for META-INF/taglib.tld in it.

The prefix attribute's value is arbitrary but required: It provides a label for identifying which library a tag is associated with. You use this prefix throughout the page to reference tags in this particular library.

WARNING   Some tag libraries, such as those provided with the Apache Struts package and JSTL, rely on runtime reflection to resolve the names and values of properties and JavaBeans in the page. IDEA has no way to accurately determine whether they're being used appropriately, beyond verifying that all required attributes have been satisfied.

11.1.7 *Implementing an ACME web application*

Let's put a web interface on top of the currency converter. The application is simplistic: You'll implement a JSP form that gathers the required data for performing a currency conversion and a single JSP that is responsible for returning the results.

The entry JSP should briefly explain its purpose and then provide an HTML form that the user can fill out to provide the data for the conversion. According to the API, this data includes the starting currency, the ending currency, and the amount of currency to be exchanged. Using the **Project** tool window, create a new JSP called index.jsp under the resources folder of your ACME web application web module. Edit it as shown in listing 11.1.

> **Listing 11.1   The static elements of a simple JSP page that presents an HTML form to the user**

```
<html>
<head>
<title>ACME Currency Converter</title>
</head>
<body>
<h1>ACME Currency Converter</h1>
```

```
<p>
Welcome to the ACME Currency converter! Please fill in the
 form below and submit it to perform a mock currency exchange.
</p>
<form method="get" action="results.jsp">
Starting currency:
<select name="startingCurrency">
</select><br>
Ending currency:
<select name="endingCurrency">
</select><br>
Amount: <input type="text" name="amount" size="6" value="10"><br>
<input type="submit" name="submit" value="Submit">
</form>
</body>
</html>
```

You need to include one piece of dynamic functionality in this file: populating the drop-down selections with the list of currencies known to your system (see listing 11.2). Because you've modeled the API of the Currency class to be able to tell what currencies exist, this JSP can use that method to dynamically populate the contents of those lists. The text on the options should be the currency's three-letter acronym, and the value can be the same.

> **Listing 11.2 Retrieving existing currencies and printing an HTML option element for each**

```
Iterator iterator = Currency.getCurrencies();
while (iterator.hasNext()) {
    String currency = (String) iterator.next();
    out.println("<option value=\"" + currency + "\">" +
            currency + "</option>");
}
```

Combining the two, the final index.jsp should look like listing 11.3. When you're implementing this JSP, don't forget to leverage IDEA's features that save you time and effort. To illustrate:

- *Use code completion*. Start implementing these changes to your file by opening a scriptlet and typing Currency.getCurr. Then invoke basic code completion (**Ctrl+Space**) to see a list of static methods on the Currency object that meet the pattern. Use your up and down arrow keys to select the get-Currencies() method, and press **Enter** to accept the choice.

- *Use the import pop-up.* If you have import pop-ups turned on (the default setting), the editor will realize that the `Currency` class isn't currently in scope. It will note the error and pop up a small intention window asking where the class comes from. Pressing **Alt+Enter** lets you choose which `Currency` class on the module's Classpath should be imported and inserts an appropriate `insert` statement for you.

- *Use refactoring.* While your cursor is still on the `getCurrencies()` method, invoke the **Introduce Variable** refactoring (**Ctrl+Alt+V**). IDEA will correctly identify the variable type as an `Iterator` and suggest a variable name based on its code style configuration. Either change the name or accept the default, but click **OK** to accept the variable.

- *Use live templates.* With the `Iterator` defined, move your cursor to the next new line and invoke the **Insert Live Template** function (**Ctrl+J**). Choose the `itit` live template, which iterates through a list of objects defined by an `Iterator` (you can choose the option by using the arrow keys to navigate the list or by typing the letters `itit` and thereby narrowing the list to a single entry). The shortest way, however, is to type `itit` in the editor and press the **Tab** key. The live template walks you through each of the variables to ensure they're contextually sound. The suggested iterator is likely correct; the object being cast to should not be a generic `Object` but rather a `Currency`, and the variable name can be anything you wish.

Listing 11.3 A complete JSP with dynamic elements implemented in scriptlets

```
<%@ page import="com.acme.conversion.currency.Currency,
    java.util.Iterator"%>
<html>
<head>
<title>ACME Currency Converter</title>
</head>
<body>
<h1>ACME Currency Converter</h1>
<p>
Welcome to the ACME Currency converter! Please fill in the
 form below and submit it to perform a mock currency exchange.
</p>
<form method="get" action="results.jsp">
Starting currency:
<select name="startingCurrency">
<%
    Iterator startIter = Currency.getCurrencies();
    while (startIter.hasNext()) {
        String currency = (String) startIter.next();
        out.println("<option value=\"" + currency + "\">" +
```

```
            currency + "</option>");
    }
%>
</select><br>
Ending currency:
<select name="endingCurrency">
<%
    Iterator endIter = Currency.getCurrencies();
    while (endIter.hasNext()) {
        String currency = (String) endIter.next();
        out.println("<option value=\"" + currency + "\">" +
            currency + "</option>");
    }
%>
</select><br>
Amount: <input type="text" name="amount" size="6" value="10"><br>
<input type="submit" name="submit" value="Submit">
</form>
</body>
</html>
```

Because this web application is extremely simple and informal, let's break a tenet of web application design and embed the business logic of the conversion into a JSP (see listing 11.4). Typically, this is a bad idea: For enterprise applications, business logic should exist in its own layer where it can be centrally managed and be presented through multiple channels without having any sort of tight coupling to the presentation layer that controls what a client sees and how they see it. But because you're looking specifically at exercising IDEA's web application and JSP features, we don't think anyone will object.

The resulting JSP, therefore, is responsible for two things: accepting the incoming parameters and performing the business logic of a currency exchange on them, and presenting the results to the client. You can implement the former by putting a scriptlet at the top of the page that reads the incoming parameters, parses them, and uses them as input to the exchange process. The latter can use a combination of static HTML and JSP expressions to show those results.

Don't forget to use some of IDEA's efficiency features (such as refactoring, code generation, live templates, and so on) as you implement this page.

Listing 11.4   The resulting JSP that does the calculation and shows the result to the client

```
<%@ page
import="com.acme.conversion.currency.service.CurrencyExchangeService,
com.acme.conversion.currency.service.CurrencyExchangeServiceFactory,
```

```
com.acme.conversion.currency.Currency,
java.text.DecimalFormat"%>
<%
    String startCurrStr = request.getParameter("startingCurrency");
    String endCurrStr = request.getParameter("endingCurrency");
    String amountStr = request.getParameter("amount");

    double amount = Double.parseDouble(amountStr);
    DecimalFormat df = new DecimalFormat("0.00");

    CurrencyExchangeService service =
        CurrencyExchangeServiceFactory.getService();;
    double rate = service.requestCurrentRate(startCurrStr,
        endCurrStr);
%>
<html>
<head>
<title>ACME Currency Converter - Results</title>
</head>
<body>
<h1>ACME Currency Converter - Results</h1>
<p>
Here are the results of your currency conversion. Enjoy!
</p>
<p>
Starting currency: <%= startCurrStr %><br>
Ending currency: <%= endCurrStr %><br>
Amount converted: <%= df.format(amount) %><br>
Exchange rate: <%= df.format(rate) %><br>
Amount after exchange: <%= df.format(amount * rate) %><br>
</p>
<p>
<a href="index.jsp">Return to main page</a>
</p>
</body>
</html>
```

With this JSP implemented, you should have a working web application front end. Running and debugging an application like this are covered later in this chapter.

11.2 *Working with EJBs*

The J2EE platform provides clear separation of architectural elements of the enterprise application; it consists of the client layer, web layer, and EJB layer. IDEA supports specific module types for each of the layers. In previous chapters, we discussed using Java modules, which can be used for development of

J2EE client-layer components such as applets or rich GUI clients. We touched on support for web layer development with web modules earlier in this chapter. Let's get closer to EJB support in IDEA.

Exploring the full extent of the EJB and other J2EE technologies is beyond the scope of this book, and we're going to assume that you have some degree of familiarity with those technologies. The following material focuses on IDEA's support for working with J2EE applications.

11.2.1 *Working with EJB modules*

The EJB module is extension of the Java module and is created separately for a group of related EJBs and their deployment descriptors. There is one EJB standard deployment descriptor (ejb-jar.xml) and a number of application server–specific ones—for instance, weblogic-ejb-jar.xml and weblogic-cmp-rdbms-ejb-jar.xml for the WebLogic application server. Deployment descriptors are XML documents describing EJBs and EJB module properties. They're designed to be used for deploying J2EE components.

Creating a new EJB module

Extending your tool functionality, let's add a new EJB module. Start by following these steps:

1   Select **File | New Module** from the main menu.

2   The first dialog in the **New Module** wizard appears and prompts you to select the type of module to create. Click the EJB Module option, and then click **Next**.

3   The next dialog prompts you to select a module name and a module content root. Enter ACMEEjb as the module name, and specify the module content root to be a sibling directory to the currency converter's Java module (for example, if the module you've been working on can be found in the C:\Projects\CurrencyConverter directory, make this module use the C:\Projects\ACMEEjb directory). Click **Next**.

4   The next dialog prompts you to specify a source directory for the EJB module. This is where the source files for any custom Java classes will reside. The default suggestion of *src* is fine, so click **Next**.

5   The next dialog prompts you to specify a compiler output path for the for the EJB module. Accept the name suggested by IDEA, and click **Next** to continue.

6 The next dialog prompts you to select the application server for which this J2EE application is being written. Select **Weblogic**. The created module is associated with the corresponding configuration and can be deployed to the WebLogic application server. WebLogic-specific deployment descriptors (weblogic-ejb-jar.xml and webvblogic-cmp-rdbms-ejb-jar.xml) are created for the module. Click **Next**.

7 In this step you can define paths to WebLogic-specific deployment descriptors (weblogic-ejb-jar.xml and weblogic-cmp-rdbms-ejb-jar.xml) and their versions created for the module. Click the **Finish** button to finish the process.

Configuring your EJB module

You can configure your EJB module settings with EJB **Module Settings** and J2EE **Build Settings** tabs of the **Paths** dialog. The EJB **Module Settings** tab, shown in figure 11.8, lets you change the binding of your EJB module to particular application server (you can add and choose another application server here by clicking the **Configure** button).

The **Deployment Descriptors** group lets you change the location of your deployment descriptors. You can also specify additional deployment descriptors required for your server (this is especially important when you define settings manually for generic application servers).

The **Module and Libraries to Package** group lets you control packaging of your EJB. Each library or module used by a given EJB module (configured in the **Libraries(Classpath)** and **Dependencies** tabs) appears in this table so you can set how to package them during build. You configure this section in much the same way as the **Modules and Libraries to Package** section of **Web Module Settings**.

The J2EE **Build Settings** tab, shown in figure 11.9, lets you control how your EJB module is built. Building an EJB module is similar to building a web module.

Naming J2EE items in IDEA

Naming J2EE items is a boring task, because you want to have more or less similar names for all components with similar functions. Creating new names and, most important, following your own conventions may be a big job, especially for large and complicated projects with lots of components, modules, and elements. Fortunately, IDEA helps you to create J2EE names that match J2EE coding practice.

You can set names for J2EE items in the J2EE **Names** tab of the **Code Style** settings dialog, shown in figure 11.10.

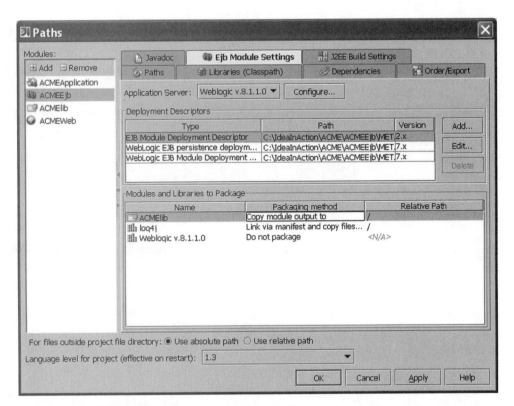

Figure 11.8 In the EJB Module Settings tab, you can select and configure the application server and manage module deployment descriptors as well as modules and libraries deployed with the current module.

In the corresponding fields on this tab, you can specify prefixes and/or suffixes for the names of bean classes, bean interfaces, the <ejb-name> tag, servlets, and filters. These prefixes and suffixes appear in the corresponding fields of the **Create EJB**, **New Servlet**, and **New Filter** dialogs. In addition, for an Entity bean, you can specify a default primary key class that appears in the **Create New CMP Field** dialog.

Names for Entity, Session, and Message beans are formed in the following manner. The prefix and suffix are taken from the J2EE **Names** settings and are shown as labels before and after the text field where you introduce the bean name. The bean name root is suggested based on the bean type—that is, Entity, Session, or Message. The name must be a valid Java identifier; otherwise the **OK** button in the creation dialog is disabled, and you can't create the bean.

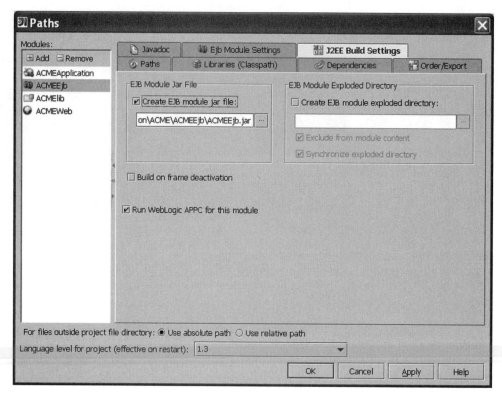

Figure 11.9 You can use the J2EE Build Settings tab to define the way the module is deployed as well as to set parameters associated with the module make process and the way it's created.

Names for enterprise bean class and interfaces of Entity and Session beans as well as Message bean class name are suggested by IDEA based on the following logic. The prefix and suffix are taken from the J2EE **Names** settings. The name root is added based on the bean name root. When you alter the bean name root, IDEA automatically changes it for the class and interfaces. If you modify any of the class or interface names, IDEA doesn't automatically change this field along with the bean name root. However, you can bring this field back to the automatically editable state: Make its prefix and suffix match the ones in the J2EE **Names** settings, and the root should be similar to the bean name root.

Creating new EJBs

EJBs are useful when you want to encapsulate business logic into separate component(s). There are several types of EJBs: Session, Message, and Entity. Session EJBs provide synchronous services, Message EJBs are designed to work with

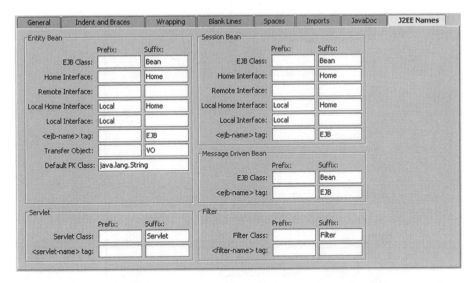

Figure 11.10   The Code Style dialog has a tab dedicated to defining the naming conventions for your J2EE implementations, which helps ensure consistency.

asynchronous requests, and Entity EJBs can handle various data and data services with no need to run a specific database application. As an example, you'll create two EJBs: a CMP Entity bean (an Entity bean to quickly restore the database data without manual SQL coding) and a Session bean.

You can create EJBs using the context menu in the **Project** view. Right-click an EJB module there or press **Alt+Insert**, and select a necessary item under the **New** submenu. Now, do the following:

1   Select a bean type (CMP Entity or Session).

2   In the resulting dialog, shown in figure 11.11, specify the bean name, package, bean class, and interfaces (local and remote).

3   For CMP beans, set the primary key class and CMP version.

Editing EJB deployment descriptors

Like web modules, EJB modules and EJBs have deployment descriptors. Deployment descriptors are essential for the deployment process success. Without the properly configured deployment descriptor, an application server doesn't know what to do with files you provide. The deployment descriptors are automatically created by IDEA and shown in a graphic way. For instance, suppose you need to add security roles, change classes/interfaces for EJBs, and so on. Changes you

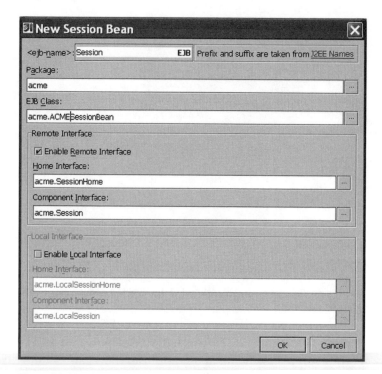

Figure 11.11 When you ask IDEA to create a new Session bean, the New Session Bean dialog prompts for all the relevant information (much like a single-step wizard process).

make to your EJB or EJB module structure are recorded in deployment descriptors. Usually, it's sufficient to utilize IDEA's visual features to edit deployment descriptors. However, for custom application server integrations (not specifically supported by IDEA), or if server-specific parameters are to be set (IDEA has visual support for most but not all widely used tags), you may need to edit deployment descriptors manually.

From the J2EE project tab, you can edit the EJB module or EJB node—not the ejb-jar.xml file, but the node directly under EJB Modules. The EJB Module editor/ EJB editor opens, as shown in figure 11.12. This interface lets you edit the most common options of an EJB module/EJB deployment descriptor as well as Web-Logic settings for Entity beans.

Several features are supported for EJB editing. First, EJBs are Java classes, so all of IDEA's features are available including convenient code editing, refactorings, automatic imports management, completions, and so on.

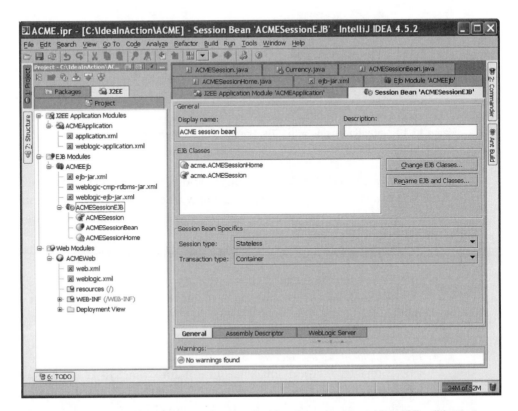

Figure 11.12 You can edit EJB properties visually. There's no need to get into XML editing to tune commonly used EJB characteristics.

Second, EJB dependencies are considered Java class inheritances. Thus, EJB class, Component interface, and Home interface dependencies are treated as if an EJB class implements the corresponding interface. In an EJB class, all method implementations have an **Implements method** icon to the left to the method declaration and in its interface, whereas implemented methods have a **Has implementation** icon.

Intention actions are another set of conveniences: If the IDE assumes your bean has something wrong in it, IDEA suggests amending it if a reasonable correction is possible. For instance, suppose you introduce a new method in an EJB class. When the caret is on the method declaration, IDEA shows a lightbulb. If you press **Alt+Enter**, IDEA suggests a way to correct this situation. In this case, IDEA proposes to insert the current method in a bean interface (see figure 11.13).

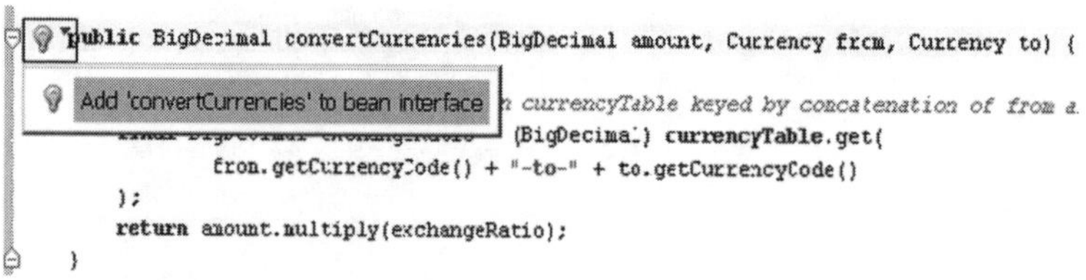

```
public BigDecimal convertCurrencies(BigDecimal amount, Currency from, Currency to) {
    Add 'convertCurrencies' to bean interface  currencyTable keyed by concatenation of from a
                                              (BigDecimal) currencyTable.get(
            from.getCurrencyCode() + "-to-" + to.getCurrencyCode()
    );
    return amount.multiply(exchangeRatio);
}
```

Figure 11.13   Intention action with EJBs. Updating bean interface from bean implementation class change.

If you have two interfaces, IDEA prompts you with the **Select interfaces** dialog, where you can choose interfaces that you may want to add to this method. IDEA's intention actions can, for instance, add a default implementation of the current method to the EJB class.

IDEA has EJB-related intention actions for three major cases:

- *EJB Declaration Intention.* This action is used to introduce an EJB class method into the corresponding EJB Interface. For instance, when you add the ejbCreateXXX(int i) method in an EJB class, IDEA suggests adding the createXXX() method to the bean interface.

- *EJB Implementation Intention.* This action is used to introduce the default EJB Interface method implementation into the EJB class. For instance, when you add the myMethod() method into EJB Home, IDEA suggests adding the myMethod() declaration to the bean class.

- *Quick-Fix Intention Actions.* These actions are used to fix errors due to violations of the EJB Specification requirements. For example, when you're editing ejbCreate() throws RemoteException in an EJB class, IDEA suggests removing the RemoteException from the ejbCreate throws list and adding CreateException there.

EJB error highlighting informs you of the types of errors in your code:

- All errors that make EJB deployment impossible are highlighted in red. However, they don't prevent compilation. If they can be corrected, IDEA suggests possible corrections using intention actions.

- Compatibility errors are highlighted as warnings—you'll find the list of possible errors and warnings in IDEA's built-in Help system.

- If there are deployment descriptor errors, the bean group and EJB with the error are highlighted in the EJB View in red. The tooltip for the group says which bean is invalid, and the tooltip for the EJB says what the error is.

Another feature is the **Select Target** pop-up. When the caret is in EJB-related Java code (EJB class, `Component` interface, `Home` interface, or deployment descriptor), pressing **Alt+F1** calls the **Select Target** pop-up with the J2EE View option.

Finally, selecting J2EE View opens (if it was closed) the J2EE tab of the **Project** view and navigates to the chosen class, interface, or deployment descriptor within it.

All editing actions are two-way: Changes in Java code and deployment descriptors are instantly displayed in the J2EE tab, and vice versa.

Refactoring EJBs

According to Martin Fowler in *Refactoring: Improving the Design of Existing Code* (Addison-Wesley, 2000), refactoring is "the process of changing a software system in such a way that it doesn't alter the external behavior of the code, yet improves its internal structure. It's a disciplined way to clean up code that minimizes the chances of including bugs." If you have some code and need to improve it, refactorings can be very useful. In this case, EJBs are complex structures, and changing the code manually is often too cumbersome.

Automated refactorings for EJBs in IDEA are as follows:

- When you refactor a method in an interface, the implementing method in an EJB class is also refactored, and vice versa. For instance, if you wish to rename a method called `createXXX()` in a `Home` interface, IDEA suggests renaming the method to `ejbCreateXXX()` in an EJB class that implements the `createXXX()` method.

- When a method is refactored, corresponding links in the deployment descriptor are updated.

- When you rename a CMP or CMR field accessor, IDEA suggests renaming the entire field with all its accessors and deployment descriptor references instead.

- You can easily rename or change all class names for particular EJB (available from the visual property editor of EJB; see figure 11.12).

11.2.2 *Working with J2EE application modules*

The J2EE application module is an umbrella for a complete J2EE server application and thus serves as a container for J2EE components, like web or EJB modules. It groups them into a single module and lets you deploy them together. Such an application can be deployed to any J2EE-compliant server in the form of a J2EE application archive file (also known as an EAR file, or EAR). The format of the EAR file is part of the J2EE Platform Specification.

An EAR file defines a provider-independent way of combining EJB JARs, WARs, and library JARs into a single deployable package. This vendor neutrality is made possible through standardized XML deployment descriptors (application.xml and a number of application server–specific deployment descriptors, such as weblogic-application.xml for the WebLogic application server) that control such elements as web module context roots. Once created, the EAR file is deployed into an application server, which reads the deployment descriptors and makes the application available.

Creating a new J2EE application module

You need to introduce a J2EE application module to have a more convenient way to deploy and run your application. The J2EE application module includes other interconnected modules (like EJB, web, and other Java modules).

Start working with J2EE modules by creating one:

1 Select **File | New Module** from the main menu.

2 The first dialog in the **New Module** wizard appears and prompts you to select the type of module to create. Click the J2EE **Application Module** option, and then click **Next**.

3 The next dialog prompts you to select a module name. Enter ACMEJ2EEApp as the module name. Click **Next** to continue.

4 The next dialog prompts you to select the application server for which this J2EE application module is being written. Select **WebLogic Server**. The created module is associated with the corresponding configuration and can be deployed to the WebLogic application server. Click **Next**.

5 Define the paths to application module and WebLogic-specific deployment descriptors created for the module. Click **Next**.

6 In this step, define which of the existing web and/or EJB modules should be included into the new J2EE application. Select the desired J2EE modules to be included in the created modules at build time in the **Packaging method** column. To alter the **Relative path** and **Web Module Context Root** values for the included J2EE modules, click in the corresponding column for the desired module.

7 Click **Finish** to finish the process.

Configuring the J2EE application module

Not all modules may exist at the time the J2EE application module is created. In this case, you can add modules manually using the **File | Settings: Project Settings: Paths:** J2EE **Application Module Settings** tab.

In the **Modules and Libraries to Package** section, mark as **Include module in build** the modules you need (see figure 11.14).

Editing J2EE deployment descriptors

Like web and EJB modules, J2EE application modules have deployment descriptors. To fine-tune the J2EE application deployment process (introducing/changing security roles), you may need to introduce changes in them either in a graphic editor or manually.

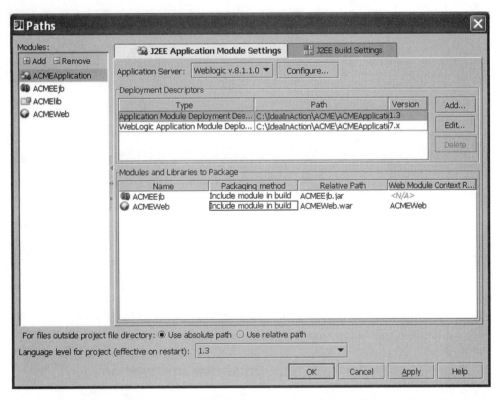

Figure 11.14 Main configuration settings for an application module. The most important field is the table where you can edit the modules and libraries that are to be packaged into the deployed module and the method of doing so.

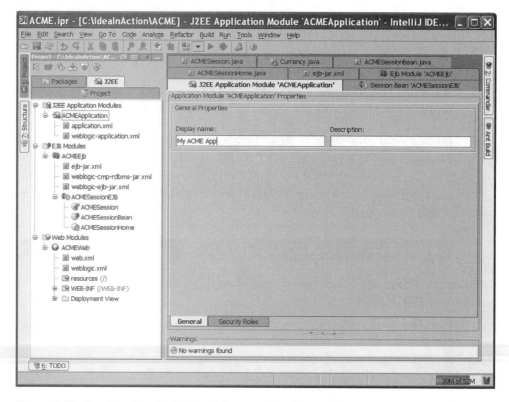

Figure 11.15 Graphic editor for J2EE module properties. If any settings are wrong, you're warned in the Warnings field.

From the J2EE project tab, you can edit the J2EE application module. Press **F4** or **Ctrl+Enter,** or right-click the module and select **Edit** from the context menu. The J2EE **Application Module** editor shown in figure 11.15 will open. This interface lets you edit the most common options of a J2EE application module deployment descriptor.

You can also alter the module properties in text form by directly editing the corresponding deployment descriptor.

11.3 *Understanding application server integration*

Running, testing, and debugging an enterprise application is a more complex process than doing the same thing to a standard Java application, because of the need for an application server. Servlets, EJBs, and similar technologies run in the context of a *container,* an environment that application servers provide.

The rules that characterize the container, as well as how it interacts with the applications it supports, are defined in the appropriate specification documents: A portion of the Servlet specification is devoted to defining how a servlet container must act, and a portion of the EJB specification is devoted to defining how an EJB container must act, for example.

IDEA comes with built-in integration support for both the Tomcat and WebLogic application servers. When properly configured, IDEA is able to start and stop these servers, deploy and undeploy enterprise applications on these servers, and remotely attach a debugging session to these servers.

If you're using an application server other than Tomcat or WebLogic, don't panic! IDEA's web server integration features are supported by a public API that allows developers to extend support to other web servers through plugins. Plugins for a number of other popular servers (including Caucho's Resin server and JBoss) either already exist or are currently in development. Once installed, an application server plugin adds additional server options to the **Application Servers** settings. The options and setup requirements depend on the server and the plugin's features.

If you can't locate support for your application server through the plugin library, you still have some options. Although they won't be as tightly integrated, you can still debug your applications and, in some cases, control your server from within IDEA by configuring a generic application server. Another alternative is to use a supported server, such as Tomcat, for development, and then do final testing on your production server.

Application server integration is managed through the **Application Servers** settings dialog. You can access this window by selecting **File | Settings | Application Servers** entry.

11.3.1 *Integrating IDEA with Tomcat*

Tomcat is a servlet container produced by the Apache Jakarta Project, part of the Apache Software Foundation dedicated to open-source server-side Java technologies. Tomcat has the distinction of being the official reference implementation for the Servlet and JavaServer Pages technologies. It's an open-source servlet container, which makes it very useful for running and testing servlets and JSPs.

When you add a new reference to an installed Tomcat server, IDEA shows the dialog as in figure 11.16. The **Tomcat home** and **Tomcat base directory** fields specify the paths used by your Tomcat installation (refer to the Tomcat documentation for a full explanation of the usage of these paths). The read-only **Detected Tomcat version** label displays the version of Tomcat located in the specified

Figure 11.16
To integrate an installation of Tomcat with IDEA, you need to specify the home and base directories of the application server.

Tomcat home directory. The new reference is given a unique name to distinguish it from other application server references that have been configured in IDEA. The Tomcat configurations are loaded by IDEA from the base directory selected.

11.3.2 *Integrating IDEA with WebLogic*

WebLogic—specifically, WebLogic Server from BEA Systems—is an industry-leading application server. It provides a comprehensive set of services, which support the technologies that form the J2EE specification.

When you add a new reference to an installed WebLogic server, IDEA shows the dialog as in figure 11.17.

The BEA **Home** field specifies the path used by your WebLogic installation; BEA **Version** specifies the version of the WebLogic suite you have installed. IDEA can usually determine which version of WebLogic Server is installed by inspecting the contents of the BEA Home directory. As before, the new reference is given a unique name to distinguish it from other application server references that

Figure 11.17 To integrate an installation of WebLogic with IDEA, you need to specify the home directory and version number of the application server.

have been configured in IDEA. IDEA requires that a WebLogic domain exists prior to running the integration. Without a domain already created, IDEA won't know how to work with WebLogic.

11.3.3 *Integrating IDEA with generic application servers*

There are a host of other application servers on the market besides Tomcat and WebLogic, and not all of them are as tightly integrated with IDEA as Tomcat and Web-Logic. But, because they're application servers, they must adhere to a specification. This level of commonality allows IDEA to provide application server support in a generic fashion.

The benefit of generic application server integration is that it can apply to any application server, so you're never left entirely out in the cold; the penalty of generic application server integration is that IDEA can't predict any application server-specific features or details and thus you're forced to configure the server manually.

When you add a new reference to an installed generic application server, it's added immediately with a unique name to distinguish it from other application server references that have previously been configured. Unlike Tomcat and WebLogic, no dialog appears to prompt for additional information: Generic application servers differ with respect to the information they demand, and there's no way for IDEA to know what information is required by the application server you have chosen.

However, a generic application server must have libraries that reference the servlet reference classes. Because IDEA knows nothing specific about a generic application server, it relies on you to configure the reference with the appropriate libraries. The newly created Generic application server reference is useless until its libraries are configured, as shown in figure 11.18. The final step to configuring a generic application server is to manually add all the server's library JARs to the reference's configuration.

11.3.4 *Installing Tomcat to support the ACME web application*

You've authored a simple web application using a couple of JSPs, but you need a servlet container if you want to run, test, and debug the web application. Let's install Tomcat locally for testing purposes and configure IDEA to associate the Tomcat installation with your web module.

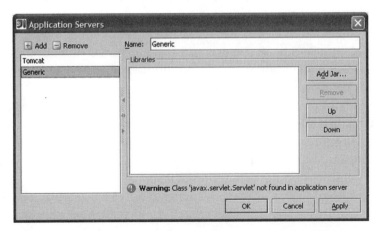

Figure 11.18 The error message at the bottom of the Libraries list indicates that this generic application server isn't yet properly configured.

Download the latest production-quality Tomcat binary release from the Jakarta web site, located at http://jakarta.apache.org/tomcat. The binary versions of Tomcat are distributed as an archive file, so installing it is usually as simple as extracting the archive file to a unique directory on your local file system.

Once Tomcat has been successfully extracted, you need to inform IDEA of its location. Within IDEA, open the **Settings** window (**Ctrl+Alt+S**) and choose the **Application Servers** configuration item. Click **Add** to add a new application server definition, and choose **Tomcat Server** from the drop-down. In the **Tomcat Server** window that appears, either type in the full path of the directory where Tomcat is installed or navigate to it using the ellipsis (**...**) button. Both paths are identical for a typical Tomcat installation, and clicking **OK** finds and registers all of Tomcat's JARs with that application server instance. The default name of this application server entry is Tomcat; you can change it if you'd like.

Finally, you have to associate your web module with that application server. Return to the **Settings** window (**Ctrl+Alt+S**) and choose the **Paths** configuration item. Select your web module from the list, and then select the **Web Module Settings** tab. The first option on this tab is **Application Server,** which you left blank earlier because no application servers were defined at that time. Now, you can click the drop-down and choose **Tomcat**. Persist your changes by clicking **OK**, and the association is complete.

11.4 Running and debugging web applications

Once you've completed your web application, you're going to want to run it, and IDEA gives you several different options depending on the type of application server you're running and how you prefer to work. You can either let IDEA deploy and run your web application, as you would run a standalone Java application, or you can handle deployment and management of the application server yourself, integrating with IDEA only for its debugging capabilities.

Running a web application is more involved than running a plain Java application. In order to run and test a web application, you need to start the web application server, deploy the web application on the server, and view the web application using a web browser. All these steps can be automated, given the right configuration. The Run/Debug configuration profiles that you used to run and debug standard Java applications earlier in the book also support running and debugging web applications, and they effectively group and simplify all these steps in a single, easily configurable location.

Configuration of each application server poses different requirements in order to run or debug applications through IDEA. Consult the documentation specific to IDEA integration with your application server in order to get up and running properly. This chapter focuses on the setup of arguably the most accessible application server, Tomcat.

You use the same **Run/Debug Configurations** screen used for other types of applications to create a web application configuration. This panel can be accessed through the **Run | Edit Configurations** menu option or by selecting **Edit Configurations** from the configuration profile drop-down on the main toolbar. You can see an example of this screen (for Tomcat users) in figure 11.19. It has tabs for each of the application servers that might be configured in IDEA: Tomcat, WebLogic, and a generic application server at the least, possibly more if your installed plugins have added them.

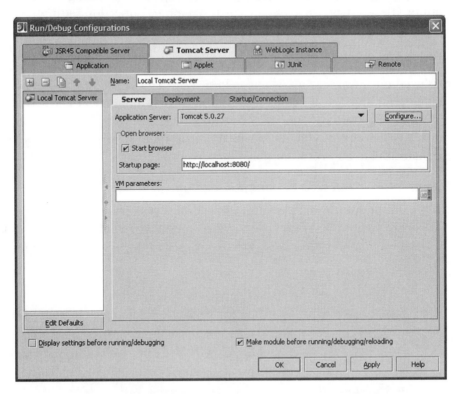

Figure 11.19   Each application server type has its own tab in the Run/Debug Configurations management window.

11.4.1 *Running your web application*

With the appropriate tab selected for your application server in the **Run/Debug Configurations** window (for example, the **Tomcat** tab), you can add a configuration by clicking the plus (**+**) button, just like adding a configuration for a plain Java application. Adding a new configuration for a web application, however, demands that you specify whether the application server is *local* or *remote*. This choice refers to the location of the web application server: whether it's installed on the local machine or on a remote one (over which you have no automated control).

The options for the Run configuration you're creating differ depending on whether you specify the configuration as being local or remote. If you specify the configuration as being local, IDEA assumes that you have full control over the server and prompts you for options such as VM parameters for the server's virtual machine and startup/shutdown scripts. If you specify the configuration as being remote, IDEA instead prompts you for the remote connection settings.

Additionally, the options for the Run configuration differ depending on the target application server. For example, local Tomcat configurations have a **Deployment** tab that lets you choose which web modules in your project are deployed on server startup, whereas local WebLogic configurations allow you to deploy J2EE and EJB modules in addition to web modules (Tomcat is a servlet container, and WebLogic is a full J2EE container), and generic application servers don't have a deployment tab at all (because there's no standard deployment mechanism that all generic application servers adhere to).

11.4.2 *Running the ACME web application on Tomcat*

It's time to see your web application in action. Let's create a new run configuration profile that is configured to start the Tomcat web application server, deploy the ACME web application, and open a browser to the appropriate page. Follow these steps:

1   Select **Run | Edit Configurations** from the main menu.

2   In the **Run/Debug Configurations** window, select the **Tomcat Server** tab.

3   Click the plus (**+**) button to create a new Run configuration. Select **Local** from the drop-down that appears. A new Run configuration (with default values) is created with a unique name.

4   In the **Name** field, enter ACME webapp.

5   Select the **Server** tab in the configuration panel if it isn't already selected.

6 From the **Application Server** drop-down, choose the Tomcat server that you previously installed. If the list is empty, no Tomcat server has been registered with IDEA. Click the **Configure** button and configure a Tomcat installation; refer to section 11.3.4 if necessary.

7 Select the **Start Browser** checkbox if it's disabled. In the **Startup page** field, enter the URL for the entry page of your web application. This URL should be `http://localhost:8080/index.jsp`, provided you're using Tomcat's default port and you've named your files as the example specified.

8 Select the **Deployment** tab in the configuration panel.

9 Select the node that represents your ACME web application. Confirm that the **Deploy Web Module** checkbox is selected. You can deploy from either a WAR or an exploded directory source, but ensure the **Application Context** is a forward slash (/).

10 At the bottom of the window, ensure the **Display settings before running/debugging** checkbox is deselected and the **Make module before running/debugging/reloading** checkbox is selected.

11 Click **OK**.

Your Run configuration has been saved. Now execute it by choosing ACME **webapp** from the **Run/Debug Configurations** drop-down in the main toolbar and clicking the **Run** button (the green arrow) next to it (**Shift+F10**). The **Run** tool window opens, as shown in figure 11.20. In addition, your primary web browser appears and shows the ACME web application (see figure 11.21). Give it a whirl!

Figure 11.20   The Run tool window shows the deployment status of the ACME web application and provides controls to undeploy and redeploy it. It also shows the server output, which helps monitor the server status and debug any problems that arise.

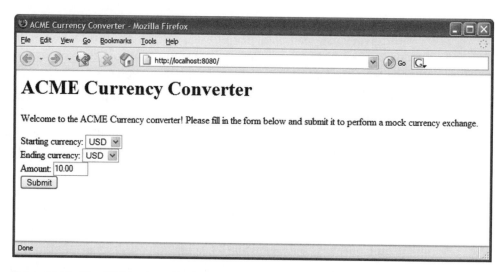

Figure 11.21 **The ACME web application, launched from IDEA's run configuration profile**

Unlike a plain Java application, the web application won't shut itself down when it executes. Tomcat continues to run, and the ACME web application continues to service incoming requests until one of two things happens: either the web application is undeployed, in which case the web application server unloads it and removes it from public consumption, or the web application server is shut down. When you're done playing with the converter, stop the Tomcat server by clicking **Stop** in the **Run** tool window or by pressing **Ctrl+F2**.

11.4.3 *Debugging your web application*

IDEA lets you debug your web application as you would debug console or Swing applications. With supported servers, IDEA even lets you set breakpoints in your JSPs, a feature that is extremely powerful. Web application server debugging is accomplished through Java's remote debugging facilities. For most application servers, debugging the application on your local host is preferable, because IDEA can have more control over server startup, showdown, configuration, and deployment in that environment.

In the **Run/Debug Configurations** window, the configurations categorized under the three integrated application servers tabs (Tomcat, WebLogic, and Generic/JSR45-compatible) have a **Startup/Connection** tab. One of this tab's responsibilities is to distinguish differences between the deployed applications running environment and its debugging environment, and this distinction is typically the command-line arguments passed to the application server that enable the Java Platform Debugger Architecture (JPDA). When running your web application, no additional arguments are required; when debugging, the application server needs to use the JPDA to broadcast the service to which IDEA's debugger may attach.

NOTE   One of the extra environment variables is a port number, but don't confuse the **Port** field with the general port number of your web or application server. This port represents a new service available in debug mode only, the remote JVM's JPDA debugging data. This is the port over which IDEA receives runtime information from your JVM, such as the current executing line number.

In the case of a local configuration, the **Startup/Connection** tab lets you specify the startup and shutdown scripts for the application server as well as any environment variables that should be passed to the application server's invocation. You can rely on debugging support for the web application as you're configuring the web application server to enable the JPDA. In the case of a remote configuration, the tab doesn't automatically enable remote debugging; rather, it tells you what command-line arguments need to be added to the remote server's JVM in order to enable remote debugging and connect via the JPDA. If the remote application server wasn't started with these arguments in its command line, remote debugging won't be possible.

Assuming that the server, local or remote, has been started with remote debugging enabled, IDEA lets you step through a web application using the same interface as debugging a standalone Java application. The **Debug** tool window is augmented to show the deployment status of the web applications and to show the server console in lieu of the JVM console, as shown in figure 11.22.

TIP   When you alter your source code, recompile, build a new WAR file, and provide it to the web application, your changes may not take effect, because the new WAR may not be automatically deployed to the server. Some web application servers support automatic hot deployment, and some don't. If you're unsure or wish to force a new WAR to be used, you can undeploy and redeploy web applications using the controls in the **Run** or **Debug** tool window.

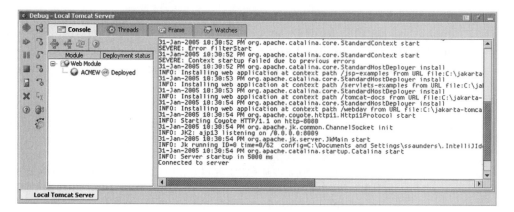

Figure 11.22 The Debug window lets you observe and control the deployment of a web application in addition to using all the familiar debugging controls.

11.5 *Working with web content (IDEA 5.0 and higher)*

One of the biggest improvements introduced in IDEA 5.0 is greatly enhanced support for web content like HTML, CSS, and JavaScript. Although IDEA has always allowed you to edit these languages, its support was limited to basic text-editing features. With IDEA 5.0, however, these languages are much more deeply integrated into the IDE and can utilize many of the features previously only available to Java source code editing. Here are some examples:

- Code structure analysis
- Move and rename refactoring
- Code completion
- Validation and syntax highlighting
- Integrated documentation

11.5.1 *Supported file types and content*

IDEA 5.0 now includes built-in support for HTML, CSS, and JavaScript files types. These are native file types, supported throughout the IDEA infrastructure. This means you can configure new file extensions for them, create file templates, control their formatting and syntax highlighting, and so forth.

HTML files

Any file type registered as belonging to the generic designation of HTML automatically inherits the ability to use all the HTML features discussed in this section. By default, IDEA maps the following extensions to the HTML file type:

- .htm
- .html
- .shtml
- .shtm
- .sht

The HTML file format supports both traditional HTML as well as the more rigidly structured XHTML. For the loosely parsed, more typical HTML file, IDEA offers warnings and errors based on the official HTML 4.01 specification from the W3C, but it doesn't complain about XML-related issues such as entity declarations and empty tags that aren't properly closed. It does, however, enforce proper structure for non-empty tags, such as `<table>` missing its `</table>` closing tag. Also be aware that most browsers have added support for their own nonstandard attributes and tags and that IDEA flags these as unrecognized, because they fall outside the core specification. More on document syntax validation later.

NOTE IDEA maintains a separate list of file type extensions for HTML and XHTML, but it only enforces XML-related structure and syntax problems in XHTML files if you've included a proper XML header. For example:

```
<!DOCTYPE html
  PUBLIC "-//W3C//DTD XHTML 1.0 Transitional//EN"
  "http://www.w3.org/TR/xhtml1/DTD/xhtml1-transitional.dtd">
<html xmlns="http://www.w3.org/1999/xhtml" xml:lang="en"
  lang="en">
```

CSS files

Cascading stylesheets are now a mainstay of web development, and IDEA 5.0 has appropriately added support for this format. By default, IDEA recognizes the .css file extension for these file types. For purposes of validation, IDEA uses the W3C's CSS 2.1 specification. As with nonstandard HTML, IDEA complains about any browser-specific stylesheet properties.

JavaScript files

If you're not familiar with JavaScript, it's important to point out that the only thing it has in common with Java is the first four letters—so, it's important to set your expectations appropriately. JavaScript doesn't have the same structure, API, or strict typing as Java, so you won't benefit from many of IDEA's Java-related features. Likewise, much of what you might think of as JavaScript has more to do with the browser than the language. For example, JavaScript concerns itself with syntax, conditionals, flow control, variable assignment, and so forth, whereas reacting to mouse events or accessing a page's form fields is functionality derived from objects exposed by the browser and outside the scope of the language—and thus outside IDEA's code assistance and other features. Although IDEA's support for JavaScript is unavoidably not as rich as its support for Java, a number of key features help JavaScript integrate into your project, as you'll see. By default, IDEA has registered the familiar .js file extension for standalone JavaScript files.

As with the other types of content, IDEA provides validation and coding assistance for JavaScript. In these cases, IDEA defers to the rules outlined for ECMA-Script-262, the formal standard for the language most people know as JavaScript.

Embedded and mixed-mode content

Often, in web development, HTML, CSS, and JavaScript are found intermingled in the same file. For example, an HTML document may have embedded CSS stylesheets or JavaScript blocks. Furthermore, JSP files consist largely of HTML with both Java and JavaScript blocks thrown in, possibly with CSS as well. IDEA handles this situation and adjusts accordingly, providing full access to most of the new features. Take, for example, CSS support, which can be accessed in an external CSS file, in a `<style>` block in HTML or JSP file, or in an HTML tag's `style` property attribute. Some features, such as the structure browser, act on the primary file type, based on the file's extension.

Organizing your web content in IDEA

When adding web content to your project, you should put it in the same location as your JSPs and other resources that make up your web application module. Doing so gives you the benefit of logical paths that can be resolved correctly during completion and validation operations undertaken by IDEA. For example, it's common to refer to the image files in HTML documents via alias names of folders that are specified in server settings, to allow deployment-time modification. Having such mappings supported right in the web module lets you use aliased paths with correct resolution.

If you're developing JSP applications, you'll most likely benefit from these new web content features either in the context of the JSP pages or through content associated with those pages as just described. Consider for a moment, however, that using IDEA as your development environment for other types of web projects also offers plenty of benefits, even for projects that don't involve any Java or JSP code. In addition to the improved integration and new features for web content in IDEA 5.0, you can take advantage of these other IDEA features:

- Integrated version control and local history
- A powerful, customizable source code editor
- Rich search, replace, and navigation features
- Familiar keystrokes and interface
- Editor bookmarks, macros, templates, and other features

11.5.2 Basic editor features

Many of the core features of IDEA's editor are available to web content files. Some of these, such as search and replace, macros, bookmarks, navigation, and selection, are language agnostic and work as well with HTML or JavaScript as they do with Java or JSP. We've covered these features in detail earlier in the book, so no additional commentary is necessary, other than pointing out that they're available when you're editing web content files. Other features, although they work similarly to the way they do in Java, are worth elaborating on.

Editor options

Most of the relevant editor options, such as Smart Keys, brace and scope highlighting, paired tags, quotes, brackets, and so forth, are now active in web content files. The standard code-folding features of the IDEA editor are also supported. These are available in HTML, CSS stylesheets and blocks, and JavaScript files and embedded scripts.

Formatting web content files

You can format JavaScript, CSS, and HTML files through the **Code | Reformat Code** feature (**Ctrl+Alt+L**). You control the formatting, as with Java files, through the **Code Style** settings panel. Although each of these file types inherits basic code style settings such as tab size, indention rules, and blank line handling from the core code style settings, HTML has its own tab under **Code Style** settings that lets you fine-tune its formatting, as shown in figure 11.23. Additional options for formatting CSS and JavaScript files were planned for the final release.

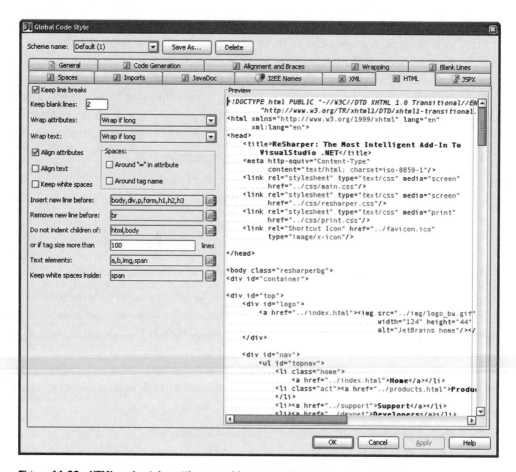

Figure 11.23   HTML code style settings provide a great degree of customizability.

The fields at the bottom of the dialog specify a list of HTML tags for which to apply the corresponding rule. For instance, in figure 11.23, we've specified that we don't want to indent the children of either the <HTML> or <BODY> tag. The **Text elements** field identifies inline tags (as opposed to block tags) so the formatter leaves them in their original context. The **Keep line breaks** option, if enabled, causes the formatter to leave any explicit line breaks you've entered. Otherwise, it decides when and where a line break is appropriate. The related option **Keep blank lines** specifies the maximum number of sequential blank lines to preserve. So, if you specify a value of 3 in this field, a series of seven blank lines is transformed into three.

Syntax highlighting

Syntax highlighting for web content files works exactly as it does in Java and JSP files. IDEA starts with reasonable defaults, but you can customize them easily through the **Colors & Fonts** settings panel, as shown in figure 11.24. All file types inherit the basic settings specified in the **General** tab, and HTML and CSS have their own tabs allowing you to further customize file type–specific syntax. JavaScript doesn't have its own tab under Colors & Fonts; but it inherits any appropriate defaults from the Java settings, such as the color of String literals or numeric constants. Additional options are planned.

11.5.3 Coding assistance for web content

Perhaps the biggest change to IDEA 5.0's web content features is that the IDE now understands the nature and syntax of JavaScript, CSS, and HTML in a way it never did before. Many of the code-aware features that make Java development so pleasurable in IDEA are now available for web development as well, including a built-in API reference and numerous code completion capabilities.

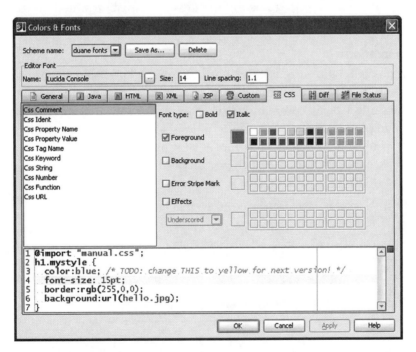

Figure 11.24   The CSS Colors & Fonts settings allow you to customize how IDEA colorizes your stylesheets.

Context sensitive help

IDEA now provides language and syntax assistance for HTML, JavaScript, and CSS elements, as it does for Java (see figure 11.25). Help is provided in a format of Quick Documentation lookup, which appears inline when you press **Ctrl+Q** with a tag, symbol, or attribute selected. This command is also available from the **View** menu. The **Quick Documentation** pop-up offers a brief summary of the symbols usage and, if applicable, links to related tags or properties.

The source of the assistance in this case isn't JavaDoc; it's the relevant W3C or ECMA specification. HTML files have context-sensitive help for both tags and attributes; CSS files offer help for individual style properties as well as the tags used in selectors; and JavaScript for the core language and the W3C Document Object model API. For help on a property, you can request help anywhere on the line, including in the property value assignment and in <style> blocks and style attributes in HTML.

IDEA can also offer assistance about attributes available for a particular HTML tag. While the cursor is positioned inside the tag, select **View | Parameter Info** or press **Ctrl+P** to view a pop-up listing the available attributes. Required attributers appear in a bold font.

Code completion

IDEA's code-completion capabilities have also been enhanced to support these new formats. To access code completion, position the cursor and use the **Code | Complete Code | Basic** command (**Ctrl+Space**) just as you would for Java code. You can complete tag names, attribute names, JavaScript symbols, CSS properties, style class and ID values, and more. Closing tags, parentheses, and braces are also automatically added, but these can be disabled or tweaked in the **Code**

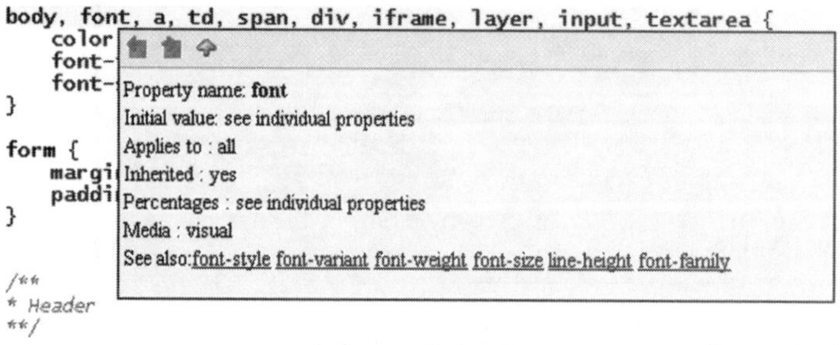

Figure 11.25   IDEA's context-sensitive help brings the CSS and HTML specifications into your source code.

Completion settings panel. Other code-completion options on this panel affect code completion with HTML and CSS as they do with other file types.

For HTML tags, any required attributes are immediately added when you use the code-completion feature. You can use the **Tab** key to jump between attributes, filling in these values. For HTML attributes and CSS properties that specify a specific set of legal values, IDEA's code-completion features offer these as suggestions. A typical example is the `align` attribute, which must be `justify`, `center`, `left`, or `right`.

Code completion in HTML and CSS also applies to file references made through `src` and `href` attributes. For example, when you include an external JavaScript file or create an anchor tag, IDEA provides you with a list of matching files and folders in the same folder as the source file. You can also provide a starting point if your resources are located in another directory, such as `../images` or `/scripts`. Note that only paths located in the current project's content roots are considered for completion, because all paths outside the project are invisible to IDEA.

Another good example of the new code-completion features for HTML and JavaScript is the HTML event handlers. IDEA offers any JavaScript methods available to the current document as candidates for a tag's event handler attributes, such as `onLoad()` or `onMouseOver()`.

For JavaScript, IDEA offers completion based on JavaScript keywords, variables, parameters, and functions defined in your script. Functions, parameters, and variables have appropriate icons in the completion drop-downs to identify them. This includes all scripts in the current page, as well as any locally included script files. However, IDEA doesn't offer code completion against objects defined outside of the core JavaScript specification. Therefore, don't expect it to complete against window, document, or other objects and methods commonly available in the browser. One notable exception is the W3C Document Object Model API (the DOM) for navigating through HTML; IDEA provides code completion and API assistance for this popular specification.

> **TIP** When a code-completion suggestion list appears to complete a tag, attribute, or property, you can use the context help feature (**Ctrl+Q**) to reference help directly within the list. Use the arrow keys to select the item you're interested in.

Syntax validation

While you type, IDEA is hard at work making sure your HTML, CSS, and JavaScript are properly formatted and following correct language syntax. Problems are flagged appropriately as warnings and errors, just as they are when you're working on a Java file. All the standard error stripe features and navigation are supported. For HTML and XHTML files, you can use the **Tools | Validate** action (also available by right-clicking inside the document) to validate the file for proper XML syntax. Here are some of the types of problems IDEA spots:

- Missing or invalid closing tags and braces
- References to invalid or missing directories, files, or local anchors by `src` and `href` attributes
- Duplicate attributes
- Invalid CSS selector format and tag references
- Missing required attributes or parameters
- Invalid HTML attributes and CSS properties
- Illegal attribute and property values
- Unused CSS class definitions

Many of these problems can be corrected for you automatically through IDEA's intention system, just as they are for other file types. Click the lightbulb icon or press **Alt+Enter** to accept the suggested fix. For example, if you assign an HTML tag a style class that hasn't been defined, IDEA ask if you would like to add an appropriate CSS selector. You can selectively enable and disable intention actions in the **Intentions** settings panel.

 A new feature of 5.0 is the ability to convert an HTML document into a valid and well-formed XHTML document. This makes it easy to move from the older HTML standard to a more rigid XML-based system.

Support for comments

All the appropriate comment designators are supported in the new file types, including C-style block comments, double slash line comments, and HTML style comment tags. You can use the **Code | Comment with Line Comment (Ctrl+/)** and **Code | Comment with Block Comment (Ctrl+Shift+/)** actions to comment out the current selection. If the current selection is already commented, the command reverses the process, removing the comments. As it is in Java and JSP files, comments have their own code style and coloring.

Find and Highlight usages

As in Java files, you can use the flavors of **Find** and **Highlight usages** actions in the **Search** menu and right-click context menu to determine where symbols are being used throughout the current file or project. You can apply these actions to a variety of different elements, including

- HTML tags
- CSS selectors and classes
- JavaScript functions, parameters, and variables

Showing the styles applied to a tag

If you right-click an HTML tag and select the **Show Applied Styles for Tag** option, IDEA opens a results window listing all the CSS styles applied to the tag. This is particularly helpful if you're including several different levels of stylesheets or have complex selectors in your stylesheet. From the results window, you can navigate back to any of the style definitions.

11.5.4 Navigating through web content files

In addition to the features we just discussed, IDEA's newfound insight into the nature of HTML, JavaScript, and CSS allows for improved navigation. Because it's now aware of the hierarchy, structure, and makeup of these languages, it can offer a consistent navigation model across the different types of files supported by IDEA.

Structural views

Each of the relevant file types supports its own variation of the **Structure** window you've used with Java files. The **Structure** window, as shown in figure 11.26, lets

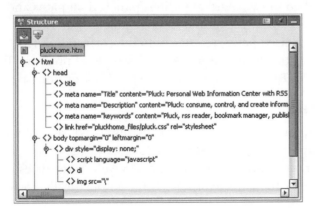

Figure 11.26
The Structure window brings a sense of order to your HTML, allowing you to quickly navigate through the hierarchy of tags.

you visualize the hierarchy of structure in the file and also allows quick navigation to its various components. Click any element to jump to its source. (Navigation control can be configured using the structure view toolbar.) The HTML view is a hierarchical tree of the page structure, the JavaScript structural view is a list of all the functions and variables defined in the file, and the CSS view is more or less a list of each the selectors specified by the file.

Go to declaration

This action works the same as it does with Java files. Selecting a symbol and executing **Go To | Declaration** (**Ctrl+B**) takes you to the symbol's initial definition, even if it's defined in another file. This feature works in the expected places in HTML, CSS, and JavaScript files, including

- JavaScript function calls, variables, and parameters
- HTML tags (takes you to the XHTML schema)
- References to external files through `src` and `href` attributes (anchors, styles, scripts, and so on)
- Stylesheet references through HTML tag `id` or `class` attributes

> **TIP** If you do a lot of HTML work for web site design, you will find the new **Image Viewer** helpful. It lets you view images directly in the IDEA editor. It even works in HTML image tags. Click the image reference, and then select **Go To | Declaration** (**Ctrl+B**). This is a good way to verify that an image you reference is the image you think it is!

Open in Browser

The **Open in Browser** feature lets you easily preview the currently open HTML file in the browser specified in the **General** settings panel. If all paths and references in the file are relative to the file location, you're able to view the file as it is. If paths are specified via aliased paths, references to the corresponding files may appear broken. (Note that this feature is just for quick general preview.) To view the file, select the **Open in Browser** command from the **View** or pop-up menu.

11.5.5 *Refactoring web content*

In addition to all the editor-related features already discussed, several refactoring operations can be applied to HTML, CSS, or JavaScript files. The first two, **Move** and **Rename**, work similarly to the way they do with other types of files. When you perform one of these refactorings, IDEA automatically corrects all affected references, even those in other files. It also takes care of any version control system actions necessary to keep your tree appropriately synchronized. These refactorings can be applied in a variety of contexts, including

- HTML, JavaScript and CSS files as well as their parent directories
- CSS `class` and `id` attributes
- JavaScript functions, parameters, and variables
- Referenced external files, including anchors, images, stylesheets, and JavaScript

The **Copy** refactoring is also supported for HTML, CSS, and JavaScript files, but only for the files themselves, not functions, selectors, and so forth. The **Copy** refactoring is a convenient way to create a clone of a file to use as a starting point, although a more generic approach is to use IDEA's file template feature to design your own JavaScript, HTML, or CSS starting points.

Another useful refactorings, **Extract Include**, makes it easy to move an inline block of JavaScript or CSS out of your HTML and into its own external file. IDEA automatically creates the new file and supplies the appropriate tag reference where the block once stood. You can select this option from anywhere in a JavaScript or CSS style block. The **Inline** refactoring does the opposite, pulling in the contents of an included file and omitting the need for an `include` statement.

Another refactoring that now extends to web content is IDEA's **Safe Delete** mechanism. As you'll recall from earlier chapters, you activate the **Safe Delete** refactoring by pressing **Alt+Delete** on a file in the project browser, or through the **Refactor | Safe Delete** command. When this refactoring is activated, IDEA searches for usages of the file to be deleted and informs you about all references to that file in other project files. The found references are shown in the **Refactoring Preview** tool window, and you may jump to the relevant places to resolve possible conflicts. This is helpful when an HTML, JavaScript, or CSS file is referenced in multiple locations and its simple deletion (via **Delete** command) may lead to multiple broken references. Note that as with other path-sensitive commands, this feature works correctly only for files referenced explicitly through relative or aliased paths within the project's content roots.

11.6 Summary

Since its inception, IDEA has promised to be the premiere Java editor on the market—the most complete, the most intelligent, and the most easy to use—and no editor could make this claim without support for enterprise application development using J2EE technologies. IDEA provides facilities for working with the central technologies in J2EE: servlets, JSPs, and EJBs. Although servlets can leverage most of the standard editor features mentioned so far, JSPs are a hybrid mix of HTML and Java and thus can't. To accommodate, the editor has built-in completion for JSP tags and attributes, along with refactoring support and syntax/error demarcation (it's quite a mature XML editor, another technology that helps bind J2EE together). IDEA's EJB wizard creates new EJBs quickly and easily, and the system knows the J2EE specification well enough to provide visual cues delineating issues that can prevent deployment.

Beyond this working-with-code perspective, IDEA also integrates with the enterprise application servers, the containers within which these technologies carry out their operations. Enterprise applications are typically more complex than their non-enterprise counterparts, due in part to their more involved mechanism for deployment and execution. IDEA's application server integration allows for much of this mechanism to be automated, freeing your time to work on the critical business logic of your application. IDEA's extensible plugin mechanism also allows for nonbundled application server support to be included—and updated—in a timely and modular fashion.

IDEA 5.0 also offers greatly enhanced support for web content, such as HTML, CSS, and JavaScript. Developers of enterprise applications often find themselves working in these technologies when implementing front-end user interfaces. Now, features such as code structure analysis, **Move** and **Rename** refactoring, and code completion are available on these file types. This is another example of how IDEA continues to grow and assist professional developers in meaningful ways.

Customizing IDEA

12

Whether you realize it or not, you have a preferred environment when you're developing software. Everyone has personal experiences—experiences with different editors, with different coding styles, with different operating systems, and so on—all of which contribute to the growth of specific patterns or habits that maximize your productivity. It's a rare developer who can drop into a totally new environment and maintain their usual pace and quality of development.

Unfortunately, it's not uncommon for corporate policy to enforce environmental change. You may not have a choice over the coding standard against which you must adhere, or what revision control system you use, or even what IDE has been mandated. Any policy that drags you away from your habits—out of your comfort zone—will have a detrimental effect on your productivity.

Luckily, one of IDEA's strongest features is its wealth of customization options. IDEA provides a number of facilities for customizing its look and feel, as well as its operation.

Suppose for a moment that you've joined the in-house development shop at ACME Incorporated, where a team of developers and architects is working on a small-scale enterprise Java application. They're trying to adhere to a test-driven development methodology and have a coding standard that is a slight variant from the Sun Java coding standard. This chapter will showcase some of IDEA's customizable settings that make a transition to this environment as painless as possible.

12.1 Configuring IDEA's options and settings

IDEA maintains two types of settings, *IDE Settings* and *Project Settings*. IDE settings pertain to all projects and control aspects of using the IDE that are project independent. Project settings, on the other hand, affect only a specific project (and are saved along with that project file). Changes to your project settings affect only the current project, allowing you to customize things like your version control and debugging preferences on a project-by-project basis.

All of IDEA's settings are accessed through the **Settings** icon of the main toolbar, through the **File | Settings** menu option, or by using the default keyboard shortcut **Ctrl+Alt+S**. Each of these approaches brings up the **Settings** panel shown in figure 12.1. The upper half of the panel is dedicated to project settings, those which apply to a specific project and have no effect outside that scope. Most of these settings panels have been introduced in their respective chapters; table 12.1 describes them briefly.

Table 12.1   The subsections of IDEA's Project Settings dialog allow you to modify the appearance and behavior of the current project without influencing other projects that you may be working on.

Project Settings group	Description
Paths (1)	Setup of project directories (source, output, and so on) and libraries
Compiler (2)	Compilation options and compiler selection
Version Control (3)	Selection and configuration of your external version control system
Project Code Style (4)	Custom, project-specific rules defining how your code should be formatted
GUI Designer (5)	Options available in the GUI Designer

The lower half of the **Settings** panel is dedicated to **IDE Settings**, which apply to all projects and control the basic appearance and behavior of the IDE; see table 12.2.

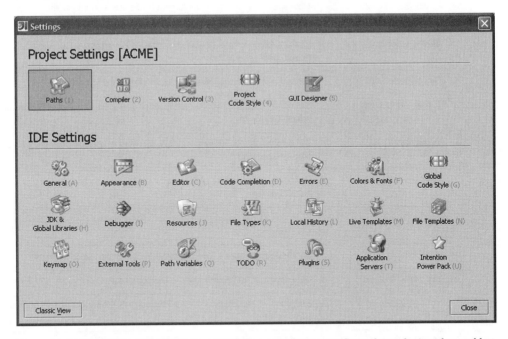

Figure 12.1   The Settings panel. Project Settings are settings specific to the project you're working on; IDE Settings apply to all projects and affect the basic operation of IDEA. With version 5.0, the Paths option is called Modules.

Table 12.2 The subsections of IDEA's IDE Settings allow you to control almost every aspect of the software's appearance and behavior.

IDE Settings group	Description
General (A)	General IDE options that fall in no other category, such as behavior during startup and frame activation/deactivation, the Check for new version behavior, and file-encoding options
Appearance (B)	General look and feel of the entire IDE, such as the default window font, toolbars and other window artifacts, and transparency of floating windows
Editor (C)	Customization of the behavior of the code editor windows, such as smart keys, margins, line numbering, code folding, brace highlighting, and cut/copy and paste behavior
Code Completion (D)	Code-completion behavior, such as enabling/disabling specific type of code completion (basic, smart type, class name), pop-up delay time, and bracket insertion
Errors (E)	How specific types of errors known to the IDE should be interpreted: as errors, as warnings, or ignored
Colors & Fonts (F)	Customization of the view of the code editor windows, such as the font, colors, and special text effects in different file types
Global Code Style (G)	Default rules defining how your code should be formatted
JDK & Global Libraries (H)	Definition, location, and organization of the JDKs and global (non-project-specific) libraries
Debugger (I)	Behavior of the debugging window, such as its default transport, and stepping patterns
Resources (J)	Definition and caching of external resources, such as XML files, DTDs, and schemas
File Types (K)	Definition of file types and extensions, and control over how IDEA interacts with them
Local History (L)	Configuration options for the built-in local version control system
Live Templates (M)	Generation of commonly-used code constructs
File Templates (N)	Definition of archetypical file structure, from empty classes to complex Java patterns
Keymap (O)	Configuration of all shortcut key bindings in IDEA
External Tools (P)	Definition and management of external tool/helper executables
Path Variables (Q)	Simple name-value editor for defining, editing, and deleting path variables

continued on next page

Table 12.2 The subsections of IDEA's IDE Settings allow you to control almost every aspect of the software's appearance and behavior. *(continued)*

IDE Settings group	Description
TODO (R)	Patterns and filters used by the IDE to find to-do references in source code
Plugins (S)	Management of external plugins that extend the scope and breadth of IDEA
App Servers (U)	Addition, configuration, and deletion of application servers in the IDE
Intention Power Pack (T)	List of intentions available in the editor

12.1.1 Customizing the interface

The **Appearance** panel, shown in figure 12.2, lets you customize the IDEA interface. You can do everything from tweak minor aspects of its behavior to change the entire look and feel.

A new settings panel, **Customizations**, has been added to allow you to customize the commands and options presented in IDEA's toolbar and pop-up menus. Using this panel, you can rearrange the toolbar, simplify it, or load it with commands to suit your preference.

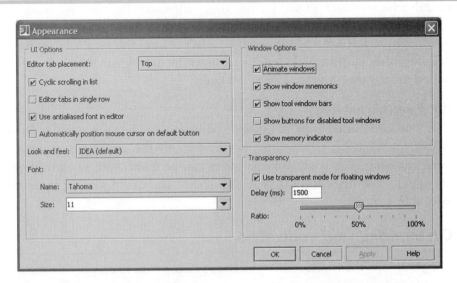

Figure 12.2 The Appearance options allow you to customize the look and feel of the interface.

Changing the overall look and feel

Under **UI Options** on the **Appearance** panel, the **Look and feel** setting controls how the IDEA interface appears on your system. This option controls aspects of the interface and layout such as buttons, scrollbars, and tabbed panes. By default, IDEA uses its own custom look, although you can change it if you wish.

This option lists all the available looks and feels for your platform. If you wish, select your platform's look and feel to make IDEA look more like a native application, or select the **Metal** option to use the default Java look and feel. You can even select another platform's look and feel; you can make IDEA on the Mac look like it's running under Windows, or vice versa. We urge you to try IDEA's look and feel, because it has been designed to be unobtrusive and clean. Although it may not be as familiar as the native look and feel of your operating system, its design is practical and usable.

IDEA 5 As mentioned in the preface, version 5.0 of IDEA ships with a new default look and feel known as Alloy.

Controlling the interface fonts

Under the **Font** options on the **Appearance** panel, select the name and size of the default font you want to use for the IDEA interface. The font you select will be used in various sizes for menus, title bars, output from running programs, dialog boxes, and so forth. This font setting doesn't control the font used by the editor, however; that's controlled through your code style settings, which were mentioned in chapter 3 and are described later.

Using antialiased fonts

The **Use antialiased font in editor** option on the **Appearance** panel lets you enable anti-aliasing, which attempts to smooth the text fonts to make them more readable. The results of this effect can be good, bad, or ugly, depending on your font settings and the type of display you have. Interface fonts are anti-aliased by default.

12.2 Customizing your code style

Everybody has their own code style. Recognizing this, IDEA provides a vast array of code-styling options that allow you to specify every nuance of your preferred code layout. You can control just about every option of your code style on the

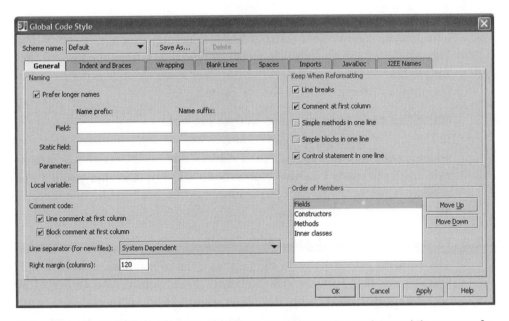

Figure 12.3 The Global Code Style panel: IDEA can model and understand very subtle nuances of a coding style.

Global Code Style panel, shown in figure 12.3, enabling IDEA to keep everything nice and neat.

 The **Global Code Style** panel has been regrouped and reordered, and the dialog looks slightly different. Some of the options shown in figure 12.3 appear on different tabs.

12.2.1 How IDEA uses your code style

Once it understands how you like your code to be formatted, IDEA can help you by automatically using your style when it generates, refactors, or reformats your code. You can even create a different code style for each project if you wish.

Creating your own code style

At the top of the **Global Code Style** settings dialog, you can select your code style from the **Scheme name** drop-down. One **Default** code style is included with IDEA, and it can't be deleted. To begin creating a custom style, click the **Save As** button to create a copy of the **Default** settings as a starting point. For a name, select whatever you want—for example, My Code Style. This name will be used here and in your Project Settings when selecting the code style for the project. You can delete a code style if you wish by selecting it from the list and clicking the **Delete** button. The editor will use the selected code style scheme, unless you've specified a different scheme for the project.

Managing code style schemes across projects

In the Project Settings, you can choose to use something other than the currently selected code style by enabling the **Project Code Style** option. Radio buttons provide the options to **Use the global code style** or **Use per-project code style scheme**. Choose the per-project option, and then select the scheme you wish to use from the drop-down list.

12.2.2 *Variable naming and general formatting*

The **General** tab of the code style settings contains a number of general formatting options that apply across the board. The **Naming** and **Order of Members** options apply to code completion operations as well as any code generation operation. IDEA doesn't use these options to rename or reorder your source code, only to generate suggested variable names and properly place inserted members. We covered the usage of the J2EE **Names** tab in chapter 11, when we talked about how to build EJBs in IDEA.

Specifying naming prefixes and suffixes

The naming prefix and suffix options allow you to specify a prefix or suffix to be used when generating suggestions for naming new symbols through IDEA's code-generation features. Enter any combination of prefixes and suffixes you desire. Any blank entries will use the default name suggestions without any special prefixes or suffixes. When you add prefix values, IDEA automatically uppercases the suggested base name. For example, if IDEA is going to suggest the name count for a new field variable, and you've specified a prefix f for field variables, IDEA suggests the name fCount. You can even enter both a prefix and suffix—both will be applied. The option **Prefer longer names** determines the default selection when multiple names are suggested.

Determining the order of inserted members

The **Order of Members** option lets you tell IDEA where you want it to place new members it inserts during code refactoring and generation operations. This option has no effect on reformatting operations as you might first expect. Use the **Move Up** and **Move Down** buttons to reorder the list to your liking.

Preserving your own formatting

The **Keep When Reformatting** option group lets you specify code scenarios that should not be reformatted with your code style settings. This lets you preserve exceptional formatting while still using the code-formatting features for the most part. You can elect to preserve these five types of formatting as is:

- **Line breaks**—If selected, IDEA leaves all your line breaks alone. Otherwise, reformatting your code automatically adds and removes line breaks as necessary to match your code style settings.

- **Comment at first column**—If selected, any comments that begin at the first column retain their position rather than being indented to match the indentation level of the code they accompany.

- **Simple methods in one line**—If selected, any methods written in one line retain their formatting when the code is reformatted rather than follow all the usual code style settings.

- **Simple blocks in one line**—Similarly, if selected, any code blocks written in one line retain their formatting when the code is reformatted rather than follow all the usual code style settings.

- **Control statement in one line**—If selected, control statements (such as `if`, `for`, and so on) are left on a single line if that's the way they're entered. Otherwise, your code style settings will be used to position the body of the control statement.

Placing comments

The **Comments** option group controls how line and block comments should appear. For each type of comment, you can enable the option to place the comments at the first column. This means that when you ask IDEA to comment out a line, it places the comment characters either at the very start of the line or just in front of the first non whitespace character.

IDEA 5 Two new options on the **General** tab of the **Code Style** settings panel allow you to control how IDEA handles the declaration of generated local variables and parameters. If either the **Make generated local variables final** or the **Make generated parameters final** option is enabled, IDEA automatically includes the final modifier in their declaration.

12.2.3 *Controlling indentation and braces*

The **Indent and Braces** tab in the **Global Code Style** panel controls the basic layout of your code structure by controlling the size of the indentation and the layout of code blocks. Your tab and indentation settings can be different for different file types if you desire.

Using tabs instead of spaces for indentation

You can use the **Tab size** option to specify the width of your tab characters. Normally, the editor uses space characters for indentation and formatting. When you press the **Tab** key, reformat your code, or indent a line, the editor inserts spaces to apply the indentation. If you enable the **Use Tab Character** option, tab characters are used instead of spaces. The **Smart Tabs** option uses a combination of tabs and spaces to achieve your desired formatting, because tabs alone are limited to multiples of whatever tab size you've specified.

Controlling indent size

The **Indent** option specifies your desired width for one level of indentation. Each additional level of indentation adds to this width. The **Continuation indent** option specifies the indentation level for statements that are split across two or more lines of source code. This lets you format the lines after the first line differently to avoid confusing source code. The **Do not indent top level class members** option is for people who don't like the first tab in their source code. Otherwise there is a tab indentation in front of members and methods. Activating this option puts no space in front of class members.

Indenting multiline parameters

Sometimes you'll encounter a line of code that doesn't fit on the current line, but long lines are undesirable in your coding standard. The code has to be split across several lines. As you learned earlier, there is a code style setting for continuation indentation; but this style can potentially be hard to read because clauses, parameters, and other artifacts don't line up with one another on the screen. Long lines split in this fashion are called *multiline* code, and IDEA provides a series of settings that lets you specify which cases should be lined up for readability and which cases should use normal continuation indentation. These settings are found under the **Align when multiline** heading.

Placing elements on a new line

The **Place on New Line** group of options is used to specify how you'd like to format the `else`, `while`, `catch`, and `finally` keywords. Each of these keywords follows a companion block of code: `else` follows an `if` block, `while` follows a `do` block, and so forth. If selected, the keywords appear on a new line following the previous block of code; otherwise, they appear on the same line as the preceding closing brace.

 The placement of bracing can now be further refined in the **Braces Placement** option group of the **Indent and Braces tab**. A new option for placement, **Next line if wrapped**, specifies that the brace should be placed on the next line if text wrapping was required. For example, if you selected this option for class declarations, the opening brace appears on the same line as the declaration—unless the declaration is so long that it wrapped across multiple lines, in which case the brace is placed on its own line immediately following the declaration.

Managing the placement of braces

In the **Braces Placement** option group, you can specify where you would like the opening brace to appear for class declarations, method declarations, and everything else. There are four possible settings for managing the placement of braces, and all options appear in the preview area of the tab:

- **End of line**—The opening brace is positioned at the end of the declaration line.
- **Next line**—The opening brace is positioned at the beginning of the line following the declaration.
- **Next line shifted**—Same as **Next line**, but the brace is shifted in one indentation level. The body of the block is at the same indentation level as the brace.
- **Next line shifted2**—Same as **Next line**, but the body of the block is shifted in an additional level of indentation.

Two additional options are related to brace placement. If you select the **Special else if treatment** option, the `else if` construct is treated almost like a single keyword and always appears on the same line. If this option is deselected, the `if` appears indented under the `else`. The remaining option, **Indent case from switch**, does exactly that. If it's selected, `case` statements and their `default` label appear indented in one level under their `switch` statement rather than at the same level.

Forcing braces

On many occasions, Java doesn't require the use of braces. For example, after an `if` expression, if you want only one line to execute, you don't need the braces. Many developers see this as bad practice and an invitation for bugs to enter the system. IDEA can enforce the use of braces using these options. Setting each scenario to **Do not force**, **When multiline,** or **Always**, you can tell IDEA exactly how you want this situation handled.

12.2.4 Controlling whitespace

Whitespace is an important element in creating a readable code style. Without ample whitespace, all your code runs together into a big mess that no one can read. You can adjust how the editor formats blank lines and spaces through the **Blank Lines** and **Spaces** tabs of the **Global Code Style** settings.

Managing blank lines

The **Blank Lines** tab specifies your code style's use of blank lines. It's divided into two option groups. The first, **Keep Blank Lines**, specifies the number of blank lines that are kept before class or method declarations after reformatting. Because this option only comes into effect when reformatting, you won't see any change reflected in the preview window as you make adjustments.

The second group, **Blank Lines**, controls the number of blank lines used before, after, and around various types of code elements. In this case, the term *around* really means *in between*. If you specify that there should be three spaces around all your methods, you'll get three spaces between method definitions, not three spaces before and after each method (which would result in six spaces). Spacing isn't added before the first item or after the last item.

> **TIP** Changes to the code style settings are reflected immediately in the preview panel. This feature makes it easy to define a global code style: Set each option, watch the effect it has on the previewed code, decide which options make the code more readable and maintainable, and save the style when you're done.

Managing spacing

The **Spaces** tab gives you an abundance of options to specify how and when spaces are used in your code. As you change your options, you can view the effects of the change in the preview window. The options break into six categories:

- **Before Parentheses** controls spacing between methods, keywords, and opening parentheses.

- **Around Operators** controls spacing around mathematical and boolean symbols.

- **Before Left Brace** controls spacing around curly braces after keywords.

- **Within Parentheses** controls spacing inside parentheses.

- **In Ternary Operator** controls formatting of the ternary operator (`condition ? true : false`).

- **Other** controls miscellaneous spacing options such as spacing around punctuation, commas, and so forth.

12.2.5 Customizing import statements

The options in the **Imports** tab control how IDEA manages import statements. IDEA can automatically import classes and packages for you, and it can optimize your import block based on the settings in this tab.

Optimizing imports

You can use the command **Tools | Optimize Imports (Ctrl+Alt+O)** to rearrange your imports as specified in your layout settings. It also removes unused imports and uses packages instead of single classes if specified in your options. You can optimize imports from the **Project** view by right-clicking a file, a package, or directory and selecting the **Optimize Imports** option from the context menu. If you wish, you can optimize imports across your entire source tree.

 The **Optimize Imports** command has been moved from the **Tools** menu to the **Code** menu.

Configuring the basic import rules

When you reference a class outside the current package, IDEA can automatically import the necessary class or package for you. The settings on the **Imports** tab of the **Global Code Style** settings control exactly what is imported and how:

- **Use single class import**—If unselected, IDEA always imports entire packages rather than single classes. If enabled, individual classes are used unless one of the package options discussed later takes effect.

- **Use fully qualified class names**—If enabled, IDEA doesn't bother importing classes and instead refers to a class reference with its fully qualified class name.

- **Insert imports for inner classes**—If enabled, IDEA provides `import` statements for inner classes contained in the Java class.

- **Use fully qualified class names in JavaDoc**—When enabled, IDEA always uses a fully qualified class name in a JavaDoc reference, even if the class is imported or package-local.

- **Class count to use import with ***—Specifies a threshold value for the number of imports from a particular package, which causes the entire package to be imported rather than individual classes.

Importing entire packages

The packages listed under the **Packages to Use Import with *** list are always imported en masse, regardless of the number of classes you import from the package (as long as you use one, of course). The Swing and AWT packages are included in this list by default, but you can remove them if you wish.

When you're entering a package, you don't need to add a wildcard or trailing period to the end of the package name. For example, the pattern for matching the Swing package is `javax.swing`—no need for a wildcard. If you don't select the **With Subpackages** option next to your package, the rule only applies to the root package. If it's selected, all subpackages below the specified package are also imported as a single unit when required.

Specifying an import layout

The **Import Layout** list specifies the preferred order in which your `import` statements appear, based on the package they come from. You can also insert blank lines between groups of `import` statements. The `<all other imports>` entry can't be removed; it specifies the location for any imported class or package not matching an entry in the layout list. As before, you can use the **With Subpackages** option to extend the scope of a match to include all the packages below it.

Order isn't technically important. Java won't let you create ambiguous class references, so order doesn't determine precedence when resolving class names. This is purely a stylistic issue. For example, you may want all your local package imports to appear first, followed by third-party packages, and finally core API packages. This way, you can get an idea of what internal dependencies exist by glancing up at your import block.

12.2.6 *Controlling line wraps*

Lines of code can become excessively long. Method declarations with many parameters, class declarations with extends and implements clauses, and array declaration and initialization are all prime candidates for causing lines to extend past the arbitrary right margin, the point where the full line of code is no longer visible on the screen. Coding standards often dictate when and how to wrap lines of code, and IDEA supports configuration options to enforce those rules.

From the **Global Code Style** window, the **Wrapping** tab controls this behavior. It identifies multiple discrete contexts, such as method call arguments and for statements, and lets you set a line wrap policy for each case. Possible settings include:

- **Do not wrap**—If selected, no special wrapping style is applied to the code. Long lines are left as is and may extend past the right margin.
- **Wrap if long**—If selected, lines that go beyond the right margin are wrapped with proper indentation.
- **Chop down if long**—If selected, elements in a list are chopped down (that is, wrapped to give one element per line with proper indentation, if they go beyond the right margin). Shorter lines are left alone.
- **Wrap always**—If selected, all elements in a list are always chopped down (wrapped to give one element per line with proper indentation, regardless of the right margin setting).

You can set the right margin on the **General** tab of the **Global Code Style** panel.

12.2.7 *Adherence to a code standard—made easy*

With the addition of all these code-formatting features, IDEA absolves you of the need to change your personal, effective coding habits in order to conform to an imposed standard. The Java compiler doesn't care about your whitespace, your layout, or how readable your code is; it just cares about syntactic accuracy. By configuring the appropriate coding style schemes in IDEA, you can write code in the style you find the most effective and then reformat your entire tree to another standard before submitting it to a revision control system and sharing it among a team.

Abiding by coding standards is made even easier with IDEA's ability to help manage JavaDoc and naming in J2EE applications. Configuration options for these are located in the **Project Code Style** dialog; consult IDEA's documentation to best take advantage of these features.

12.3 *Customizing your color scheme*

You've already seen the syntax highlighting features in the editor. As with code styles, IDEA recognizes that everyone has their own color preferences. With this in mind, IDEA provides a flexible system for specifying the color and style of code in the editor. The color scheme you define determines not only the color used in your source code, but also interface-related color properties such as the current row, the cursor, line numbers, and so forth.

12.3.1 *How IDEA uses color schemes*

Syntax highlighting does more than make your code look pretty. It reveals code structure, increases readability, and can alert you to errors in both syntax and logic. IDEA uses your selected color scheme in the editor window and (to a lesser extent) in your search results.

To get to the color scheme settings, bring up the **Settings** and click the **Colors & Fonts** option. The color scheme editor is shown in figure 12.4. You can select the scheme to edit through the **Scheme name** drop-down at the top of the panel. A default scheme is provided, but it isn't editable; so, the first thing you should do is to use the **Save As** button to save a copy of the default scheme using whatever name you choose. Select the name to begin editing. You can change your color scheme at any time, or define several and switch between them.

12.3.2 *Editor properties*

There are several sets of color scheme properties, organized into tabs by the type of document they affect. Click the corresponding tab in the **Colors & Fonts** window to access the properties you can configure:

- **General**—Default text and backgrounds, editor markup, interface elements
- **Java**—Syntax and API usage used in Java files, and Java code in JSPs
- **HTML**—Tags and comments in HTML files, and HTML tags in JSPs
- **XML**—Tags in XML documents
- **JSP**—Tags specific to the JSP API

- **Custom**—Used when working with a user-defined file type
- **Diff**—Used in the diff viewer to color different types of changes
- **File Status**—Lets you configure the color of the filenames depending on their status in version control

Working with the preview window

A preview window in each tab in the **Colors & Fonts** window shows you how your color scheme will appear in the editor. The preview window mirrors as closely as possible the editor window, including optional components like line numbers, method separators, and so forth. Each preview window contains sample content that covers most, but not all, of the available style properties. If you want, you can

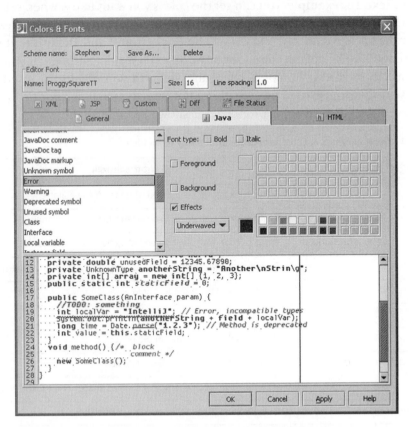

Figure 12.4   Colors and fonts customization in the IDEA Editor. You can configure the specific color highlighting of all common java application file types individually.

use the **Apply** button to see your changes reflected in the real editor window without leaving the style editor. Note that the style-editing window is modal, so although you'll see your new styles take effect, you won't be able to work in the editor until you close the style editor.

TIP You can click anything in the preview window to select the property that manages its style. This makes it easy to design your own color scheme; click the items you don't like, and change them.

Configuring general properties

The **General** properties tab controls the colors used by the editor interface rather than your text. For example, you can set the colors you want to use when selecting text, or the color of the line numbering. This tab also contains the default text settings for the background and text color. The **Background** and **Default text** properties are used as the default values for any unspecified color settings. If you don't specify a background color for a particular style, these defaults are used. The default settings are also used by everything not directly tied to a color property. A summary of the **General** color properties is shown in table 12.3.

Table 12.3 General Colors & Fonts properties that apply to all files

Property name	What it controls
Background	Editor background color, used when the file is editable
Background in read-only files	Editor background color, used when the file isn't editable
Read-only fragment background	Areas of code that can't be edited as they were generated
Default text	Default font styling for any text not covered by another property
Selection	Color of selection in the text area
Caret	Cursor color
Caret row	Highlights the current row in the editor
Right margin	Color of the right margin line, if enabled
Whitespaces	Color of whitespace characters such as spaces and tabs, if visible
Line number	Line numbers in the editor window, if enabled
CVS annotations	CVS annotations shown in the gutter area

continued on next page

Table 12.3   General Colors & Fonts properties that apply to all files *(continued)*

Property name	What it controls
Folded text	Text representing a block of folded code
Folding outline	Code folding controls, if enabled
Selected folding outline	Currently selected code-folding control
Added lines	Color used in the gutter to indicate added lines, if using a VCS
Modified lines	Color used in the gutter to indicate changed lines, if using a VCS
Search result	Matching terms for search operations and refactorings
Search result (write access)	Write matches found by highlight usages in the file
Text search result	Color used to highlight the results of a text search in the file
Template variable	Color of template variables in live templates and file templates

Configuring Java properties

The **Java** tab is used to configure the color scheme for Java code, including JSP scriptlets (this is the dialog shown in figure 12.4). If you review the list of color scheme properties in table 12.4, you'll notice a lot more options than constants and keywords. A number of properties are dedicated to error conditions, warnings, and scoping. These options make it possible to use syntax highlighting as a means for spotting errors not only in syntax, but in logic as well.

Let's illustrate this with a scenario we've experienced repeatedly. Unused symbols are shown in their own color. This indicates that although a symbol (such as an instance variable) is syntactically correct, it isn't referenced anywhere. When you see an unused variable, you should be suspicious. Is it an obsolete reference? Did you forget to implement the code that uses it? Did you use the wrong variable name somewhere else? Because IDEA's color highlighting is aware of syntax, scope and references, it can be a valuable tool for catching bugs early.

Table 12.4   The Colors & Fonts properties that apply when editing a Java source file

Property name	What it controls
Keyword	Java keywords, such as `public`, `class`, `return`
Number	Numeric constant values, such as `12`

continued on next page

Table 12.4   The Colors & Fonts properties that apply when editing a Java source file *(continued)*

Property name	What it controls
String	String constants, such as `"Hello World"`
Valid escape in string	Valid escape character within a string, such as `\n` for a carriage return
Invalid escape in string	Invalid escape character within a string, such as `\g`
Operator sign	Symbol representing an operator, such as +, =, and <
Parenthesis	All method definitions, and the calling of methods
Braces	Braces that define the limits of a code block
Brackets	Square brackets used in the definition and use of primitive array types
Comma	Commas used in any argument notation, including array declaration
Semicolon	Character used to signify the end of all lines of code in Java
Dot	Dots used in package notation
Line comment	Comments of the `//` variety
Block comment	Comments of the `/* */` variety
JavaDoc comment	JavaDoc comments, `/** */`
JavaDoc tag	JavaDoc tags, such as `@return` and `@see`
JavaDoc markup	HTML in JavaDoc comments
Unknown symbol	Reference to a variable, method, or other symbol that isn't defined
Error	Invalid Java syntax
Warning	Java code that is circumspect, such as assigning a static to a non-static
Deprecated symbol	Attempts to use deprecated classes, methods, or fields
Unused symbol	Symbols that have no known references
Class	Java class names
Interface	Java interface names
Local variable	Local variables (variables within a method body)
Instance field	Instance variables (variables within class scope)
Static field	Static field variables

continued on next page

Table 12.4 The Colors & Fonts properties that apply when editing a Java source file *(continued)*

Property name	What it controls
Parameter	Method parameters
Method call	Java code that calls a method
Method declaration	Identifier of a method in a method declaration
Constructor call	Java code that calls a constructor
Constructor declaration	Identifier of a constructor in a constructor declaration
Static method	Static methods
ToDo item	Comments that match a ToDo item pattern
Matched brace	Used by the brace matching feature
Unmatched brace	Used by the brace matching feature
Bad character	Invalid character not allowed in a `String` constant
Method separator	Lines drawn between methods for visual separation, if enabled
Breakpoint line	Line with a breakpoint set on it
Execution point	Current suspended execution point (used while debugging)
Annotation name	Name of an annotation of Java 1.5 program code
Annotation attribute name	Attribute name of an annotation in Java 1.5 program code

12.3.3 *Changing font settings*

The editor uses the same basic font and point size for all the file types IDEA supports. Only the font's color, weight, and effects (such as underlining) can be modified.

Choosing an editor font

The editor font can be different from the font used by the main interface, menus, and dialogs. You specify the interface font through the **Appearance** options of the **IDE Settings**. You can use any font installed on your system with the editor. When you click the font browser for the first time in any given IDEA session, it takes a few seconds to scan your system for fonts before displaying the font dialog. Make your selection from the list.

Although you can use any font in the editor, it's important to understand the difference between *proportional* and *monospace* fonts. Proportional fonts vary the width of the font depending on the character. For example, in a proportional font, the letter m is wider than the letter i. This makes the font easier to read, which is why the majority of fonts installed on your system are proportional fonts. Proportional fonts have a shortcoming, however: Because the width can vary from character to character, it's not always possible to achieve exact alignment and indentation, which can be a problem when you're editing code.

Monospace fonts, also known as *fixed-pitch* or *fixed-width* fonts, use the same width for every character, eliminating this alignment problem. Courier is the most common example of a monospace font. The font browser has a **Show only mono-space fonts** option: Selecting it hides all the proportional fonts on your system.

This doesn't mean that you shouldn't consider selecting a proportional font for your editor. Many proportional fonts have only subtle differences between characters widths, making alignment problems less apparent. Personal preference and font availability will determine the best choice for you.

> **TIP** You may want to consider using anti-aliased fonts in the editor. Anti-aliasing attempts to smooth the text fonts to make them more readable. You can enable anti-aliased fonts for the editor through the **Appearance** options in your **IDE Settings**.

Adjusting the font size and line spacing

Next to the font selector are options for adjusting the size and spacing of the font. The font size is specified in points and defaults to a value of 12. You may want to adjust this value up or down depending on your preferred resolution and selected font.

The **Line spacing** option controls the amount of space between each line of text in the editor. By default, the line spacing is 1.0, which is normal spacing. The line spacing value adjusts the spacing relative to normal spacing, so 2.0 means twice as much space and 0.75 means 75% spacing. You can specify any value here, including fractional values, but numbers between 0.5 and 2.0 work best. By reducing line spacing, you fit more rows of text onto the screen at any one time; we tend to bring our spacing down to 0.9 or so.

Controlling font styling and color

For each color scheme property that supports foreground text (some properties only affect the background), you can enable bold, italics, or both. If neither is selected, the normal font weight is used. These options are combined with the three-color options, foreground color, background color, and text effects, to determine the final font style for the selected property.

TIP Although you can't disable a color scheme property, you can achieve the same effect by deselecting all three of the style color options. For example, if you don't want the current row highlighted, deselect the **Caret** row property's background option. Doing so causes this property's font to revert to the default text style and background.

You can also select a text effect, also known as *text decoration*, for your color scheme property by enabling the **Effects** option and selecting one of the following effects from the drop-down:

- **Underscored**—Basic underlined text with a straight underscore in the selected color

- **Underwaved**—Alternative underlining with a rippled underscore in the selected color

- **Bordered**—Solid border in the selected color around the element on all four sides

- **Strikeout**—Line of the selected color through the center of the text

To choose a color, click an entry in the color palette to the right of each option. The currently selected color is shown in the larger square to the property's immediate right. Double-click this square to choose a color from the color wheel.

TIP These non-color-based visual effects are extremely useful for drawing attention to code that needs attention, sometimes in unforeseen ways. We've known at least two software developers with red-green color blindness who, using IDEA's highly configurable color and fonts settings, were able to demarcate errors and warnings using underscored, underwaved, bordered, and struck-out text. Doing so allowed them to enjoy the full range of IDEA's contextual code analysis.

12.4 *Customizing keyboard shortcuts*

One of IDEA's strong suits is its keyboard support. IDEA provides keyboard access to just about every feature in its arsenal and also lets you customize them to your liking. If you wish, you can use IDEA almost entirely from the keyboard, never having to touch your grubby little mouse. This lets you keep your hands on the keyboard, where they belong! (You can't code with the mouse, after all.) Once you start navigating with the keyboard, you'll quickly find it more efficient than constantly reaching for the mouse.

12.4.1   Using keyboard shortcuts

A keyboard shortcut (sometimes called an *accelerator*) is a keystroke combination (such as **Ctrl+F**) that activates a menu item or other action from the keyboard. If a menu item has a keyboard shortcut assigned to it, the shortcut is listed next to the menu item. Some commands have multiple shortcuts assigned to them, but only one is shown in the editor.

12.4.2   Navigating the interface with the keyboard

You can also use the keyboard to navigate around the interface. Most menu titles, menu items, buttons, and other components in IDEA are equipped with mnemonics. A *mnemonic* is an underlined letter that appears in the component's text and reminds you that you can activate the equivalent command by pressing the **Alt** key and the character key of the underlined letter. For instance, you can use a mnemonic to activate a button or select a checkbox. You can also use the **Tab** key to jump between fields in most dialogs and the arrow keys to navigate lists and select boxes.

12.4.3   Selecting a keymap

IDEA lets you select one of its built-in keymaps or define your own using one as a starting point. Either way, you can change your keymap selection at anytime by executing the **File | Settings** command and choosing the **Keymap** option in the **IDE Settings** category. This brings up the keymap editor, shown in figure 12.5. To select your keymap, click its name in the list and click the **Set Active** button. Your selected keymap is shown in bold and has the (*active*) modified name. Briefly, you can choose from these built-in keymaps:

- **Default**—Default keymap on which all other keymaps are based.
- **Mac OS X**—Keymap appropriate for Mac OS X. The command key is represented as the **Meta** key.
- **Emacs**—Keymap designed to approximate many of the settings of the popular UNIX editor Emacs. Note that this isn't a full emulation of Emacs; this setting affects only the keymap, not the behavior of the editor.
- **Visual Studio**—Keymap configured to match that of Microsoft's Visual Studio.

TIP   If you're an aficionado of the UNIX editor vi (you know who you are), never fear. Due to vi's command mode/editor mode nature, no vi keymap is provided with IDEA; but a third-party plugin is available that will do the trick. See http://www.intellij.org/twiki/bin/view/Main/VimPlugin for details.

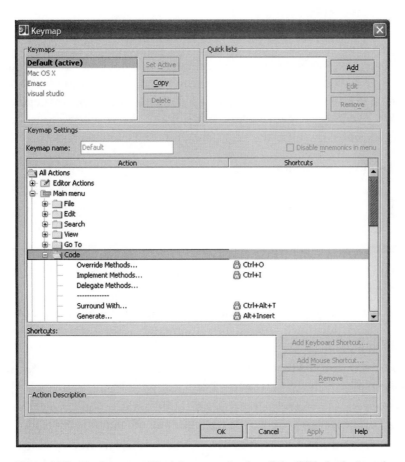

Figure 12.5   The keymap editor lets you customize all the IDEA shortcuts and define your own. This flexibility lets you use IDEA without ever taking your hands off of the keyboard.

The keyboard shortcuts listed in menu items change dynamically to reflect your selected keymap. To learn the other key assignments for your keymap, use the keyboard settings browser.

> **TIP**   You can download a handy keymap reference card from the IntelliJ website, http://www.jetbrains.com/idea/documentation/documentation.html.

12.4.4 *Creating a new keymap*

The keymaps included with IDEA are listed in grey, indicating that they aren't editable. To customize a keymap, you first create a copy of an existing keymap and then edit it to your liking. Select the keymap you want to start from, and click the **Copy** button. You'll be asked to provide a name for your new keymap, and you can elect to make it the active keymap. You can also delete a keymap (other than the default keymaps) by selecting it and clicking the **Delete** button.

12.4.5 *Defining keyboard shortcuts*

All the actions for which you can create shortcuts are organized in the keymap editor by type. Any entry shown in blue text has been modified from its parent keymap or, in the case of the categories, contains modified entries. The categories are as follows:

- **Editor Actions**—Editor-related keys such as navigation, selection, deletion, and so on

- **Main menu**—All the actions available through the main menu, including any plugins that have created new menus or added entries to the existing menus

- **Version Control Systems**—Keys that handle basic VCS operations, such as check-in, check-out, revert, and so on

- **Ant Targets**—If you're using the Ant build tool in your project, lets you assign keystrokes to any specific target in any of your Ant build files

- **Debugger Actions**—Debugger-related keys, such as freeze, resume, and watch manipulation

- **GUI Designer**—GUI designer–related keys, such as layout commands and the data-binding wizard

- **Bookmarks**—Keystrokes for setting, unsetting, returning to, and listing bookmarks

- **External Tools**—Lets you assign shortcuts to any external tools you've defined (see chapter 13)

- **Macros**—Keystrokes for running user-created macros

- **Quick Lists**—Keystrokes for bringing up user-made short menus of useful commands

- **Other**—A dumping ground for miscellaneous actions that don't fall into the other categories

For each action, you can see the currently assigned shortcuts (if any) and, for some entries, a description of the action. Below the list is the shortcut list for the currently selected action. Note that each action can be assigned to as many shortcuts as you wish. The first shortcut in the list is shown on the menu items corresponding to the action, but beyond this appearance there is no difference in the shortcuts.

You can't edit an existing shortcut; you must delete the existing shortcut by selecting it and clicking **Remove** and then add a new one to replace it. To add a shortcut, select an action from the action tree, and then click **Add Keyboard Shortcut**. You're presented with a dialog like one shown in figure 12.6. To define the shortcut, press the shortcut combination on your keyboard, including any modifier keys

Figure 12.6 Adding a keyboard shortcut is straightforward. Conflicts with existing keyboard shortcuts are indicated in the dialog.

such as **Ctrl**, **Alt**, or **Shift**. If there are any conflicts with existing shortcuts, they're shown, but you aren't prevented from assigning the shortcut. When you accept a shortcut that conflicts with another shortcut, you're given three choices of how to resolve the conflict:

- **Remove** deletes the existing shortcut, keeping the new one you just defined.
- **Leave** leaves the conflict in place but disables the existing shortcut.
- **Cancel** deletes the new shortcut and leaves the existing shortcut unmodified.

WARNING IDEA will happily let you assign a shortcut to a normal letter key like D without complaining that it's already assigned (to the action of placing the letter *D* on the page!). However, such an assignment is usually done only by mistake, because it means you can't use that letter while typing (because doing so will trigger the command).

You can also create shortcuts that require two key presses to activate. Emacs users should be familiar with this concept, because many of its commands follow this format. Two-stroke shortcuts are listed with a comma. For example, the shortcut **Escape, Ctrl+F** means to press **Escape**, then release it, and then press **Ctrl+F**. Although it may sound inconvenient to enter two key combinations rather than one, doing so increases the number of keystroke combinations considerably.

To create a two-stroke shortcut, add a shortcut as before, but click the **Enable** box above the **Second Stroke** field. Enter your first stroke in the first box, and then mouse over to the **Second Stroke** field and enter the second key combination.

> **TIP** If you turn on the **Disable mnemonics in menu** option for your keymap, the main IDEA menu won't be accessible via the **Alt** key, freeing up the dozen or more key combinations used to access the menus.

12.4.6 *Defining mouse shortcuts*

Another alternative is the mouse shortcut. It lets you define shortcuts that include mouse button clicks, with or without modifier keys. When a mouse click is included in a shortcut, the action affects the item you click. For example, if you hold down **Alt** and single-click the middle mouse button, you can view the Quick JavaDoc for the item that you click in the editor. Although you can't assign an action to turning the wheel on a wheel mouse (it's used for scrolling), if your wheel is also a button, IDEA considers it button 2.

To assign a mouse shortcut, select the action and click the **Add Mouse Shortcut** button to bring up the dialog shown in figure 12.7. This dialog works similarly to that for adding keyboard shortcuts. First select either a single-click or a double-click shortcut. Then, hold down any combination of modifier keys (**Alt, Ctrl,** and **Shift**) you want to include, and press your mouse buttons on the **Click Pad** area of the dialog (where the icon of the mouse is). The button you pressed and the resulting shortcut definition are shown in the **Shortcut Preview** area. You can repeat the process until you're happy with your shortcut and click **OK**. As before, you may need to resolve a conflict with an existing shortcut.

Figure 12.7   Mouse shortcuts add a new dimension to shortcuts, allowing you to perform operations with a click rather than a keystroke.

12.4.7 *Defining quick lists*

Another configurable option IDEA offers is quick lists, which are basically pop-up menus of IDEA commands that you design yourself and assign to a keystroke or mouse gesture. You can select from any of the commands available in IDEA, and you can create as many quick lists as you like.

To create a quick list, bring up the **Keymap** settings panel and locate the **Quick List** section to the right of the keymaps you've defined. Click its **Add** button, and specify a name and description. Then pick the options you wish to include, in the order you want them to appear.

An additional option in the quick list editor available to 5.0 users only lets you add menu separators. These help visually group your actions into related functions, making long lists easier to use.

Once you've defined a quick list, you need to map it to a keystroke or mouse gesture in order to use it in IDEA. All the quick lists you've created appear under the Quick Lists node of the **Action** tree in the **Keymap Settings** area. You assign keys to quick lists just as you do for other types of actions. An example of a quick list in action is shown in figure 12.8.

Figure 12.8 Quick lists let you create custom pop-up menus anywhere in IDEA.

12.5 *Working with non-Java file types*

IDEA lets you work with files other than Java, including XML, HTML, JSPs, and plain text files. Although the editor's convenience features are primarily geared around Java, it has notable support for XML files and JSPs (discussed in chapter 11).

IDEA uses the file's extension to determine the type of file it's dealing with. If the extension is unrecognized, IDEA won't allow you to open the file in the editor. A file's type also determines how the code is displayed in the editor and what color scheme settings are used. In the **IDE Settings**, you can use the **File Types** options to control how IDEA works with such files.

12.5.1 *Modifying file types settings*

IDEA comes with a number of predefined file types, but not all of them are editable. Java class and source files, JSP files, text files, archive files, XML files, HTML files, and IDEA GUI designer form files are all integral to the editor and are therefore off limits to editing or removal. You can edit the remaining file type definitions, including JavaScript, IDL, and user-defined file types.

12.5.2 *Registering file extensions*

You can use the **File Types** panel to add to and remove from the list of extensions registered to a file type, although you can't register the same file extension to more than one file type. For example, if you want to be able to edit your SQL files in the editor, you can add the extensions .sql and .ddl to the list of extensions registered to text files. A better way, though, is to create a custom file type for SQL files.

12.5.3 *Creating a custom file type*

Custom file types allow you to extend the kind of files the editor is aware of by providing information about what keywords are relevant to the file type, what comments look like, and so forth. Editing a custom file type is like editing a plain-text file, with the addition of keyword and comment syntax highlighting and number recognition. To create a new file type, click the **Add** button in the **File Types** panel to bring up the **Add/Edit File Type** dialog, as shown in figure 12.9.

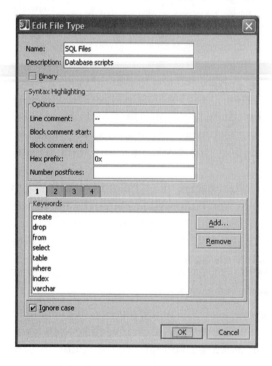

Figure 12.9
Create your own custom file types to extend the editor's capabilities.

Configure the options that most closely match your file type:

- **Ignore case**—If selected, keyword matching (discussed in a moment) is case insensitive.

- **Line comment**—Specify the pattern that signifies the start of a single-line comment.

- **Block comment start and end**—Specify the pattern that marks the beginning and end of a block comment.

- **Hex prefix**—Specify the pattern that indicates a value is a hexadecimal number, such as `0x`.

- **Number postfixes**—Numbers are recognized automatically if they're surrounded by whitespace, but this setting lets you extend the matching to include numbers with postfixes. A postfix is any trailing text such as `e-5`, `kg`, `ft`, and so on.

If you're defining a binary file type, all the syntax highlighting options are unavailable because they don't mean anything. Any option that doesn't apply to your new file type should be left blank.

Next, define any keywords that you want to receive special attention through the four sets of keyword tabs at the bottom of the dialog. The coloring of keywords is determined by your color scheme settings, discussed earlier in this chapter. All custom file types share the same color scheme, so you use the tabs to define four logical sets of keywords that each receive different coloring. If you're designing a file type to support cascading stylesheets, for example, you can put all the selector types into one category of keywords and all the properties in another. There is no way to teach IDEA how to interpret your new file type's syntax; you can only teach it to recognize keywords and symbols. Once you've created your new file type, don't forget to register file extensions for it.

12.6 *Using file templates*

Traditionally, when you're adding a new class or interface to a Java source tree, you determine the appropriate package and create an empty file in that directory. It's then your responsibility to add the appropriate Java code, such as the `package` statement and the class declaration, to format and structure the class to meet your needs. When you're working with software design patterns—well documented, tried and true data structures and algorithms for solving common problems—this task is amplified, because you have to reimplement an already-defined structure by hand from scratch.

IDEA attempts to minimize this boilerplate work with the concept of *file templates*. File templates define a starting point for new files, Java or otherwise. When you create a new file from within the **Project** window, IDEA looks up and presents you with a set of templates that can be created in that context. For example, if you try to create a new file in a package in a Java source tree, IDEA asks if you want to create a new Java class, Java interface, or Singleton, among others. Choosing one of these options invokes its associated file template, which includes a basic framework for the type of file you're creating. Using this strategy, you can start with your file's basic framework already defined, rather than with a blank document.

12.6.1 *Creating a new file from a template*

In the **Project** window, right-click the folder where you want to create the new file. From the context menu, select an entry from the **New** submenu to create your new file. You have several choices as to the type of file you're creating; but IDEA will suggest creating Java files only under the existing configured sourcepaths:

- **Class** creates a standard Java class.
- **Interface** creates a standard Java interface.
- **File** creates a non-Java file, such as a text file or JSP.
- **Package** or **Directory** creates a new package if you're under a source tree or otherwise a plain old directory.
- **Singleton** creates a class that implements the Singleton pattern, ensuring that a single instance is constructed.
- **Enumeration Class** creates a class that models enumerated types.

You're asked to name the file, and, in the case of non-Java files, you must provide the file extension. For example, if you create a new class or interface, it automatically gets a .java extension.

Editing the default file templates

To edit a default template for a file type, select the **File Templates** option of the **IDE Settings** to bring up the **File Templates** dialog. This dialog gives you access to all the templates in the system. The **Code** tab is used with IDEA's code-generation features; the J2EE tab is used for developing web applications. For now, we'll concentrate on the **Templates** and **Includes** tabs, which are used to create new files. An example of the file template editor is shown in figure 12.10.

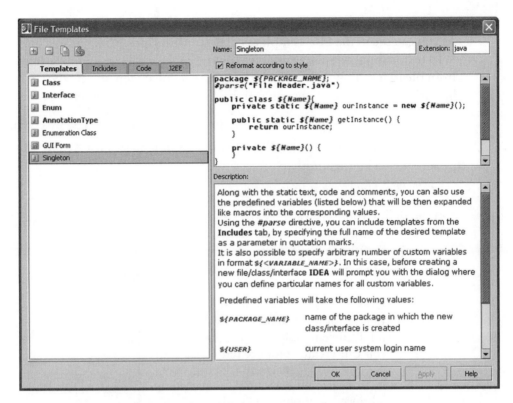

Figure 12.10 The File template editor lets you manage your file templates.

The **Templates** tab lists all the templates in the system. The color of the template name indicates the type of template and its status, and the icon tells you the file type:

- **Bold**—A default template that can be edited but not removed
- **Black**—A default template that can be edited or removed
- **Blue**—A user-defined or -edited template

To edit a template, select it from the list. Doing so loads the template into the edit window in the upper-right corner. You can see that a template is a combination of static text and scripting variables.

TIP To restore one of the bundled templates to its default values, shut down IDEA and delete the template file from IDEA's config folder under the `fileTemplates` directory. The next time you start IDEA, the default template will be restored.

Using template variables

As you can see in the **File Templates** dialog's **Description** box and accompanying help text, special template variables fill in the pieces of the template that change from file to file. Template variables start with a dollar sign and can be surrounded by curly braces. Java classes can use the following predefined template variables:

- *PACKAGE_NAME*—The name of the package in which the class was created
- *USER*—The user creating the class (as determined by Java system properties)
- *DATE*—The current date
- *TIME*—The current time

You can define your own variables by using them in your template text. When you create a new file using your template, IDEA prompts you to define any variable it doesn't recognize, as shown in figure 12.11.

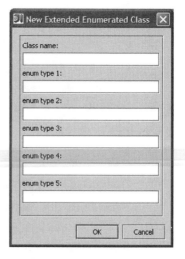

TIP IDEA uses Jakarta's Velocity Template Engine for its file templates. Velocity is a full-featured scripting language, and you can create complex templates with it. Visit http://jakarta.apache.org/velocity/ to learn more about Velocity and its advanced scripting capabilities.

Figure 12.11   Custom templates request data for parameters they don't implicitly understand.

Template formatting

Each template has a **Reformat according to style** option. If it's enabled, any source file created from the template is automatically reformatted according to the user's code style settings. This means you don't have to worry about things such as indentation and spacing, because they're corrected at creation time. It also means templates are portable across projects and users, regardless of their code formatting preferences. If this option is deselected, the template creates files unchanged from the template's formatting.

Defining a new file template

To create a new template, click the **Create Template** icon (the plus sign) in the **File Templates** dialog and specify a meaningful name for the template. This name will be the label used to identify the template when creating new files. Make sure the file extension field is set to the appropriate type; for a Java class, the extension is .java; for a text file, it's .txt; and so forth. You can then edit your template in the dialog's editor field.

Saving the current file as a template

You can create a template from an existing source file by executing the command **Tools | Save File as Template**. A new file template is created based on your source file. The template editor appears with your new template selected, ready to customize. All references to the class and package names are already replaced by template variables, but you may want to tweak the template text further.

12.6.2 *Working with template includes*

The **Includes** tab of the template editor lets you define a series of includes that can be loaded into other templates by name. For example, you may want to create a standard header include to use with your company's copyright notice or other legal mumbo jumbo. You can then include your header into your other class templates, saving you the headache of maintaining it across multiple templates. To include a template, use the `#parse` directive, passing the full name of the include file (with the extension) in quotation marks. For example, if your include file is named File Header.java, you use `#parse("File Header.java")` in your class file template to include the contents of the header.

12.7 *Increasing the amount of memory allocated to IDEA*

By default, IDEA allocates 16MB of heap to start, and it's allowed to grow to 128MB. If you have plenty of memory on your machine, you can improve the performance of IDEA significantly by moving the upper limit to 256MB or more. If you want to adjust this setting, you need to modify the files used to start IDEA.

Under Windows, go to the IDEA installation folder. Under bin, load the file idea.lax into your favorite text editor. This file is the configuration file used by the IDEA application launcher. Find the line that begins as follows (we've omitted the other options on this line for clarity):

```
lax.nl.java.option.additional=-Xms16m -Xmx128m
```

This line passes options to the JVM that is used to start IDEA and accepts any Java VM option. The `-Xms` option specifies the minimum heap size, and `-Xmx` specifies the maximum. In this case, to raise the maximum from 128MB to 256MB, change the line to read

```
lax.nl.java.option.additional=-Xms16m -Xmx256m
```

If you know what you're doing, you can also use this option line to tweak the VM's garbage-collection strategy and other settings, although it's recommended that you leave everything other than the memory allocation to the default values.

IDEA 5 The memory options have been removed from the .lax file and put into the idea.exe.vmoptions file. The same options are used, one option per line.

On the Mac, things work a little differently. In the IDEA installation directory, open the file bin/idea.app/Contents/Info.plist in a text editor, and look at the bottom of the XML under the key VMOptions. It looks something like this:

```
<key>VMOptions</key>
<string>-Xms16m -Xmx128m</string>
```

Change the VM options to whatever minimum and maximum values you want, and then restart IDEA to see the changes take effect.

> **WARNING**   If you rerun the installer or update your IDEA installation to a newer version, you'll lose your memory configuration changes.

12.8 *Summary*

IDEA is the most highly configurable IDE on the market today. It has been designed so that everything can be customized, resulting in a natural feel for any developer. You can configure and access all options via keyboard shortcuts, including your custom-written Ant targets. IDEA, unlike any other IDE, lets you configure how you want to interact with the IDE, instead of the IDE dictating how it wants to be used.

Beyond the bounds of the developer, IDEA also helps work within a team standard. A high level of code management and code formatting means you can follow standards with a minimum of fuss. All of IDEA's code-generation features are run through the code formatting rules, so you can rest assured that while you're developing, the style of the code is consistent.

Although IDEA is one of the most capable IDEs on the market, and the most configurable, it's also the easiest on the eyes. You're probably going to have to stare at it all day, every day. IDEA doesn't leave you high and dry here either, because you can configure every color on the screen for everything that loads into the editor. All this customizability lets IDEA lives up to its tag: Develop with pleasure.

Extending IDEA

13

The process of software development is rarely an uninterrupted one. General annoyances hamper productivity on most sizable development efforts.

One common problem is the difficulty in navigating between a large number of disparate source files. Some tasks are pervasive by nature, and the developer assigned to handling them has no choice but to trace through source code in multiple packages, in multiple directories, potentially throughout the source tree. In addition, developers often have many open issues assigned to them, such as new features to implement, pilot implementations to test functionality, introduction of new cross-cutting concerns, and bugs to fix.

Another common issue is functionality deferred out of necessity. Often, while working on one deliverable, you happen across another that hasn't been previously thought of or included on the project plan. Sometimes you may encounter a flaw in a piece of code that demands fixing, but scheduling and scope pressures prevent you from making the necessary changes right away. The task has to be deferred until its risk, scope, and ultimate impact can be assessed. The danger is that the task, which arose from a code inspection, may easily be forgotten as you work on your deliverables, and project management may never acknowledge its existence.

IDEA provides a series of tools to help overcome these (and other) barriers to productivity. Bookmarks allow rapid movement between diverse areas of the code base. ToDo lists give you an informal way to use comments to denote unresolved issues. The IDEA Commander provides a convenient panel interface for performing basic file refactorings (such as moving, copying and cloning) on packages, classes, files, and the like. And, in the event that you use external tools for auditing, for pre- or post-processing of source or object files, or even for source code generation, IDEA includes a generic tool integration mechanism that is flexible enough to meet most needs. This chapter will explore each in turn.

13.1 Working with bookmarks

IDEA's bookmarks don't alter your source code; they're reference points that let you navigate back to a particular area of code. Once placed, bookmarks stay with your project until you remove them. There are two types of bookmarks: numbered and anonymous. They're revealed in the editor through gutter icons as well as black lines in the marker bar, as shown in figure 13.1.

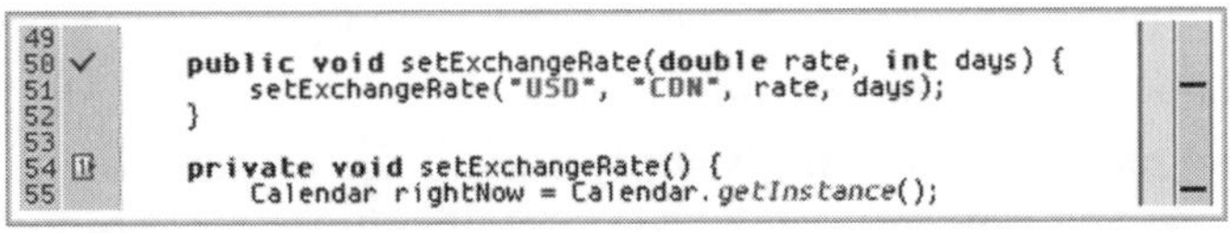

Figure 13.1
An anonymous bookmark
and a numbered bookmark

13.1.1 Placing and using numbered bookmarks

To place a numbered bookmark to the current line of code in the editor, hold down **Ctrl+Shift** and press one of the digit keys, 0–9. The bookmark icon with that number appears in the gutter next to the current line. Once placed, numbered bookmarks are accessible via a quick, one-step navigation sequence: hold down the **Ctrl** key and press a digit key to instantly jump to the corresponding bookmark.

The nature of the shortcuts means you're allowed a maximum of 10 numbered bookmarks in any one project, so use them wisely! You can always remove a bookmark and set it again somewhere else once you're through with it. Holding **Ctrl+Shift** and pressing a number for a bookmark that already exists will remove it; you can also select **Edit | Toggle Bookmark** or pressing **F11** while on the same line as the bookmark.

13.1.2 Placing and using anonymous bookmarks

An anonymous bookmark is indicated by a checkmark icon. Unlike numbered bookmarks, you can create as many anonymous bookmarks as you like. To place an anonymous bookmark on the current line of code, select the **Edit | Toggle Bookmark** command or press **F11**. A bookmarked line has a checkmark icon in the gutter area to the left of the line. Pressing **F11** again turns off the bookmark. You can also toggle a bookmark on a line of code by holding down the **Ctrl** key and left-clicking in the gutter next to the line. You can't set a numbered bookmark and an anonymous bookmark on the same line.

Although numbered bookmarks have a special shortcut (that's the real benefit of numbered bookmarks—the ability to navigate to them with a split-second keystroke), anonymous bookmarks don't. You have to use another bookmark navigation method.

IDEA gives you two ways to jump to any bookmark entry in the current document. First, you can click the bookmark's black mark in the right-hand marker bar. The cursor then scrolls to the selected bookmark.

IDEA also lets you navigate through your bookmark collection sequentially. Select **Go To | Next Bookmark** or **Go To | Previous Bookmark** to move back and forth among all the bookmarks in the current document. When you reach the end of your bookmarks, IDEA loops around to the first one. There are no predefined shortcut keys for these two commands, but you can assign some through the **Keymap** settings. These navigation methods apply only to the current document; to visit other bookmarks in your collection, you must bring up the bookmark list we'll cover next.

13.1.3 *Managing your bookmarks collection*

To access the bookmark list, select the **Edit | Show Bookmarks** command or press **Shift+F11** to bring up the dialog shown in figure 13.2. The bookmarks list lets you recall any of your bookmarked locations and also manage the list. The list displays an entry for each bookmark defined in the current project. The Description column is editable and can be used to jot down a quick note to remind you of the significance of the bookmark. The buttons function as follows:

- **Go to** closes the bookmark list and navigates the editor to the selected bookmark.

- **View Source** navigates to the selected bookmark like the **Go to** button but doesn't close the list.

- **Move up** / **Move Down** reorder the bookmark list for the purposes of the Next and Previous bookmark navigation feature discussed earlier.

- **Remove** deletes the selected bookmark.

- **Remove All** deletes all bookmarks from the project.

- **Close** closes the bookmark list.

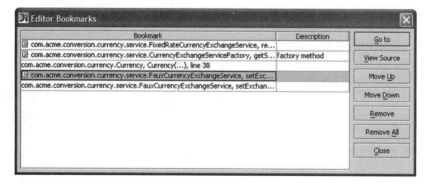

Figure 13.2 The Editor Bookmarks dialog allows you to manage and navigate to all your bookmarks.

13.2 Working with ToDo lists

The strategy of leaving comments in source code to help remind the reader of unfinished work or unresolved problems has been in practice for years. These comments remain part of the source code, so anyone reading the code has access to them. If the work you're doing may be handed off to other developers before you get a chance to finish it, or if you're working in a substantial system of code that you're not intimately familiar with, consider using IDEA's ToDo support.

IDEA uses a simple pattern-matching strategy to track ToDo items. The default settings match against the pattern ToDo. When it encounters this pattern, IDEA interprets it as an item to be added to your ToDo list. IDEA can detect the pattern when it's placed within a valid comment. IDEA colors the matched pattern to alert you to its presence. You can control the style and color of the highlighting through the editor's color scheme, discussed in chapter 12. A typical example of a ToDo item is shown in figure 13.3.

> **NOTE** IDEA can detect ToDo patterns in all supported file types that have defined comments syntax. Make sure you insert ToDo items inside comments that are valid for the current file type.

As you work, IDEA constantly keeps up with any ToDo entries it finds; you don't have to execute a search to view your list. The list is available at any time through the **TODO** tool window, which you can access by clicking its icon or pressing **Alt+6**. A ToDo tool window is shown in figure 13.4.

This tool window displays all of your ToDo entries and their location in your source tree. The window has two tabs: the default tab, **Project**, shows your project's ToDo entries; the second, **Current File**, limits the list to those found in the file you're currently editing. You can use the toolbar controls listed in table 13.1 to organize or explore your ToDo items. The numbers next to each entry tell you the row and column number of the match.

```
public static CurrencyExchangeService getService() {
    // The body of this method should decide on and return to us
    // a valid CurrencyExchangeService of some sort.

    // Until we either write one (or are provided one), we can only
    // return null here.

    // todo change this factory method so it returns different service impls
    return new FixedRateCurrencyExchangeService();
}
```

Figure 13.3 ToDos are special comments that are handled differently within IDEA.

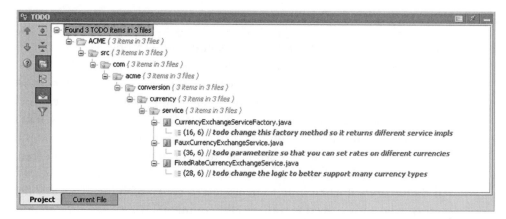

Figure 13.4   The TODO window shows you all the remaining ToDo references in your source tree.

Double-clicking an item in the list loads that item in the editor. If you've enabled the **Autoscroll to Source** option, then all you have to do is select the entry to view it in the editor. You can move sequentially through your list with the **Next** and **Previous** buttons on the toolbar or their shortcuts, **Ctrl+Alt+Up** and **Ctrl+Alt+ Down**. You don't have to have focus in the ToDo window for the Next and Previous actions to be available; these controls work even while you're working in the editor, making it easy to move through your ToDo list.

Table 13.1   The ToDo tool window is controlled by these icons.

Icon	Shortcut	Purpose
⬆ ⬇	Ctrl+Alt+Up, Ctrl+Alt+Down	Scrolls to the next/previous ToDo item
⑦	F1	Access the online help
⬍	Ctrl+Numpad -	Expand all
⬍	Ctrl+Numpad +	Collapse all
▣	Ctrl+P	Group by package
▤	Ctrl+F	Flatten packages
⬇		Autoscroll to source
▽		Select a filter

13.2.1 *Creating custom ToDo list items*

IDEA lets you take the ToDo concept a step further by adjusting its ToDo search pattern and defining your own. For example, you may need to embed questions in your comments, and keep track of those questions in the code. You can configure IDEA's ToDo mechanism to be aware of any pattern; you can even give a unique pattern its own icon. This pattern and its icon are specified in the **TODO** section of the IDE Settings, as shown in figure 13.5. By default, only the single pattern for matching ToDo items is present, but you can easily add additional patterns.

You specify each pattern using a *regular expression*, a type of shorthand for specifying complex pattern matches. IDEA uses the regular expression library included with JDK 1.4 for its pattern matching both here and in document searching and replacing. Refer to the JDK 1.4 JavaDoc for details on creating regular expressions. Along with the pattern itself, each entry also specifies an icon and its case sensitivity. When you create or edit an entry, you can specify these options. The icon is used by the entry in the **TODO** window. Unfortunately, there are only three icons to pick from, but you can reuse icons across several patterns if you wish.

NOTE In one respect, saying that IDEA has ToDo support is a misnomer. IDEA doesn't really have special support for ToDo comments; rather, it has a facility for recognizing regular expressions in source code that carry significant meaning. The IDE is also able to parse all its project source files, and it supports defining, highlighting, managing, and navigating to any instance of those regular expressions. The expression *ToDo* just happens to be commonly used and is of most immediate use to IDEA's user base.

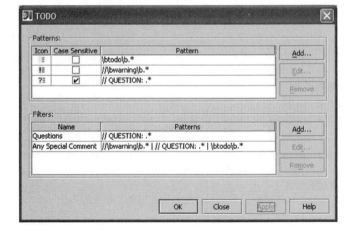

Figure 13.5
The TODO settings let you create your own entries.

This feature can be helpful in team environments, because it lets you create your own lists of tasks and issues within your code tree. If you're working with a team of developers, it's a good idea to coordinate on your naming scheme and conventions for creating ToDo items. Here are some ideas for ToDo items:

- Unresolved issues or questions that need to be answered
- Possible bottlenecks and areas that may need to be optimized
- Code that needs to be refactored
- Bug fix references or change lists

WARNINGS   Most major software development efforts use a software suite for tracking bugs and feature requests. Using ToDo comments in source code is no replacement for the visibility, workflow, and project management benefits that a more sophisticated solution provides.

Immediately after you add or edit your ToDo patterns, IDEA must search your entire source tree to update your ToDo list. This may take a while on a large project, so be prepared.

13.2.2 *Using ToDo filters*

The lower half of the **TODO** settings panel lets you create logical collections of the patterns you've defined. In the **TODO** window, you can click the filter icon and select any of the filters you've defined to control the type of items displayed. You can view just warnings, just the items that were recent bug fixes, and so on. To define a filter, use the **Add** and **Edit** buttons. All you need to do is specify a name and select the patterns you want to include. You don't have to type the regular expressions again—you get to pick the patterns from the list you've already defined. Left-clicking the filter icon also provides a shortcut to the **TODO** settings, called **Edit Filters**.

13.3 *The IDEA Commander*

The Commander provides an alternate view of your project files. Although the operations you can perform through the Commander mirror those available through the **Project** and **Structure** views, the Commander is a more useful tool when you're performing file-oriented tasks.

13.3.1 *Working with the IDEA Commander*

To activate the Commander, select the **Window | Commander** command, press **Alt+2**, or click the **Commander** icon in the main window. As you can see in figure 13.6, the **Commander** window has a dual-pane layout. Each pane shows an independently controllable view of the files in your project. Unlike the **Project** window, however, the Commander lets you display any two of these views simultaneously.

Controlling the views

Unlike the **Project** view's hierarchical tree view of your files, the Commander displays only the contents of a single layer of the hierarchy. If you're working exclusively within a given package or folder, this can be convenient. Being able to manipulate the contents of the two panes independently lets you see the contents of any two folders in your project side by side for easy comparison. The biggest benefit, however, comes when you're moving and copying files between folders, as we'll discuss shortly.

You can swap the contents of the two panes with the **View | Swap Panels** command (**Ctrl+U**).

Figure 13.6
The Commander window is subdivided into two panes.

Navigating within the views

In the Commander, you can double-click folders to open them, revealing their contents. To go back up a level, double-click the **Up Arrow** icon at the top of each panel. You can use the arrow keys to navigate between entries and the **Enter** key to move between directories. To jump back to the root folder, press **Ctrl+**. The Commander remembers your position, so you don't need to worry about losing your place. You'll always be returned to the last folder you visited. To switch the focus between the two views, press the **Tab** key or make a selection in the other view with your mouse. The keyboard shortcuts for the commander are shown in table 13.2.

Table 13.2 Keyboard shortcuts in the Commander

Shortcut	Action	Description
Alt+F6	Synchronize Views	Sets the contents of both panels to the folder selected in the active panel
Tab	Change Active Panel	Switches the focus between panels
Ctrl+\	Toggle Root Folder	Loads the root folder in the active panel
Ctrl+U	Swap Panels	Swaps the contents of the two panels

If you double-click a file, it's loaded into the editor, provided it's a supported file format. The one exception is Java classes. Instead of loading the files into the editor, the Commander shows you the contents of the class (its methods, fields, and so on), as in the **Structure** view. Double-clicking a method or field loads the file into the editor with the cursor at the start of the selected element.

> **TIP** To load a class file into the editor without drilling down into its structure view, select the class in either pane and press **Ctrl+Enter** (or **F4** to move focus to the editor).

The command **View | Synchronize Views** (**Alt+F6**) ensures that both panes display the same folder. This command is available only when you have the **Commander** window active and have selected one of the two panes. When you execute the command, the non-active pane's contents change to show the folder currently visible in the selected one. Note that the folders won't remain synchronized if you switch to another folder in either of them—this operation is a one-shot deal.

A nice improvement to the Commander in 5.0 keeps track of your navigations, allowing you to step backward or forward through your recent actions.

13.3.2 *File operations*

The benefit of the Commander's two-pane interface becomes evident when you're copying or moving files within your project. Any time you execute the copy or move command, the default destination for the new file is set to the location of the other pane. This makes the Commander a useful tool when you need to copy or move a number of files—for example, when rearranging your source tree. By performing these operations through IDEA rather than by directly against the local file system, you're technically utilizing IDEA's refactoring subsystem, and you therefore garner a number of substantial benefits:

- IDEA automatically handles any version control system additions and deletions.
- IDEA provides undo capabilities.
- IDEA automatically adjusts package references as necessary.

Copying files between panes

To copy files between two panes, first select the file or files you want to copy. You can select files from either the left or right pane. Choose the **Refactor | Copy** command from the main menu, by right-clicking the selected file, or by using the keyboard shortcut **F5**. You'll be presented with a dialog like the one shown in figure 13.7. The destination is automatically set to the location referenced by the other frame. You can specify a different location by entering into the field provided or clicking the browse button to select with the file chooser.

Moving files between panes

Moving files in the Commander is nearly identical to using the **Copy** command. The only difference is that the **Move** command deletes the original file after

Figure 13.7
An example of the Copy files dialog.

copying it into the other pane. If you're moving Java classes or packages, IDEA automatically adjusts any references to the affected classes to account for their new package.

Other operations

Any of the commands that act on multiple selections take both panes into account. For example, you can select files in both panes and use the **Compile**, **Compare Two Files**, **Reformat Code**, and other commands from the context menu. This is a convenient way to act on files located in different parts of your project.

13.4 *Integrating external tools with IDEA*

IDEA's external tools support provides a degree of integration between IDEA and third-party standalone applications without requiring the development of a plug-in. The external tools configuration options let you pass contextual information (like the currently selected file, or your project's source directory) to the external program through command-line arguments. This flexibility lets you easily integrate virtually any application into the IDE: for example, code generators, source analyzers, pre- or post-processors, database utilities, and so forth. Tools appear as new menu items in IDEA, depending on how they're configured.

13.4.1 *Managing the tool list*

To configure, edit, or remove external tools definitions in IDEA, select **File | Settings** from the main menu (**Ctrl+Alt+S**). This command brings up the **Settings** pane. Click the **External Tools** icon to open the dialog shown in figure 13.8.

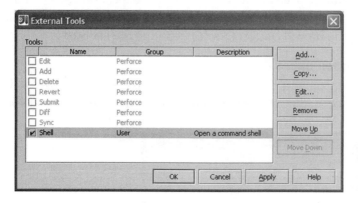

Figure 13.8
The External Tools Editor assigns general names to external tool invocations.

IDEA's external tool settings are saved as part of your IDE Settings and are shared among all projects. Each external tool that you've configured appears in this list. IDEA ships with several entries in the **Tools** menu already, to support the Perforce version control system. If you aren't using Perforce, you can delete them if you wish (although they're disabled by default, so you'll never see them anywhere except in this dialog). You can use the buttons on the right to create new tools, edit or reorder existing ones, or remove them. As an alternative to remove an entry, the checkbox beside each tool enables or disables it temporarily, meaning it isn't available for use in IDEA.

Creating a new tool entry

To define a new tool, click the **Add** button to bring up the **Edit Tool** dialog box shown in figure 13.9. Enter a short name in the **Name** field; this name will be used to identify the tool in IDEA's menus. If you wish, you can enter a more complete explanation of the tool's purpose in the **Description** field.

Another optional field, **Group**, lets you organize your tools into discrete groups of commands. To add a tool to a group, type the name of the group in the tool's **Group** field, or select an existing group from the drop-down list. If the name doesn't exist, IDEA adds it to the list for you. Groups have no properties and aren't something you have to manage directly. If you delete all the tools from a group, the group disappears from the selection box. Consequently, if you want to rename a group, you must edit the **Group** setting for each tool that is part of that group.

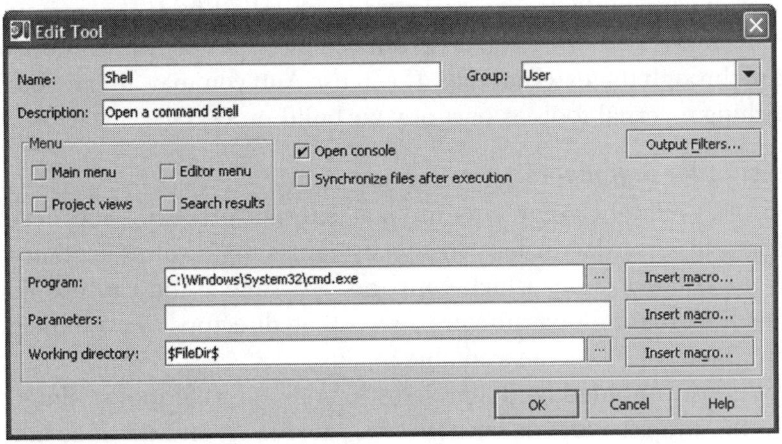

Figure 13.9   Creating a new tool entry is done from the Edit Tool dialog.

TIP   If you're using IDEA on a Mac, you may have difficulty launching applications that are distributed in Apple's application bundle format (.app files). To launch this type of application, launch the application with the `/usr/bin/open` command. Enter `/usr/bin/open` in the command field, and use the `-a` parameter to specify the path to the application bundle. For example, to launch the OSX file merge tool, enter `-a /Developer/Applications/FileMerge.app` in the **Parameters** field.

Specifying which program to run

Enter the name of the external executable in the **Program** field to specify which program to run. If the executable isn't in your system's normal execution path, enter the full path to the program. To pass arguments or parameters to the program, enter them in the **Parameters** field just as you enter them on the command line. If there are spaces in any of the arguments, surround the entire argument in double quotes. In the **Working directory** field, you can select the current working directory within which the program is executed. If this field is left blank, IDEA's default project directory is used. You can use the browse buttons next to the **Program** and **Working directory** fields to make a selection from your local file system.

Setting up external tools in IDEA is most useful when the tool is designed to act on a file in your project. Otherwise, it's just a glorified shortcut. IDEA's ability to pass contextual information from your project, such as the currently selected file, to the program makes this feature useful. To integrate with an application in this way, the program must be able to accept arguments from the command line. Fortunately, most of the types of applications you might want to integrate, such as compilers and code builders, are designed to be called from the command line and operate in this fashion. There's no limit to the types of applications you may want to use through the external tool. If you use Ant, you may already be familiar with launching external tools as part of your build process.

Using macros for arguments

To pass project-relevant arguments to your external program, you need to use IDEA's macro facility. Macros let you specify values that are resolved at runtime based on the context under which your tool was called. You can use macros to help define the program's parameters, its working directory, or even the program executable. Table 13.3 lists the available macros.

Macros are surrounded by dollar signs in your external tool settings. So, the macro for the project name is written $*ProjectName*$. In addition, macros are case sensitive. You can type macros by hand, if you'd like, but it's easier to click the **Insert macro** button to select one from the list provided.

Table 13.3   Macros enable contextual scripting of repeatable operations.

Category	Macro	Description
Project Settings	`ProjectFileDir`	Project file's directory
	`ProjectFilePath`	Absolute path of the project file
	`ProjectName`	Name of the project file without an extension
	`Projectpath`	Project's content paths
	`JavaDocPath`	JavaDoc output directory
	`Classpath`	Project's Classpath
	`JDKPath`	Home directory of the project's JDK
	`OutputPath`	Output path for compiled classes
	`Sourcepath`	Project's source paths
Selected/ Current File	`FileClass`	Fully qualified class name of the selected file
	`FileDir`	Absolute path of the selected file's directory
	`FileDirRelative-ToProjectRoot`	Path of the selected file's directory, relative to the project root
	`FileDirRelative-ToSourcepath`	Path of the selected file's directory, relative to its sourcepath's root
	`FileExt`	Selected file's extension
	`FileName`	Selected file's name, including any extension
	`FileNameWithout-Extension`	Selected file's name, minus any extension
	`FilePackage`	File's package
	`FilePath`	Absolute path of the selected file
	`FilePathRelative-ToProjectRoot`	Path of the selected file, relative to the project root
	`FilePathRelative-ToSourcepath`	Path of the selected file, relative to the its sourcepath's root
	`FileRelativeDir`	Selected file's directory, relative to the project root
	`ClasspathEntry`	Entry in the Classpath that the selected file belongs to
	`SourcepathEntry`	Entry in the sourcepath that the selected file belongs to

continued on next page

Table 13.3   Macros enable contextual scripting of repeatable operations. *(continued)*

Category	Macro	Description
Miscellaneous	ColumnNumber	Column number of the cursor in the editor
	LineNumber	Line number of the cursor in the editor
	Prompt	Displays a string input dialog used to complete the macro

TIP   When you're selecting a macro, the **Macro preview** area shows you what the macro will evaluate to under the current circumstances. For this reason, it's best to configure your external tools while operating under circumstances like those in which you expect to use it.

Prompting the user for values

Although most of the macros replace themselves with a value derived from the project or selected file, one macro behaves differently. The Prompt macro prompts you for its value when you execute the tool. If you have multiple Prompt macros, you're asked to supply a macro for each. Unfortunately, you have no control over the message displayed when you're prompted for a value; it always asks you vaguely to *Enter parameters*. Nevertheless, the Prompt macro is handy for call programs whose arguments must change regularly or when you don't want to include sensitive information in your tool settings, such as a database password.

13.4.2   Accessing external tools from within IDEA

Once you've configured a set of tools within IDEA, you need to define how those tools will be launched. Typically, external tools are accessed either via a menu option or by a user-defined keyboard shortcut.

Adding your tools to IDEA's menus

To access your tools, add them to one or more of IDEA's menus by selecting the appropriate options from the **Menu** options listed in the **Edit Tool** panel. If you've specified groups for your tools, they're arranged in submenus by group name. Any commands that aren't part of group appear as top-level menu items. The order of the items in the menu is determined by the order in which the tools appear in the External Tools settings. To change their order, bring up the External Tools settings, select a tool entry, and use the **Move Up** and **Move Down** buttons to reorder the entries. (If you don't add your tool to any of the menus, the only way to run the tool is through keyboard shortcuts, as described next.) The available menu options are as follows:

- **Main menu** adds the tool (or the group of tools, if they're grouped) to the end of the **Tools** menu.

- **Project views** adds the tool (or the group of tools, if they're grouped) to the end of the Project view's context menu.

- **Editor menu** adds the tool to the end of the editor's context menu.

- **Search results** adds the tool to the context menu in the results tree from IDEA's search tools.

Assigning keyboard shortcuts to your tools

As with IDEA's other commands and functions, you can assign keyboard shortcuts to your external tools, as shown in figure 13.10. All of your external tools appear in the Keymap settings under the External Tools hierarchy. Adding shortcuts for external tools works exactly as it does for other commands. Refer back to chapter 12 for information on editing keymap entries.

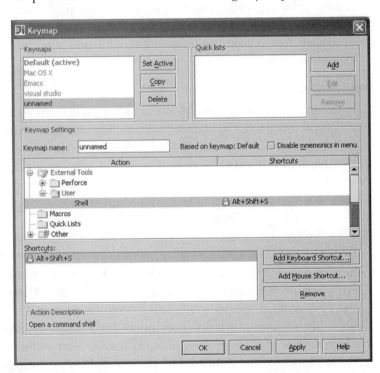

Figure 13.10 You can assign keyboard shortcuts to any of your external tools, giving you one-touch access to them.

13.4.3 *Reacting to the results of external tools*

Some external tools provide you with information, in which case the output from the tool needs to be captured and displayed. Some tools, however, respond with detailed output that references specific files, lines, and even columns in your source tree: for example, an external pre- or post-process code analyzer. Some even alter the source code they used as input or generate new source code from metadata files. IDEA has facilities for intelligently integrating with each of these situations.

Opening a console

If the external application you're running displays output that you wish to view, enable the **Open console** option in the tool's settings. This option tells IDEA to open a message window to display the results of executing the program. This output window works similarly to the output from running a Java application through IDEA. If there are any problems, such as bad arguments or an invalid pathname, these are also displayed in the output window, making it a useful option to enable when debugging your settings. If your application doesn't produce any output, or launches its own interface, you can leave this option deselected.

Using output filters to link program output

Many Java-related programs you run through the external tools feature generate output messages that reference a file in your source tree. For example, a program may reference an error in a particular source file. Through the use of output filters, you can train IDEA to interpret these types of messages, allowing it to hotlink the messages with the editor just as it does when you encounter compilation errors when building your project. You do this by defining one or more output filters for your tool using regular expressions.

Begin by clicking the **Output Filters** button in the tool editor to bring up the current list of output filters. You can add as many filters as you'd like, but only the first matching filter for each line will be used. You should design your filters to be as unambiguous as possible. You can use the buttons in the **Output Filters** window to reorder and edit items in the list; click **Add** to define a new one.

When requested, specify a name and description for the filter. The most important part, however, is creating the regular expression that identifies the linkable reference in the program's output. In these regular expressions, you embed placeholder variables to identify key components of the output:

- `$FILE_PATH$`—The portion of the output that corresponds to a source file
- `$LINE$`—A line number reference
- `$COLUMN$`—A column reference

Only the `$FILE_PATH$` parameter is required; the line and column references are optional, giving you a finer degree of integration if provided by your application. Depending on your application's output, designing the output filter can be trivial or impossible. Let's take an easy example:

```
Error parsing /src/scanner/RadioInterface.xml:103 Missing Closing Tag
```

One output filter that can match this output is

```
$FILE_PATH$:$LINE$
```

However, if colons aren't unique to the error message, you must get more creative.

> **TIP** Many development tools and compilers are designed to produce machine-readable output, but they often default to a friendly, more verbose style for human users. If the output from the program you want to integrate with appears too complex to parse, look for a command-line option that lets you change the output to something more easily digestible by IDEA. Some programs call this *emacs mode*, after the popular UNIX editor that uses a similar output parsing scheme.

Understanding synchronization considerations

Tools like XDoclet and Castor can generate Java source code from metadata (in JavaDoc attributes and XML, respectively). Running these tools, or other tools like them, causes significant changes in your source tree—changes that IDEA needs to be aware of. You should select the option **Synchronize files after execution** on the **Edit Tool** dialog when creating a tool entry if your external tool will be creating, altering, or deleting any files in your project path. This will ensure that IDEA picks up the changes and updates its internal cache files appropriately. This update applies to both source files and object files.

13.5 *Using IDEA's open APIs*

IDEA provides a set of open APIs that allow third parties to integrate their solutions and extend existing functionality. JetBrains maintains the online plugin repository, which holds more than 200 plugins. IDEA users can conveniently access the repository with the help of the Plugin Manager, accessible through the **Plugins** button in the IDE Settings pane.

With the help of the provided open API, you can extend almost every aspect of IDEA's functionality. For example, it's possible to do the following:

- Add new intention actions
- Add new code inspections
- Integrate new code editing features
- Implement new refactorings
- Incorporate new tool windows
- Integrate with new version control systems, or extend existing VCS integrations
- Provide integration with application servers
- Embed new types of editors (for example, for viewing images or other file types)

We obviously don't have enough room in this book to list all the opportunities provided by the open API, because there are almost no restricted areas for extensions. To learn more about IDEA plugin development, visit the dedicated community-driven web site at www.intellij.org/twiki/bin/view/Main/IntelliJPluginsHome.

13.6 Summary

On projects of any significant magnitude, the software development process always encounters interruptions in its smooth and steady flow. The act of introducing new features and eliminating bugs requires you to simultaneously edit files from all over the source tree; unforeseen features and refactorings reveal themselves deep in code, and you can't immediately address them without affecting the project schedule; part of the build, test, and audit process involves running third-party tools that aren't integrated with the development environment and yet affect it considerably.

These problems, although significant, are commonplace and can be reduced in scope with the proper support. IDEA has included features such as source code bookmarks, cataloging and highlighting of ToDo comments in source code, the Commander for large-scale file-based refactorings, and a generic external tool integration mechanism to alleviate a large portion of these headaches. In addition, the Open API gives you the power to extend IDEA in a coherent way.

appendix: Getting help with IDEA

IDEA has a number of built-in features to provide user assistance, whether you have a problem with IDEA itself, with the Java API, or even your own Java code. This appendix deals with help with IDEA itself; Java code completion and API browsing features are covered in chapters 2 and 3.

We've written this book with the assumption that you won't be reading the whole thing cover to cover before using IDEA. We assume you'll read the first few chapters to get a handle on the basic way IDEA works and then hit the various details as you encounter them. We hope the book proves to be a handy reference as well as a useful tutorial.

A.1 Using the integrated help text

IDEA uses the standard JavaHelp interface to provide application help text in the product. To bring up the help text, execute **Help | Help Topics** to bring up the Help tool, shown in figure A.1. You can browse the topic tree or click the search

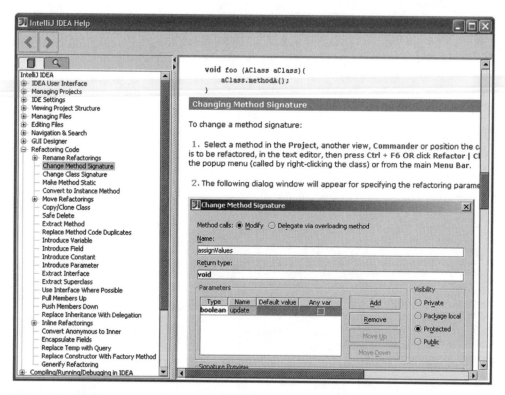

Figure A.1   IDEA features a well-written and hierarchical user manual, suitable for browsing.

icon and search for help by keyword. The arrows at the top of the help browser let you move back to previous topics.

For most dialogs in IDEA, you can get context-sensitive help by pressing **F1** or clicking the **Help** button or icon. If help is available for the current context, the help window appears at the relevant portion of help text.

A.1.1 Using Tip of the Day

Each time you start IDEA, it shares a handy tip with you, as shown in figure A.2. If you find this feature more annoying than helpful, deselect the **Show Tips on Startup** option. You can re-enable the tips (or see another tip) by selecting **Help | Tip of the Day**. The **Previous Tip** and **Next Tip** buttons let you browse through the tip collection if you want to review or skip ahead. If you have a few minutes, why not zip through the lot of them?

A.1.2 Using the Productivity Guide

IDEA provides a very important helper called the **Productivity Guide.** This tool analyzes the productivity features you may have missed in your everyday coding and shows you useful advice that is, in effect, *personal* tips of the day. These tips appear only during long processes, such as loading projects, compiling, and

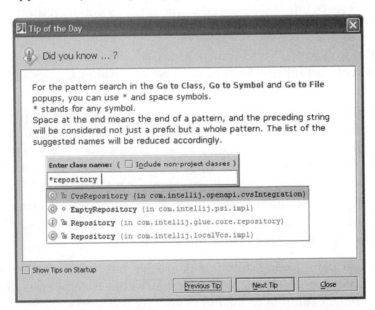

Figure A.2   IDEA's Tip of the Day is a good way to introduce yourself to new and useful features.

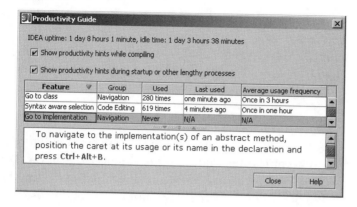

Figure A.3
Your personal Productivity Guide in IDEA is available from the Help menu.

other times when you typically only see a progress bar. You can access general statistics about used and missed features by calling the **Help | Productivity Guide** command to open a dialog like the one shown in figure A.3. Here you can easily discover features that you have been missing—features that could increase your productivity dramatically.

A.2   Seeking help through online resources

Several good sources of information on IDEA are available online. JetBrains manages three IDEA web sites that you may want to visit:

- **www.jetbrains.com**—The official home of IDEA provides product information, updates, and other information. This site includes articles and other useful tips on running IDEA.

- **www.intellij.net**—The IntelliJ network site, run by the folks at JetBrains, includes discussion forums, feature request forms, and more. The forums can be a useful source of tips and tricks, as well as a place you can get your questions answered. From time to time, JetBrains makes beta copies of new versions of IDEA available here for testing by the user community.

- **www.intellij.org**—JetBrains' community site features downloadable plug-ins, developer information, and other goodies. The dozens of plug-ins on this site can add all sorts of new features to IDEA.

IDEA maintains an ever-growing collection of articles, tutorials, and other documentation on its website, which you can access from within IDEA by executing the **Help | Online Documentation** command.

A.2.1 *Reporting bugs and requesting features*

If you find a bug in the software, or you have an idea about how to make IDEA better, the folks at JetBrains want to hear from you. At the JetBrains network site (www.intellij.net), you can log in to the bug-tracking system to submit bugs and feature requests or check on the status of previously filed requests. You can even vote on which requests you're most interested in getting resolved.

If something bad happens while IDEA is running, you'll see a dialog that lets you automatically report the problem to the IDEA technical staff. You can track the status of the problem through tracking tools on the website, if you sign up for a bug-tracking account.

> **NOTE** If you find a valid bug in the IDE, we encourage you to submit the bug to JetBrains. Doing so only takes a second; and, thanks to JetBrains' commitment to publishing and addressing its bug list, you'll help improve the product for everyone.

A.2.2 *Technical support from actual people*

If you have a maintenance and support agreement with JetBrains, you can access special support features on the web site. (Consult your licensing contract for the details of your specific support terms.) Technical support from JetBrains (at the time of this writing) is provided as unlimited email support on installation and operation of the software in accordance with its documentation. In addition to the direct channel, JetBrains' user forums at www.intellij.net host a community of IDEA-savvy users who actively discuss the JetBrains line of products.

index

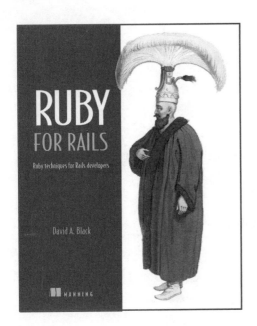

MORE TITLES FROM MANNING ...

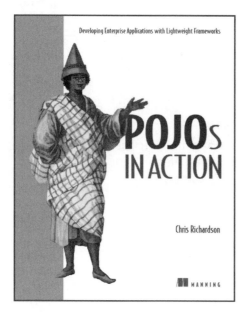

POJOs in Action: Developing Enterprise Applications with Lightweight Frameworks

by Chris Richardson
ISBN: 1-930114-58-3
592 pages
$44.95
January 2006

WebWork in Action

by Patrick Lightbody and Jason Carreira
ISBN: 1930114-53-2
400 pages
$44.95
September 2005

For ordering information go to www.manning.com

Hibernate in Action

> by Christian Bauer and Gavin King
> ISBN: 1-930114-15-X
> 400 pages
> $44.95
> August 2004

Hibernate Quickly

> by Patrick Peak and Nick Heudecker
> ISBN: 1-930114-41-9
> 456 pages
> $44.95
> August 2005

MORE TITLES FROM MANNING ...

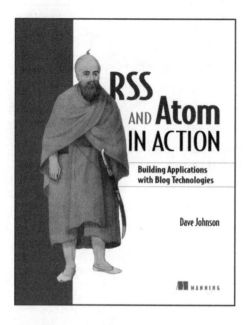